The JEFFERSON LIES

Exposing the Myths You've Always Believed
About Thomas Jefferson

DAVID BARTON

WND Books

THE JEFFERSON LIES

Unless otherwise noted, Scripture quotations are taken from THE ENGLISH STANDARD VERSION. © 2001 by Crossway Bibles, a division of Good News Publishers. Scripture quotations marked NIV are taken from HOLY BIBLE: NEW INTERNATIONAL VERSION®. © 1973, 1978, 1984 by International Bible Society. Used by permission of Zondervan Publishing House. All rights reserved. Scripture quotations marked KJV are taken from the King James Version of the Bible.

Published by WND Books, Washington, D.C. WND Books is a registered trademark of WorldNetDaily.com, Inc. ("WND")

Book designed by Mark Karis. Cover illustration by Vi Yen Nguyen.

WND Books are available at special discounts for bulk purchases. WND Books also publishes books in electronic formats. For more information call (541) 474-1776 or visit www.wndbooks.com.

Hardcover ISBN: 978-1-944229-02-3
eBook ISBN: 978-1-944229-03-0

Library of Congress Cataloging-in-Publication Data Available Upon Request

Printed in the United States of America
16 17 18 19 20 PAH 9 8 7 6 5 4 3

CONTENTS

FOREWORD

Irony: when people make bald faced lies and impugns someone's character based on a book with the word *lie* in the title.

When *The Jefferson Lies* was first published, the book and David Barton were attacked relentlessly. There were no facts to back up the attacks. They were just more of the same; progressives must not let the truth of our nations founding be told. They will fight the truth with lies, good with evil, honesty with deceit.

Many people could have taken the abuse, the accusations, the lies, and walked away. They could have decided that it is not worth the aggravation to fight for the truth. That it is not worth the heartache for themselves (or their family). But some people are wired differently. *Courage* is when you are willing to take the arrows for what you believe. David Barton is one of those people. He is a man of principle and courage.

When David and *The Jefferson Lies* came under attack he never considered retreating. He doubled down. He did more research, cited more sources, ultimately using the attacks as a way to make *The Jefferson Lies* even more important reading. The irony, those who threw stones could not break this house; they made it stronger.

I recently learned that the United States government was actually trying to strip God out of a private homeless shelter for previously incarcerated women struggling in Colorado. That's

V

right, Marilyn Vyzourek, the woman who runs an organization called Gospel Shelters for Women, was told that she could no longer offer Bible studies at her shelter. Why did they have that ability? Because our government, which happily funds all kinds of programs championed by the secular left, decided that the shelter's acceptance of two twenty-five-thousand-dollar federal grants made them subservient to their will.

It's not surprising. In fact, it's just the latest in a decades-old attempt by progressive secularists to keep religion entirely separate from the government. Everyone knows that's just what Thomas Jefferson intended when he penned the words "separation of church and state," right?

Well, not quite.

My friend, historian David Barton, takes on this long-held falsehood about the separation of church and state and proves once and for all that Jefferson was no secularist. Not even close. Did you know, for instance, that when Jefferson was vice president in 1800, he helped start church services inside the US Capitol? Those services grew to include more than two thousand people attending each week, and it became one of the biggest churches in America at the time.

And that's just the beginning.

Why does the Left continue to misquote Jefferson, accuse him of being anti-God, and attribute evil deeds to him? Because they know that if they are able to discredit and dismiss Jefferson and our other Founders, then we are that much closer to surrendering our birthright and our natural freedoms. These myths have flourished in our educational institutions in recent years and have become accepted as truth. It's a poison in our nation's system that can only be flushed out by light and truth.

There are three things I've learned from Thomas Jefferson and have tried hard to apply in my own life: (1) Question with boldness, (2) Hold to the truth, and (3) Speak without fear. In *The Jefferson Lies*, David Barton boldly questions the modern myths about Jefferson and arms you with the well-researched truth. I ask you to read it, learn from it, and then to go speak without fear.

Oh, by the way, Marilyn Vyzourek refused to back down from the government's demands. They may have stripped her of federal money, but that would not be the end of Gospel Shelters for Women. When I heard about her story I decided to replace the money they'd lost with a personal contribution. After all, sometimes questioning with boldness involves more than just words; it requires action.

I like to think Thomas Jefferson would have smiled just a little if he were still around.

—GLENN BECK

EDITORS' NOTES

Many early American historical quotes have been used in this book—quotes made at a time when grammatical usage and spelling were quite different from what is practiced today. In an effort to improve readability and flow, we have modernized all spellings and punctuations in the historical quotes used throughout this work, leaving the historical content unimpaired.

As an example of the very different colonial spelling of words, consider the opening language of the Pilgrims' Mayflower Compact of 1620 (the words misspelled by today's standards are underlined):

> We whose names are <u>undwriten</u>, the <u>loyall</u> subjects of our dread <u>soveraigne</u> Lord King James, by the grace of God, of Great <u>Britaine</u>, <u>Franc</u>, & Ireland king, defender of the faith, &c., <u>having</u> undertaken, for the <u>glorie</u> of God, and <u>advancemente</u> of the Christian faith, and <u>honour</u> of our king & <u>countrie</u>, a voyage to plant the first <u>colonie</u> in the <u>Northerne</u> parts of Virginia, <u>doe</u> by these presents solemnly & <u>mutualy</u> in the presence of God, and one of another, covenant & combine <u>our selves togeather</u> into a <u>civill</u> body <u>politick</u>.

The use of modern spellings will not change any meanings. By referring to the sources in the footnotes, the reader will be able to examine the original spelling should he or she so desire.

Similarly distracting to today's readers is the early use of capitals and commas. For an example of the copious use of commas, refer to the previous example; to see the excessive use of capitals, notice this excerpt from a 1749 piece written by signer of the Declaration Robert Treat Paine (underlined words would not be capitalized today):

> I <u>Believe</u> the Bible to be the written word of God & to <u>Contain</u> in it the whole <u>Rule</u> of <u>Faith</u> & manners; I consent to the Assemblys <u>Shorter</u> Chatachism as being <u>Agreable</u> to the '<u>Reveal'd Will</u>' of God & to contain in it the <u>Doctrines</u> that are <u>According</u> to Godliness. I have for some time had a desire to attend upon the Lords Supper and to <u>Come</u> to that divine <u>Institution</u> of a <u>Dying</u> Redeemer, And I trust I'm now convinced that it is my <u>Duty Openly</u> to profess him least he be ashamed to own me <u>An Other</u> day; I humbly therefore desire that you would receive me into your <u>Communion & Fellowship</u>, & I beg your <u>Prayers</u> for me that Grace may be carried on in my soul to <u>Perfection,</u> & that I may live answerable to the <u>Profession</u> I now make which (God <u>Assisting</u>) I purpose to be the main <u>End</u> of all my <u>Actions</u>.

In a further effort to improve readability, the modern rules of capitalization and punctuation have also been followed in the quotes throughout this book. These changes will not affect or alter the meaning of the content in the quotes.

Finally, the author personally chooses to capitalize all nouns or pronouns referring to the Bible or Biblical Deity as a sign of his personal respect for Biblical faith; and for exactly the opposite reason he chooses not to capitalize words such as *satan*, *lucifer*, or the *devil*.

Responding to the Critics

In 2011, Thomas Nelson contracted with me to pen *The Jefferson Lies: Exposing the Myths You've Always Believed About Thomas Jefferson*. After its release on April 10 of that year, it promptly became a *New York Times* bestseller.

Thomas Nelson had given a pre-release copy of the work to Grove City psychology professor Warren Throckmorton and fellow professor Michael Coulter. They hastily prepared and released their own ebook attacking my work: *Getting Jefferson Right: Fact Checking Claims about Our Third President.** It was released just three weeks after my book. Four other conservative academics joined them to attack the work and together the six initiated a highly publicized media campaign against me and the book.

But what didn't make the headlines is the fact that only one of those six had previously published any work on early American history—my area of expertise and the subject of

---

* Although the work is co-authored, Throckmorton seems to be the main critic as indicated by his extensive writing about me (over a span of four years, he has attacked me in over three hundred articles). As such, throughout this essay I refer to him as the author of *Getting Jefferson Right*.

numerous best-selling books I have written, including several used in universities and law schools. My personal archives contain more than 100,000 originals, or copies of original documents that predate 1812, including handwritten letters, documents, and artifacts belonging to Founding Fathers such as Thomas Jefferson.

Thomas Nelson was left with a choice: defend the title against these unqualified critics, or desert it. They chose the latter.

Despite having in their possession the full documentation for the facts presented in the book, in an act of corporate cowardice, Thomas Nelson pulled the book while it was still on the best-seller list. Nelson did not even have the courtesy to notify me of their decision. In fact, the first I learned that the book had been banished from shelves was when a reporter called to get my response to the publisher's national press release.

"As iron sharpens iron, so one man sharpens another" (Proverbs 27:17). I welcome criticism of my work. Indeed, whenever I receive word of a possible inaccuracy in any of my works, I investigate the claim and, if warranted, I make the necessary corrections in subsequent printings. This has been my established practice for twenty-five years.

Throckmorton's work, however, was relentlessly negative and, as I show below, many of his charges are simply wrong. He did point out a few passages in the first edition of *The Jefferson Lies* that might have been more carefully worded or better argued, so I have made appropriate revisions for this edition. I am grateful to Throckmorton for helping improve the work (although that was not his intention).

Throckmorton, a psychologist who has demonstrated no previous expertise in American history, specifically listed twenty-three items from the more than two thousand facts in my book with which he took issue. I will not address many of his objections as they are grounded in minutia, semantics, or personal interpretations, but I will address several criticisms that may seem, at least to impartial observers, to have some merit. (I address other of his arguments and present more historical evidence at www.TheJeffersonLies.com.)

Before I respond to Throckmorton, however, I would like to suggest that one reason that *The Jefferson Lies* became so controversial was the handful of conservative critics who entered the conflict to echo Throckmorton's claims. As the editor of a conservative national news magazine affirmed:

> Left-wing historians for years have criticized Barton. We haven't spotlighted those criticisms because we know the biases behind them. It's different when Christian conservatives point out inaccuracies.[1]

Although it may no longer be accurate to describe Throckmorton as a conservative (see www.TheJeffersonLies. com for details), who are these other Christian conservatives and, more importantly, are they in a good position to fairly criticize the book?

Throckmorton admitted that he had recruited scholars for this purpose,[2] led by Jay Richards, a philosopher/theologian with the Discovery Institute, who, according to media outlets had asked "10 conservative Christian professors to assess Barton's work."[3] Although he reported that their responses were "negative," several of them actually refused to participate in his quest. Only three of the ten contacted by Richards were listed in several articles: Glenn Moots, Glenn Sunshine, and Gregg

Frazer. Of these three, only Frazer specializes in religion and the American Founding,* and it is not clear that Frazer even bothered to read *The Jefferson Lies.* Instead, he watched and criticized a 1992 video entitled *America's Godly Heritage.*[4]

I am not a journalist, but if media outlets are going to rely on expert criticism, then shouldn't those experts not only specialize in relevant subjects but also take the time to read the work in question? By way of analogy, imagine the case of a journalist who came to *Time* magazine with a story about how even liberal professors object to President Obama's Iran policy. As evidence, he offers three examples, two of whom are experts on Latin America and the third who gives no evidence of being aware of Obama's current policies. Would *Time* run such a story?

In any case, answering Throckmorton's accusations against this book provides a welcome opportunity not only to expose historical mistakes common among writers like him but also to allow Americans to have an even firmer grasp on the nonsecularist nature of Jefferson.

So before delving fully into *The Jefferson Lies,* here are six of Throckmorton's attacks, and you will quickly see why they are wrong. But they do serve as excellent appetizers for the additional (and today largely unknown) very interesting historical information about Thomas Jefferson yet to come.

---

* By "specializes in religion and the American Founding" I mean someone who has spent a great deal of time researching and writing about religion and the American Founding. I do not mean to suggest that the critics mentioned above are not good scholars and teachers, just that they are not experts on this particular subject.

ISSUE #1: JEFFERSON, CONGRESS, AND MISSIONARIES

In the first edition of *The Jefferson Lies* (and also in this edition), I listed numerous official measures sponsored or endorsed by Jefferson that involved government support and even funding of religious endeavors, all demonstrating that Jefferson did not hold the sort of strict separation between church and state favored today by secularist groups such as the ACLU, Freedom From Religion Foundation, Americans United for Separation of Church and State, Military Religious Freedom Foundation, and others.

For example, it will be seen later that Jefferson facilitated church services inside the US Capitol on Sunday[5] and also in government buildings such as the War Department and Treasury Department.[6] He also personally attended church in the Capitol both as vice president[7] and president.[8] And while in the Continental Congress, he recommended a Bible image for the Great Seal of America[9] and was a leader in the call for a nationwide day of fasting and prayer,[10] even helping arrange a public religious service on such days.[11] As Governor of Virginia, he placed "God" directly into the state seal,[12] introduced unabashed Biblical practices and standards directly into state law,[13] and also called for a statewide day of public thanksgiving and prayer.[14]

There are many additional similar acts, but Throckmorton protests my characterization of Jefferson as something less than an ardent secularist. So, attempting to make a mountain of a molehill, he attacks one of the lesser of my numerous examples on this point, reconfiguring it as if it was the entirety of my historical presentation on this issue. But even if he was correct in his mischaracterization of the single event that he selected (which, as will be shown below, he is not), I could remove that example and my main point would remain unaltered.

Throckmorton strongly objects to my claim that Jefferson signed "federal acts setting aside government lands so that missionaries might be assisted in 'propagating the Gospel' among the Indians (1802, and again in 1803 and 1804)."[15] Even though the name of the group to which Congress entrusted those government lands was "The Society of United Brethren for Propagating the Gospel among the Heathen," Throckmorton forcefully asserts that the three laws signed by Jefferson relating to this group had nothing to do with propagating the Gospel, but instead were part of a congressional restitution measure passed in response to an atrocity committed against the Delaware Indians.

By way of background on that specific incident, Moravian missionaries began working with the Delaware around 1740, and by the early 1780s a sizeable percentage (albeit a minority) of the tribe had become Christian. But according to Moravian Bishop John Holmes, in 1782 a group of local Pennsylvania "fanatics" arose and "demanded the total extirpation of all the Indians, lest God's vengeance should fall upon the Christians for not destroying the Indians, as the Israelites were commanded to do in the case of the Canaanites."[16] This group approached the Christian Delaware, falsely presenting themselves as friends sent to protect and move them to a place of safety.

Local whites warned the Delaware about the danger posed by this group, but those warnings went unheeded. The Delaware instead "cheerfully delivered their guns, hatchets, and other weapons" to their apparent "Christian" protectors.[17] After doing so, a slaughter was carried out against them,[18] in which about one-third of the Christian Delaware were systematically murdered. The butchers' plans to slaughter the rest failed,[19] and much of the remnant of these Delaware moved north into Canada for safety.

What happened to the cold-blooded killers? According to Bishop Holmes, "Divine justice overtook them, for being attacked by a party of English and Indian warriors, the greater part of them were cut to pieces."[20]

The War for Independence ended the following year, in September 1783. Two months later in November, the Confederation Congress began setting aside from the territory they had just acquired from the British the portions previously occupied by the Christian Delaware, inviting them back to those lands. In May 1785, Congress officially approved a federal land trust for them, reauthorizing the measure in 1787, 1788, and several times thereafter. According to Throckmorton:

> The Land Ordinance of 1785 and the acts of 1787 and 1788 were efforts to make right the damage done to the Christian Indians by the Pennsylvania militia in 1782. Congress provided land in the trust of the United Brethren society organized for this purpose in September of 1787.[21]

Throckmorton asserts that Congress officially viewed "The Society of United Brethren for Propagating the Gospel among the Heathen," to whom Congress entrusted the land, only as a corporate real estate management company and nothing more, explaining:

The Brethren [i.e., Moravians] had already promoted Christianity to the Indians. Now they were empowered to act as trustees for this land . . . [and] federal action referred to this entity as an entity and not as a description of an activity.[22*]

He therefore concludes:

So the claim made by . . . Barton about federal funds authorizing evangelism and/or the "propagation of the Gospel to the heathen" is simply false.[23]

According to Throckmorton:

If there had not been an atrocity and subsequent displacement of the Christian Indians, there would have been no need for federal legislation in this case.[24]

Throckmorton thus makes clear his view that:

---

* It is striking that in the section in his book wherein Throckmorton asserts that the United Brethren had "already promoted Christianity" and that the congressional act was only a real estate transaction, he cites George Henry Loskiel, *History of the Mission of the United Brethren Among the Indians in North America*. In Three Parts (London: The Brethren's Society, 1794). But he apparently did not read much in that source, for it contains numerous accounts documenting that Christian evangelism was indeed active and ongoing both before and after the transaction, including baptisms, evangelism, and similar activities (cf. pp. 201, 206, 210, ff.). Other books from that time affirm the same, including John Heckenealder, *A Narrative of the Mission of the United Brethren among the Delaware and Mohigan Indians, &c.* by John Heckenealder, who was many years in the service of that Mission (Philadelphia, 1820); and Rev. John Holmes, *Historical Sketches of the Missions of the United Brethren for Propagating the Gospel Among the Heathen, From Their Commencement to the Year 1817* (Dublin: R. Napper, 1818; reprinted London, 1827). The evidence is overwhelming that Christian evangelism was part and parcel of what occurred with that land tract.

1. Congress helped the Christian Delaware only because of
   a the 1782 atrocity; and

2. Congress in general, and Jefferson in particular, had no
   interest in and were not involved with missionary or
   evangelistic work among native peoples, including the
   Delaware.

But Throckmorton's claims in these two areas are exactly
the opposite of what actually occurred. The abundant evidence
establishing this will be presented chronologically so that the
1785 Ordinance regarding the Delaware can be seen in its
overall historical context of similar governmental acts.

In November 1775, a decade before the congressional act
in question, the Continental Congress of which Jefferson was a
member provided monies "out of the continental treasury" to the
Rev. Samuel Kirkland for the specific purpose of "the propagation of the Gospel among the Indians."[25] (Also related to the Rev.
Kirkland, in January 1777 Congress gave more money for his
missionary work among native peoples,[26] and in October 1779
appropriated even additional funds to expand his missionary work
into other tribes,[27] funding him yet again in December 1784.[28])

In December 1775 a Delaware chief appeared before
the Continental Congress, and John Hancock, president of
Congress, told him:

> We are pleased that the Delaware intend to embrace
> Christianity. We [Congress] will send you, according to your
> desire, a minister and a schoolmaster to instruct you in the
> principles of religion and other parts of useful knowledge.[29]

Notice here that: (1) Congress is providing Gospel ministers and missionaries to the Delaware tribe, on their lands; (2) Jefferson was part of this Congress; and (3) Congress provided these services to the Delaware seven years *before* any atrocity had been committed.

In February 1776, as tensions were increasing between America and Great Britain, Congress identified specific means to solidify its relationship with potential native allies, explaining:

> [A] friendly commerce between the people of the United Colonies and the Indians, and *the propagation of the Gospel* and the cultivation of the civil arts among the latter, may produce many and inestimable advantages to both.[30] (emphasis added)

Congress therefore directed:

> That the Commissioners for Indian Affairs in the northern department be desired to inquire of Mr. Jacob Fowler, of the Montauke tribe of Indians, on Long Island, and Mr. Joseph Johnson, of the Mohegan, upon what terms they will reside among the Six Nations of Indians and instruct them in the Christian religion.[31]

Congress thus again provided funding for missionaries; and significantly, Jefferson was also part of this Congress and this policy; and there is no evidence in the congressional records, Jefferson's own correspondence, that of other delegates in Congress, or Jefferson's own autobiography that he objected to or opposed any of these acts.

(Similar congressional funding for missionaries was regularly passed by subsequent Congresses, including in 1776, 1777, 1779, three times in 1785, and so forth.[32])

In April 1776, Congress ordered the Commissioners for Indian Affairs to employ "a minister of the Gospel to reside among the Delaware Indians and instruct them in the Christian religion."[33] So again: (1) Congress directly funded missionaries to the Delaware on their lands; (2) Jefferson was part of this Congress; and (3) this act was unrelated to any atrocity.

In May 1779, George Washington gave a speech to the Delaware Indian chiefs (yes, once again, the Delaware), telling them:

> You do well to wish to learn our arts and ways of life, and above all the religion of Jesus Christ. These will make you a greater and happier people than you are. Congress will do everything they can to assist you in this wise intention.[34]

According to George Washington, Congress would assist the Delaware in learning "the religion of Jesus Christ." Later that year he met with the Rev. Hyacinthe de la Motte, whom he identified as "employed by order of Congress as missionary to the Indian tribes in the Eastern department."[35]

In May 1785, Congress, having already firmly established its practice of supplying Christian missionaries to the Delaware, approved the land trust in question for the use of the Christian Delaware and the Moravian missionaries.[36] And just seven days later, it directed "[t]hat the Board of Treasury advance to Jacob Fowler the sum of one hundred dollars to encourage him to instruct the Indians."[37] (This is the same Fowler previously funded by Congress in 1776 to do missionary work among the Mohawk and Oneida Indians.[38])

In 1788, John Hancock, then serving as governor of Massachusetts, issued an official proclamation to assist "The

Society for Propagating the Gospel among the Indians and others in North America" by urging "the good people of this Commonwealth to contribute" for the "purpose of propagating the knowledge of the Gospel among the Indians and others in America."[39]

Also in 1788, George Washington wrote Moravian Bishop John Ettwein (one of those directly involved in securing the original land trust from Congress in 1785), telling him that "if an event so long and so earnestly desired as that of converting the Indians to Christianity and consequently to civilization can be effected, the Society of Bethlehem [i.e., the Moravians] bids fair to bear a very considerable part in it."[40]

In 1789, President Washington again wrote Bishop Ettwein and "the Directors of the Society of the United Brethren for Propagating the Gospel among the Heathen," telling them that "it will be a desirable thing for the protection of the Union to cooperate, as far as the circumstances may conveniently admit, with the disinterestedness endeavors of your society to civilize and Christianize the savages of the wilderness."[41] In 1795, Washington approved a treaty with the Oneida, Tuscarora, and Stockbridge Indians, building them a church.[42]

In 1803, President Thomas Jefferson approved a treaty with the Kaskaskia Indians, providing them "annually for seven years, one hundred dollars towards the support of a priest" and "the sum of three hundred dollars to assist the said tribe in the erection of a church."[43] And, as mentioned previously, he also signed the 1802, 1803, and 1804 land acts renewals for "The Society of United Brethren for Propagating the Gospel among the Heathen."[44]

In 1819, President James Monroe approved a treaty with the Ottawa, Chippewa, and Potawatomy Indians delivering several sections of federal land in Michigan "to the rector of the Catholic church of St. Anne of Detroit, for the use of the said church," stipulating that those federal lands could be "retained or sold" by the Catholic Church, doing whichever would best aid Christian education to the native children of those tribes.[45]

In 1825, President John Quincy Adams approved a treaty with the Osage Indians that set aside federal lands "to include the Harmony Missionary establishment," specifying that those lands were to be disposed of "for the benefit of said Missions . . . so long as said Missions shall be usefully employed in teaching, civilizing, and improving the said Indians."[46]

Such treaties and acts continued to be negotiated and regularly passed over subsequent decades and into the twentieth century.[47] Those numerous additional examples need not be presented here, for the pattern of Congress in this area is already clearly established.

Perhaps the best summation of the national governmental policy that spanned some one hundred and thirty years of both presidential and legislative actions on this issue was delivered by President Grover Cleveland when he declared:

> No matter what I may do, no matter what you may do, no matter what Congress may do, no matter what may be done for the education of the Indian, after all, the solution of the Indian question rests in the Gospel of Christ.[48]

Notice how Congress repeatedly connected providing federal lands for native tribes with the explicit purpose of carrying out Christian missionary work on those lands—something Throckmorton denies occurred, especially with the Delaware. Nevertheless, this official conjoining of federal lands for native tribes and missionary activity on those lands was regularly repeated in the 1700s, 1800s, and 1900s.

Clearly, Throckmorton's claim that Congress in general, and Jefferson in particular, had no interest in and were not involved with missionary or evangelistic work among native peoples, including the Delaware, is demonstrably false. But what about his claim that Congress helped the Christian Delaware only because of a specific atrocity?

Significantly, when Congress originally designated those lands in the 1785 act, there was *no* reference in the legislative actions to *any* atrocity—*no* official congressional records even mentioned the tragedy. In fact, the modern editors of published works from the federal archives that contain those particular records, and who apparently entertained the same supposition as Throckmorton, candidly confessed that "the silence of the journals on this matter is . . . puzzling."[49] But the silence is puzzling only if one insists on seeking a purely secular motivation for the congressional actions, ignoring Congress' lengthy prior and succeeding record of sponsoring explicit missionary activity among native tribes, including the Delaware.

The records are clear that from 1776 until Jefferson's death in 1826 (and then long afterward, on into the twentieth century), the national government directly funded Christian missionaries and churches for native peoples; and the designation of federal lands for the use of native peoples was repeatedly joined with explicitly Christian missionary endeavors on those lands.

But despite both the clarity and the abundance of readily available historical evidence, Throckmorton still asserts:

In other words, the federal government never provided money to missionaries to evangelize the Indians. Instead, the government attempted to right a wrong by protecting land claims by missionaries on behalf of their native converts.[50]

Clearly, Throckmorton is wrong. But having missed the mark on his primary claim, he then makes four subsequent erroneous claims based on his original error.

First, in reference to the 1802, 1803, and 1804 renewal acts signed by Jefferson for the Moravian "Society of the United Brethren for Propagating the Gospel among the Heathen," Throckmorton asserts that the name of the Society was irrelevant to congressional intentions, explaining that "federal action referred to this entity as an entity and not as a description of an activity."[51] But in 1788, not long after the measure was first enacted and at a time when Congress was re-extending it, a significant phrase was deleted (shown in strikethrough) and a replacement inserted (indicated by italics), thus causing that law to state that Congress

> ordered the property of the said towns and reserved lands to be vested in the Moravian Brethren at Bethlehem in Pennsylvania, or the Society of the said brethren for ~~Propagating the Gospel among the Heathen~~ *civilizing the Indians and promoting Christianity* (or as they are called The Society of the United Brethren for Propagating the Gospel among the Heathen) in trust and for the uses expressed in the said Ordinance.[52]

Congress specifically replaced the name of the entity with a description of its Christian activity, thus explicitly referring to the activity of the Moravian missionaries rather than the entity of their corporate organization. This change therefore made abundantly clear that the land trust was definitely given for the unambiguous missionary purpose of "promoting Christianity."

In his second dependent error, Throckmorton claimed that because the Delaware were already evangelized, Congress would not have undertaken missionary work among them,[53] but such was definitely not the case. According to the records of the United Brethren, those congressional land trusts were specifically used for explicit missionary and Christianization efforts with the Delaware.[54]

In Throckmorton's third related error, he claims:

> Eventually, the Society ceded the land back to the federal government because the converts did not return in sufficient numbers to make the mission viable. In fact, the largest settlement of about 60 Christian Indians was in the Schoenbrun location (renamed Goshen).[55]

While the number living at the mission was definitely larger than what Throckmorton claims,[56] there were intervals when the native population in particular areas on the land trust was indeed smaller. Why? In part because the more spiritually mature among the Christian Delaware were periodically sent out to plant new churches and do mission work among neighboring native tribes.[57] Thus, the settlements in the federal land trust served as centers of activity to convert the Delaware and then to train and send them out to do missionary work among their own brethren and other native peoples. During those periods when a group of Delaware was dispatched to start a new mission, the permanent population on the land trust was definitely reduced.

In his fourth supplementary error, Throckmorton claimed that by Jefferson signing the three acts for the Moravians. . .

> Jefferson did not authorize the propagation of the Gospel; he simply maintained existing policy.[58]

> A review of the three bills which Jefferson signed reveals nothing new in them about Indians or religion.[59]

Throckmorton is generally correct in these statements—but not for the reason he thinks. Jefferson did indeed "maintain existing policy," which, as has already been demonstrated, consistently authorized the propagation of the Gospel on federal lands. And Throckmorton is also spot on in his claim that Jefferson's signing of those three bills "reveals nothing new in them about Indians or religion," for Jefferson was simply continuing the practice of Congresses of which he had been a part in providing missionaries to native peoples, including through congressional land grants.

If Jefferson had objected to these practices, he certainly did not have to sign any of the three acts into law; or he could have required any provisions offensive to him to be altered before signing them. And if compensation for an atrocity had indeed been the sole object for giving the Christian Delaware the land trust, it would have been simple enough to craft such legislation without involving the Moravians at all. But Jefferson made no objections and requested no changes; he signed the bills to continue existing policy, which definitely included missionary and evangelistic work.

Throckmorton may not personally like what Congress and Thomas Jefferson did in regard to missionaries among native peoples; he may even vehemently disagree with their actions; but there is no excuse for being so disingenuous as to assert that neither Congress nor Jefferson directly facilitated missionary work among native peoples.

Perhaps Throckmorton's refusal to acknowledge so many self-evident and even irrefutable facts on this subject is because he himself holds a negative view of Christian missionary work among native peoples. After all, he specifically complains that

> [T]he federal government pushed Christianity on Native American tribes until early in the 20th century. Native children were removed from their families in elementary school and sent away to board schools, sometimes run by church groups. They were forbidden to speak their language or follow their native customs. Some recall harsh punishments if the rules were violated. Christian Native Americans agree that the treatment was demeaning and offensive.[60]

Throckmorton, as with many Negativists, sees Christian missionary work among native peoples as atrocity-filled—something that broke up families, coerced faith and western culture, and harshly punished those who committed even minor violations of the missionaries' inflexible pharisaical beliefs. Yet the Moravians clearly state that their missionaries had long before learned that "nothing is effected with Indians by force or constraint."[61] Furthermore, rather than requiring native peoples to conform to English beliefs and practices, Moravians acknowledged that their missionaries "lived and dressed in the Indian manner, so that in travelling they were often taken for Indians."[62]

I am not arguing that the national government's policy toward native people has always been perfect. To the contrary, many policies and actions have been undeniably atrocious. But the policies under consideration here were aimed at spreading the Gospel in an indigenous, voluntary, and non-coercive manner, and in many instances were successful.

A further indication of Throckmorton's generally negative view of Christian Anglo/Indian relations is his claim that it was threats from the white man that kept the Christian Delaware from returning to the lands reserved for them by Congress.[63] But the Moravians who lived and worked with those Delaware firmly avow otherwise, succinctly reporting that it was the "pagan Indians"[64] from both the "Delawares and Shawanose"[65] who repeatedly demonstrated such "hostility"[66] toward the Christian Delaware that they were finally forced to abandon "their present location."[67] So the greatest impediment to the return of the Christian Delaware was not Anglo but rather Indian opposition; and that opposition was very real. In fact, on multiple occasions, known Delaware converts were targeted, hurt, or killed by their unconverted brethren.[68]

Throckmorton's misguided analysis of the relations between Congress, missionaries, and native peoples is typical of today's Modernists. He finds it inconceivable that there could have ever been a time wherein the federal government would have acted differently on religion than the secularist manner in which it does today. He thus interprets historical events and persons as if they occurred and lived today rather than in the past, which has resulted in a misrepresentation of historical beliefs and events, especially concerning Jefferson and the Delaware.

ISSUE #2: JEFFERSON AND MIRACLES

An important contribution of *The Jefferson Lies* is to help dispel the common misconception that Jefferson did not include miracles in his 1804 abridgement of the Bible. I am not the first person to make this argument, and I openly acknowledged the work of earlier scholars who made similar points. I understand that arguments can be made for and against the inclusion of miracles in Jefferson's 1804 abridged work for Native Americans, and I discuss each position. But in the final analysis, I believe that I made a compelling case that Jefferson included miracles in that work.

But rather than engage in a serious debate about these questions, Throckmorton simply announces that I am wrong because "Dickinson Adams' *definitive work* demonstrates that these texts were not included in either of Jefferson's abridgments"[69] (emphasis added). He then asserts:

> For these claims [about the inclusion of the miraculous], Barton cites Charles Sanford's book, *The Religious Life of Thomas Jefferson*, in a footnote. For some reason, Sanford erroneously included these four texts in his summary of Jefferson's abridgments. However, these miraculous healings and events were not included by Jefferson.[70]

Why does Throckmorton consider Dickinson Adams' reconstruction of Jefferson's work "definitive" but Charles Sanford's "erroneous"? Or, more precisely, why would one of the reconstructions include Jefferson's passages on the miraculous but not the other?

When Jefferson originally compiled his 1804 work, he wrote out the list of verses he planned to include and then began to cut those passages from the Bible in order to assemble them in a simple abridgment of the Gospels for the use of native peoples.

But as his work progressed, Jefferson ended up snipping sixteen additional Bible passages for inclusion that he had not listed in his original handwritten draft. So in 1983 when Dickinson Adams reconstructed Jefferson's work, he included all the passages that Jefferson had identified in his written outline, but he struggled over what to do with the additional sixteen passages that Jefferson had clipped but not initially listed. Should he include them or not? Adams finally decided to use only eleven-and-a-half of those sixteen Jeffersonian passages, excluding the four-and-a-half that included (in Adams' own words):

> M[atthew] 8:9–10 (the cure of the centurion's servant); M[atthew] 9:33–34 (the casting out of a demon); M[atthew] 10:3–4 (the call of the Apostles); M[atthew] 11:2–9 (Jesus and John the Baptist); and a duplicate of M[atthew] 11:9.[71]

Why did Adams decide to exclude these passages on the miraculous that Jefferson himself had clipped for inclusion? He admitted that he had done so specifically "because of their miraculous or supernatural content,"[72] explaining that, in his view, "The remaining four and a half clippings, however, consist of verses Jefferson is unlikely to have used and are thus excluded from the reconstructed text."[73]

Strikingly, even though Jefferson had personally selected and clipped for inclusion these passages containing the miraculous, Dickinson Adams decided *not* to use them because they did not comport with his own personal opinion about Jefferson's beliefs on the subject. He was willing to include the extra eleven-and-a-half non-miraculous passages but not the remaining four-and-a-half, even though Jefferson had personally chosen all sixteen of them.

In 1993, Dr. Mark Beliles also did a reconstruction of Jefferson's 1804 work. It offers an excellent overview of the difference in the three modern reconstructions, concisely explaining:

> Unfortunately, there is no surviving copy of Jefferson's first compilation of 1804. What has survived is a copy of the front page, an initial table of Scripture texts that he planned to use, and most importantly, the two *New Testaments* from which Jefferson clipped out the verses for his work. Dickinson Adams made a valuable reconstruction of Jefferson's work in 1983 using two *New Testaments* identical to those that Jefferson used. This reconstruction showed there were sixteen passages that Jefferson clipped from the two *New Testaments* but did not include in the beginning table of texts. In his edition, Adams included eleven and one half of these passages. Some were not included based on his own assumptions about Jefferson's beliefs, including two significant texts referring to the miracles of Christ. Others were left out because they were difficult to fit into the flow of the text. My edition partially rectifies this by including one text—Matthew 11:2–9, under my own heading: "Miracles Authenticate Christ's Claims." (Charles Sanford in his *The Religious Life of Thomas Jefferson*, goes further and claims that all of Matthew 9:18–34 was in Jefferson's first compilation. This would have included the resurrection of Jarius' daughter, the healing of the bleeding woman, and the healing of two blind men, in addition to the casting out of a demon.)[74]

Thus, the basis for Throckmorton's pronouncement that I (along with Sanford and Beliles) was wrong about Jefferson having included miracles in his work for native peoples was not Jefferson's own actions from 1804 but rather a modern scholar's personal opinion from 1983. So even if one rejects the complete inclusion made by Sanford (as Throckmorton does), he is still left with the four-and-a-half passages that Jefferson himself selected and which undeniably included the miraculous. And as will be seen when Lie #3 is covered, even if all of these sixteen passages are excluded, Jefferson still included numerous other passages that incontestably did contain multiple references to the spiritual and supernatural.

ISSUE #3: JEFFERSON AND THE VIRGINIA BIBLE SOCIETY

Not surprisingly, Throckmorton objects to my statement that Jefferson "was an active member of the Virginia Bible Society,"[75] complaining:

> Even though the claim that Jefferson had anything to do with the founding of the Virginia Bible Society is false, it is worth noting that Jefferson's actions in support of the Bible could be viewed as contradicting his clear contempt for the dross and the dunghill that he believed much of the Bible was. Just two years prior to denouncing the concept of taking Bibles to other nations, Jefferson donated $50 to the fledgling Bible Society of Virginia and one of the society's leaders portrayed him as a member.[76]

By way of background, America's first Bible Society was formed in Philadelphia in 1808, and over the next eight years, 121 additional Bible Societies were established across the country,[77] with the Virginia Bible Society being formed in 1813. The purpose of each Society was to provide a Bible without cost to anyone who could not afford or did not have a Bible, including prisoners, the sick, elderly, poor, or unconverted. Their goal was for everyone in America, community by community, and state by state, to have a Bible.

In November 1813, Samuel Greenhow, the treasurer of the Virginia Bible Society, contacted Jefferson concerning the new organization. (Greenhow was also Jefferson's agent at the Mutual Assurance Society, a Virginia fire insurance company founded in 1794.) He approached Jefferson with great deference:

> Sir, I [am] very unwilling to be considered as impertinent [presumptuous and rude] and have therefore hesitated before I determined that I might without impertinence enclose to you a copy of the address and constitution of an association in Virginia for the distribution of Bibles gratuitously [without charge] to those who are not able to purchase them. . . . I shall hope for your patronage of the Association. We should be much pleased to number you among the members of the Society; but if you should prefer it, we will thankfully receive any donation that you may be pleased to aid us with.[78]

Jefferson read the constitution of the new Society, and then responded to Greenhow:

> I had not supposed there was a family in this state not possessing a Bible, and wishing without having the means to procure one. When in earlier life I was intimate with every class, I think I never was in a house where that was the case. However, circumstances may have changed, and the Society, I presume, have evidence of the fact. I therefore enclose you

cheerfully an order on Messrs. Gibson & Jefferson for fifty dollars for the purposes of the Society, sincerely agreeing with you that there never was a more pure and sublime system of morality delivered to man than is to be found in the four evangelists. Accept the assurance of my esteem and respect.[79]

Notice that Jefferson says he gives his gift "cheerfully," and that it is "for the purposes of the Society." What was the purpose of the Society? The answer was succinctly set forth in the document Jefferson had just read:

The object of the Society is the distribution of Bibles and Testaments to the poor of our country, and to the Heathen.[80]

Jefferson said that he had given his contribution to support this purpose. Throckmorton ignores this, however, instead explaining that:

Jefferson's donation was apparently a one-time contribution. There is no evidence in Jefferson's writings that he accepted Greenhow's invitation to join the organization.[81]

But the document that Greenhow sent, and that Jefferson read, proves just the opposite. For example, why did Jefferson give the specific amount of fifty dollars to the Society? Why not twenty-five, or forty, or some other greater or lesser amount? The answer is found in the rules of the Society that Jefferson had just examined:

Persons of every religious creed or denomination may become Members of this Society upon paying five dollars subscription money, and binding themselves to pay four dollars annually so long as they choose to continue in the Society. The payment, however, of *fifty dollars* in advance, shall without any further contribution constitute a person *member for life*.[82] (emphasis added)

Jefferson gave fifty dollars; and according to the document he had just read, that specific one-time amount "without any further contribution" made him a "member for life" of the Virginia Bible Society. Throckmorton incorrectly interpreted this as an insignificant "one-time contribution" on the part of Jefferson; but it was "one-time" because it was such a large amount that the Society asked nothing more from such major donors.

John Holt Rice, an officer of the Society, based on its written rules, had therefore accurately reported Jefferson as a member.[83] But amazingly, Throckmorton says such a claim is false, suggesting that it might be nothing more than what he described as "puffery" on the part of Rice.[84]

Throckmorton may not like the rules of the Virginia Bible Society; he may not like the fact that Jefferson read those rules and contributed accordingly; he may not like that Rice said Jefferson was a member; but none of that changes the historical facts. Throckmorton is simply wrong on this subject.

(Incidentally, other scholars have reached the same conclusion on this point as I did, including Dr. Thomas Buckley, perhaps the foremost expert on church-state relations in Virginia, and respected by scholars from all sides of the political spectrum. He, too, affirms that "Jefferson, Madison, and Monroe paid fifty dollars apiece to join [the Virginia Bible Society] as life members."[85])

ISSUE #4: JEFFERSON AND BIBLE SUBSCRIPTIONS

Throckmorton strenuously objects to my statement that Jefferson helped "finance the printing of one of America's groundbreaking editions of the Bible"—the John Thompson hot-pressed Bible. He launches into a lengthy exegesis about how Jefferson did not help "finance" or "fund" that Bible but rather only paid a subscription for it.[86] He concludes that this was "hardly a way to provide 'financial backing' for a project,[87] explaining:

> Buying a Bible by subscription was common then and was a way to provide the printer with some idea of how many copies to print. An analogy today might be to think of a magazine subscription as a purchase of a year's volume of issues. You are committing to pay one price but might pay in payments instead. Another analogy would be pre-ordering a book. Selling by subscription allowed journeymen printers to manage a large project but the result was that the subscribers got what they paid for. The subscribers were not investors in the project. The investors in the project were printers, John Thompson and Abraham Small. The Bible would have been printed whether or not Jefferson and the other Founders subscribed.[88]

Not only is Throckmorton wrong with these assertions but by them he demonstrates his unfamiliarity with the printing business in the Founding Era. For example, if Throckmorton is correct about what a subscription means (i.e., "to think of a magazine subscription"), then how does he explain these entries from Jefferson's ledger book?

> I have subscribed to the building of an Episcopalian church ($200), a Presbyterian ($60), a Baptist ($25) . . .[89]

Subscribed towards building an Episcopal church in Washington, $100 . . .[90]

Subscribed to church (Episcopal) near Navy Yard ($50).[91]

Subscribed $50 towards Methodist church in Georgetown.[92]

How does Throckmorton translate his analogy of "think of a magazine subscription" (a payment to purchase something that is already published) into providing advance funding and capital for the construction of a church? He can't. His modernistic analogy is problematic because a subscription at the time of Jefferson is not even remotely related to what it has become today.

Founding Father Noah Webster noted that a subscriber was one who pledged or promised to contribute a certain sum to an undertaking.[93] This was true whether it was for printing a book, building a church, or backing some other project. In the case of printing books, subscribers in the Founding Era gave the publishers a pre-publication promise of money—that is, a small IOU—to thus guarantee to the printer the funds necessary to remain solvent in the production of that work.

Since early publishers worked diligently to avoid debt, numerous proposed books were never published because of an insufficient number of subscribers, or prefunders.[94] In fact, there were works to which Jefferson actually subscribed that were never printed due to lack of subscribers or other problems.[95] So, Throckmorton is not correct in his claim that the book would be printed regardless of whether or not Jefferson and others subscribed. And he is equally errant in his claim that the printers were the investors; so very often in the Founding Era, it was the subscribers who were the investors.

But in a further effort to make Jefferson's subscription to John Thompson's Bible seem irrelevant and meaningless, Throckmorton asserts:

> It is not surprising that Jefferson would order one of these Bibles. Jefferson had an intellectual and personal interest in the Bible, as he did with many religious and philosophical books.[96]

This suggestion is also problematic. Jefferson had over 6,000 books in his personal library,[97] but in his life he subscribed to only 24 books.[98] Jefferson, like most citizens, simply purchased books after they were printed; so why not do the same with the Thompson Bible, as Throckmorton posits, if he were only seeking to add it to his library? One likely possibility is that Jefferson found the John Thompson Bible so important and of such unique interest to him that it was one of the few books to which he subscribed.

Significantly, Jefferson did not subscribe to many books, but he did subscribe the John Thompson Bible.[99] He similarly subscribed Thomas Scott's Bible,[100] and he also offered to subscribe Charles Thomson's Bible.[101] So, contrary to Throckmorton's claims, Jefferson definitely did help finance the printing of a Bible—on multiple occasions.

ISSUE #5: JEFFERSON AND A BIBLE FOR INDIANS

As will be seen later in Lie #3, in 1804 Jefferson made an abridgement of the Bible for use by Native Americans, and around 1820 a second one for his own personal study. Throckmorton objects to the commonly accepted view that the 1804 version was intended for Native Americans.[102] This claim is particularly odd given the title that Jefferson himself penned and placed on that work:

The Philosophy of Jesus of Nazareth. Extracted from the Account of His Life and Doctrines Given by Matthew, Mark, Luke and John. *Being an Abridgement of the New Testament for the Use of the Indians,* Unembarrassed [Uncomplicated] with Matters of Fact or Faith beyond the Level of their Comprehensions.[103] (emphasis added)

In attempting to justify his belief that Jefferson did not really intend this work for Native Americans, Throckmorton explains:

Another reason to think that Jefferson did not really intend his work to be shared directly with native people is that he initially hoped to do the job using Greek, Latin, and French in addition to English but time constraints kept him to a more modest effort in 1804. As indicated by his own words and his purchases of Bibles in the four languages, Jefferson has planned this multilingual effort by as early as 1805. Surely, he did not intend the Indians to master Greek, Latin, French and English in order to comprehend the moral teachings of Jesus.[104]

The title Jefferson placed on his four-language work (compiled around 1820) was *The Life and Morals of Jesus of Nazareth, Extracted Textually from the Gospels in Greek, Latin, French, and English.*[105] But Throckmorton concludes that those two works are really just two different phases of the same work.[106] This is truly astounding, considering that:

1. Jefferson personally assigned a distinctly different title to each of the two works;

2. Jefferson indicated a separate purpose for each work: the first for the use of native peoples, the second for his own use;

3. Jefferson's first work was in English only; the second was in four languages: English, French, Latin, and Greek; and

4. Bible verses Jefferson placed in each work were distinctly different from verses in the other.

Concerning this latter point, the 1804 work includes 717 Bible verses[107] and the 1820 work 1090 verses.[108] A combined total of 574 of these verses appear in both works,[109] so 516 verses (or 47 percent) of those found in the 1820 work are *not* found in the 1804 one;[110] and 143 verses (or 13 percent) of those in the 1804 work do *not* appear in the 1820 one.[111] It is therefore obvious that the two works are distinctly different. In fact, since Jefferson specifically announced that his 1804 abridgment was "for the Use of Indians" at "*the Level of their Comprehension*," it would certainly *not* include the French, Latin, or Greek passages that he placed in his second work more than a decade later. In this, as in so many areas, Throckmorton seems to miss or reject the obvious in his quest to find something hidden and obscure.

ISSUE #6: JEFFERSON AND EMANCIPATION

Despite the abundant documentation that I present showing that Jefferson, even though a slave owner, repeatedly attempted to restrict and end slavery both in his state of Virginia and in the nation, Throckmorton completely ignores that evidence and attempts to portray Jefferson as a hypocritical racist who could have freed his own slaves but refused to so do. I demonstrate that Virginia slave laws did not permit Jefferson, in his situation, to free his own slaves, but Throckmorton claims otherwise, asserting that Jefferson could have indeed freed his slaves under a particular clause in a 1782 statute, which stated that "any person, by his or her last will and testament, or by any other instrument in writing . . . [may] emancipate and set free his or her slaves, or any of them."[112]

But Throckmorton ignored the portion of this law immediately preceding the clause he invoked, which clearly states that the emancipation provision was only "expedient *under certain restrictions.*"[113] Throckmorton discounted those restrictions, and he also disregarded Jefferson's own declaration that "the laws do not permit us to turn them loose . . ."[114] Notice Jefferson's use of the word *laws*—that is, there were "laws" (plural), and "certain restrictions" already in place, not just a single "law" (singular) governing emancipation in Virginia, as Throckmorton naïvely seems to believe.

The state's slave code was very complicated, with laws adding new requirements or altering previous ones being passed regularly, including during the legislative sessions of October 1776, May 1777, October 1778, May 1779, October 1779, May 1780, October 1780, May 1782, October 1783, October 1784, October 1785, October 1786, December 1787, November 1788, December 1788, November 1789, December 1789, December 1790, November 1792, as well as in 1794, 1797, 1803, etc.[115] Each of these laws interfaced with others to make a very complicated legal gridwork pertaining to the subject of slavery—much like the three-million-word IRS code has become today.

Particularly relevant to Jefferson's case was a law requiring the economic bonding of certain emancipated slaves. Jefferson, who suffered severe economic difficulties throughout his lifetime, was unable to meet the added financial requirements of that emancipation law. Another Virginia law applicable to him stipulated that "all slaves so emancipated shall be liable to be taken . . . to satisfy any debt contracted by the person emancipating them."[116] Thus, emancipated slaves could be seized by creditors to pay off any debt owed by the owner, thus legally negating their emancipation.

Dumas Malone, the Pulitzer Prize–winning biographer of Jefferson, calculated Jefferson's indebtedness at $107,273.63 at the time of his death[117] (or nearly $2.5 million in today's money). He concluded that for Jefferson, in his financial condition, to have emancipated his slaves "in view of his indebtedness may have been illegal" under Virginia law.[118] Noted historian Paul Johnson agrees that Jefferson's economic difficulties were indeed a significant impediment to emancipating his slaves.[119] Simply put, Jefferson did not have the financial resources necessary to free his 260[120] slaves, most of which he had inherited at a very young age or had received through his marriage to his wife, Martha.

Perhaps the case of Robert Carter best demonstrates the overall complexity of the Virginia emancipation process. Carter, whose wealth was considerable and who had as many as 500 slaves, emancipated them all in 1791. Yet, due to the difficulties of his executor process, and the intricacies of Virginia slave laws, *sixty years later* in 1852 (and long after Carter's death), his heirs were still working to free his slaves as per his original directive.[121] When it came to emancipation, Virginia law was definitely convoluted and restrictive.

There are numerous additional examples demonstrating that the simplicity in emancipation that Throckmorton attempts to portray simply did not exist in many cases, including that of Jefferson. It is regrettable that his fixation on criticizing me causes him to miss the major point I made on this subject, which was that (as will be demonstrated below) given Jefferson's lengthy record of repeated efforts to secure emancipation for all slaves, the modern characterization of Jefferson as a racist advocate of slavery is highly misleading, if not altogether false. In fact, the truth was so well known to previous generations that civil rights leaders across the decades, both black and white, invoked Jefferson as a model for his tireless emancipation efforts—a fact rarely acknowledged today.

* * *

It is certainly proper for Throckmorton to offer a robust critique of *The Jefferson Lies*, but I wish he had engaged the substance of my arguments. Instead, he repeatedly focuses on narrow and almost obscure facts, which he wrongly asserts are vital to my premise.

For example, Throckmorton calls my reference to the John Thompson Bible one of the "key claims" in my book.[122] I covered that entire topic in fewer than seven of the 6,417 lines in the book—certainly not enough to constitute his characterization of it as being a "key claim." Furthermore, the mention of that Bible was just one item from a list of nearly a dozen similar ones, so that even if the reference to the Thompson Bible were completely removed, the overall point made in the chapter remains unaltered. But Throckmorton repeatedly ignores, or perhaps avoids, the major point being made.

Similarly, I also made a brief reference to an 1803 treaty that Jefferson approved which provided funding for the ministry of a Catholic priest and the building of a church for the Kaskaskia tribe. That entire topic is covered in only sixteen lines, but Throckmorton again titles it a "key claim."[123]

Many of Throckmorton's criticisms are of this nature. In this Preface, I have not attempted to respond to each and every criticism he levels at me but rather I have addressed a sampling of them. (To view more of his objections, and the historical responses, go to www.TheJeffersonLies.com, A Response to Critics.) But while Throckmorton and I do have our differences, I sincerely appreciate the fact that he at least read the book before criticizing it—something that many who attacked this book did not do.

In fact, when Jay Richards (the speaker from the Discovery Institute who was enlisted by Throckmorton to find and recruit critics to attack my works) confronted me about what he claimed were errors in *The Jefferson Lies*, I repeatedly asked him if he had read the book. He refused to answer. But it was clear from his mischaracterization of my arguments that he had not read it (or at least all of it). For instance, he repeatedly asserted that I said that Jefferson was an evangelical, but as is clear in the chapter on Jefferson's faith, I do not make that claim.

Although they did not intend to help me, I am grateful to Richards, Throckmorton, and other critics for helping to improve *The Jefferson Lies*. I am also grateful that WND Books agreed to bring this book back into print—especially with the caveat that I include this new preface exposing the many irresponsible and wrong claims made by the Grove City professors. I happily did so, for this provides an opportunity to expose even more of the modern falsehoods currently circulating about Jefferson.

Anytime that a work of this magnitude is produced—a work that includes nearly a thousand footnotes drawn from thousands of historical sources—there are many who must be acknowledged, and among those worthy of public recognition are:

- Early American historians (such as Jared Sparks, Benson Lossing, George Bancroft, Richard Frothingham, Charles Coffin, John Fiske, and others) who believed that they should objectively report history without spin or personal opinion—that it was their duty to record everything that occurred, including not only the bad and the ugly (which is too often the limit of historical examination today) but also the good.

- Current websites that invested extensive time and money in placing thousands of original unedited historical documents online so that they can now be read in their entirety by any citizen without the extraneous personal opinions with which many scholars seek to bias readers. Such praiseworthy websites include the Avalon Project, the Library of Congress, the American Presidency Project, a Century of Lawmaking, and many others.

- Jefferson scholars such as Dr. Mark Beliles, who in 1993 not only researched Jefferson's faith by reading scores of Jefferson's own writings but also studied countless letters, writings, diaries, and memoirs from scores of clergymen who personally interacted with Jefferson. Beliles thus presents remarkable insight into Jefferson's complex relationship with the clergy, reaching conclusions that, although consistent with primary source historical data, are dramatically different from the opinions of many today who call themselves Jefferson scholars but have read few of Jefferson's own writings. (Beliles also recently penned *Doubting Thomas: The Religious Life and Legacy of Thomas Jefferson,* and also *The Selected Religious Papers and Writings of Thomas Jefferson.*) Others who demonstrate the same sound historical approach include Dr. Daniel Dreisbach, Dr. Mark David Hall, and Dr. Philip Hamburger.

- My own research staff, who took hundreds of tedious questions I posited them and provided answers from primary source documents. Among the many who were vital in the research and writing of this book were Sarah Freeman, Caroline Henry, Tim Stackpole, Kristy Stedman, Brian Freeman, Damaris Schuler, Timothy Barton, Gabriella Barton, Derringer Dick, Mary Coran, and Jennifer Farley.

- The various professors and PhDs who not only spent so much time reviewing this work, graciously offering their comments and openly endorsing it, but also the many other professors who reviewed and provided recommendations but declined endorsing it for the certainly that if they did so, they would be attacked by the likes of Throckmorton and Richards.

- Also, my sincere appreciation is due my wife, Cheryl, who graciously and flexibly accommodated the countless hundreds of hours I spent researching and writing this work, often at irregular times and in unusual settings.

- Of course, my highest gratitude is humbly offered to my Creator and Redeemer without Whose daily sustenance and mercy my life would not exist. It is only in His loving Providence that we live, move, and have our being.

- I extend my heartfelt thanks to each of these; their contributions, most of which will never be fully known by the public, have been indispensable.

So here it is. The book you almost didn't get to read!

Now you know the true story behind *The Jefferson Lies*. But more importantly, you will now learn truth about Thomas Jefferson at a time when truth itself is under attack. I hope that this book kindles within you a new veneration for Thomas Jefferson as a cherished American hero. Hopefully this book will play some small role in helping to rehabilitate the public's perception of one of America's greatest civic leaders.

Rediscovering Thomas Jefferson

When I speak at universities and law schools across the nation—schools full of America's best and brightest students—I like to display a slide of the famous painting of the signers of the Declaration of Independence that hangs inside the Rotunda of the US Capitol. While showing that picture, I often comment that it is unfortunate that the Founding Fathers were a collective group of racists, bigots, and slaveholders. Almost always I receive nods of sad affirmation from the students.

I then ask them to identify which of the signers in the painting owned slaves. Everyone immediately points to Thomas Jefferson, but to date no one has ever pointed out a second example. They have been taught that the Founding Fathers were racists. They know that Jefferson owned slaves. Apparently this means that the rest of the fifty-six also owned slaves. Yet many of these men did not own slaves, and some who did freed them. In fact, a majority of the Founders spoke or wrote against slavery, introduced or passed antislavery legislation, and/or were involved in antislavery societies.[1] And even though Jefferson owned slaves, as we shall see, he was profoundly troubled by the institution and in fact worked to end it. But students are usually not told this part of the story.

Because of the many modern attacks on the Founders and the often incomplete and usually negative information students receive, most have no idea that very few individuals in history have received as many titles of honor as Thomas Jefferson, including "Apostle of Liberty,"[2] "Man of the People,"[3] "Pen of the Revolution,"[4] "Father of the Declaration of Independence,"[5] "The Defender of the Rights of Man and the Rights of Conscience,"[6] the "Sage of Monticello,"[7] and "The Apostle of Democracy."[8] As well, he is one of a handful of Founders honored with a major national monument in Washington, DC, and he has been featured on more postage stamps than any other Founder save George Washington and Benjamin Franklin.[9]

He is truly a national icon of significant note and accomplishment—a visionary and an innovator—a Renaissance man in the classical sense of the term. He was masterful and skilled in many diverse areas, and his multidimensional abilities were profusely praised by those who knew him. For example:

- Marquis de Chastellux, a French general who served with Jefferson during the American Revolution, described him as "a musician, skilled in drawing, a geometrician, an astronomer, a natural philosopher, legislator, and statesman."[10]

- Dr. Benjamin Rush, one of Jefferson's fellow signers of the Declaration of Independence, said he was "enlightened at the same time in chemistry, natural history, and medicine."[11]

- The Reverend Ezra Stiles, president of Yale of College from 1778–1795, called him a "naturalist and philosopher, a truly scientific and learned man."[12]

- John Quincy Adams knew him as "a man of very extensive learning and pleasing manners."[13]

- General Marquis de Lafayette considered him a "great statesman, zealous citizen, and amiable friend."[14]

- Alexis de Tocqueville, the French historian and political leader who penned the famous Democracy in America as a result of his visit to America in 1831, called Jefferson "the greatest [man] whom the democracy of America has as yet produced."[15]

Perhaps the best summation of Jefferson's extensive abilities was given by President John F. Kennedy, who once quipped to a group of Nobel Prize winners dining with him at the White House:

> I think this is the most extraordinary collection of talent, of human knowledge, that has ever been gathered together at the White House—with the possible exception of when Thomas Jefferson dined alone. Someone once said that Thomas Jefferson was a gentleman of 32 who could calculate an eclipse, survey an estate, tie an artery, plan an edifice, try a cause, break a horse, and dance the minuet.[16]

Jefferson was truly a remarkable man, and it is an understatement to say that his positive influence on America and even the world has been enormous. He helped shape America for the better, and more recently, across the world wherever tyranny has been opposed and freedom pursued, Jefferson and his words are regularly held forth as the embodiment of liberty and limited government. This fact was especially reaffirmed in the later part of the twentieth century.

For example, Chinese students who strove to force democratic reforms under their totalitarian government regularly invoked Jefferson, even as the world watched the Communist tyrants massacre those students at Tiananmen Square.[17]

And then when Czechoslovakians rose to throw off forty years of Soviet Communist tyranny, Czech leader Zdenek Janicek quoted Jefferson and his words to encourage the revolting Czech workers.[18] And after Vaclav Havel became the first president of the freed Czech Republic, he, too, pointed to Jefferson and his governing philosophy as the standard for his new nation.[19]

During Poland's struggle for independence from the Soviet Union, Jefferson was cited so often that award-winning Polish author Jerzy Kosinski observed, "In every Pole, there is Jefferson more than anyone else."[20]

Reform-minded Soviet leader Mikhail Gorbachev spoke openly of Jefferson's positive influence upon him, explaining: "For myself, I found one thing to be true: having once begun a dialogue with Jefferson, one continues the conversation with him forever."[21]

When the Soviet Union fell in 1991 and Russia became free from its Communist oppressors, Andrei Kozyrev, the foreign minister of the new Russian republic, openly acknowledged that he was indebted to Jefferson and his governing philosophy.[22]

This pattern has been regularly repeated around the globe. As former prime minister of England Lady Margaret Thatcher affirmed, "[I]n the history of liberty, he's a great figure everywhere in the world."[23]

Jefferson and his ideas of freedom, limited government, and God-given inalienable rights literally changed the world, and historians across the generations consistently praised his influence and contributions:

> American history presents few names to its students more attractive and distinguished than that of Thomas Jefferson, and rarely has a single individual in civil station acquired such an ascendancy over the feelings and actions of a people.[24]
>
> —BENSON LOSSING, 1848

> Thomas Jefferson . . . [was] singled out to draft the confession of faith of the rising empire. He owed this distinction to . . . that general favor which follows merit, modesty, and a sweet disposition. . . . No man of his century had more trust in the collective reason and conscience of his fellowmen, or better knew how to take their counsel.[25]
>
> —GEORGE BANCROFT, "FATHER OF AMERICAN HISTORY," 1864

> [He] had a faith in humanity that never wavered. He aimed to secure for it law that should deal out equal and exact justice to all men, and he sought to lift all men up to their native dignity by lifelong labor in the cause of education.[26]
>
> —RICHARD FROTHINGHAM, 1872

> Of all the men of that time, there was perhaps none of wider culture or keener political instincts.[27]
>
> —JOHN FISKE, 1891

[O]ne of the finest traits of his character was his magnanimity.... His dearest aim was to bring down the aristocracy and elevate the masses.[28]

—EDWARD ELLIS, 1898

Jefferson often made mistakes, but as he said of Washington, he "erred with integrity." If he changed his mind, it was because he had new light or a clearer understanding; if he altered his course, it was because he believed he could accomplish greater good.[29]

—WILLIAM ELEROY CURTIS, 1901

Democracy has won in the United States, and the spirit of its founder lives in all our political parties. He has stamped his individuality on the American government more than any other man.[30]

—HENRY WILLIAM ELSON, 1904

[Jefferson] is a kind of Rosetta Stone of the American experience, a massive, tectonic intelligence that has formed and rattled the fault lines of our history, our present moment, and, if we are lucky, our future.[31]

—KEN BURNS, 1996

This once nearly universal praise of Jefferson has certainly diminished in recent years. Mention some of Jefferson's accomplishments today and most Americans who have been through American history classes since the 1960s will retort, "Yeah, he may have done some of those things, but he was also a racist and a bigot—a slaveholder. And he slept with his fourteen-year-old slave Sally Hemings and made her pregnant. And he hated religion so much that he founded the first secular university in America, even writing his own Bible from which he cut out the Scriptures with which he disagreed."

Why can today's Americans list so many negatives about Jefferson but so few positives? The answer is found in the way American history is now presented, which has become so appallingly poor that among both recent graduates and citizens in general:[32]

- One-half failed to recognize Patrick Henry as the man who said, "Give me liberty or give me death!"[33] and more students thought that Ulysses S. Grant rather than George Washington led the troops at Yorktown[34]

- Eight in ten Americans could not name even two of the rights listed in the Declaration[35] and some nine in ten could not name even one writer of the *Federalist Papers*[36]

- Six in ten could not identify the three branches of government (legislative, executive, judicial),[37] three of four did not know what the Judiciary Branch does,[38] and eight in ten could not name even one of the federal government's powers.[39] Two in three did not know that the Constitutional Convention produced the US Constitution,[40] and seven in ten did not know that the Constitution was the supreme law of the land[41]

- Only one in four can actually name one fundamental freedom protected by the First Amendment,[42] and just 1 in 1000 can name all five freedoms protected by it (speech, religion, press, assembly, and petition).[43]

Over the past two decades, I have worked as an official consultant in drafting social studies and history standards for various states, and I am often asked to serve as an expert historical witness in federal and state legislatures and courts. In doing so, I have had extensive interactions with thousands of teachers and scores of college professors. Based on those experiences, I have identified six modern historical malpractices that undermine the knowledge of our own history. I call them: Negativism, Relativism, Antinationalism, Modernism, Minimalism, and Rigid Secularism.*

Although these six isms might suggest that an ivory-tower discussion is about to commence, such is not the case. Once the six are described, you may have an aha! moment and recognize how they have shaped your own opinion. In fact, if you now think poorly of Jefferson, you will almost assuredly hold a very different opinion at the end of this book—and that is its object: to reverse the effect of these six malpractices that have distorted not only the presentation of Jefferson in particular but of American history in general. So let's first identify the recent influences that have affected the way Jefferson is currently viewed before looking at the historic truth about him.

---

* These six categories can also be identified by their more academic descriptors. For example, Negativism is a historical manifestation of Critical Theory, which is a derivative of the Frankfurt School and the Cultural Marxism that it propounded. Relativism is akin to German Historicism; Antinationalism is comparable to modern Post-Colonialism; and so forth. I have chosen to use more informal and colloquial terms, which will be preferable for most audiences, but academics will also recognize the corollary to these terms as they are used within the academic field.

HISTORICAL NEGATIVISM

Historical Negativism is a steady flow of belittling and demeaning portrayals of Western heroes, beliefs, values, and institutions.

An accurate presentation of history depends on telling the good, the bad, and the ugly about any event, person, or period, but Negativists stress the bad and the ugly while routinely ignoring the good. They can identify every blemish that has appeared on the face of the country over the past four centuries but not what has made America the envy of almost every people in the world—every people, that is, except many modern Americans, who can now recite more of what's wrong with America than what's right.

For example, every public school textbook I have seen teaches students about the infamous American witch trials in which twenty-seven individuals died.[44] This is certainly appropriate, but these trials should be put in context. I have never seen a contemporary history book that informs students that witch trials were also occurring across the world at that time with 500,000 put to death in Europe,[45] including 30,000 in England, 75,000 in France, and 100,000 in Germany.[46] Why do modern texts point out the twenty-seven deaths in America but ignore the 500,000 elsewhere? Historical Negativism.

Students should also know that the American trials lasted only eighteen months, while the European trials lasted for years.[47] And the American trials were brought to a close when Christian leaders such as the Reverend John Wise, the Reverend Increase Mather, and Thomas Brattle confronted civil leaders that Biblical rules of evidence and due process were not being followed in the courts, thus convincing officials to end those trials.[48]

Furthermore, students should learn that the Puritans established some of the freest societies governed by the rule of law that the world had ever seen,[49] including early elective forms of government in America.[50] They also originated America's practice of written constitutions[51] and constructed the first bills of rights to protect individual liberties.[52] Moreover, they encouraged widespread education (literacy rates in New England were among the highest on the globe)[53] and founded what became two of the greatest universities in the world: Harvard and Yale. Like all humans they were far from perfect, but there is much to celebrate in their accomplishments. School children deserve to learn more about the Puritans than just the Salem witch trials.

Another long venerated group that has now become a frequent target for attack by Historical Negativists is America's Founding Fathers. Popular media, educational sources, and curricula regularly assert that they were (according to programming on A&E) petty and profane,[54] sex maniacs and selfish egotists (according to, for example, The History Channel, NBC, and A&E)[55] who abused those not from their own elitist group (from a popular national public school curriculum)[56]—propagandists without conscience (as per numerous works and encyclopedias).[57] In fact, the Founders were actually terrorists (public school curriculum in Texas)[58]—precursors to the Nazis (Journalism Professor Robert Jenson)[59]—who gave us "our imbecilic Constitution" (Law Professor Sanford Levinson in *The New York Times*).[60] (My own history teacher once told me, "George Washington had twenty-six illegitimate children, giving new meaning to the phrase 'Washington slept here'.") There are countless more examples of similar negativity expressed toward the Founding Fathers in modern classrooms and educational materials.

In short, Historical Negativists relentlessly attack that which was historically venerated, including the country, its Founders, and traditional faith and morality. They teach things that undermine American values, institutions, traditions, and heroes, but virtually nothing that honors or affirms them. And this is certainly true with many modern portrayals of Thomas Jefferson.

HISTORICAL RELATIVISM

The second historical malpractice is *Relativism*, which asserts that in history, religion, culture, and law there are neither absolutes nor transcendent principles. Values are to be determined individually, and personal standards trump traditional ones; thus subjectivity and feelings prevail over objectivity and facts.

In the legal arena, this malpractice has led Relativist judges to redefine laws and constitutions to reflect their own personal beliefs and values. US Supreme Court Chief Justice Charles Evans Hughes accurately encapsulated the essence of this belief when he said: "We are under a Constitution—but the Constitution is what the judges say it is."[61]

For instance, the religion clauses of the First Amendment were clearly written to protect religious belief and practice and prohibit only the creation of a state-established and enforced religion. But in the hands of activist Relativist judges the purpose of that Amendment has been reversed so as now to ban religious exercises and expressions that were long part of our public life.

Relativists in education, like their counterpart in the Judiciary, also hold that beliefs are relative and not absolute. They therefore teach students that all forms of governments are good, with textbooks even equating communistic, socialistic, and totalitarian governments favorably with free ones.* Relativists also assert that while most religions are equal, that any religion—or even *no* religion—is actually better than a Judeo-Christian one.[62]

But in the real world, all governments and all beliefs are definitely *not* equal. Some things work and some don't. Comparisons can and should be made. As signer of the Declaration John Witherspoon urged two centuries ago in a slightly different context, "Let us try it by its fruits. Let us . . . see which of them best merits the approbation of an honest and impartial judge."[63] But Relativists refuse to make assessments, or to judge the fruits or consequences of various systems and ideas.

For example, it seems clear that America's free-market, private enterprise-driven economic system has produced excellent financial results. Not only does America's four percent of the world's

---

* This problem has been particularly visible in the state of Texas over the past few decades. It is not that Texas is the source of the problem but rather that because Texas and California have nearly one-fourth the nation's public school students, textbook publishers generally flock to these two states to have their textbooks approved, thus providing a significant market in which to sell their materials. As part of the approval process in Texas, texts submitted by publishers are reviewed both by citizens and content-area specialists appointed by the State Board of Education, who then testify as to any problems they find within those books. Much testimony has been given about textbooks that not only present all governments as equal (see, for example, *World Geography Today, Teachers Annotated Edition,* Stephanie Abraham Hirsh and Karen Tindel Wiggins, editors (Holt, Rinehard, & Winston, 1989), 92, 173) but also some that even state that Socialism and Communism were the best governments devised by man. Former Texas state legislator Rick Green speaks openly of his appearances before the State Board of Education (as do many others) testifying about such textbooks, and recommending they be rejected for use in Texas schools. Texas therefore provides an excellent survey of the textbook content and educational philosophy, both good and bad, presented in student textbooks across the country.

population produce almost a quarter of the world's gross domestic product (GDP)[64] but other nations that have embraced this same system have begun to soar economically, including South Korea, the Czech Republic, Estonia, Ireland, Singapore, and Guyana. Nevertheless, in one state where I was appointed to help write their standards, when it was suggested that students in economics classes be taught the repeatedly proven superior performance of the free-market system among the world's various economic approaches, university professors came to the state capitol to lead the protest against that proposal.[65]

But just as economic systems can and should be compared and judged, so, too, should governments.

America has only had one form of government since the US Constitution went into effect in 1789, but in that same period of time, France has had fifteen constitutions;[66] Brazil, seven since 1822;[67] Poland, seven since 1919;[68] Afghanistan, five since 1923;[69] Russia, four since 1918;[70] South Korea, six since 1948;[71] and so forth. This type of instability characterizes nations in Europe, Africa, South America, and the rest of the world—except America. Why? Because the specific values set forth in the Declaration of Independence and subsequently embodied in the Constitution have, under God, produced this remarkable stability. Yet Relativists refuse to acknowledge such self-evident facts, instead holding that there is nothing special about either America or its form of government.

Sadly, Relativists now dominate both classroom instruction and curricular writing, but regardless of their claims, all beliefs are not equal. Differing ideas and values do produce distinctly different outcomes and consequences, whether in law, government, culture, or morality.

ANTINATIONALISM

The third device for pulling down what is traditionally honored is *Antinationalism*, which undermines patriotism, or the love of one's country. While this can occur through a direct denunciation or demeaning of America (as with Historical Negativism), it usually occurs through the more subtle means of emphasizing a loyalty to things either larger or smaller than the nation.

As an example of the former, I was recently appointed by a state to review its history standards as drafted by 240 of its leading classroom teachers. The very first standard they penned announced, "In Kindergarten, the study of the self, home, family, and classroom establishes the foundation for responsible citizenship in a *global society.*"[72] And this same objective also topped the first grade standards, along with recommendations that icons such as the Liberty Bell and individuals such as Nathan Hale no longer be taught.[73] Thus, the focus is turned away from the nation and placed on something much larger, such as "a global society."

Promoting a global focus is one form of Antinationalism. Another results from urging a loyalty to something smaller than the nation, such as one's subgroup—what is today known as "Identity Politics." Hence, many individuals no longer identify themselves as Americans first but rather as Feminists, Union Members, Latinos, LGBT, African-Americans, Evangelicals, Seniors, and so on. In fact, Congress now passes "hate crime" laws determining which subgroups will receive extra protection (such as gays and lesbians) and which will not (such as veterans and seniors).[74] Congress has also passed tax laws determining which subgroups will be economically rewarded and which punished.* Thus, many laws no longer apply equally to all Americans.

America was long characterized by the Latin phrase on the Great Seal of the United States: *E Pluribus Unum*, meaning "out of many, one." This acknowledged that although there was much diversity in America, there was a common national culture and unity that transcended all differences. But Antinationalism reverses that emphasis to become *E Unum Pluribus*—that is, "out of one, many," thus dividing the nation into separate groups and components with no unifying or overarching commonality between them.

The earlier approach was described by a Chief of Naturalization who explained to World War I and II immigrants seeking American citizenship that:

> An American is a man who is greater in his soul than in his class, creed, political party, or the section in which he lives. To be an American, a man must have an American soul and believe in the spiritual realities upon which America rests

---

* The Constitution originally established capitation taxation, whereby taxes were spread evenly per capita, or per head, much like the Biblical tithe. Significantly, under the Biblical approach, everyone paid the tax at the same ten percent rate; whether rich or poor, the percentage was the same. So if a wealthy man made one million dollars, his tithe, or tax, was one hundred thousand dollars; and if a poor man made only one hundred dollars, his tithe, or tax, was only ten dollars. So under this uniform tax, the rich actually paid more than the poor, but each was treated exactly the same under the law. This changed in 1913 when the progressive income tax became the replacement for capitation taxation. At that point, it became necessary for the government to determine the group to which one belonged before knowing how to treat that person. Thus, the poor were handled differently from the middle class, and both of them differently from the rich. So no longer are all citizens treated equally under tax laws, but instead they are handled differently according to the particular group to which they belong.

15

and out of which America was born. America was created to unite mankind by those passions which lift and not by the passions which separate and debase. We came to America . . . to get rid of the things that divide and make sure of the things that unite. . . . [T]he man who seeks to divide men from men, group from group, interest from interest in this great Union is striking at its very heart.[75]

The current emphasis both on globalism and subgroups has replaced the former teaching of a love for and a loyalty to the country. This de-emphasis on the nation, combined with the overemphasis on negatives about it, has weakened a veneration and respect for those things that promote and make it unique and distinctive, including its Constitution, form of government, religious faith, traditional morality, and also its venerated heroes—such as Thomas Jefferson.

REJECTION OF AMERICAN EXCEPTIONALISM

Before examining the final three modern historical malpractices, it should be noted that the greatest casualty of the combined influence of Historical Negativism, Historical Relativism, and Antinationalism is American Exceptionalism—the belief that America is blessed and enjoys unprecedented stability, prosperity, and liberty as a result of the institutions and policies produced by unique ideas such as God-given inalienable rights, individualism, limited government, republicanism, and an educated and virtuous citizenry.

Americans *truly* are blessed. Statistically speaking, America is an exceptional nation, for in so many important categories among the other nations of the world she represents the exception rather than the rule. This exceptionalism encompasses great diversity of race, ethnicity, and religion, and has benefited every American. But today, following several decades of indoctrination in both education and politics, American Exceptionalism is no longer recognized, understood, or venerated. To the contrary, many Americans now seem ashamed of their country and feel compelled to apologize to others for it;[76] they are particularly conscious of America's flaws but seem obliviously ignorant of its matchless benefits and opportunities.

In fact, when I was recently appointed by a State Superintendent of Public Education to serve as a historical consultant in the writing of standards for that state's curriculum—a state considered very conservative—I reminded the teachers about the importance of acknowledging American Exceptionalism and identifying the specific causes for it. One would think that educators in this conservative state would have been open to this suggestion, but I was quickly rebuked; these teachers found it reprehensible to think of teaching that America was different from other nations. Strangely, some educators now claim that it is "un-American" to say the Pledge of Allegiance, and some schools have gone forty years without reciting it.[77]

The combined effects of Historical Negativism, Historical Relativism, and Antinationalism have allowed nothing respected and traditional to stand unattacked and untainted, whether it is the country itself, its Constitution and form or government, or even its heroes. Hence, in the case of Thomas Jefferson, Americans can readily point out what they have been told are his multitude of unpardonable sins but can list nearly none of his invaluable and timeless contributions that undeniably changed America and the world for the better.

MODERNISM (PRESENTISM)

A fourth common historical malpractice is *Modernism*,* which examines historical events and persons as if they occurred and lived today rather than in the past. It thus severs history from its context and setting, therefore misrepresenting historical beliefs and events.

For example, it seems self-evident to twenty-first century Americans that slavery is immoral, and I certainly agree. But the problem comes when modern writers condemn America's Founders for not immediately abolishing the practice[78] even invoking this as evidence that America did not have a Christian Founding.[79] Such claims reflect Modernism (that is, Presentism)—measuring eighteenth-century Americans by twenty-first century standards.

Modernists fail to recognize, or at least to acknowledge, that slavery had been widely accepted for millennia before the Founding Fathers, and that during the Founding Era numerous American Gospel ministers cited Biblical texts from both Old and New Testament in support of the institution,[80] even owning slaves themselves.[81] Our current belief about slavery has literally taken centuries to gradually develop.

By way of analogy, a century from now Modernists may condemn our generation for its failure to abolish abortion, especially since it has been irrefutably proved that the procedure kills a living human being. But as one who lives in this generation, I understand that our inability (thus far) to end this moral

---

*   The term Modernism is used here not in the context of Post-Modernism but rather in regards to the practice of using the present as the filter for the past. Some works identify this term as "Presentism."

reprehension does not mean that all of us in this generation are not Christians, or even that some of those who have actually had an abortion and have now reversed their previous views toward it, are not Christians. Yet Modernist writers of future generations who might reach similar conclusions about the abortion issue today as Modernist writers now do about slavery and previous generations will be similarly wrong.

Another illustration of Modernism is the current claim that because the Founders frequently used terms such as "Providence," they were therefore deists.[82] After all, this word is rarely used by Christians today, and few modern editions of the Bible even contain the term.* But in the most popular Bible of early colonial America, the Geneva Bible, the term appeared 144 times and it was routinely used by some of America's most famous and even evangelical Gospel ministers. For almost three centuries, today's supposedly "deistic" term "Providence" was deeply implanted in the thought and speech of mainstream Christianity before eventually falling into modern disuse.

Similarly, Modernist critics complain about what they see as a liberal use of the death penalty in the early colonies.[83] But as nineteenth-century historian Daniel Dorchester pointed out, when those settlers left England to come to America, the death penalty was applied to 223 separate offenses in the Mother

---

* Current versions of the Bible that have no mention of the word *Providence* include those such as the *English Standard, The Message, New English Translation, New Life Bible, New Living.* Versions with one mention include the *New International* (Job 10:12), *20th Century KJV* (Acts 24:2), *American Standard* (Acts 24:2), and *New American Standard* (Acts 24: 2). The *New King James* has 3 mentions (Psalm 65:1, Psalm 104:1, Psalm 147:1), and the *Amplified Bible* has 4 (Job 10: 12, Ecclesiastes 12:13, Ezekiel 3:20, and Zechariah 3:9).

Country, but after their arrival in America, "not a single colony code recognized more than fifteen capital crimes."[84] He therefore correctly concluded, "Such are the facts of modern history which should moderate our denunciations and charges of severity, brutality, and narrow-mindedness against the colonial forefathers who, it clearly appears, were much in advance of their times."[85]

All of this is not to say that there is no absolute truth or that historical eras, movements, and individuals should not be judged by the immutable standards of right and wrong that transcend all generations—the standards that Jefferson and the Founding Fathers identified in the Declaration of Independence as "the laws of nature and of nature's God." But just because those in previous generations may have "seen some things imperfectly" (1 Corinthians 13:12) does not mean that everything they did that differs from today's practices can therefore be dismissed out of hand.

Presenting history through the filter of Modernism produces many flawed conclusions, including about Jefferson.

MINIMALISM (REDUCTIONISM)

The fifth modern malpractice is *Minimalism*,* which is an unreasonable insistence on oversimplification—on reducing everything to monolithic causes and linear effects. Minimalism is easily recognizable in political campaign rhetoric: candidates take behemoth problems facing the nation—complicated difficulties that often have been decades in the making—and reduce them to one-line platitudes and campaign slogans.

---

*   This term is also described in some works as "Reductionism," "Reductionist," or "Misgeneralization."

Minimalism is also very evident in the modern portrayal of history. For example, if you ask most citizens today why America separated from Great Britain, the overwhelming response will be "taxation without representation." This is certainly what we have been taught in school; and that answer is acceptable—as far as it goes; but taxation without representation was only one of twenty-seven grievances set forth in the Declaration of Independence. Listed in the Declaration eleven times more often than taxation without representation was the abuse of representative powers; the abuse of military powers appeared seven times more often; the abuse of judicial powers four times as often; and stirring up domestic insurrection twice as often. Taxation without representation was merely grievance number seventeen out of the twenty-seven, listed alongside Great Britain's suppression of immigration and her interference with our foreign trade. And when one turns from the Declaration to other documents approved by Congress, it also becomes crystal clear that Great Britain's direct threat to religious liberty in America was also a prominently listed cause for the separation.[86] So taxation without representation was merely one grievance among many, and not even one of the most significant, yet it is often the only one that Minimalists recite.

Minimalism causes major themes in history to be neglected or ignored either by oversimplification of major things or a pre-occupation with minor things—the proverbial not seeing the forest for the trees. So regardless of whether it is through under-stating or overcomplicating, Minimalists fail to report many crucial aspects of history that provide perspective and context.

So how does this relate to Jefferson? Any proper examination of his life definitely will not accommodate Minimalism, for he was far more complex than most other individuals from the same period. As affirmed by Pulitzer Prize–winning historian Henry Adams:

> A few broad strokes of the brush would paint the portraits of all the early Presidents—with this exception [Jefferson]; and a few more strokes would answer for any member of their many cabinets; but Jefferson could be painted only touch by touch, with a fine pencil, and the perfection of the likeness depending upon the shifting and uncertain flicker of its semitransparent shadows.[87]

Minimalists try to squeeze Jefferson into a simplistic monolithic mold that he does not fit, thus the image of him as presented by one modern writer often varies greatly from the image of him presented by another.[88]

RIGID SECULARISM

The sixth and final error that undermines historical accuracy is an *unrelenting Secularism*, which presents an inaccurate and distorted view of religious influences in American history. This malpractice manifests itself in several shrewd and clever ways, including the use of omission as well as the selective presentation of specific historical eras, events, and persons.

For example, even though there are some two hundred major Founding Fathers (including signers of the Declaration, drafters of the US Constitution, framers of the Bill of Rights, and so forth), many modern books purporting to examine the faith of the Founders present only a small handful of them. And the ones they do select are almost exclusively those who at some point in their lives questioned a basic tenet of orthodox

Christianity (usually Thomas Jefferson, Benjamin Franklin, John Adams, Ethan Allen, and Thomas Paine), or who did not express their religious convictions in a manner deemed to be orthodox by the authors (often George Washington, James Madison, and Alexander Hamilton).[89] So, unless readers know something about the scores of other Founding Fathers (which few today do), most accept the writers' depiction that the overall body of Founders was generally not orthodox Christian.

Recall the students at the beginning of this chapter who believed that all the Founders were pro-slavery? When I ask students to point out in that same painting the numerous openly religious and even evangelical signers, they look at me quizzically and can't offer a single name. They have been trained to identify Jefferson and Franklin, two of the least religious among the Founders, but not the scores of others who held a distinctly religious view.

By the way, *least religious* is a comparative rather than an absolute term. So when paralleling Jefferson to many of his fellow signers of the Declaration, he did not give Gospel altar calls in the courtroom like Thomas McKean.[90] Nor did he call his state to prayer on 22 separate occasions using Christ-centered language like John Hancock.[91] And he did not start the Sunday school movement in America or help found its first Bible society, as Benjamin Rush did.[92] Neither did he compile a church hymnal in which he set the entire book of Psalms to music, like Francis Hopkinson.[93] Nor was he a military chaplain, like Robert Treat Paine;[94] a theologian, like Roger Sherman;[95] or a Gospel minister, like John Witherspoon.[96] Jefferson certainly did not do in the religious realm what many others of his fellow signers did, so he truly is one of the "least" religious among that group; but this definitely does not mean that he was non- or anti-religious, as commonly claimed today.

In fact, as will be fully documented later, Jefferson's actions in promoting religious activities in the public realm go far beyond what most religious folks today would ever consider doing. This is not to suggest that Jefferson was an evangelical, for such was not the case; he was an active Anglican/Episcopalian, but his numerous pro-religious actions in the public realm are not insignificant.

So by an overemphasis on the least religious Founders and an exclusion of the others, students are taught the exception, not the rule—a practice also common to Negativism.

Another tactic associated with Rigid Secularism includes outright deception. Consider Ken Davis' best-selling *Don't Know Much About History*. In that work, he reminds readers of Patrick Henry's famous speech:

> Is life so dear or peace so sweet as to be purchased at the price of chains and slavery? . . . I know not what course others may take, but as for me, give me liberty or give me death![97]

Strikingly, the only phrase missing from the quotation (indicated by the ellipse) is Henry's fervent appeal to God: "Forbid it, Almighty God!"[98]

Similarly, Davis likewise edited the Mayflower Compact so that it reads:

> We whose names are underwritten . . . doe by these presents solemnly and mutually in the presence of God, and one of anotherr, covenant and combine our selves togeather into a civil body politick, for our better ordering and perservation

and furtherance of the ends aforesaid; and by vertue hearof to enacte, constitute, and frame such just and equal lawes, ordinances, acts, constitutions, and offices, from time to time, as shall be thought most meete for the generall good of the Colonie, unto which we promise all due submission and obedience . . .[99]

The portion omitted by Davis in the quotation is the Pilgrims' unequivocal declaration that their work was "undertaken for the glory of God and the advancement of the Christian faith."[100]

A similar secularist bias is evident in a modern reprint of the *Maxims of Washington*.[101] In 1834–1837, the first major collection of George Washington's writings (twelve volumes) was published by noted historian Jared Sparks. Drawing from those writings, in 1855 John Frederick Schroeder compiled Washington's short and pithy statements into four categories: political, social, moral, and religious.[102] He introduced each section with testimonials about Washington from contemporaries who personally knew him, including Ben Franklin, Marquis de Lafayette, John Paul Jones, John Hancock, Alexander Hamilton, and numerous others.

But when the modern reprint was released, John Riley, a scholar at Mount Vernon and the White House Historical Association, replaced the original 1855 introductions to each category with his own personal views. Therefore, in the section on Washington's religious maxims, he proclaimed that Washington was a deist;[103] but to do that, he had to delete from the original work the direct testimony of numerous of Washington's friends and associates who unequivocally avowed that Washington was a Christian.[104]

Perhaps the best example of an obsessive secularism is seen in *The Godless Constitution*. In that work, professors Isaac Kramnick and Laurence Moore assert that the Founding Fathers were largely a group of atheists, agnostics, and deists, with a few religious Founders sprinkled in among them. The two then aver that all the Founders—both the religious and non-religious ones—set out to deliberately create a thoroughly secularist government.[105] Strikingly, at the end of the book where footnotes customarily appear to delineate the evidence supporting the claims, the professors candidly acknowledge that "we have dispensed with the usual scholarly apparatus of footnotes."[106] Not even a high-school student would be permitted to submit a research paper with the same lack of primary source documentation, but these professors are willing to do so to advance their personal secularist views.

Many academics today find faith irrelevant or inconsequential in their own personal lives and therefore are blinded to its presence in earlier times. They often wrongly assume that since religion is not an important factor to them, that it was also inconsequential to intelligent folks of earlier times. Thus, they frequently neglect, ignore, dismiss, or understate its historical presence, or are only aware of its occasional shortcomings rather than its much more plentiful positive contributions. But primary source evidence and not professors' or anyone else's personal opinions or agenda is the proper standard for truth, including with any examination of Jefferson's life and beliefs.

The six modern malpractices of Negativism, Relativism, Antinationalism, Modernism, Minimalism, and Rigid Secularism have had far too great an influence over recent decades. But in the following chapters, we will move beyond those practices and embark on a search for historical truth about Jefferson, reclaiming many of the puzzle pieces of his image that have been discarded and lost in this present era. Specifically, we will delve into seven contemporary claims about Jefferson's faith and morals:

- Did he father a child (or children) by his young slave girl, Sally Hemings?

- Did he found a secular university as a reflection of his own supposedly secular lifestyle and beliefs?

- Did he write his own Bible, excluding the supernatural parts of Christianity with which he disagreed?

- Was he a racist who opposed civil rights and equality for black Americans?

- Did he, in his pursuit of separation of church and state, advocate secularizing the public square and expelling faith and religious expressions from the public arena?

- Did he hate the clergy?

- Did he repudiate religion? Was he an atheist, deist, or secularist, or was he a Christian?

In these seven areas, we will examine Jefferson's own words and actions as well as the eyewitness testimony of those who knew him best. Fortunately, Jefferson was candid and forthright on these subjects, which thus allows him to speak for himself. The image of him that will emerge will undoubtedly differ dramatically from what most Americans today have been told about him in each of these areas.

So notwithstanding the discomfort that may beset some modern agendas, the time has come to examine the seven issues raised against Jefferson today and begin recovering historical truth concerning each.

LIE #1

Thomas Jefferson Fathered Sally Hemings' Children

*I*n 1998 the journal *Science* released the results of a DNA investigation into whether Jefferson had fathered any children through his slave Sally Hemings, specifically her first child, Thomas, or her fifth child, Eston.[1] In conjunction with its announcement, Pulitzer Prize–winning historian Professor Joseph Ellis wrote an accompanying article in the journal *Nature* announcing that the question was now settled—that DNA testing had conclusively proved that Thomas Jefferson had indeed fathered a Hemings child, thus scientifically affirming a two-centuries-old rumor.[2]

That 1998 announcement was actually relevant to events occurring at the time, for it came at the commencement of President Bill Clinton's impeachment proceedings for lying under oath to a grand jury about his sexual activities with a young intern inside the Oval Office. News reports immediately pounced on the fortuitous DNA announcement, arguing that if a man as great as Thomas Jefferson had engaged in sexual trysts, then President Clinton should not face inquiries about his sexual misbehavior. After all, such conduct had not diminished the stature of Jefferson, they argued, so it should not be allowed to weaken Clinton's.

Professor Ellis agreed, candidly admitting, "President William Jefferson Clinton also has a vested interest in this [DNA] revelation."[3] (Shortly before his bombshell announcement about Jefferson, Ellis had added his signature as a cosigner of a *New York Times* ad opposing the impeachment of Clinton.[4]) Henry Gee, a staff writer for *Nature* who also wrote a piece as part of the initial revelation, similarly acknowledged that the DNA report provided much-needed cover for President Clinton:

> The parallels between the story of Jefferson's sexual indiscretions and the travails of the current President are close. Thomas Jefferson came close to impeachment—but the scandal did not affect his popularity and he won the 1804 Presidential election by a landslide. And if President William Jefferson Clinton has cause to curse the invention of DNA fingerprinting, the latest report shows that it has a long reach indeed—back to the birth of the United States itself.[5]

Dr. David Mayer, professor of law and history and a member of an independent Scholars' Commission later convened to review the Jefferson-Hemings issue, also believed that the timing of the DNA article had not been by accident:

> Professor Ellis' accompanying article also noted, quite frankly, "Politically, the Thomas Jefferson verdict is likely to figure in upcoming impeachment hearings on William Jefferson Clinton's sexual indiscretions, in which DNA testing has also played a role." In television interviews following release of the article, Professor Ellis elaborated on this theme; and Clinton's

apologists made part of their defense the notion that every President—even Jefferson—had his "sexual indiscretions."[6]

As far as Clinton defenders were concerned (especially his supporters in the media), the announcement of Jefferson's alleged moral failings was a gift from heaven. Thus, the entire nation was bombarded with the Jefferson paternity story for weeks, and the news of his supposed immorality was burned deeply into the consciousness of Americans.

Many groups beyond Clinton supporters also welcomed the test results as useful to their particular agendas. For example, the Jefferson-Hemings affair became the perfect platform for the feminist movement to discuss the nature of sexual relations. Many in that movement had already asserted that any type of sexual relations between a male and a female constituted rape,[7] but this development seemed to especially prove their point.[8] It was questioned whether any sex could be consensual if it was between individuals from different stations in life—such as Hemings and Jefferson had been.[9] Many feminist writers, including Fawn Brodie, Barbara Chase-Riboud, and Annette Gordon-Reed, had even authored books about the older Jefferson and the younger Hemings.[10]

Others who benefited from the Jefferson-Hemings story included activists who desired to keep open the racial wounds of previous generations. They pointed to Jefferson and his sexual exploitation of the slave Hemings as proof of how all African American slaves were treated by all white American slave owners not only in Jefferson's day but across subsequent American history,[11] and that the effects of this behavior[12] by Jefferson and others were still keenly felt in the black community today.[13] The Jefferson announcement therefore reinforced demands for restitutionary policies that would provide preferential treatment and elevation of status and opportunity as repayment for past wrongs.[14]

However, only eight weeks after the initial blockbuster DNA story was issued, it was pulled and rewritten, quietly and without fanfare, with the scientific researcher who had conducted the DNA test acknowledging that the test actually had *not* proven that Jefferson fathered any children with Hemings.[15] It turned out that the results had been dramatically overstated: there were twenty-six Jefferson males living in the area, of whom ten might have been the father of a Hemings child, and Thomas was only one possibility. But the admission of the misportrayed DNA testing results did not make the same splash in the national headlines, for it aided no agenda. Doing justice to Jefferson's reputation was not deemed in and of itself to be a worthy national consideration, so the retraction story was generally buried or ignored.

Consider the damage done by this false and inflammatory reporting. Ask any citizen today whether it has been scientifically proven that Jefferson fathered illegitimate children with Hemings, and they will likely answer with a resounding "Yes!" The nation certainly heard the repeated barrage of news headlines following the initial report, but the silence surrounding the correction has been deafening. Many today still believe that the original announcement was the only word ever given on the issue.

Yet, notwithstanding the 1998 DNA testing results, the fact remains that charges of a Jefferson moral failure with Hemings had circulated for almost two centuries before the DNA testing was undertaken. So even without the DNA testing results, it is still appropriate to ask why such charges were originally leveled against Jefferson. Did he actually commit the sexual misbehavior with which he has long been charged? After all, we're often told that where there's smoke, there's surely fire; so if it had not been for the charges raised long ago, no one today would have even considered undertaking DNA testing.

By way of historical background, Sally Hemings was a young slave girl who served Jefferson's daughters at the family home, Monticello. Jefferson had five daughters: Martha (nicknamed "Patsy"), Mary (nicknamed "Maria" but also called "Polly"), Jane (who died very young), Lucy Elizabeth I (who also died very young), and Lucy Elizabeth II.

During the American Revolution Jefferson was frequently away from his beloved family, serving in the Virginia legislature, the Continental Congress, and as state governor. In 1784, following the Revolution, Jefferson was sent by Congress as an American diplomatic envoy to Paris. His wife had recently died, so he took along Patsy, the oldest of his three remaining daughters. The other two, Mary and Lucy Elizabeth II, stayed behind with their aunt. But after Jefferson departed Monticello with Patsy, the toddler Lucy Elizabeth II unexpectedly died, so Jefferson sent for his only remaining daughter, Mary, to join him in France. Accompanying the eight-year-old Mary on the voyage as her companion was the fourteen-year-old Sally Hemings, whom Jefferson described as "Maria's maid."[16]

Critics charge that after the girls arrived in Paris, Jefferson began a sexual relationship with Hemings, who was nearly thirty years his junior and the same age as his oldest daughter, fourteen-year-old Patsy[17]—a relationship that produced some or all of Sally's children. (Most scholars believe that Hemings had five children.[18])

Following the initial DNA testing announcement that Jefferson was the father of Hemings' fifth child, Eston, some historians, including many who had previously believed Jefferson to be innocent of the paternity charges, reversed their positions and declared Jefferson guilty, with the two-century-old debate finally closed.[19] But the subsequent admission of a significant overstatement certainly changed matters.

Yet, regardless of the on-and-then-off DNA testing results, was there a sexual moral failure between Jefferson and Hemings?

The evidence for consideration may be divided into three areas:

1. The original 1998 DNA report. While this category of evidence is now discredited, it is important to understand why the announcement was subsequently rescinded and rewritten.

2. Oral tradition from two of Sally's children, the strongest of which involved Thomas Woodson, her first child. Two centuries ago, he claimed (and others repeated) that Sally Hemings was his mother and Thomas Jefferson his father. The fact that Sally named the boy Thomas was used as evidence to confirm that he had indeed been fathered by Jefferson. Sally's fourth child, Madison, made similar claims.

3. Published newspaper reports from Jefferson's day specifically charging him with fathering Hemings' children.

Let's consider the evidence in each category.

CATEGORY 1: THE DNA EVIDENCE

To delve further into the story behind the retraction of the 1998 DNA testing results, begin with Professor Ellis' original announcement in *Nature*, which claimed:

> Almost two hundred years ago Thomas Jefferson was alleged to have fathered children by his slave Sally Hemings. The charges have remained controversial. Now, DNA analysis confirms that *Jefferson was indeed the father* of at least one of Hemings' children [Eston].[20] (emphasis added)

In the two weeks following that announcement, 221 printed news articles repeated the claim, embedding it deeply in the minds of Americans.[21] Typical articles declared:

> Jefferson affair no longer rumor. . . . The DNA tests end nearly two centuries of speculation. . . . The evidence has shifted so startlingly that it now appears likely that Jefferson fathered four or five children by Hemings.
>
> —*USA TODAY*[22]

> Did the author of the Declaration of Independence take a slave for his mistress? DNA tests say yes. . . . The evidence here, in other words, removes any shadow of a doubt that Thomas Jefferson sired at least one son by Sally Hemings.
>
> —*U.S. NEWS & WORLD REPORT*[23]

> [G]enetic testing almost certainly proves that our third president fathered at least one child by Sally Hemings.
>
> —*WASHINGTON POST*[24]

DNA Test Finds Evidence of Jefferson Child by Slave.
—*NEW YORK TIMES*[25]

The opportunity to announce these results afforded many Negativists in the media a welcome occasion to denigrate Jefferson. One national columnist gloated, "What a relief. Now Jefferson can be brought down off the god-like pedestal on which some have tried to elevate him."[26] He continued, "How are we to view Jefferson now? How about 'deadbeat dad'? That's what you call fathers who run away from their responsibilities to their children."[27]

Another described him as a "slave-owning, serial flogger, sex maniac."[28] Others portrayed him as a child molester, using an innocent adolescent girl for sex:

> We have recently learned through DNA testing that Jefferson was probably the father of Sally Hemings' youngest child, a boy, and maybe the father of the other four children as well. . . . He took her to Paris when she was 13, and when she returned two years later, she was pregnant.
> —RICHARD COHEN, *WASHINGTON POST*[29]

> What type of relationship could this have been, considering the profound power differences between master and slave? . . . [S]he was 13 or 14 and he was 43.
> —CLARENCE PAGE, *CHICAGO TRIBUNE*[30]

> In 1789, Sally Hemings returned with the Jefferson family to Virginia. By then, Sally was 16 or 17 and pregnant.
> —DINITIA SMITH AND NICHOLAS WADE, *NEW YORK TIMES*[31]

The hysterics against Jefferson became so great that some questioned why his image appeared on our coins;[32] others clamored for "the dismantling of the Jefferson Memorial" in Washington, DC, and "the removal of his face from Mount Rushmore."[33]

The DNA evidence as originally presented by Professor Ellis and reported by the media had seemed both unassailable and irrefutable, but there were several critical factors that most Americans never heard.

For example, the original 1998 report contained a significant finding about which scholars and the media remained conspicuously silent:

> President Thomas Jefferson was accused of having fathered a child, Tom [Woodson], by Sally Hemings. Tom was said to have been born in 1790, soon after Jefferson and Sally Hemings returned from France, where he had been minister. Present-day members of the African-American Woodson family believe that Thomas Jefferson was the father of Thomas Woodson, whose name comes from his later owner. . . . [But DNA testing shows] Thomas Woodson was *not* Thomas Jefferson's son.[34] (emphasis added)

So, the longest rumored charge against Jefferson, originally printed two centuries ago in publications of the day, was proven wrong. Jefferson was completely exonerated of that longstanding claim.

Furthermore, when *Nature* later issued its embarrassing correction, editors confessed, "The title assigned to our study was misleading."[35] Why? Because no DNA sample used in the testing had been taken from the Thomas Jefferson family line— and the public was never told of this significant omission. (It does seem that if someone wanted to test Thomas Jefferson's paternity that his own DNA should be used.)

Genetic DNA paternity testing requires the testing of a Y chromosome from a male descendant of the subject because the Y chromosome in males remains virtually unchanged from generation to generation. But Thomas Jefferson had no male descendants from which to take a DNA sample. His only son had died at birth. Since Jefferson had no surviving male descendants, the researchers therefore chose to test the Y chromosomes from the descendants of Field Jefferson, Thomas's uncle.

The researchers found that the configuration of the Y chromosomes in the descendants of Field Jefferson—a general configuration common to the entire Jefferson family—was indeed present in the descendants of Sally Hemings' youngest child, Eston. Therefore, on the basis of DNA testing, the most that researchers could conclusively say was that some Jefferson male—and there were twenty-six Jefferson males living in the area at the time—had a relationship with Sally Hemings that resulted in the birth of Eston. But which Jefferson was it?

A blue-ribbon commission of thirteen leading scholars was assembled to examine the Jefferson paternity issue. Those scholars were all PhDs from prestigious schools such as Harvard, the University of Virginia, the University of North Carolina, the University of Kentucky, Indiana University, and others.[36] This Scholars' Commission reported:

> There are at least ten possible fathers for Sally Hemings' children who could have passed down genetic material that might produce children physically resembling Thomas Jefferson and who are thought to have visited Monticello regularly during the years Sally Hemings was having children.[37]

After investigating the ten possible fathers, the group concluded that the "case against some of Thomas Jefferson's relatives appears significantly stronger than the case against him."[38] It was these other nine unaddressed paternity alternatives that made the DNA testing announcement suspect. Thomas Jefferson's own DNA was not checked; and with the exception of Field Jefferson, the DNA for the rest of the Jefferson males living in the area was *not* checked. *World* therefore correctly reported:

> According to the genetic evidence, the father *could* have been Jefferson. Or it could have been his brother Randolph. Or one of Randolph's sons. Or, presumably, his uncle Field, or his son George or one of his sons. . . . Any of these men had access to Monticello and could have been culpable.[39] (emphasis added)

National columnist Mona Charen accurately summarized the scope of the testing results:

> The DNA data did rule Jefferson out as the father of Thomas Woodson, the eldest of Sally's sons, and shed no light on the rest. That leaves a scenario in which Jefferson's sexual liaison with his slave [that produced Eston] is estimated to have begun when he was 65 years old. Possible certainly, but likely? While the DNA data adds to our knowledge—it is clear that there was mixing of Hemings and Jefferson genes sometime in the past 200 years—they do not provide names or dates. They most definitely do not "prove" anything about Thomas Jefferson himself.[40]

Herbert Barger, the Jefferson family historian and genealogist who assisted in the DNA testing, explained:

My study indicates to me that Thomas Jefferson was NOT the father of Eston or any other Hemings child. The DNA study . . . indicates that Randolph [Thomas' younger brother] is possibly the father of Eston and maybe the others. . . . [T]hree of Sally Hemings' children, Harriet, Beverly, and Eston (the latter two not common names), were given names of the *Randolph* family.[41] (emphasis added)

The Scholars' Commission arrived at the same conclusion. Significantly, that group had *not* been composed of Jefferson supporters; in fact, several of the scholars had believed that Jefferson might indeed be the father of Hemings' children.[42] But after spending a year investigating the evidence, they *all* concluded that Randolph, Jefferson's younger brother, was indeed the most likely father, explaining:

[T]he circumstantial case that Eston Hemings was fathered by the President's younger brother is many times stronger than the case against the President himself. Among the considerations which might point to Randolph are:

- In "Memoirs of a Monticello Slave," former slave Isaac Jefferson asserts that when Randolph Jefferson visited Monticello, he "used to come out among black people, play the fiddle and dance half the night . . ." In contrast, we have not a single account of Thomas Jefferson spending his nights socializing with the slaves in such a manner. . . .

- [W]e have Jefferson's letter inviting Randolph (and presumably his sons as well) to come to Monticello shortly before Sally became pregnant with Eston. It was common for such visits to last for weeks.

- Pearl Graham, who did original research among the Hemings descendants in the 1940s and believed the story that Thomas Jefferson fathered Sally Hemings' children, wrote in a 1958 letter to a leading Jefferson scholar at Princeton University that a grand-daughter of one of Sally Hemings' children had told her that Randolph Jefferson "had colored children" of his own.

- Until Fawn Brodie [recently] persuaded the descendants of Eston Hemings that President Jefferson was his father, their family oral history had passed down that Eston was fathered by "Thomas Jefferson's uncle." That is not possible, as both of his paternal uncles died decades before Eston was conceived. But [according] to Martha Jefferson Randolph [Jefferson's oldest daughter], who was generally in charge of Monticello during Eston Hemings' entire memory there, her father's younger brother was "Uncle Randolph"—and he was referred to as such in family letters.

- We don't know exactly when Randolph's first wife died, but we do know that he remarried—to a very controlling woman—shortly after Eston Hemings was born. About the same time, Thomas Jefferson retired from public office and spent the rest of his life at Monticello, where he could presumably have had access to Sally Hemings any night he wished. But Sally, although only in her mid-thirties, gave birth to no known children after Eston was born in 1808. Even the Thomas Jefferson Memorial Foundation report acknowledges that Sally's childbearing years may have corresponded to the years in which Randolph Jefferson was a widower.[43]

Significantly, when correcting its original announcement, even *Nature* ruefully conceded, "It is true that men of Randolph Jefferson's family could have fathered Sally Hemings' later children."[44] But that important admission as well as the subsequent scholars' report were both widely ignored by the media. In fact, PBS's *Frontline*, A&E's *Biography*, the *Washington Post*, and others actually had in their possession information that tended to exonerate Jefferson but deliberately omitted it from their reporting.[45]

Incidentally, Dr. Eugene Foster, who conducted the DNA testing, had been very clear about the limitations of his testing, but his findings were misrepresented by Joseph Ellis, historian and professor at Mt. Holyoke College. Ellis, who opposed what was happening to President Clinton at the time, had written the sensationalistic "announcement" for *Nature*, but his personal spin went well beyond Foster's scientific findings, making his claim unfactual.

But perhaps this should not have been surprising. Four years later, in 2002, it was revealed that Ellis had been guilty of publicly lying to his classes on multiple occasions. For example, he told students that he went to Vietnam as a platoon leader and paratrooper in the 101st Airborne and served on General Westmoreland's staff during the war; he did neither. He also said that he did active civil rights work in Mississippi during the Civil Rights Movement and was harassed by the state police for his efforts; again, not true. He even claimed that he scored the winning touchdown in the last football game of his senior year in high school; it turns out he wasn't even on the team.[46] As one columnist properly queried, "How can you trust a historian who makes up history?"[47]

Looking back over the entire fiasco, the *Wall Street Journal* correctly noted of the unreported retraction, "[T]he backtracking comes a little late to change the hundreds of other headlines fingering Jefferson."[48] The effect of the original news flood was toxic. One reporter who covered the story accurately noted, "[D]efective scholarship is difficult to recall."[49] The *Jewish World Review* therefore properly asked, "Was Jefferson libeled by DNA?"[50] The evidence answers "Yes!"

In short, the DNA testing did not show Jefferson to be guilty of any sexual liaison with Hemings. The so-called smoking gun turned out to be a waterlogged pea shooter.

CATEGORY 2: THE EVIDENCE OF ORAL TRADITION

The second type of evidence used against Jefferson is oral tradition, but the DNA findings significantly weakened this source.

The strongest evidence in this category had long been the two-century-old charge that Jefferson had fathered Thomas Woodson, but the DNA findings were conclusive that no Jefferson—not any of the twenty-six Jefferson males—had fathered Woodson. That original test was later repeated by Dr. Foster with the same results.[51] Consequently, that oral tradition is now authoritatively disproved. (Incidentally, DNA testing has been conducted on descendants from two of Hemings' five children. As already noted, testing on the Thomas Woodson branch was negative for any Jefferson genes. The Eston Hemings branch showed some Jefferson genes, but it did not show from which of the twenty-six Jefferson males they came. The remaining three branches of Hemings' progeny have thus far declined to participate in DNA testing.)

The other major oral tradition challenging Jefferson's sexual morality came from Sally Hemings' son Madison (the fourth Hemings child, born in 1805). In an article published in an Ohio newspaper in 1873, Madison Hemings claimed that in France "my mother became Mr. Jefferson's concubine, and when he was called back home she was enceinte [pregnant] by him" with Thomas Woodson.[52] But the DNA testing disproved two of Madison Hemings' major claims: (1) there were no Jefferson genes in Sally's first child, Thomas; therefore, (2) Sally did not return home pregnant by Jefferson.

Several of Madison's other claims about Jefferson have also been shown to be erroneous, including that Jefferson was not interested in agriculture.[53] Yet modern authors such as Professor Annette Gordon-Reed believe that Jefferson was guilty of all that Madison charged him with. In fact, Reed not only dismisses outright all evidence to the contrary but she even concocts evidence in her attempts to "prove" her (and Madison's) claims.

For instance, in her book *Thomas Jefferson-Sally Hemings: An American Controversy*, she "reprinted" a letter written in 1858 by Ellen Randolph Coolidge (Thomas Jefferson's granddaughter) describing the rooms at Monticello. According to Reed, Coolidge had written: "His [Jefferson's] apartments had no private entrance not perfectly accessible and visible to all the household. No female domestic ever entered his chambers except at hours when he was known not to be in the public gaze."[54]

So, based on Reed's quotation of Jefferson's granddaughter, female domestics such as Hemings entered Jefferson's apartment only at hours when no one was watching. But Coolidge's letter had actually said exactly the opposite:

His [Jefferson's] apartments had no private entrance not perfectly accessible and visible to all the household. No female domestic ever entered his chambers except at hours when he was known not to be *there; and none could have entered without being exposed to* the public gaze.[55] (emphasis added)

The emphasized portion above is what Gordon-Reed omitted, thus completely reversing its message.

Significantly, the granddaughter had actually said that (1) no one could have entered without being seen, and that (2) no female staff entered Jefferson's room unless he was not there. But Reed rewrote what his granddaughter had actually said. She changed the quotation, cutting out the most important part without the use of an ellipse or any other indication that she had purposely removed that key segment.

Sadly, when someone dismisses Madison Hemings' claims because of their many provable and obvious inaccuracies, writers such as Gordon-Reed cry "Racism!" and lament that black witnesses from history are automatically given less credence.[56] Other writers such as Jan Lewis and Peter Onuf believe that those who do not accept the testimony of Madison Hemings carte blanche are simply racists.[57]

Refusal to consider the substantial evidence that contradicts Madison Hemings' claims indicates that personal predilections and political agendas have been placed above an honest search for the truth. Genuine scholars require verifiable documentation—something completely lacking in the case of Thomas Woodson's and Madison Hemings' oral testimonies. In fact, crucial elements of their oral testimonies are factually disprovable, which serves to repudiate the second category of "evidence" currently used to "prove" Jefferson's paternity through Hemings.

CATEGORY 3: THE CHARGES PUBLISHED TWO CENTURIES AGO

The earliest printed charges alleging Jefferson's paternity with Hemings appeared in newspaper articles written from 1801 to 1803 by James T. Callender (1758–1803).

Callender first rose to attention in 1792 in Scotland when he authored *The Political Progress of Great Britain.* That work, highly critical of the British government, led to his indictment for sedition (that is, for inciting insurrection against or the overthrow of a government). After being "oftimes called in court, he did not appear and was pronounced a fugitive and outlaw."[58] Facing prison, in 1793 Callender and his family of young children fled to America for refuge, arriving with no means or prospect of support. American patriots, learning of Callender's plight, sympathetically embraced him as a man suffering British persecution. Many, including Thomas Jefferson, personally provided charitable contributions to help Callender, especially his children.

In 1796 Callender secured a job writing for a Republican (that is, an Anti-Federalist, pro-Jefferson) newspaper in Philadelphia. Promising "a tornado as no government ever got before,"[59] Callender resumed the defamatory writing style that had landed him in trouble in Great Britain, only this time it was against prominent Federalist Americans such as Alexander Hamilton, John Adams, and George Washington. By attacking the Federalists, Callender considered himself to be the mouthpiece for Jefferson's Republican Party and believed he was rendering it a valuable service.

The northern states tended to be Federalist and the southern states Anti-Federalist (Republican). Callender was therefore in a northern state writing against Federalist statesmen highly regarded in that region. His writings not only raised great ire but were so malicious as to invite litigation even in that land of free speech. Fearing legal punishment, Callender fled from Philadelphia to Richmond in 1799.

Arriving there, he took a job with another Republican newspaper where he continued his attacks on the Federalists. But in 1800, because of his vicious writings, Callender was convicted under the federal Sedition Law, fined $200 (about $3,000 today), and imprisoned for nine months. Still he did not relent. While in prison he authored two more attack pieces in the same scurrilous style that previously had caused him so much difficulty. Callender proved to be a troublesome hothead with no sense of discretion.

During this time, Jefferson was serving as vice president under President John Adams. Callender wrote Jefferson twenty-nine letters (and two more when he was not vice president), but Jefferson largely ignored him, replying only three times in a two-year period.[60] Because of Jefferson's lack of response, Callender complained to James Madison that he "might as well have addressed a letter to Lot's wife"[61] (the Biblical character who was turned into a pillar of salt). Jefferson avoided Callender but continued occasional charitable gifts for the support of his young children.

When Jefferson became president in 1801, he deemed the Sedition Law to be unconstitutional and pardoned everyone who had been prosecuted under it (about two dozen individuals, including Callender).[62] Jefferson also ordered that the fines collected under that law be returned, with interest. But the Federalist sheriff who had collected the $200 fine from Callender refused, and even ignored direct orders from Secretary of State James Madison to refund the fine.

Callender, now free, was unaware of these difficulties with the sheriff and became infuriated against Jefferson, blaming him for not returning his $200. Secretary of State Madison reported to Virginia governor James Monroe, "Callender, I find, is under a strange error on the subject of his fine, and in a strange humor in consequence of it."[63]

Callender became enraged at Jefferson. Believing that Jefferson's party owed him something for what he considered his long "service" on their behalf, he demanded a presidential appointment as the US postmaster for Richmond[64]—an appointment that both President Jefferson and Secretary of State Madison properly refused him.[65]

Meanwhile, Jefferson, still unable to obtain the return of the fine from the Federalist sheriff, took steps to repay Callender's fine from private funds. As he told Governor Monroe: "I think with you we had better refund his fine by private contributions. I enclose you an order on Gibson & Jefferson for $50, which I believe is one fourth of the whole sum."[66]

Only three days later, following a meeting in which Callender responded viciously against Jefferson's offer of personal help, the formerly sympathetic Jefferson understandably underwent a complete change of heart toward Callender. As he explained to Monroe:

> Since [my last letter, three days ago], Callender is arrived here. He did not call on me; but understanding he was in distress, I sent Captain [Meriwether] Lewis to him with $50

to inform him we were making some inquiries as to his fine, which would take a little time; and lest he should suffer in the meantime I had sent him &c. His language to Captain Lewis was very hightoned. He intimated that he was in possession of things which he could and would make use of in a certain case: that he received the $50 not as a charity, but a due, in fact as hush money; that I knew what he expected, viz. a certain office [Richmond postmaster], and more to this effect. Such a misconstruction of my charities puts an end to them forever. You will therefore be so good as to make no use of the order I enclosed you [to repay the fine by private funds].[67]

Jefferson's instructions to withhold further relief from Callender arrived too late. As Governor Monroe told Jefferson, "Your [letter] just received. It is to be regretted that Capt[ain] Lewis paid the money. . . . [Y]our resolution to terminate all communication with him is wise."[68]

On the same day that Monroe wrote Jefferson, Madison wrote Monroe describing the outrageous nature of his own meeting with Callender:

Callender made his appearance here some days ago in the same temper which is described in your letter. He seems implacable [bull-headed] towards the principle object of his complaints and not to be satisfied in any respect without an office. It has been my lot to bear the burden of receiving & repelling his claims. . . . It is impossible however to reason concerning a man whose imagination & passions have been so fermented [soured].[69]

Madison then explained to Monroe part of the reason why

he believed Callender was so irrational:

> Do you know, too, that besides his other passions, he is under
> the tyranny of that of love? . . . The object of his flame is in
> Richmond. . . . He has flattered himself, and probably been
> flattered by others, into a persuasion that the emoluments
> [compensations] and reputation of a post office would obtain
> her in marriage. Of these recommendations, however, he is
> sent back in despair. With respect to the fine even, I fear
> that delays, if nothing more, may still torment him and lead
> him to torment others. . . . Callender's irritation, produced
> by his wants, is whetted constantly by his suspicion that the
> difficulties, if not intended, are the offspring of indifference
> in those who have interposed in his behalf [Jefferson].[70]

Five days later Governor Monroe responded to Madison's
letter, telling him of his own meeting with Callender:

> I have your [letter] and have since seen Mr. Callender, with
> whom I had much conversation. . . . I dwelt particularly on
> the remission of the fine. . . . Still he added that some little
> office would greatly accommodate him, and without one he
> did not know how he should subsist. That he was tired of
> the press &c.[71]

But even while Jefferson was working to obtain the return of
the fine, Callender announced his intention to punish Jefferson.
Having obtained neither the postal appointment (or any other
"little office") nor the full return of his fine, he became incensed
against Jefferson. Complaining that Jefferson had turned his back
on him, he grumbled "I now begin to know what ingratitude is"[72]
and issued the ominous warning that he was "not the man who

is either to be oppressed or plundered with impunity."[73]

The disgruntled Callender who previously had written only for Republican newspapers—that is, pro-Jefferson and Anti-Federalist publications—actively sought a job with the *Recorder*, a Federalist newspaper in Richmond that was openly critical of President Jefferson. Callender then launched a series of virulent attacks against Jefferson in articles written throughout 1801, 1802, and 1803, accusing him, among other things, of "dishonesty, cowardice, and gross personal immorality."[74] It was in these defamatory articles that Callender charged that Jefferson had fathered a child by Hemings.

Callender's charge about Hemings received broad circulation when some of the Federalists of Massachusetts—strident and vocal opponents of President Jefferson, who used every opportunity to attack him—reprinted the charges about Jefferson and Hemings in a series of articles entitled "Commonwealth of Massachusetts vs. Thomas Jefferson."[75]

Significantly, the claims about Jefferson and Hemings were always associated with partisan smear politics. Callender died less than a year after publishing his charges. During that time he was constantly drunk, and after threatening suicide on several occasions, he eventually drowned in three feet of water in the James River. A coroner's jury ruled his death accidental, due to intoxication.[76]

Before his death, however, Callender acknowledged that his attacks against Jefferson had been motivated by his belief that Jefferson had refused to repay his $200 fine.[77] In fact, in his article that first "exposed" the Jefferson-Hemings "relationship," Callender confirmed his own personal, vindictive motivation by closing the article with these stinging words: "When Mr.

Jefferson has read this article, he will find leisure to estimate how much has been lost or gained by so many unprovoked attacks upon J. T. Callender."[78]

History has proved Callender's charges against Jefferson to be one inaccuracy after another. For example, in his initial article in which he first "revealed" the Jefferson-Hemings "affair," Callender had asserted:

> It is well known that the man whom it delighteth the people to honor [President Jefferson] keeps, and for many years past has kept as his concubine one of his own slaves. Her name is Sally. The name of her eldest son is Tom. His features are said to bear a striking, although sable [dark-skinned] resemblance to those of the president himself. The boy is ten or twelve years of age. His mother went to France in the same vessel with Mr. Jefferson.[79]

This story was widely circulated, and the "striking resemblance" hearsay was often repeated to adduce Jefferson's guilt. For example, the 1802 *Frederick-Town Herald* declared: "Other information assures us that Mr. Jefferson's Sally and their children are real persons. . . . Her son, whom Callender calls president Tom, we also are assured, bears a strong likeness to Mr. Jefferson."[80]

Interestingly, the "striking resemblance" charge is still invoked today as "proof" that Jefferson fathered Hemings' children,[81] but since the DNA testing unequivocally proved that Sally's son Tom was not the son of Thomas Jefferson, Callender's allegations (as well as the modern ones) that Tom bore a "striking resemblance to the president himself" are meaningless.

Furthermore, Callender claimed that Jefferson and Sally

"went to France on the same vessel," which was also wrong; they went on two separate vessels, one in 1784 and the other in 1787. He also wrongly predicted that Americans—especially the Federalists—would widely embrace his charges against Jefferson as true. Only three weeks after his first article, he forewarned:

> More About Sally and the President. For two days after the publication of the *Recorder* of September 1st, the [Jefferson's supporters] were at a loss what to say or think. The Philistine priesthood were not more confounded when they saw their idol Dagon prostrate and broke to pieces [1 Samuel 5:1–4]. . . . Sally's business makes a prodigious [monumental] noise. . . . After this discovery, I do not believe that at the next election [of 1804], Jefferson could obtain two votes on the eastern side of the Susquehanna [the general location of Jefferson opponents], and I think hardly four upon this side of it [the area of Jefferson supporters]. He will, therefore, be laid aside [i.e., not reelected].[82]

But Jefferson was easily reelected and even many of his Federalist opponents rejected Callender's ludicrous charges.

For example, David Humphreys of Philadelphia wrote in that city's newspaper, the *Aurora*, that he had "shown that the story of Sally was a falsehood,"[83] and Henry Lee, an ardent Federalist, declared that "there is no foundation whatsoever for that story."[84] And a Boston newspaper openly declaring itself to be "far . . . from revering the political or moral character of Mr. Jefferson" similarly spurned the charge, telling its readers that "In the *Richmond Recorder*, of the 8th inst. there is a publication, signed *J. T. Callender*, containing a charge against the President of the United States of so black a nature that we are unwilling to sully our pages with the filthy tale."[85]

Callender was also wrong when he believed that he could besmirch the character of other popular national leaders. For example, he charged President George Washington with filling the American governmental process with "confusion and iniquity" and with "corrupt[ing] the American judges."[86] And he charged President John Adams with attempting to overthrow the Constitution, betraying the nation to foreign powers, committing voter fraud and ballot tampering, allowing the slaughter of Americans by the Indians, ruining American morals, and even wishing that the British had won the American Revolution.[87] But the charges Callender made against Washington and Adams were so ridiculous that they were never believed by objective historians—or, for that matter, by thoughtful citizens.

So why have Callender's charges against Jefferson survived when his charges against all the others deservedly perished long ago? Because a few Negativist writers in recent years now cite the allegations made by Callender (called the "single poisoned spring" of Jefferson history[88]) as if they were indisputably proved. They fail to report that the originator of these claims had an established and well-documented pattern of false reporting, just as they fail to mention the scurrilous, self-serving motives behind his published accusations. The Negativists who today embrace Callender's claims have kept alive what so many others in previous generations long ago rejected.

As Pulitzer Prize–winning historian James Truslow Adams affirmed, "Almost every scandalous story about Jefferson which is still whispered or believed can be traced to the lies in Callender's book"[89]—that is, to the lies that appeared in the series of newspaper articles he wrote. Merrill Peterson, professor of history at the University of Virginia, holds the same opinion,[90] and Pulitzer Prize–winning historian Dumas Malone described Callender as "one of the most notorious scandalmongers and character assassins in American history."[91] Stanford University historian John C. Miller describes Callender as "the most unscrupulous scandalmonger of the day . . . a journalist who stopped at nothing and stooped to anything."[92] He explains:

> Callender made his charges against Jefferson without fear and without research. He had never visited Monticello; he had never spoken to Sally Hemings; and he never made the slightest effort to verify the "facts" he so stridently proclaimed. It was "journalism" at its most reckless, wildly irresponsible, and scurrilous. Callender was not an investigative journalist; he never bothered to investigate anything. For him, the story, especially if it reeked of scandal, was everything; truth, if it stood in his way, was summarily mowed down.[93]

Even historian Benjamin Ellis Martin—a strident, nineteenth-century Jefferson-bashing critic who might easily have accepted Callender's charges—found no basis for believing them. To the contrary, he described Callender as a writer who did "effective scavenger work" in "scandal, slanders, lies, libels, scurrility" and one who excelled in "blackguardism" (unprincipled, vile writing).[94] Martin, a confirmed anti-Jeffersonian, therefore concluded:

> I am unable to find one good word to speak of this man [Callender]. . . . He was a journalistic janizary [mercenary], his pen always for sale on any side, a hardened and habitual liar, a traitorous and truculent [malicious] scoundrel; and

the world went better when he sank out of sight beneath the waters of the James River.[95]

Significantly, Jefferson's long political career had been characterized by numerous personal attacks launched against him, especially during his presidential election. In fact, Jefferson placed the number of attacks in the thousands,[96] of which Callender's had been just one. After surveying the charges published against Jefferson by his opponents, Pulitzer Prize–winning historian Charles Warren concluded that "no other presidential campaign in American history ever brought forth such vicious and scurrilous personal attacks."[97] And Pulitzer Prize–winning historian Dumas Malone similarly observed that Jefferson "suffered open personal attacks which, in severity and obscenity, have rarely if ever been matched."[98]

Jefferson knew that he could never rebut the falsehoods as rapidly as they could be concocted. So long before Callender leveled his charges against him, Jefferson had made it his standing personal policy to ignore all ridiculous claims made against him by his enemies.

He gave three reasons for this policy. First, any response he made might seem to dignify the charges.[99] Second, he was convinced that his personal integrity would eventually prevail over the false accusations made against him.[100] And third, Jefferson trusted the good judgment of the people.[101]

Jefferson acknowledged that he could have successfully taken legal action against libelers like Callender, but he refused to lower himself to that level, instead turning them over to the Judge of the Universe, to Whom they would eventually answer. As he explained:

I know that I might have filled the courts of the United States with actions for these slanders, and have ruined perhaps many persons who are not innocent. But this would be no equivalent to the loss of [my own] character [by retaliating against them]. I leave them, therefore, to the reproof of their own consciences. If these do not condemn them, there will yet come a day when the false witness will meet a judge Who has not slept over his slanders.[102]

Amazingly, Jefferson's lifelong policy of refusing to answer false claims has today been translated into culpatory evidence against him. In fact, one prominent national news outlet pointed out that since Jefferson "never directly denied"[103] having an affair with Sally, it was proof that he had fathered her children! (Consider the unreasonableness of declaring that an individual is guilty of whatever he does not deny.)

Even though Jefferson's public policy was silence, twice he took pen in hand to privately recount to two of his personal friends his relationship with Callender. One was a lengthy letter to Governor James Monroe in which Jefferson explained:

I am really mortified at the base ingratitude of Callender. It presents human nature in a hideous form. . . . When the *Political Progress of Britain* first appeared in this country [in 1794] . . . I was speaking of it in terms of strong approbation to a friend in Philadelphia when he asked me if I knew that the author [Callender] was then in the city, a fugitive from prosecution on account of that work and in want of employ for his subsistence. This was the first of my learning that Callender was the author of the work. I considered him as a man of science fled from persecution, and assured my friend of my readiness to do whatever could serve him. . . . In 1798, I think, I was applied . . . to contribute to his relief. I did so. In 1799 . . . I contributed again. He had, by this time, paid me two or three personal visits. When he fled in a panic from Philadelphia to General Mason's [in Virginia], he wrote to me that he was a fugitive in want of employ. . . . I availed myself of this pretext to cover a mere charity [and sent him] fifty dollars. . . . I considered him still as a proper object of benevolence. The succeeding year, he again wanted money. . . . I made his letter, as before, the occasion of giving him another fifty dollars. He considers these as proofs of my approbation [approval]. . . . Soon after I was elected to the government, Callender came on here, wishing to be made postmaster at Richmond. I knew him to be totally unfit for it; and however ready I was to aid him with my own charities (and I then gave him fifty dollars), I did not think the public offices confided to me to give away as charities. He took it in mortal offense. . . . This is the true state of what has passed between him and me.[104]

In the second private letter about the Callender situation, written to Abigail Adams, Jefferson substantially repeated what he had said in his letter to Monroe and then closed by telling her: "I am not afraid to appeal to the nation at large, to posterity, and still less to that Being Who sees Himself our motives, Who will judge us from His own knowledge of them."[105] In fact, Jefferson repeatedly affirmed that he believed in a personal God Who would render judgment, and that he had nothing to hide.[106]

Therefore, *none* of the three sources of evidence often invoked against Jefferson (the DNA testing, oral tradition, or the early published claims of Callender) provides any credible basis for believing that Jefferson fathered any of Hemings' children. Nevertheless, Negativist attempts to convict Jefferson not only continue but have even expanded into new venues.

For example, Jefferson is now being subjected to the tests of "psychohistory" in order to "prove" that he had an affair with Hemings. ("Psychohistory" occurs when, rather than accepting what someone actually said, a psychological counter-analysis of that person's words is attempted in an effort to establish their "true" motives. The result of such a flawed analysis is sometimes called psychobabble.) Fawn Brodie used this method in her book *Thomas Jefferson: An Intimate History* in order to extract an implied confession from Jefferson. She explains:

> The first evidence that Sally Hemings had become for Jefferson a special preoccupation may be seen in one of the most subtly illuminating of all his writings, the daily journal he kept on a seven-week trip through eastern France, Germany, and Holland in March and April of 1788. . . . Anyone who reads with care these twenty-five pages must find it singular that in describing the countryside between these cities he used the word "mulatto" eight times.[107]

Since Sally Hemings was mulatto, Brodie concludes that Jefferson's use of that word when describing the agriculture condition of land proves that he had a sexual relationship with her. Yet *mulatto* is used by Jefferson—who was by profession a farmer, scientist, and botanist—in his diary to describe the specific type and color of the soil.

Notice the examples Brodie provides—examples that she

claims "prove" Jefferson's sexual infatuation with Hemings:

> "The road goes thro' the plains of the Maine, which are mulatto and very fine . . ."; "It has a good southern aspect, the soil a barren mulatto clay . . ."; "It is of south western aspect, very poor, sometimes gray, sometimes mulatto . . ."; "These plains are sometimes black, sometimes mulatto, always rich . . ."; ". . . the plains are generally mulatto . . ."; ". . . the valley of the Rhine . . . varies in quality, sometimes a rich mulatto loam, sometimes a poor sand . . ."; ". . . the hills are mulatto but also whitish . . ."; "Meagre mulatto clay mixed with small broken stones . . ."[108]

Since the word *mulatto* is primarily used in a racial sense today, Modernist Brodie concludes that it was only used this way two centuries ago. She therefore claims that her psycho-analysis of Jefferson's observation of soil in Europe is actually "proof" of an affair with Hemings, but by so doing, she shows herself unfamiliar with both agriculture and linguistic etymology. Consider a few examples of the word mulatto as commonly used for generations in American agriculture:

> The soil. . . . changes into what is called the *mulatto* soil, consisting of a black mold and red earth. . . . The *mulatto* lands are generally strong and yield large crops of wheat, tobacco, corn, &c.
>
> —GEORGIA, 1792[109]

> Land rich—very rich; a deep stiff *mulatto* soil.
>
> —TEXAS, 1846[110]

Both the deep black soil of the uplands and the light colored or *mulatto* soil peculiar to the bluff deposit are alike noted for productiveness.

—IOWA, 1875[111]

The soil . . . is a sandy, *mulatto*-colored soil; it has been called the corn soil, though it produces wheat, cotton, tobacco, potatoes, etc.

—TENNESSEE, 1879[112]

Highland is in the center of a tract of dark, "*mulatto*" soil of exceptional fertility, whence comes a large amount of farming trade.

—KANSAS, 1883[113]

[T]he soil is called a "*mulatto* soil," and is that kind best adapted to the raising of cotton. It is a loamy clay, composed largely also of vegetable mold.

—ARKANSAS, 1889[114]

As Jefferson biographer Willard Sterne Randall correctly notes, Brodie's entire supposition is farcical:

[W]hen Jefferson used the term *mulatto* to describe soil during his French travels, Sally was still on a ship with Polly, accompanying her to France. If he [Jefferson] had ever noticed her or remembered her at all, Sally had been only ten years old when Jefferson last visited Monticello hurriedly in 1784. . . . She was only eight when Jefferson last resided at Monticello and was mourning his wife's death. Unless Brodie was suggesting that Jefferson consoled himself by having an affair with an eight-year-old child, the whole chain of suppositions is preposterous.[115]

Pulitzer Prize–winning historian Garry Wills similarly observed of Brodie's work:

> She has managed to write a long and complex study of Jefferson without displaying any acquaintance with eighteenth-century plantation conditions, political thought, literary conventions, or scientific categories—all of which greatly concerned Jefferson. She constantly finds double meanings in colonial language, basing her arguments on the present usage of key words [i.e., Modernism].[116]

In summary, there currently exists virtually no sound evidence, either modern or ancient, that Thomas Jefferson fathered even one child with Sally Hemings, much less five. In fact, if Jefferson were alive today, and were charged with a crime and taken to court for allegedly having had sex with the young Hemings, it would be an open-and-shut case: he would be promptly acquitted by any impartial jury.

LIE #2

Thomas Jefferson Founded a Secular University

*J*efferson was involved in many educational endeavors throughout his life, but his greatest, and certainly the one dearest to his heart, was his founding of the University of Virginia—the final major work of his long and fruitful life.

If one accepts the modern mischaracterization that Jefferson was antireligious and hostile to Christianity, it then becomes logical to assert that he would promote the secular and oppose the religious in his educational endeavors—especially at his beloved university. The following quotations represent assertions regularly made by many modern writers:

> Jefferson also founded the first intentionally secularized university in America. His vision for the University of Virginia was for education finally free from traditional Christian dogma. He had a disdain for the influence that institutional Christianity had on education. At the University of Virginia there was no Christian curriculum and the school had no chaplain. Its faculty was comprised of Deists and Unitarians.
> —PROFESSOR DARYL CORNETT, MID-AMERICA THEOLOGICAL SEMINARY[1]

After Jefferson left the presidency in 1809, he embarked on . . . the University of Virginia. . . . A Deist and a secular humanist, Jefferson rejected the religious tradition that had provided the foundation for the colonial universities.
—PROFESSOR ANITA VICKERS, PENN STATE UNIVERSITY[2]

No part of the regular school day was set aside for religious worship. . . . Jefferson did not permit the room belonging to the university to be used for religious purposes.
—PROFESSOR LEONARD LEVY, CLAREMONT GRADUATE SCHOOL[3]

The university which Thomas Jefferson established at Charlottesville in Virginia was . . . distinctly and purposely secular.
—PROFESSOR JOHN BRUBACHER, YALE UNIVERSITY, UNIVERSITY OF MICHIGAN

—PROFESSOR WILLIS RUDY, FAIRLEIGH DICKINSON UNIVERSITY[4]

These quotations, along with the numerous others that could be added, raise the following questions:

1. Did Jefferson have a disdain for the influence of Christianity on education?

2. Did he found the first intentionally secular university in America?

3. Did he hire only Deists and Unitarians for his faculty?

4. Did he exclude religious content from the curriculum of the school?

Most Americans would probably answer "yes" to these four questions, for they have been told repeatedly by many of today's writers, both academic and journalistic, that Jefferson was an ardent secularist. But what if this is wrong? What if Jefferson's own education—an education that thoroughly prepared him for the national and international scene—had not only been heavily religious but also personally satisfying to him? If such was the case, then it is illogical to assert that Jefferson would seek to exclude from others that which had so benefited him; so let's begin with a look at Jefferson's own education.

Born in 1743, as a youngster he attended St. James' Anglican Church of Northam Parish with his family. The church was pastored by the Reverend William Douglass, and from 1752 to 1758 the young Thomas attended the Reverend Douglass' school. In 1758 his family moved to Albemarle County, where they attended the Fredericksville Parish Anglican Church, pastored by the Reverend James Fontaine Maury. From 1758 to 1760 Thomas attended the Reverend Maury's school, and then entered William and Mary, yet another school affiliated with the Anglican Church.

Part of Jefferson's daily routine at the college included morning and evening prayers from the *Book of Common Prayer* with lengthy Scripture readings.[5] Scottish instructor Dr. William Small, the son of a Presbyterian minister, was Jefferson's favorite instructor. Jefferson later acknowledged: "It was my great good fortune, and what probably fixed the destinies of my life, that Dr. William Small of Scotland, was then professor . . ."[6]

It's interesting that many of the best instructors in early America were Scottish Presbyterians. As historian George Marsden affirmed, "[I]t is not much of an exaggeration to say that outside of New England, the Scots were the educators of eighteenth-century America."[7] These Scottish instructors regularly tutored students in what was known as the Scottish Common Sense educational philosophy—an approach under which not only Jefferson but also other notable Virginia Founding Fathers were trained, including George Washington, James Madison, George Mason, Peyton Randolph, Richard Henry Lee, and Thomas Nelson. In fact, Gaillard Hunt, head of the manuscript division of the Library of Congress, observed: "One reason why the ruling class in Virginia acted with such unanimity [during the Revolution] . . . was that a large proportion of them had received the same kind of education. This usually came first from clergymen."[8]

Scottish Common Sense was originated to counter the skepticism of stridently secular European writers and philosophers. This approach asserted that common sense should shape philosophy rather than vice versa, and that normal, everyday language could express philosophical principles in a way that could be understood by ordinary individuals and not just academic elites.

Key tenets of Scottish Common Sense included:[9]

1. There is a God.

2. God placed into every individual a conscience—a moral sense written on his or her heart (cf. Jeremiah 31:33, Romans 2:14–15, Hebrews 8:10, 10:16, and others).

3. God established "first principles" in areas such as law, government, education, politics, and economics; and these first, or transcendent guiding principles could be discovered by the use of common sense, logic, and reason.

4. There was no conflict between reason and revelation.
The two were not inherent enemies; both came directly
from God, and revelation fortified and clarified reason.

This is the philosophy under which Jefferson was largely
educated.

Interestingly, Jefferson's own personal education, including
at the elementary, secondary, and postsecondary levels, all
occurred at religious schools and consistently incorporated
religious instruction. Yet many of today's writers insist that it
was not the Scottish Common Sense philosophy under which
he had been trained that influenced his thinking but rather it
was the secular European Enlightenment. For example:

> Perhaps no one among the Founding Fathers was a fuller-
> fledged subscriber to the Enlightenment tradition than
> Thomas Jefferson.[10]

> Jefferson. . . . was an Enlightenment thinker who emphasized
> natural law above all else.[11]

> In Europe, the Enlightenment centered around the salons
> of Paris and was famous for the "philosophes" popular
> philosophers—such as Voltaire, Montesquieu, Diderot,
> Rousseau. . . . American political leaders like Jefferson . . .
> were heavily influenced by Enlightenment thinking.[12]

Far too many of today's writers, consumed by the spirit of
Rigid Secularism, regularly regurgitate each other's claims that
Jefferson's philosophy (and thus the Declaration of Independence
that he largely penned) were products of the secular European
Enlightenment. But Jefferson himself repudiated that notion.

When it was suggested that he had based the Declaration on the writings of other philosophers, he responded, "[W]hether I had gathered my ideas from reading or reflection I do not know. I know only that I turned to neither book nor pamphlet while writing it."[13] In fact, he specifically asserted that the Declaration of Independence was "an expression of the American mind"[14] rather than a lexicon of European ideas, and even proclaimed that "the comparisons of our governments with those of Europe are like a comparison of heaven and hell."[15]

This is not to say that the Enlightenment had no influence in the American Founding; it certainly did. However, the crucial distinction regularly overlooked (or ignored) by many writers today is that some of the leading Enlightenment writers had ideas compatible with orthodox Christianity (such as Baron Puffendorf, Charles Montesquieu, Francis Hutcheson, John Locke, Thomas Reid, Hugo Grotius, and William Blackstone). Others of them certainly embraced ideas antithetical to traditional Christianity (such as Voltaire, Denis Diderot, David Hume, Claude Adrien Helvetius, Jean-Jacques Rousseau, Sir Nicholas Malby, and Guillaume Thomas François Raynal).

Modern authors regularly assert that America's Founders were influenced by the latter group; but to the extent that they were influenced by Enlightenment thinkers at all, they drew almost solely from the first group.[16] Indeed, of the four Enlightenment writers cited most frequently in the political literature of the Founding Era, three (Charles Montesquieu, William Blackstone, and John Locke) are from the first group. Only David Hume is from the second group, and the Founders were primarily interested in his political, not religious, ideas.[17]

In fact, many Founders were openly critical of Hume's

theological and human-knowledge ideas. For instance, John Adams described him as an atheist, deist, and libertine;[18] James Madison placed him among "bungling lawgivers";[19] and John Quincy Adams denounced Hume as "the Atheist Jacobite."[20] John Witherspoon,[21] Benjamin Rush,[22] Patrick Henry,[23] James Wilson,[24] and other Founders joined in such criticisms.

But if Jefferson really was antireligious (as so many currently claim), then perhaps he, unlike the other Founders, would be drawn toward Hume's philosophical and theological ideas. But such was definitely not the case. To the contrary, Jefferson found Hume "endeavoring to mislead, by either the suppression of a truth or by giving it a false coloring."[25] He even regretted the early influence that Hume's works had upon him, candidly lamenting, "I remember well the enthusiasm with which I devoured it [Hume's work] when young, and the length of time, the research, and reflection which were necessary to eradicate the poison it had instilled into my mind."[26]

Jefferson was similarly forthright in his criticism of other secular Enlightenment writers, including Guillaume Thomas François Raynal (known as Abbé Raynal). Jefferson described his works as "a great deal of falsehood"[27] and being "wrong exactly in the same proportion."[28]

Such denunciations of leading secular Enlightenment writers are certainly not consistent with the modern image of a Jefferson who was supposedly greatly influenced by them. But if secular Enlightenment writers were not a primary force in shaping Jefferson's thinking, then who was?—to whom did he look?—who were his heroes?

Jefferson himself answered that question, declaring that "Bacon, Newton and Locke . . . [are] my trinity of the three greatest men the world had ever produced."[29] Consider the philosophy of these three.

Francis Bacon, a British philosopher, attorney, and statesman called the "Father of Modern Science,"[30] is known for developing the process of inductive thinking and creating the scientific method. Historians have declared that "The intellect of Bacon was one of the most powerful and searching ever possessed by man."[31] But Bacon was by no means secular; rather he was quite the opposite.

In his noted work *De Interpretatione Naturae Prooemium* (1603), Bacon declared that his threefold goal was to discover truth, serve the church, and serve his country. He openly asserted that the vigorous pursuit of truth would always lead one directly to God: "[A] little philosophy inclineth man's mind to atheism; but depth in philosophy bringeth men's minds about to religion."[32]

Bacon penned many noted religious works, including *Essays, Ten in Number, Combined with Sacred Meditations and the Colors of Good and Evil* (1597); *The Proficiencies and Advancement of Learning, Divine and Human* (1605); *On the Unity in Religion* (1612); *On Atheism* (1612); *Of Praise* (1612); as well as a translation of some of the Biblical psalms (1625). This outspoken and famous Christian writer who never separated God or religion from science or government was the first of Jefferson's triumvirate of the world's greatest thinkers.

The second was Isaac Newton, an English statesman, mathematician, and scientist credited with birthing modern calculus and discovering the laws of universal gravitation. Newton did extensive work in physics, astronomy, and optics and was the first scientist to be knighted for his work. Strikingly, however, according to modern academic biographers of Newton:

He spent more time on theology than on science; indeed, he wrote about 1.3 million words on Biblical subjects. . . . Newton's understanding of God came primarily from the Bible, which he studied for days and weeks at a time. . . . Newton's theology profoundly influenced his scientific method. . . . His God was not merely a philosopher's impersonal First Cause; He was the God in the Bible Who freely creates and rules the world, Who speaks and acts in history.[33]

Among Newton's theological works were his *Observations Upon the Prophecies of Daniel and the Apocalypse of St. John* (1733), *Notes on Early Church History* (c. 1680), and many others. And throughout his scientific works, Newton maintained a distinctly Biblical view.[34] This Christian scientist and writer was the second of Jefferson's trinity of personal heroes.

The third was English philosopher and political theorist John Locke. Locke was intimately involved with politics in England and also greatly influenced America, including through his work on the 1669 constitution for the Carolina Colony.[35] He also penned numerous works on education, philosophy, government, empiricism, and religion that were highly popular with Americans.

Today's writers frequently describe Locke as a deist (or at least a follower of an early form of deism),[36] but Locke clearly thought of himself as a Christian and he dedicated an enormous amount of time to carefully studying the Bible. For instance, he wrote a verse-by-verse commentary on Paul's Epistles[37] and compiled a topical Bible, called a *Common Place-Book to the Holy Bible*,[38] which listed verses by subject for easy study reference. And in his *Two Treatises of Government* (1689—a work about the proper role of government that was openly praised by Jefferson and other Founders[39]), Locke invoked the Bible over 1,500 times.[40]

Much ink has been spilled debating Locke's religious views, but according to Jefferson:

> Locke's system of Christianity is this: Adam was created happy & immortal. . . . By sin he lost this so that he became subject to total death (like that of brutes [animals])—to the crosses & unhappiness of this life. At the intercession, however, of the Son of God this sentence was in part remitted. . . . And moreover to them who believed, their faith was to be counted for righteousness [Romans 4:3, 5]. Not that faith without works was to save them; St. James, chapter 2 says expressly the contrary [vv. 14–26], and all make the fundamental pillars of Christianity to be faith and repentance. So that a reformation of life (included under repentance) was essential, & defects in this would be made up by their faith; i.e., their faith should be counted for righteousness [Romans 4:3, 5]. . . . [A]dding a faith in God & His attributes that on their repentance He would pardon them [1 John 1:9]; they also would be justified [Romans 3:24]. This then explains the text "there is no other name under heaven by which a man may be saved" [Acts 4:12], i.e., the defects in good works shall not be supplied by a faith in Mahomet, Fo [i.e., Buddha], or any other except Christ.[41]

So, Jefferson openly embraced and highly venerated Francis Bacon, Isaac Newton, and John Locke—each an outspoken Christian thinker and philosopher; none an anti-Christian secularist. And when it came to morality and ethics, Jefferson repeatedly and openly affirmed that his preferred source was Jesus Christ.[42]

1. DID JEFFERSON HAVE A DISDAIN FOR THE INFLUENCE OF CHRISTIANITY ON EDUCATION?

Jefferson's own education as well as many of the major educational influences on his life had been thoroughly Christian. He did not despise or reject his own favorable educational experience, so it is therefore not surprising that in his subsequent educational endeavors he repeatedly incorporated the same general religious instruction.

For example, in 1783 when a grammar school was being established in his area, he wrote to the Reverend Dr. John Witherspoon, the president of the College of New Jersey (now Princeton), a Presbyterian university that trained many clergy, to request one of Witherspoon's students or staff as an instructor for the school.[43] In 1792 Jefferson again wrote the Reverend Witherspoon about another local school "in hopes that your seminary . . . may furnish some person whom you could recommend" to be the assistant to "the head of a school of considerable reputation in Virginia."[44]

What would Jefferson expect from students trained by the Reverend Dr. Witherspoon? Certainly not a secular approach to education. On the contrary, not only did Witherspoon teach the Scottish Common Sense philosophy but he also specifically instructed his students:

> That he is the best friend to American liberty who is most sincere and active in promoting true and undefiled religion, and who sets himself with the greatest firmness to bear down profanity and immorality of every kind. Whoever is an

avowed enemy of God, I scruple not to call him an enemy to his country.[45]

So when Jefferson needed teachers for schools in his area, he called on a leading Christian theologian and educator to send him religiously trained instructors. He certainly could have turned to other sources for help; he did not.

In 1794, after Jefferson had returned home from serving as secretary of state for President George Washington, he contacted a member of the Virginia legislature about bringing the Geneva Academy from Europe to Virginia.[46] The Geneva Academy was established in 1559 by Reformation theologian John Calvin.[47] In this school, the Bible was an indispensable textbook, with students from the school serving in the role of missionaries all over Europe.[48] It was this famous religious school that Jefferson wanted to bring to his state.

Then in 1803, while serving as president, Jefferson met with Presbyterian minister Gideon Blackburn at the White House about opening a missionary school for Cherokees near Knoxville, Tennessee. The school was to include religious instruction as a primary part of its studies, and President Jefferson directed Secretary of War Henry Dearborn to give federal money to help the school achieve its objectives.[49]

In 1804, President Jefferson negotiated the purchase of the Louisiana Territory. With authority over that region transferring from the French to the Americans, those living there were uncertain as to what changes might result. Sister Therese Farjon, Mother Superior of a Catholic school and convent in New Orleans, therefore wrote President Jefferson asking what the status of their religious school would be under the American government. Jefferson responded: "[Y]our institution . . . by training up its young members in the way they should go [Proverbs 22:6], cannot fail to ensure it *the patronage [support] of the government* it is under. Be assured that it will meet all the protection which my office can give it."[50] (emphasis added)

In 1805 President Jefferson was elected head of the board of trustees for the brand new Washington, DC, public schools.[51] He told the city council that he would "willingly undertake the duties proposed to me—so far as others of paramount obligation will permit my attention to them";[52] that is, he would do what he could for the city schools with the caveat that his presidential duties came first. Robert Brent therefore served as head of the trustees instead of Jefferson; but as a trustee, Jefferson contributed much to the new school system. In fact, James Ormond Wilson, the first superintendent of the Washington, DC, public school system, affirmed that Jefferson was "the chief author of the first plan of public education adopted for the city of Washington."[53] When the first report of the Washington public schools was prepared and released to document the progress of students, it announced:

> Fifty-five have learned to read in the Old and New Testaments and are all able to spell words of three, four, and five syllables; twenty-six are now learning to read Dr. Watts' *Hymns* and spell words of two syllables; ten are learning words of four and five letters. Of fifty-nine out of the whole number admitted [enrolled] that did not know a single letter, twenty can now read the Bible and spell words of three, four, and five syllables; twenty-nine read Dr. Watts' *Hymns* and spell words of two syllables; and ten, words of four and five letters.[54]

Most can probably visualize the Bible as a text to teach reading,[55] but what of Watt's *Hymns?*

Isaac Watts was a Christian theologian and hymn writer, penning some of the strongest doctrinal anthems in Christendom, including classics such as "Jesus Shall Reign," "Joy to the World," "O God our Help in Ages Past," "When I Survey the Wondrous Cross," "Am I a Soldier of the Cross," "At the Cross," and others. It was this hymnal, along with the Bible, that was used to teach reading to students in the school system whose plan of education was directly attributed to Thomas Jefferson.

Additionally, during the same time that Jefferson was working with the DC public school system, the board on which he served approved two of the schools being run by ministers: the Reverend Robert Elliott and the Richard White.[56] The Reverend Elliott was also allowed to use the school building concurrently as a meeting place for his church.[57]

In short, Jefferson was involved with many educational endeavors prior to establishing the University of Virginia in 1819, and in none of them was there any attempt to exclude Christian religious instruction. To the contrary, in each case he took steps to include or preserve such instruction and on no occasion objected to it. Jefferson certainly demonstrated no disdain for the influence of Christianity on education.

2. WAS THE UNIVERSITY OF VIRGINIA FOUNDED AS A SECULAR UNIVERSITY?

Universities in Jefferson's day were often: (1) founded and controlled by a particular denomination, (2) trained ministers for that specific denomination, and (3) had prominent ministers from that denomination serve as the chaplain, professor of Divinity, and president of the university.

Reflective of this pattern, in 1636 Harvard was founded by and for *CONGREGATIONALISTS* (so, too, with Yale in 1701 and Dartmouth in 1769). In 1692 the College of William and Mary was founded by and for *ANGLICANS* (as was the University of Pennsylvania in 1740, Kings College in 1754, and the College of Charleston in 1770). In 1746 Princeton was founded by and for *PRESBYTERIANS* (as was Dickinson in 1773 and Hampden-Sydney in 1775). In 1764 the College of Rhode Island (now Brown University) was founded by and for the *BAPTISTS*. In 1766 Queens College (now Rutgers) was founded by and for the *DUTCH REFORMED*. In 1780 Transylvania University was founded by and for the *DISCIPLES OF CHRIST*, and so on. With few exceptions, America's earliest universities were closely associated with particular denominations and were typically run by ministers from that denomination.

Departing from this pattern, Jefferson and his Board of Visitors (that is, the school's regents) specifically founded the University of Virginia to be America's first transdenominational school. It was designed to be a school not affiliated with any specific denomination but one that would train students from all denominations, fully pursuing denominational non-preferentialism but definitely not secularism. By adopting this unique and unprecedented approach, Jefferson was actually implementing a plan that had been advocated by evangelical Presbyterian clergyman Samuel Knox of Baltimore.

In 1799, the Reverend Knox penned a policy paper proposing the formation of a state university that would invite many denominations to establish multiple "theological schools" on the campus rather than just the traditional single one. The many denominations would thereby work together in mutual

Christian cooperation rather than competition.[58] Jefferson's philosophy was the same, and this was the model that he eventually employed at his University of Virginia. In fact, Jefferson even invited the Reverend Knox to be the very first professor at the university,[59] but because of a miscommunication, Knox did not respond to the offer in a timely fashion, so his teaching slot was finally offered to someone else.[60]

Throughout his career in politics, Jefferson had been a powerful advocate for religious liberty for all denominations and an ardent opponent of governments favoring one denomination over another. His famous Virginia Statute for Religious Liberty, drafted in 1777 and enacted in 1786, as well as his efforts with the 1776 Virginia constitution and its "Declaration of Rights," are well-known examples of his efforts to prevent denominational favoritism. It should therefore come as no surprise that the University of Virginia's charter, greatly influenced by Jefferson and approved by the state legislature in 1819, similarly required the school to treat all denominations equally.

Many modern writers misinterpret this denominational nonpreferentialism as secularism. In fact, those who believe Jefferson to be anti-religious often point to what he did with the Professor of Divinity position at William and Mary, his own alma mater, as "proof" of their erroneous claim.

In 1779, Jefferson introduced legislation to modify the school—an accomplishment known as the Jefferson Reorganization. According to Professor Leonard Levy:

> Jefferson's first proposal on higher education came in 1779. His Bill for the Amending of the Constitution of the College of William and Mary stated that the college consisted of "one

school of sacred theology, with two professorships therein, to wit, one for teaching the Hebrew tongue, and expounding the Holy Scriptures; and the other for explaining the commonplaces of Divinity and controversies with heretics." . . . Jefferson proposed to abolish . . . the school of theology with its professorships of religion.[61]

Did Jefferson actually propose abolishing "the school of theology with its professorships of religion"? Apparently so, for Jefferson himself acknowledged, "I effected, during my residence in Williamsburg that year, a change in the organization of that institution by abolishing . . . the two professorships of Divinity."[62]

So it appears that Professor Levy was right—that Jefferson did seek to secularize higher education. At least it appears that way until one reads the rest of Jefferson's own account of his actions, and then it becomes evident that his intention was exactly the opposite. Jefferson explained:

The College of William and Mary was an establishment purely of the Church of England [i.e., the Anglicans]; the Visitors [Regents] were required to be all of that Church; the professors to subscribe its thirty-nine [doctrinal] Articles; its students to learn its Catechism; and one of its fundamental objects was declared to be to raise up ministers for that church. The religious jealousies, therefore, of all the Dissenters [those from other denominations] took alarm lest this might give an ascendancy to the Anglican sect.[63]

Jefferson had abolished the School of Divinity because it was solely an arm of the state-established Anglican Church, and he wanted to open the college to greater involvement from "the

Dissenters" —those from other Christian denominations such as Methodists, Baptists, Presbyterians, Quakers, and so forth.

Further evidence that Jefferson's reorganization of the college was not motivated by any notion of secularism was the stipulation within his plan that "the said professors shall likewise appoint from time to time a missionary of approved veracity to the several tribes of Indians."[64] (In that day, missionaries, like ministers, taught both religious and academic subjects, and most schools were headed by ministers or missionaries.) Jefferson was not against Christian education, nor was he seeking to secularize it; he simply opposed favoring the Anglican Church over all others, and for this reason abolished the Anglican Professorship of Divinity at William and Mary.

Four decades later, Jefferson sought to ensure that the University of Virginia would reflect the same denominational nonpreferentialism that he had repeatedly promoted throughout his life. He therefore reported to the state authorities that chartered the university:

> In conformity with the principles of our Constitution which places all sects of religion on an equal footing, with the jealousies of the different sects in guarding that equality from encroachment and surprise; and with the sentiments of the legislature in favor of freedom of religion manifested on former occasions, we have proposed no Professor of Divinity; and the rather as the proofs of the being of a God—the Creator, Preserver, and Supreme Ruler of the Universe—the Author of all the relations of morality and of the laws and obligations these infer—will be within the province of the Professor of Ethics; to which adding the developments of

these moral obligations of those in which all sects agree, with a knowledge of the languages Hebrew, Greek, and Latin, a basis will be formed common to all sects. Proceeding thus far without offence to the Constitution, we have thought it proper at this point to leave every sect to provide as they think fittest the means of further instruction in their own peculiar tenets.[65]

Jefferson and the Board of Visitors (regents) decided that there should be no specific Professor of Divinity since it might give the impression that the university favored the denomination with which the professor was affiliated. But this certainly did not mean that the university would be secular or have no religious instruction. To the contrary, Jefferson simply transferred the responsibility of teaching "the proofs of the being of a God, the Creator, Preserver, and Supreme Ruler of the Universe, the Author of all the relations of morality and of the laws and obligations these infer" – the things that a professor of Divinity would normally teach – to the Professor of Ethics. So religious instruction definitely would occur.

Jefferson also reported:

It is supposed probable that a building of somewhat more size in the middle of the grounds may be called for in time, in which may be rooms for religious worship, under such impartial regulations as the Visitors shall prescribe . . . [66]

Despite Jefferson's unambiguous declarations in these provisions, critics nevertheless claimed that the university was anti-religious. As Jefferson reported to one friend at the time, "In our university you know there is no Professorship of Divinity. A handle has been made of this to disseminate an idea that this is an institution not merely of no religion but against all religion."[67] In 1822 Jefferson therefore issued another report to state authorities refuting any such notion. He began by repeating the lengthy section above from his original 1818 report, and then added:

> It was not, however, to be understood that instruction in religious opinion and duties was meant to be precluded by the public authorities as indifferent to the interests of society. On the contrary, the relations which exist between man and his Maker and the duties resulting from those relations are the most interesting and important to every human being and the most incumbent on his study and investigation. The want of instruction in the various creeds of religious faith existing among our citizens presents, therefore, a chasm in a general institution of the useful sciences. But it was thought that this want, and the entrustment to each society [denomination] of instruction in its own doctrine, were evils of less danger than a permission to the public authorities to dictate modes or principles of religious instruction, or than opportunities furnished them by giving countenance or ascendancy to any one sect over another. A remedy, however, has been suggested of promising aspect which, while it excludes the public authorities from the domain of religious freedom, will give to the sectarian schools of Divinity the full benefit the public provisions made for instruction in the other branches of science.[68]

What was the "remedy" Jefferson suggested? As he explained to a friend:

> [W]e suggest the expediency of encouraging the different religious sects [denominations] to establish, each for itself, a professorship of their own tenets on the confines of the university so near as that their students may attend the lectures there and have the free use of our library and every other accommodation we can give them. . . . [B]y bringing the sects together and mixing them with the mass of other students, we shall soften their asperities [harshness], liberalize and neutralize their prejudices, and make the general religion a religion of peace, reason, and morality.[69]

The remedy was that each of the various denominations be invited to establish its own seminary on the campus. Jefferson told the state that that this particular "arrangement would complete the circle of the useful sciences embraced by this institution and would fill the chasm now existing on principles which would leave inviolate the constitutional freedom of religion, the most inalienable and sacred of all human rights."[70]

So while there was not just one exclusive professor of Divinity at the university, the effect of Jefferson's plan that each denomination have "a professorship of their own tenets" at the school was that it greatly increased the total number of Professorships of Divinity that would be at the university. This transdenominational approach caused Presbyterians, Baptists, Methodists, and others to give the University of Virginia the early friendship and cooperative support necessary to make it a success. Consider Presbyterian minister John Holt Rice as an example.

Rice was a nationally known religious leader with extensive

evangelical credentials. He founded the Virginia Bible Society,[71] started the *Virginia Evangelical and Literary Magazine*, was elected national leader of the Presbyterian Church, and was offered the presidency of Princeton (but instead accepted the chair of theology at Hampden-Sydney College). Rice fully supported and promoted the University of Virginia,[72] and specifically did so because it was not solely affiliated with just one denomination. As he explained:

> The plan humbly suggested is to allow Jews, Catholics, Protestants, Episcopalians, Methodists, Baptists, any and all sects, if they shall choose to exercise the privilege, to endow professorships and nominate their respective professors. . . . [T]he students shall regularly attend Divine worship, but in what form should be left to the direction of parents; or in failure of this, to the choice of the students. In addition to this, the professors in every case must be men of the utmost purity of moral principle and strictness of moral conduct.[73]

Further affirming the overall pro-religious tone present at the creation of the University of Virginia is the fact that when its physical construction finally began, the special ceremony at the laying of its cornerstone—a ceremony specifically arranged by Jefferson and the Board of Visitors—included both the reading of Scripture and a prayer. Notice the desires expressed in that founding prayer:

> May Almighty God, without invocation to Whom no work of importance should be begun, bless this undertaking and enable us to carry it on with success. Protect this college, the object of which institution is to instill into the minds of

youth principles of sound knowledge, *to inspire them with the love of religion and virtue,* and prepare them for filling the various situations in society with credit to themselves and benefit to their country.[74] (emphasis added)

Clearly, then, both Jefferson's own writings as well as the records of the university absolutely refute any notion that the University of Virginia was a secularist institution. Instead, it was the nation's first prominent transdenominational school.

3. WAS JEFFERSON'S FACULTY COMPOSED OF UNITARIANS?

Jefferson established ten teaching positions at the university,[75] and some modern academics and writers assert that Jefferson filled the university staff with Unitarians.[76] This charge is not new. In 1837, a publication in New York charged that Jefferson intended for the University to theologically "poison the stream at the fountain" with "unsuspecting youth" who were to be Jefferson's targets for religious "corruption"[77] by indoctrinating them with Unitarianism.

In 1858 when Henry Randall prepared his famous three-volume biography of Jefferson, he specifically inquired into this claim. He therefore "took pains to ascertain from the two surviving original professors, who remain in the United States, what were the religious opinions of themselves and their colleagues, and how far they had reason to believe those opinions influenced their selection."[78] The question of Unitarian corruption was thus posed to those two remaining original professors, George Tucker, professor of moral philosophy, and Robley Dunglison, professor of anatomy and medicine. Dunglison succinctly answered:

I have not the slightest reason for believing that Mr. Jefferson was in any respect guided in his selection of professors of the University of Virginia by religious considerations. . . . In all my conversations with Mr. Jefferson, no reference was made to the subject. I was an Episcopalian, so was Mr. Tucker, Mr. Long, Mr. Key, Mr. Bonnycastle, and Dr. Emmet. Dr. Blaetterman, I think, was a Lutheran, but I do not know so much about his religion as I do about that of the rest. *There certainly was not a Unitarian among us.*[79] (emphasis added)

Professor Tucker agreed, declaring:

I believe that all the first professors belonged to the Episcopal Church, except Dr. Blaetterman, who, I believe, was a German Lutheran. . . . I don't remember that I ever heard the religious creeds of either professors or Visitors [Regents] discussed or inquired into by Mr. Jefferson, or anyone else.[80]

Jefferson did not select his professors with the view of "corrupting" the religious faith and principles of youth, and the professors he chose affirmed that "There certainly was not a Unitarian among us," thus specifically rebutting today's errant claims. Jefferson simply did not delve into the denominational affiliations or specific religious beliefs of his faculty; what he sought was professors who were competent and qualified in knowledge and deportment. As he once told his close friend and fellow educator Dr. Benjamin Rush:

For thus I estimate the qualities of the mind: 1. good humor [i.e., friendliness and likeability]; 2. integrity; 3. industry; 4. science. The preference of the first to the second quality may not at first be acquiesced in [agreed with], but certainly we had all rather associate with a good-humored, light-principled man than with an ill-tempered rigorist in morality.[81]

It was by applying such standards that Jefferson once invited Thomas Cooper to be professor of chemistry and law,[82] but when it became known that Cooper was a Unitarian and a public outcry arose against him, the university withdrew its offer to him.[83]

Obviously, this type of primary-source evidence concerning Jefferson and the religious views of his faculty is ignored by many of today's writers. But Roy Honeywell of Eastern Michigan University actually *did* review the original historical evidence and thus correctly concluded:

> In general, Jefferson seems to have ignored the religious affiliations of the professors. His objection to ministers was because of their active association with sectarian groups, in his day, a fruitful source of social friction. The charge that he intended the University to be a center of Unitarian influence is totally groundless.[84]

4. DID JEFFERSON EXCLUDE RELIGIOUS INSTRUCTION FROM THE ACADEMIC PROGRAM?

As already noted, in 1818 Jefferson and the university Visitors publicly released their plan for the new school announcing that it would be transdenominational and making clear that religious instruction would be provided to all students. But Jefferson insisted on additional steps to ensure that religious training would occur at the university.

For example, he directed the professor of ancient languages to teach Biblical Greek, Hebrew, and Latin so that students would be equipped to read and study the "earliest and most respected authorities of the faith of every sect [denomination]."[85] Jefferson also wanted the writings of prominent Christian authorities to be placed in the university library, so he asked Visitor (or regent) James Madison to prepare a list of Christian theological writings (which he described as writings on "Divinity") to be placed on its shelves.[86]

Madison recommended the inclusion of the early works of the Alexandrian Church Fathers, such as Clement, Origen, Pantaenus, Cyril, Athanasius, and Didymus the Blind. He also recommended Latin authors such as Saint Augustine; Saint Aquinas, and other Christian leaders from the Middle Ages; and the works of Erasmus, Luther, Calvin, Socinius, and Bellarmine from the Reformation era. Madison's list also contained more recent theologians and religious writers including Grotius, Tillotson, Hooker, Pascal, Locke, Newton, Butler, Clarke, Wollaston, Edwards, Mather, Penn, Wesley, Leibnitz, Paley, and others.[87]

And in addition to the religious lessons that Jefferson stipulated be given to students by the professors of ethics and ancient languages, Jefferson further ensured that religious instruction would occur by making religious instruction an inseparable part of the study of law and political science. As he explained to a prominent judge: "[I]n my catalogue, considering ethics as well as religion as supplements to law in the government of man, I had placed them in that sequence."[88]

And as already noted, Jefferson acknowledged "that a building . . . in the middle of the grounds may be called for in time in which may be rooms for religious worship,"[89] but he also ordered that in the university Rotunda, "one of its large elliptical rooms on its middle floor shall be used for . . . religious worship."[90] He further declared that "the students of the university will be free and *expected to attend religious worship* at the establishment of their respective sects"[91] (emphasis added).

Clearly, Jefferson took many deliberate steps to ensure that religious instruction was an integral part of academic studies. So the claim that there was no Christian curriculum or instruction at the University of Virginia is demonstrably false and easily disproved by Jefferson's own writings.

* * *

In short, first-hand source documents, especially Jefferson's writings, refute all four modern assertions about any allegedly secularist educational orientation of Jefferson in general or of his University of Virginia in particular. But there is one other aspect of Jefferson's philosophy toward religion in education that draws much attention from those who would paint him as irreligious and atheistic, and it must be addressed.

In a highly publicized 1787 letter to his nephew Peter Carr, Jefferson tells him to "question with boldness even the existence of a God."[92] Taken out of context this admonition does seem condemning—which is why Negativists, Minimalists, and Secularists have surgically lifted and regularly use just this one line from his long epistle. They then deliberately misrepresent that extracted statement so as to make it seem that he was recommending exactly the opposite of what he was actually telling his nephew.

Jefferson had raised Peter as the son he never had (Jefferson's only son was stillborn in 1777). Peter's father, Dabney, was Jefferson's brother-in-law and one of Jefferson's closest friends. While Peter was still a young boy, Dabney died and was buried on the grounds at Monticello. Jefferson then stepped in to help raise young Peter.

In 1785, when Peter was fifteen years old and Jefferson was on an overseas assignment, he began writing the boy from Europe, addressing the direction that the young man's education should take. He instructed him not only about the importance of character ("give up science, give the earth itself and all it contains, rather than do an immoral act"[93]) but also about diligently pursuing the study of history, philosophy, and poetry, especially recommending that Peter read

> . . . Virgil, Terence, Horace, Anacreon, Theocritus, Homer. . . . Read also Milton's *Paradise Lost,* Shakespeare, Ossian, Pope's and Swift's works, in order to form your style in your own language. In morality, read Epictetus, Xenophontis *Memorabilia,* Plato's Socratic dialogues, Cicero's philosophies.[94]

The next year (1786) Peter was accepted to William and Mary, and the following year (1787), George Wythe agreed to tutor Peter in Latin and Greek.[95] (Wythe had been Jefferson's instructor in law, and later, along with his former student, Jefferson, signed the Declaration of Independence.) When Jefferson learned that Wythe would tutor Peter, he was thrilled and told the boy, "I am sure you will find this to have been one of the most fortunate events of your life."[96] A year later Wythe went further and accepted Peter as a law student, just as he had done with Jefferson some twenty-five years earlier.

The famous letter containing the phrase so abused today was written by Jefferson to his nephew during his second year at William and Mary. The letter contains recommendations to Peter about his studies in four areas: Italian, Spanish, moral philosophy, and religion. The latter section was by far the longest, and it is in that part of his extensive missive that Jefferson advised Peter to "question with boldness even the existence of a God."[97]

Secularist and antireligious authors have made this short phrase the sole focus of that letter,[98] but the rest of the lengthy correspondence makes abundantly clear that Jefferson was actually instructing Peter in apologetics. The term *apologetics* first appeared in English in 1733, but it is derived from a Greek word that literally means "speaking in defense," and indicates an intelligent presentation and defense of major traditional elements of religious faith.[99]

Jefferson believed that the time had come for the seventeen-year-old Peter to know not just *what* he believed but also *why* he believed it—and to be able to defend his beliefs. Peter believed in God and Christianity, but Jefferson urged him to examine both sides of the question concerning the existence of God, study opposing arguments, and then come to a conclusion he could ably defend. (This is exactly what the Bible advises in 1 Peter 3:15: to be able to get the *reason* for one's belief.)

The Founding Fathers regularly encouraged their own children and other youth to learn and use apologetics—to learn both sides of a religious issue. For example, Elias Boudinot, a president of Congress and a framer of the Bill of Rights, wrote about this to his daughter, Susan, after Thomas Paine had attacked the Bible in his famous *Age of Reason*.[100] Boudinot assured her that an open-minded examination of the evidence easily proved the existence of God and the truth of the Bible.

> God in His infinite wisdom has given us sufficient evidence that the revelation of the Gospel is from Him. This is subject to rational inquiry and of conviction from the conclusive nature of the evidence; but when that fact is established, you

are bound as a rational creature to show your full confidence in His unchangeable veracity and infinite wisdom by firmly believing the great truths so revealed.[101]

Founding Father John Witherspoon, a signer of the Declaration and the president of Princeton, similarly endorsed this type of apologetics.[102] And the Reverend Ezra Stiles, a conservative theologian and the president of Yale, also encouraged direct challenges to traditional religious beliefs. He, too, was fully convinced that through apologetics one could withstand and answer all attacks. As he acknowledged:

> Religious liberty is peculiarly friendly to fair and generous disquisition [systematic inquiry]. Here, Deism will have its full chance; nor need Libertines [morally unrestrained individuals] more to complain of being overcome by any weapons but the gentle, the powerful ones of argument and truth. Revelation will be found to stand the test to the ten-thousandth examination.[103]

Jefferson, by telling his nephew Peter to "question with boldness even the existence of a God," was doing exactly what the leading theologians and educators of his day regularly encouraged. Yet for making the same recommendation made by prominent Christian leaders at the time, Jefferson today is somehow proved to be an antireligious secularist? Ridiculous.

Jefferson was thoroughly convinced that the existence of God was self-evident and irrefutable, being proved simply by what God had made:

> [W]hen we take a view of the universe in its parts, general

or particular, it is impossible for the human mind not to perceive and feel a conviction of design, consummate skill, and indefinite power in every atom of its composition. The movements of the heavenly bodies, so exactly held in their course by the balance of centrifugal and centripetal forces; the structure of our earth itself with its distribution of lands, waters, and atmosphere; animal and vegetable bodies examined in all their minutest particles; insects—mere atoms of life—yet as perfectly organized as man or mammoth; the mineral substances, their generation and uses; it is impossible, I say, for the human mind not to believe that there is in all this design, cause, and effect up to an Ultimate Cause—a Fabricator of all things, from matter and motion—their Preserver and Regulator . . .[104]

In fact, Jefferson believed that arguing the existence of God from a position of blind faith without resort to the proofs of reason actually hurt Christianity. As he explained:

[I] think that every Christian sect [denomination] gives a great handle to atheism by their general dogma that without a revelation there would not be sufficient proof of the being of a God. . . . So irresistible are these evidences of an intelligence and powerful Agent, that of the infinite numbers of men who have existed through all time, they have believed in the proportion of a million at least to unit [i.e., a million to one] in the hypothesis of an eternal pre-existence of a Creator.[105]

Jefferson's own education had been under the Scottish Common Sense approach. It attacked European skepticism, praised the compatibility of reason and revelation, and demonstrated the superiority of evidence in all challenges. Jefferson had been trained in this vein of apologetics and it was in the same spirit that he challenged Peter to question—that is, to examine and consider—the evidence of God's existence. In light of this background, consider the now infamous section from Jefferson's letter.

Note first that in opposition to Minimalism (where everything is reduced to one-line platitudes that require no thought or reasoning), the complete and lengthy controversial religious section of Jefferson's letter will be fully presented here so that its context will be clear. Second, notice that throughout the letter Jefferson attempted to take a neutral position on many religious issues. He set forth the popular arguments both for and against various religious doctrines, presenting the major arguments to which Peter would undoubtedly be exposed. Yet despite his well-intentioned attempt to be position neutral, Jefferson's bias in favor of his own personal belief in God comes through.

Here, in its entirety, is the section of the letter in question.

4. Religion. Your reason is now mature enough to examine this object. In the first place, divest yourself of all bias in favor of novelty and singularity of opinion. Indulge them in any other subject rather than that of religion. It is too important, and the consequences of error may be too serious. On the other hand, shake off all the fears and servile prejudices under which weak minds are servilely crouched. Fix reason firmly in her seat and call to her tribunal every fact, every opinion. Question with boldness even the existence of a God, because if there be One, He must more approve the homage of reason than that of blindfolded fear. You will naturally examine first

the religion of your own country. Read the Bible then, as you would Livy or Tacitus. The facts which are within the ordinary course of nature, you will believe on the authority of the writer, as you do those of the same kind in Livy and Tacitus. The testimony of the writer weighs in their favor in one scale, and their not being against the laws of nature does not weigh against them. But those facts in the Bible which contradict the laws of nature must be examined with more care and under a variety of faces. Here you must recur to the pretensions [claims] of the writer to inspiration from God. Examine upon what evidence his pretensions are founded and whether that evidence is so strong as that its falsehood would be more improbable than a change of the laws of nature in the case he relates. For example, in the book of Joshua we are told the sun stood still several hours. Were we to read that fact in Livy or Tacitus, we should class it with their showers of blood, speaking of statues, beasts, &c. But it is said that the writer of that book was inspired. Examine, therefore, candidly what evidence there is of his having been inspired. The pretension [claim] is entitled to your inquiry, because millions believe it. On the other hand, you are astronomer enough to know how contrary it is to the law of nature that a body revolving on its axis, as the earth does, should have stopped, should not, by that sudden stoppage, have prostrated animals, trees, buildings, and should after a certain time have resumed its revolution, and that without a second general prostration. Is this arrest of the earth's motion, or the evidence which affirms it, most within the law of probabilities? You will next read the New Testament. It is the history of personage called Jesus. Keep in your eye the opposite pretentions. 1. Of those who say He was begotten by God, born of a virgin, suspended and reversed the laws of nature at will, and ascended bodily into Heaven; and 2. Of those who say he was a man, of illegitimate birth, of a benevolent heart, enthusiastic mind, who set out without pretensions to Divinity, ended in believing them, and was punished capitally for sedition by being gibbeted according to the Roman law, which punished the first commission of that offence by whipping, and the second by exile or death in furca. See this law in the Digest, Lib. 48, tit. 19, 28. 3. and Lipsius, Lib. 2. De Cruce, cap. 2. These questions are examined in the books I have mentioned under the head of religion and several others. They will assist you in your inquiries, but keep your reason firmly on the watch in reading them all. Do not be frightened from this inquiry by any fear of its consequences. If it ends in a belief that there is no God, you will find incitements to virtue in the comfort and pleasantness you feel in its exercise, and the love of these which it will procure you. If you find reason to believe there is a God, a consciousness that you are acting under His eye and that He approves of you will be a vast additional incitement. If that there be a future state, the hope of a happy existence in that increases the appetite to deserve it; if that Jesus was also a God, you will be comforted by a belief of His aid and love. In fine, I repeat you must lay aside all prejudice on both sides, and neither believe nor reject anything because any other person or description of persons have rejected or believed it. Your own reason is the only oracle given you by Heaven, and you are answerable not for the rightness but uprightness of the decision. I forgot to observe when speaking of the New

Testament that you should read all the histories of Christ, as well of those whom a council of ecclesiastics have decided for us to be pseudo-evangelists, as those they named Evangelists, because these pseudo-evangelists pretended to inspiration as much as the others, and you are to judge their pretensions by your own reason and not by the reason of those ecclesiastics. Most of these are lost. There are some, however, still extant, collected by Fabricius, which I will endeavor to get and send you.[106]

By way of note, Jefferson's reference to the "pseudo-evangelists" and "Fabricius" is almost completely foreign to today's Modernists; it therefore can be misinterpreted as an attack on the Scriptures or the Epistles. It was not. The term *evangelists* was a concrete and well understood term in the Founding Era, often utilized in courts of law,[107] specifically meaning the four Gospels as written by Matthew, Mark, Luke, and John.[108] So what does "pseudo-evangelists" mean? Does it mean the writings of the other Apostles such as Paul and Peter? And who is Fabricius?

In 397 and 419 AD, the Synods of Carthage met and canonized the books that form what is traditionally considered within Christendom to be the inspired Scriptures.[109] At that time, many other books, including what were known as the Gnostic Gospels (such as the Gospel of Marcion, the Gospel of Apelles, the Gospel of Bardesanes, the Gospel of Basilides, and others) were rejected as not being Divinely inspired. They were thus considered to be written by "pseudo evangelists." In 1713 and 1723 German scholar Johann Albert Fabricius made compilations of these Gnostic Gospels; and just as Jefferson urged Peter to read the canonized Scriptures, he also encouraged him to read and investigate noncanonized books (such as those compiled by Fabricius) in order to understand the debate over which parts of the Bible were actually inspired.

Jefferson was not being antireligious in his letter to Peter; he was simply trying to be neutral so as to encourage Peter to reach his own conclusions. In fact, his enclosure in this letter recommended books on many topics to Peter, including: "Religion. Locke's Conduct of the mind – Middleton's works – Bolingbroke's philosophical works—Hume's essays—Voltaire's works—Beattie."[110] Significantly, three of these writers were pro-religion (Locke, Middleton, and Beattie), and the other three anti-religion.

As Jefferson scholar Dr. Mark Beliles accurately points out concerning Jefferson's letter to Peter:

> Since Jefferson used in the letter the words "some people believe" when expressing *both* orthodox and unorthodox opinions, it cannot be proven that he was personally in favor of either. Scholars often quote excerpts from it to prove his unorthodoxy, but one could just as easily quote Jefferson's phrase from this letter which said "Jesus . . . was begotten by God, born of a virgin, suspended and reversed the laws of nature at will, and ascended bodily into heaven."[111]

And Jefferson historian Robert Healey even points out what he sees as a positive bias toward faith in the letter, explaining that "after saying to Peter Carr, 'Question with boldness even the existence of a God,' he writes a few lines further on, 'Your own reason is the only oracle *given you by Heaven*"[112] (emphasis added). Additionally, in the section of the letter immediately preceding his advice on religion, Jefferson told Peter: "He Who made us would have been a pitiful bungler if He had made the rules of our moral conduct a matter of science. . . . The moral sense, or conscience, is as much a part of man as his leg or arm."[113]

This is a clear declaration by Jefferson that man was created by God and endowed by Him with a conscience—two of the primary tenets of Scottish Common Sense. His statement that our reason was given us by Heaven is yet another of its four precepts. And as already shown above, Jefferson had no personal doubts about the existence of God; to him it was self-evident that God existed, and it was also a belief held worldwide by what Jefferson had called a margin of a million to one.[114] So while Jefferson attempted (and largely succeeded) in remaining neutral while setting forth to Peter the possible options of belief, he definitely held a strong personal pro-God position.

Jefferson's advice to Peter about discovering and confirming for himself the foundation for his own personal religious beliefs might just as easily have come from today's leading Christian apologists, whether Josh McDowell, Lee Strobel, Frank Turek, or Ravi Zacharias. Like Jefferson, these apologists similarly advise Christian youth to know *what* they believe, *why* they believe it, and *how* to defend those beliefs.[115]

In summary, Jefferson's letter to Peter definitely does *not* prove irreligion on the part of Jefferson, nor can it be used to show he was promoting secular education among his own family members. Jefferson has a long record of deliberately, purposefully, and intentionally including religious instruction in the educational endeavors of which he took part, and this is especially true concerning his beloved University of Virginia.

LIE #3

Thomas Jefferson Wrote His Own Bible and Edited Out the Things He Didn't Agree With

The notion that Jefferson so disliked Christianity and the Scriptures that he made his own Bible is commonly bandied about in both secular and religious circles:

> Hunched over his desk, penknife in hand, Thomas Jefferson sliced carefully at the pages of Holy Scripture, excising select passages and pasting them together to create a Bible more to his liking. The "Jefferson Bible." A book he could feel comfortable with. What didn't make it into the Jefferson Bible was anything that conflicted with his personal world-view. Hell? It can't be. The supernatural? Not even worth considering. God's wrath against sin? I don't think so. The very words of God regarded as leftover scraps.[1]

> Jefferson . . . wrote his own Bible that excluded all references to miracles, wonders, signs, virgin birth, resurrection, the God-head, and whatever else conflicted with his own religious thought.[2]

> Jefferson . . . rejected the superstitions and mysticism of Christianity and even went so far as to edit the Gospels, removing the miracles and mysticism of Jesus.[3]

> Thomas Jefferson . . . actually took scissors to the Gospels and cut out all references to anything supernatural.[4]

Many others make similar claims.[5] Are they accurate?

This alleged hostility of Jefferson toward the Bible is inconsistent with many established facts in this area. For example, Jefferson made frequent positive use of Bible references and passages throughout his own writings[6] and gave Bibles as gifts to family members.[7] And during a period of personal economic crisis so severe that he arranged a personal loan[8] and even offered to sell his own cherished private library to Congress to raise additional funds,[9] he made a generous contribution to, and became a lifetime member of the Virginia Bible Society.[10]

Additionally, in 1798 he helped finance the printing of the John Thompson Bible—a groundbreaking American edition of the Bible.[11] (In this era, books were sometimes financed through a process known as "subscription." The publisher would approach potential financial backers and if they approved his project, they would pre-purchase copies of the work for themselves, thus providing the upfront money necessary to publish the work. Publishers often honored these funding subscribers by individually listing their names on a special page within the book.) That Bible was a massive, two-volume folio set that was not only the largest Bible ever published in America to that time but it was also America's first hot-pressed Bible.[12] (Several signers of the Constitution and Declaration as well as other major Founders also helped fund the printing of that Bible.[13])

In addition to helping fund the John Thompson Bible, Jefferson also offered to subscribe Charles Thomson's Bible[14]—the first American translation of the Greek Septuagint into English. (The Septuagint was a third century BC translation of the Hebrew Bible into Greek for the use of Jews who no longer spoke Hebrew.) Jefferson's offer came too late, but Thomson nevertheless sent Jefferson a copy after it was published. Receiving it shortly before he retired from the presidency, Jefferson told Thomson: "I shall use it with great satisfaction on my return home. I propose there, among my first employments, to give to the Septuagint an attentive perusal, and shall feel the aid you have now given me."[15]

Furthermore, Jefferson personally possessed and studied many Bibles from his own personal library, including famous ones such as:

- the Eliot Bible, printed in 1661 in the Algonquin Indian language by John Eliot, the apostle to the Indians (the first Bible printed in America in any language)

- the Bible in the Nattick Indian language (1666)

- the earliest Latin Bible printed in England (1580)

- the earliest French Geneva Bible printed in England (1687)

And many others.[16]

So . . . Jefferson owned many Bibles, studied them in original languages, belonged to a Bible society and contributed to it for the distribution of Bibles, gave copies of the Bible as gifts, and assisted in publishing and distributing a special edition of the Bible. Jefferson could have easily avoided any of these actions without hurting himself politically, but he did them anyway. Why? The most logical explanation is that he thought the Bible to be a valuable work that should be carefully studied by all citizens. In fact, he once told a noted political leader: "I have always said, and always will say, that the studious perusal of the Sacred Volume will make better citizens, better fathers, and better husbands."[17]

But what about the so-called Jefferson Bible?

In the first place, there actually is no "Jefferson Bible." This is a modern pejorative usually directed at one of two religious works that Jefferson prepared about Jesus. He compiled the first in 1804 and the second around 1820. Jefferson assigned an explicit title to each, accurately describing the scope and purpose of that particular work. Neither was a "Bible," and Jefferson would have objected to today's modern characterization of either work as such. Each was just what he had said it was in its title. His title for his 1804 work was: *The Philosophy of Jesus of Nazareth: Extracted from the Account of His Life and Doctrines Given by Matthew, Mark, Luke and John; Being an Abridgement of the New Testament for the Use of the Indians, Un-embarrassed [Uncomplicated] with Matters of Fact or Faith beyond the Level of their Comprehensions.*[18]

Notice several important points from Jefferson's description of this work. First, it was prepared for the use of Indians. Second, it was about Jesus and was drawn solely from the four Gospels, or what Jefferson often called "The Evangelists."[19] Third, it was not a Bible but rather an abridgment of the major teachings of Jesus found in those four books.

It is not surprising that Jefferson should have prepared such a work for native peoples. For years preceding its compilation, Jefferson had shown a keen interest and taken an active role in promoting Christianity among various tribes. Recall that he owned several Bibles in differing Indian languages, and also corresponded with leaders and ministers on Indian related issues.[20]

In fact, in 1802 while serving as president, he signed a law renewing the authorization for the "The Society of United Brethren for Propagating the Gospel among the Heathen" to continue pursuing their ministry and missionary work on federal tribal land trusts in the Northwest Territory.[21] (Specific detailed information about Jefferson's long public participation in promoting Gospel ministry and missionary efforts among native peoples was already presented in the Preface.)

Shortly after signing that act, Edward Dowse, one of Jefferson's long-time friends, sent him a copy of a sermon preached by the Rev. Reverend William Bennet of Scotland in which Bennet addressed the importance of promoting Christian knowledge, including among the native peoples of North America.[22] He affirmed that the emphasis of many groups was to teach morality, or holiness among Indians, and that no source and no religion, ancient or modern, surpassed the teachings of Jesus on this subject—that both history and reason combined to display "the matchless superiority of the morality of the Gospel."[23] Concerning that sermon, Dowse, who knew Jefferson well, told him: "[I]t seemed to me to have a claim to your attention. At any rate, the idea struck me that you will find it of use and perhaps may see fit to cause some copies of it to be reprinted, at your own charge, to distribute among our Indian missionaries."[24]

Jefferson replied to Dowse: "I now return the sermon you were so kind as to enclose me, having perused it with attention. . . .

I concur with the author in considering the moral precepts of Jesus as more pure, correct, and sublime than those of the ancient philosophers . . ."[25]

Of this exchange between the two, one author observed:

> Mr. Dowse apparently understood Jefferson's interest in Christian missions to the Native Americans in a way that many modern scholars have dismissed as irrelevant. This dismissal has led to the misunderstanding of Jefferson's motives for his compilation of Christ's teachings. Jefferson had a deep, genuine commitment to missionary efforts among the Indians. His account books show that he consistently donated his own money to missionaries and to societies that distributed Bibles to both Americans and Indians.[26]

As an additional affirmation of that statement, in 1803 President Jefferson signed a federal act renewing provisions related to propagating the Gospel among the Delaware tribe,[27] and he also approved a treaty with the Kaskaskia tribe to provide them Christian ministry and teaching.[28] Of that treaty former US Supreme Court Chief Justice William Rehnquist explained:

> Jefferson's treaty with the Kaskaskia Indians . . . provided annual cash support for the Tribe's Roman Catholic priest and church. . . . The treaty stated in part: "And whereas the greater part of said Tribe have been baptized and received into the Catholic church, to which they are much attached, the United States will give annually for seven years one hundred dollars towards the support of a priest of that religion . . . [a]nd . . . three hundred dollars to assist the said Tribe in the erection of a church."[29]

In 1804 President Jefferson signed yet another federal act related to the propagation of the Gospel among Indians on federal land trusts.[30]

But Jefferson not only personally undertook initiatives to help propagate Christianity and Christian teachings among native peoples, he also praised others who did the same. For example, after telling the Quakers that his own policies with all nations, including American tribal nations, had been "dictated by the principles of humanity [and] the precepts of the Gospel," he then noted that native peoples were "our brethren—our neighbors" and praised the Quakers for working among them in "religious instruction and the cultivation of letters."[31]

Across an extended period of years, Jefferson repeatedly demonstrated his interest in promoting Christianity and Christian civilization and morality among native peoples.[32*] So it is not surprising that in 1804 he prepared a work for that purpose. Taking two Bibles he had in the White House, he cut from them passages of Jesus' words and pasted those teachings into a separate folio. According to Jefferson, this work was a "digest of His [Jesus'] moral doctrines, extracted in His own words from the Evangelists."[33] Jefferson arranged the work so that the selected passages of Jesus' teachings could be read by native peoples in a nonstop, end-to-end fashion.

---

* It is not always clear whether Jefferson's objective in promoting Christianity among Native Americans was for the purpose of spiritual conversion or for civilizing and educating. For example, in his letter of April 7, 1809, to Governor James Jay, he said education should occur first, followed by "religious missionaries"; but he included both. (He indicated a similar sequence in his April 3, 1814, letter to Benjamin Smith Barton.) So regardless of whether it was one, the other, or both, Jefferson included the promotion of Christianity by means of missionaries and missionary groups as integral to what he envisioned for native peoples.

While this work is sometimes called the "Jefferson Bible," it is actually and only what Jefferson said it was: an *abridgement* of the four Gospels for the use of Native tribes. (For centuries, abridgments of the Bible have been a significant and an accepted part of the Bible market, especially popular for use among the young and new learners.[34])

No original copy of Jefferson's 1804 work survives, but what does remain is his handwritten title page for the work, the list of passages he selected for inclusion, and the two White House Bibles from which he clipped the Gospel passages. In 1983 historian Dickinson Adams took those documents and reconstructed Jefferson's *Philosophy of Jesus . . .* for the *Use of the Indians*,[35] as did Charles Sanford in 1984,[36] and Mark Beliles in 1993.[37] From those three reconstructions, it is clear that Jefferson definitely did include:

> [M]iracles such as the healing on the Sabbath in Luke 14:1–6, and the commission of Jesus to His disciples in Matthew 10 to go and heal the sick and raise the dead. It ncludes Jesus' teaching about the resurrection of the dead, about His own second coming, about His role as judge of all men at the end of time, and about His place as Son of God and Lord of a heavenly kingdom. He is also shown forgiving the sins of men and women in a manner reserved for God alone.[38]

That work also contained the miraculous resurrection of Jarius' daughter (Matthew 9:18–25), the healing of the bleeding woman (Matthew 9:20–22), and the healing of two blind men (Matthew 9:27–31),[39] all of which are also clearly acts of a miraculous or supernatural character. Other passages that reflected the spiritual and metaphysical, or supernatural included:

- Jesus declaring Himself the Son of God (Mark 14:61–62)

- Jesus healing the blind, lame, lepers, and deaf, and raising the dead (Matthew 11:4–5)

- Jesus' teaching about Hell (Matthew 10:28)

- Jesus' teaching on eternal life (Matthew 19:29)

- And many additional passages on Heaven, Hell, the resurrection, and other supernatural subjects (including Matthew 13:40–42, 49–50; 22:29–32; 25:31–34, 41, 46; Luke 14:14; and so forth).[40]

So the charge that Jefferson clipped the supernatural and miraculous from his 1804 work is false.

Jefferson understood that the words of Jesus would change Native Americans just as they had changed people throughout the history of the world. And even though Jefferson acknowledged that it required "the work of one or two evenings only"[41] to prepare this abridgment, Pulitzer Prize–winning Jefferson biographer Dumas Malone nevertheless observed that "it is a notable fact that this chief of state devoted even that time to such a task."[42]

The 1804 work is exactly and only what Jefferson said it was; and it did include teachings on the miraculous and supernatural.

By the way, Throckmorton posits that this work is *not* what Jefferson said that it was—that Jefferson's use of the word *Indians* was actually an allusion to his political adversaries.[43]

To justify this rather strained interpretation, Throckmorton points[44] to the last line of Jefferson's notes on his Second Inaugural Address, in which he states, "I have thought it best to say what is directly applied to the Indians only, but admits by inference a more general extension."[45] Yet even in this statement, Jefferson acknowledges that the word "Indians" is not simply a cryptic replacement for the traditional meaning of the word. So even if Jefferson's 1804 abridgment was somehow a coded cryptograph for his adversaries, it still remained primarily a work for Native Americans.

As Dr. Mark Beliles explains in his book *Doubting Thomas:*

> This note by Jefferson led editors Dickinson Adams and Ruth Leser to say the term "Indians" was really nothing more than a "code word" for referring to his New England Federalist religious critics. . . . That prejudice existed in more than the Indians is obvious, but to leap from that to say that Jefferson's title for his digest was therefore not intended for the Indians is wholly lacking in scholarly foundation, and was rejected by other Jefferson scholars such as [Dumas] Malone.[46]

If Throckmorton is correct that "Indians" is a code word for Jefferson's political adversaries, then evidently this abridgement of Jesus' words was actually intended for the use of John Adams, John Marshall, Alexander Hamilton, and other Federalists. Really? Jefferson family accounts as reported by Henry Stephens Randall further refute such a notion.

Randall was the only Jefferson biographer approved by the family and given full access to the family papers, family members, and family remembrances. His resulting 1858 three-volume set is still considered the most authoritative work written on Jefferson, and in it, Randall reports:

> This [i.e., the 1804 work] is sometimes mentioned as Mr. Jefferson's "Collection for the Indians," it being understood

that he conferred with friends on the expediency of having it published in the different Indian dialects as the most appropriate book for the Indians to be instructed to read in.[47] (emphasis added)

So, the 1804 work is exactly what Jefferson said it was; and it did include teachings on the miraculous and supernatural. Since it therefore does not fit the modern description of a so-called Jefferson Bible, then how about the 1820 work? Could that be the alleged Jefferson Bible that demonstrates a deliberate rejection of Jesus' supernatural works? After all, late in life Jefferson clearly did reject some orthodox Christian doctrines.

With the second work Jefferson took a much different approach from his earlier one, spending several years planning and preparing it. But like the first one, it, too, had a specific objective. He titled it *The Life and Morals of Jesus of Nazareth*, and on numerous occasions he avowed that its *sole* purpose was to collect and present the major *moral* teachings of Jesus in one short, simple collection.[48]

In fact, Jefferson made clear in multiple letters that in this particular work, he did not want to address anything beyond the moral teachings of Jesus – everything else was to be excluded as outside the scope of this specific examination. For example, in describing the work to Joseph Priestley, he told him that it "would purposely omit the question of His Divinity, and even His inspiration."[49] He also told Benjamin Rush and then William Short that "the question of His being a member of the Godhead, or in direct communication with it, as claimed for Him by some of His followers, and denied by others, *is foreign to the present view, which is merely an estimate of the intrinsic merits of His doctrines*"[50] (emphasis added).

It is rarely reported today, and thus a little-known fact that Jefferson spent literally *decades* of his life studying and comparing the moral teachings of dozens of history's most famous teachers and leaders, including Ocellus, Timæus, Pythagoras, Aristides, Cato, Socrates, Plato, Epicurus, Cicero, Xenophon, Seneca, Epictetus, Antoninus, and many others.[51] How many today even recognize these names, much less have read their works? Jefferson had. He read and critiqued the moral teachings of *each* of these famous pagan philosophers and then compared their moral teachings with those of Jesus. He repeatedly declared those of Jesus to be far superior because, unlike the others, Jesus "pushed His scrutinies into the heart of man; erected His tribunal in the region of his thoughts, and purified the waters at the fountain head."[52]

To modern secular Americans, Jefferson's study of historic morality seems eccentric and out of the ordinary—nothing more than what critics might consider a thinly veiled subterfuge masking his true hatred of the Bible. After all, they themselves surely would not have undertaken such an arduous comparison of moral writings across the millennia, so they can't imagine that Jefferson would have done so either. Yet the subject of morality was indeed a genuine theme of academic inquiry not only for Jefferson but for most Americans in his day. In fact, it was a required, stand-alone course in nearly every American university in the Founding Era.

For example, Princeton had a Professor of *Moral* Philosophy,[53] and its president, John Witherspoon, a signer of the Declaration, delivered to students systematic "Lectures on *Moral* Philosophy."[54] Harvard likewise had a Professor of Natural, Intellectual, and *Moral* Philosophy[55] as well as a Professor of Christian *Morals*.[56]

Washington Academy (named for George Washington in 1796, later known as Washington and Lee University) had daily courses on "*Moral* Philosophy."[57] William and Mary, Jefferson's alma mater, had a Professor of *Moral* and Intellectual Philosophy,[58] and Jefferson's own University of Virginia likewise had a Professor of *Moral* Philosophy.[59] Similar moral instruction was common throughout other colleges at that time,[60] and each taught the superiority of Biblical and Christian morality over all others.

Furthermore, in Jefferson's day, works on morals were of such public interest that they were penned by individuals from a broad spectrum of professions, ranging from economists such as Adam Smith in his *Theory of Moral Sentiments* (1759)[61] to political pamphleteers such as Richard Price with his *Review of the Principal Questions in Morals* (1757).[62] Many Founding Fathers also wrote full works on morality[63] or offered lengthy declarations about its importance;[64] and morals were a frequent object of legislation during their era[65] and for generations afterwards.

In Jefferson's first term as president as he was dealing with various national issues affected by morality, he began expressing his desire to prepare a work contrasting the moral teachings of non-Christian philosophers with those of Jesus. In one of his many letters to friends on this topic, he explained:

> I should first take a general view of the moral doctrines of the most remarkable of the ancient philosophers of whose ethics we have sufficient information to make an estimate—say Pythagoras, Epicurus, Epictetus, Socrates, Cicero, Seneca, Antoninus. I should do justice to the branches of morality they have treated well, but point out the importance of those in which they are deficient. I should then take a view of the

deism and ethics of the Jews and show in what a degraded state they were, and the necessity they presented of a reformation. I should proceed to a view of the life, character, and doctrines of Jesus. . . . [H]is system of morality was the most benevolent and sublime probably that has been ever taught, and consequently more perfect than those of any of the ancient philosophers.[66]

Additionally, some schools of thought in the Christian world in Jefferson's day attempted to combine the morality of ancient philosophers with that of Jesus. Jefferson therefore examined each of those systems as well, again reaching the same conclusions:

We must dismiss the Platonists and Plotinists, the Stagyrites and Gamalielites, the Eclectics, the Gnostics, and Scholastics, their essences and emanations, their Logos and Demiurgos, Aeons and Daemons, male and female, with a long train of etc. etc. etc. or, shall I say at once, of nonsense. We must reduce our volume to the simple Evangelists; select even from them the very words only of Jesus . . . . There will be found remaining the most sublime and benevolent code of morals which has ever been offered to man.[67]

Jefferson asserted that the moral teachings of Jesus needed nothing added to them from any other philosopher, Pagan or Christian.

Jefferson regularly and repeatedly effused about the preeminence of Jesus' moral teachings,[68] and it was never his intention for his work to do anything except present the morals of Jesus—a point he had made clear for years.[69] By 1813 he had finally begun compiling this work, reporting to his friend John Adams: "I have performed this operation for my own use by cutting verse by verse out of the printed book. . . . The result is an octavo of forty-six pages."[70]

Two years later, in 1815, he told his close friend and Virginia evangelical leader, the Reverend Charles Clay, about the work:

> Probably you have heard me say I had taken the four Evangelists, had cut out from them every text they had recorded of the *moral* precepts of Jesus, and arranged them in a certain order; and although they appeared but as fragments, yet fragments of the most sublime edifice of *morality* which had ever been exhibited to man.[71] (emphasis added)

The next year, in 1816, Jefferson wrote to fellow Founding Father Charles Thomson, who had earlier produced the translation of the Greek Septuagint Bible that Jefferson so admired. Thomson had just published his second work—the *Synopsis of the Four Evangelists*, in which he had taken all the passages from each of the four Gospels and arranged them chronologically. The result was basically one long Gospel, with all of Jesus' words and acts arranged sequentially.

Having seen Thomson's newest work, Jefferson told him of his own project, which he called "a wee little book," describing it as "a paradigma [example] of His doctrines made by cutting the texts out of the book [the Bible], and arranging them on the pages of a blank book in a certain order of time or subject."[72] Jefferson added, "If I had time, I would add to my little book the Greek, Latin, and French texts in columns side by side."[73] (Jefferson read seven languages: Greek, Latin, French, Italian,

Spanish, German, and English.[74]) By 1820, Jefferson had added those three additional languages in parallel columns to his "wee little book," thus completing his *Life and Morals of Jesus of Nazareth* as a four-language polyglot.

Writers who claim that this is the "Jefferson Bible" from which he excluded the supernatural are either ill-informed or ill-intentioned. Jefferson did not produce and had no intention of producing a theological or doctrinal work of exclusion; rather it was a moral work of inclusion in which he compiled at least eighty-one different moral teachings of Jesus into one easily readable collection.[75] But the secular bias of many of today's writers and scholars refuse to allow that work to be just what Jefferson said it was; they instead insist on converting it into an attack on the Bible and the supernatural.

But contrary to common belief, Jefferson's 1820 work, just like the 1804 one before it, contained *numerous* passages on the miraculous and the supernatural, including:

- Healing on the Sabbath (John 7:23)

- The Second Coming of Christ (Matthew 24:20-21, 29, 32-36, 36-44; 25:31–34)

- Resurrection of the dead (Matthew 22:28–30; Luke 14:14)

- The Holy Spirit (Luke 11:13)

- Hell (Matthew 5:29–30; 10:28; 13:37–41, 50; 18:8–9; 23:33; 25:46; Luke 12:4–5; 16:23)

- Heaven (Matthew 19:16–26; 25:34; Luke 12:33; 15:7; 16:1-15, 18-31; John 18:36–37)

- Angels (Matthew 13:39, 41, 49; 22:30; Luke 15:10)

- The devil (Matthew 13:39)

- Eternal life (Matthew 19:16; 25:46; Luke 10:25–28)[76]

So neither the 1804 or the 1820 work fits the critics' characterization of an alleged "Jefferson Bible."

But if the 1804 work was prepared for the use of Indians, then who was the intended audience for his 1820 work? That question was answered by Jefferson's eldest grandson, Thomas Jefferson Randolph:

> [H]e [my grandfather] left two codifications of the morals of Jesus—*one for himself,* and another for the Indians; the first of which I now possess: a blank volume, red morocco, gilt, letters on the back, "The Morals of Jesus"—into which he pasted extracts in Greek, Latin, French, and English, taken textually from the four Gospels and so arranged that he could run his eye of the reading of the same verse in four languages. . . . His codification of the *morals of Jesus* was not known to his family before his death, and they learnt from a letter addressed to a friend that he was in the habit of *reading nightly from it* before going to bed.[77] (emphasis added)

This is another problem with the modern characterization that this work was a "Jefferson Bible." It was *not* for public use; it was simply an assemblage of Jesus' moral teachings from the Gospels for Jefferson's personal study. So how did this private work—a work long unknown even to his family—become public?

In 1886, Cyrus Adler, the librarian for the Smithsonian, located Jefferson's personal copy, which was in the hands of his grandson; he arranged for its purchase by Congress in 1895. In 1900, US representative John Lacey of Iowa was so inspired by Jefferson's compilation of Jesus' moral teachings that he brought the work to national attention through a newspaper article widely reprinted across the country.[78] In describing that work to Congress, Lacey explained:

> [It] is a consolidation of the beautiful, pure teachings of the Savior in a compact form . . . and the opportunity is given, plain and unadorned, to compare these teachings with Marcus Aurelius's and other pagan "morals." They are in striking contrast to Plutarch's "morals" (or rather his immorals). No greater practical test of the worth of the tenets of the Christian religion could be made than the publication of this condensation by Mr. Jefferson. . . . A verse of John is combined with a verse of Matthew with no interlineations, but is blended into a harmonious whole. . . . The work was intended to place the morals of Jesus in a form where, simple and alone, they could be contrasted with the teachings of the pagan philosophers. In doing this work, Mr. Jefferson has builded . . . this beautiful little volume in a form to be accessible to the Christian world.[79]

In 1902, Representative Lacey sponsored a congressional resolution that the government reprint *Jefferson's Morals of Jesus of Nazareth* for use by the nation's senators and representatives.[80] Congress agreed and printed nine thousand copies at government expense,[81] and for the next fifty years, a copy of that work was given to every senator and representative at his or her swearing in.[82]

So what is the origin of the modern charge that Jefferson

so hated the traditional Bible that he therefore made his own? A contemporary scholar who investigated this claim concluded:

> Unfortunately, all those who have published the "Jefferson Bible" since 1903 have been almost universally either Unitarian or rationalist and secular in their approach, and their introductions to the book have . . . misrepresented Jefferson's motivations and beliefs to conform to their own theological assumptions or agendas.[83]

In summary, there is *no* "Jefferson Bible," and Jefferson did *not* produce any work solely for the purpose of deleting the miraculous and supernatural. He did, however, make two works that compiled the teachings of Jesus—one for use as a beginning reader for Native Americans and the other for his own personal use. Each was exactly what he said it was.

So the next time someone refers to a so-called Jefferson Bible, ask them to identify the specific work about which they are talking; most won't be able to do so. Then ask them where they got their information. The chances are high that it was some recent Negativist, Minimalist, Modernist, or Secularist source, but certainly not any original documentary source.

In fact, when individuals confront me about the "Jefferson Bible" and its exclusion of the supernatural, I respond, "Which 'Jefferson Bible' are you talking about?" To date, no one I have talked with knew there were two. I then ask, "Have you read either one for yourself?" All have answered, "No." So I then query, "Then how do you know it excluded the supernatural?" Without exception, the answer has been, "Because that's what everyone says"—clearly an unacceptable basis for establishing historical truth.

Thomas Jefferson Was a Racist Who Opposed Equality for Black Americans

*I*n previous generations, leading civil rights advocates, both black and white, regularly invoked Jefferson as an inspiration for their own efforts, pointing to his lengthy record of legislative proposals and writings on the subject of emancipation and civil rights.[1] But the modern portrayal of Jefferson's views on these issues has become quite different:

> Thomas Jefferson was demonstrably a racist—and a particularly aggressive and vindictive one at that. . . . His flaws are beyond redemption. . . . Jefferson is a patron saint far more suitable to white supremacists than to modern American liberals.[2]

> Jefferson . . . did not believe that all were created equal. He was a racist.[3]

[T]he third president was a creepy, brutal hypocrite. . . . always deeply committed to slavery, and even more deeply hostile to the welfare of blacks, slave or free. His proslavery views were . . . deeply racist.[4]

Jefferson was a racist. There is no question about that.[5]

While the modern charge abounds that Jefferson was an overt, unrepentant racist, an examination of his actual writings and actions on civil rights will demonstrate the error of these claims. It will also make evident why civil rights leaders in previous generations praised Jefferson for his repeated emancipation efforts.

Some people assume that America was generally homogenous in Jefferson's day, but such was not the case. Despite the small size of the nation and its meager population, there were marked and significantly passionate differences in many areas, and this was especially true with respect to slavery and civil rights.

In northern states, citizens tended to abhor slavery, and the institution was well on its way to extinction by the early 1800s. Blacks were elected to public office (e.g., Wentworth Cheswill in New Hampshire and Thomas Hercules in Pennsylvania) and both blacks and whites voted in elections.[6] Blacks also distinguished themselves for their exploits in military service (such as Peter Salem, Lemuel Haynes, Prince Estabrook, and Prince Whipple); could be found pastoring or preaching to largely white churches and congregations (such as Lemuel Haynes, Richard Allen, and Harry Hoosier); attended church and worshipped together with whites; and abolition societies abounded and exerted significant influence. In the North, both ministers and political leaders could be boldly and unapologetically outspoken for civil rights, and the general stance was for emancipation and equality. While there was definitely racism in the North, it was largely the exception rather than the rule.

The Southern colonies were quite different, however. Churches where both blacks and whites worshipped together, such as those pastored by black minister Andrew Bryan of Georgia, were uncommon. The possibility of blacks holding office was nonexistent, and political and spiritual leaders who spoke out against slavery were attacked. Freedom for slaves? Never! Equality for blacks? Unthinkable! This was the dominant southern view with only a few individual exceptions, such as Founding Father John Laurens of South Carolina. Abolition societies were rare, and the ones that existed were impotent. Racism was institutionalized.

The Middle colonies were somewhat a mix of the two other regions, but much closer in philosophical alignment and practice to the Southern colonies than the Northern ones. (As a result of the Civil War, Virginia is listed as a Southern Colony today, but as will be seen in his letter below, Jefferson considered it as a Middle Colony in his day, or what he described as one of the Chesapeake Colonies.) While the majority in this middle region supported slavery, and often strongly so, there was definitely a vocal minority advocating civil rights. Institutionalized racism was present but not as rigidly enforced as in the Southern colonies. Many ministers and some civil leaders—such as Jefferson, George Washington, Richard Bland, George Mason, Richard Henry Lee, William Hooper, William Few, and others—spoke openly for emancipation. But when doing so they often received a cool if not an outright hostile reception, albeit usually with less of the virulent reaction and rigid intolerance common in the Southern colonies.

While the Northern colonies wanted emancipation immediately and the Southern colonies not at all, the Middle colonies believed that if emancipation was to occur, it must be gradually, and with relocation. Thus the Middle colonies had colonization rather than abolition societies, with some such societies also in the South. They sought emancipation for slaves, and then offered to transport them back to Africa from whence so many had originally been stolen. This Middle colony approach acknowledged that slavery was wrong, but it also recognized that blacks had greater freedom and opportunity in Africa than in the prejudice-filled Middle and Southern colonies.

These regional dissimilarities required different political tactics in each area, for manumission laws introduced in the North would never have seen the light of day in the South. Therefore, Americans who wanted to change the national culture on slavery had to start at varying levels, depending on the geographic section in which they lived.

Jefferson was acutely aware of these distinct regional differences, as demonstrated by a 1785 exchange with the Reverend Richard Price of England. Price had sided with America during the Revolution and written several pro-American pieces, but one of his pamphlets, "because it recommend[ed] measures for . . . abolishing the Negro trade and slavery," met with a very cold reception after arriving in South Carolina.[7] Based on the negative reaction it received there, Price was concerned that he had misread American intentions toward liberty; he therefore asked Jefferson whether South Carolina was typical of the other states.

Jefferson assured Price that South Carolina was definitely not representative of the entire country on the issue of slavery, predicting the three different regional reactions his pamphlet would likely receive. He first affirmed what Price had already discovered: "Southward of the Chesapeake, it will find but few readers concurring with it in sentiment on the subject of slavery."[8]

(Jefferson used the Chesapeake Bay as the geographic dividing line for the three views toward slavery. Since the Bay began in southern Virginia, then "southward of the Chesapeake" meant the Southern Colonies. Because it extended north across Virginia, upward through Maryland, and near Delaware, Pennsylvania, and New Jersey, then the "mouth of the Chesapeake" meant the Middle Colonies; and "northward of the Chesapeake" indicated the Northern Colonies.)

Having affirmed to Price the hostile reaction his pamphlet would receive in the Southern Colonies, Jefferson then told him of the other two regions and the reactions he might expect:

> From the mouth of the head of the Chesapeake, the bulk of the people will approve it in theory, and it will find a respectable minority ready to adopt it in practice. . . . Northward of the Chesapeake, you may find here and there an opponent to your doctrine as you may find here and there a robber and murderer, but in no greater number. In that part of America, there being but few slaves, they can easily disencumber themselves of them; and emancipation is put into such a train that in a few years there will be no slave northward of Maryland.[9]

Having explained these differences, Jefferson reassured Price: "Be not therefore discouraged. What you have written will do a great deal of good. . . . I wish you to do more, and wish it on assurance of its effect."[10]

Jefferson expounded on these geographic distinctions to others as well. For example, he lamented to the Reverend David

Barrow, who had lived in Virginia but moved to Kentucky and helped found the Kentucky Abolition Society, that emancipation would be slower in the Southern and Middle colonies than the Northern ones:

> Where the disease [slavery] is most deeply seated, there it will be slowest in eradication. In the Northern states, it was merely superficial and easily corrected. In the Southern, it is incorporated with the whole system and requires time, patience, and perseverance in the curative process.[11]

Nevertheless, Jefferson remained optimistic about change in Virginia, even though, as he had acknowledged to the Reverend Price, his own desire to abolish slavery had placed him in the "respectable minority" in his own state.

But before chronicling Jefferson's many emancipation declarations and actions, the elephant in the room must be addressed: if Jefferson was truly antislavery, then why didn't he release his own slaves? After all, in his will in 1799 George Washington had made provision to free the slaves he owned (which were about half of the slaves at Mount Vernon; by law, the other half were dower slaves and could not be freed), so why didn't Jefferson at least do the same at his death in 1826? The answer is: Virginia law.

As previously acknowledged, Virginia was rigid in its pro-slavery laws and had been so for more than a century before Jefferson. As early as 1691–1692, it began placing significant economic hurdles in the way of those wanting to emancipate slaves, requiring:

[N]o Negro or mulatto slave shall be set free—unless the emancipator pays for his transportation out of the country within six months.[12]

The emancipation process in Jefferson's area and southward was not as simple as in the Northern areas, which generally required not much more than simply issuing a notice of manumission, or freedom. In southward regions, it could financially cost an emancipator to free his or her slaves, thus serving as an economic disincentive that discouraged emancipation.

Subsequent laws imposed even harsher economic restrictions, mandating that a slave could not be freed unless the owner guaranteed a bond for the education, livelihood, and support of the freed slave.[13] Then, in 1723, a law was passed that forbade the emancipation of slaves under *any* circumstance—even by a last will and testament. The only exceptions were for cases of "meritorious service" by a slave—a determination that could be made only by the state governor and his council on a case-by-case basis.[14]

At the close of the American Revolution, for a short time Virginia began to move in a new direction. In 1782 the General Assembly passed a law that permitted emancipation, but it still retained some difficult economic burdens for emancipators, requiring that freed slaves whom the state considered as young, old, weak, or infirm "shall respectively be supported and maintained by the person so liberating them, or by his or her estate."[15] The laws were regularly changed in subsequent years, allowing a wife to reverse an emancipation made by her husband in his will.[16] Furthermore, it required that a freed slave depart the state within twelve months or else reenter slavery, thus making it almost impossible for an emancipated slave to remain near his or her spouse, children, or family members who had not been freed.[17] In 1806 (after Washington's death), that law was again amended,[18] making it even more difficult for would-be emancipators. It was under this complicated slave code that Jefferson lived and operated.

Jefferson inherited about twenty slaves as a very young man, later recalling that: "[A]t fourteen years of age, the whole care and direction of myself was thrown on myself entirely without a relation or friend qualified to advise or guide me."[19] He received 135 more slaves through his marriage to his wife, Martha.[20] With such a large number, Jefferson simply did not have the economic resources to conform to restrictive state laws that required him to provide a livelihood, support, or transportation for freed slaves. In fact, at one point his own personal debt was so great that in order to generate much-needed operating cash he approached Congress about buying his cherished library.[21] (Additional detail about these laws, including the illegality of emancipating slaves while in debt, was already presented in the Preface.)

Part of Jefferson's cash shortage was due to his lifestyle as a large landowner, but there were other factors as well. For example, his wife Martha inherited a sizeable debt on the death of her father John Wayles in 1773. Her portion of the debt was £3,749, or more than half-a-million dollars in today's money. Jefferson tried to pay the debt before the Revolution by selling off lands and then giving to his British creditors the IOUs he had received for those lands as payment of his debt, but those arrangements were rejected by his debt holders. During the Revolution, Jefferson placed the funds from the land sales into a state loan office that had been set up to repay British creditors at the close of the war, but the state used the monies from that loan office to help fund the war instead. Additionally, because of extreme hyperinflation during the Revolution, the funds remaining in the loan office lost 97.5 percent of their original value in international currency exchange and were virtually worthless to British creditors.[22] Jefferson was thus left not only deeply in debt, but now he was also left without the money he had originally placed into the loan office.

Jefferson's economic hardship was further exacerbated by his practice, unlike other slave owners, of paying his slaves for the vegetables they raised, meat obtained while hunting and fishing, and for extra tasks performed outside normal working hours. He even offered a revolutionary profit-sharing plan for the products that his enslaved artisans produced in their shops.[23]

In short, Jefferson was required to operate under numerous oppressive state laws. As he once lamented to an abolitionist friend, "[t]he laws do not permit us to turn them loose."[24] But even though he did not have the economic resources that would allow him to free his slaves under Virginia law, Jefferson was nevertheless a local, national, and even a global voice advocating emancipation. He helped slowly turn the culture in a direction that would allow equal civil rights to eventually be secured for all Americans regardless of race.

Early blacks, knowing Jefferson's words and actions (which are largely unknown today), thus viewed Jefferson in a much more favorable light than they did many other leaders from the South. In fact, one of the earliest black Americans to acknowledge Jefferson's relatively advanced views on race—at least when compared to the dominant views of others in the Middle and Southern colonies—was Benjamin Banneker, whom Jefferson hired to survey the brand-new city of Washington, DC.

Banneker was a highly accomplished and self-taught mathematician and astronomer. He prepared scientific almanacs that were in high demand because of his accurate predictions for sunsets, sunrises, eclipses, weather conditions, and even for his remarkable calculation of the recurrence of locust plagues in seventeen-year cycles. Banneker sent a handwritten copy of one of his almanacs to Jefferson, beginning his letter by acknowledging that Jefferson had secured a reputation of favoring civil rights:

> [I] hope I may safely admit in consequence of the report which hath reached me that you are a man far less inflexible in sentiments of this nature than many others—that you are measurably friendly and well-disposed towards us [i.e., blacks] and that you are willing to lend your aid and assistance for our relief from those many distresses and numerous calamities to which we are reduced.[25]

Banneker then appealed to Jefferson to further exert himself in behalf of blacks and throw off any remaining prejudice he might hold:

> Now, sir, if this is founded in truth, I apprehend you will readily embrace every opportunity to eradicate that train of absurd and false ideas and opinions which so generally prevails with respect to us; and that your sentiments are concurrent with mine, which are that one universal Father hath given being to us all, and that He hath . . . made us all of one flesh [Acts 17:26]. . . . Sir, if these are sentiments of which you are fully persuaded, I hope you cannot but acknowledge that it is the indispensable duty of those who maintain for themselves

the rights of human nature and who possess the obligations of Christianity to extend their power and influence to the relief of every part of the human race from whatever burden or oppression they may unjustly labor under.[26]

Having thus affirmed to Jefferson the unequal position of blacks across much of the nation, Banneker then returned to his original purpose in writing, presenting Jefferson with "a copy of an almanac which I have calculated for the succeeding year . . . in my own handwriting."[27] Upon receiving it, Jefferson responded:

> I thank you sincerely for your letter of the 19th instant and for the almanac it contained. Nobody wishes more than I do to see such proofs as you exhibit—that nature has given to our black brethren talents equal to those of the other colors of men, and that the appearance of a want [lack] of them is owing merely to the degraded condition of their existence both in Africa and America. . . . I have taken the liberty of sending your almanac to Monsieur de Condorcet, Secretary of the Academy of Sciences at Paris and member of the Philanthropic Society, because I considered it as a document to which your whole color had a right for their justification against the doubts which have been entertained of them. I am with great esteem, sir, your most obedient humble servant.[28]

When Jefferson sent the almanac to Marquis de Condorcet, a leading anti-slavery voice in France, he told him:

> I am happy to be able to inform you that we have now in the United States a Negro . . . who is a very respectable mathematician. . . . [H]e made an almanac for the next year, which he sent me in his own hand-writing, and which I enclose to you.

I have seen very elegant solutions of geometrical problems by him. Add to this that he is a very worthy and respectable member of society. He is a free man. I shall be delighted to see these instances of moral eminence so multiplied as to prove that the want [lack] of talents observed in them [blacks] is merely the effect of their degraded condition, and not proceeding from any difference in the structure of the parts on which intellect depends.[29]

Despite such statements, many of those today who call Jefferson an unrepentant racist also claim that he believed blacks were inferior to whites. For example, in the true spirit of collective Negativism:

Jefferson . . . was convinced . . . blacks had to be seen as lower beings because of their inferiority.[30]

Jefferson thought . . . blacks were inferior to whites in body and mind.[31]

Thomas Jefferson . . . thought black people intellectually inferior to whites.[32]

Thomas Jefferson was not interested in abolition. . . . Thomas Jefferson considered blacks inferior.[33]

To "prove" this charge, such writers regularly point to comments Jefferson made in his *Notes on the State of Virginia* (1781) in which he not only expressed his ardent desire for the emancipation of slaves but also twice questioned whether blacks *might* be inferior.[34] But the sweeping conclusion reached by modern Minimalist and Negativist writers is possible *only* if they cite just those two Jefferson comments from that extensive work and ignore the rest of the lengthy emancipation treatise from which those statements are lifted.

In fact, in order to mitigate his own two comments that he had made in that work, Jefferson openly acknowledged in the very same work that his personal experience with blacks had been limited almost exclusively to the context of slavery—that is, his personal dealings had been with oppressed blacks who had been denied education. Very few analysts either then or now would dispute that under such conditions blacks might well appear inferior in intellectual abilities, for they had absolutely no opportunity to prove otherwise.

Jefferson candidly acknowledged his own subjective situation and his lack of objective data on which to base any fixed opinion. In fact, a decade before his exchange with Banneker, he had openly lamented:

> To our reproach, it must be said that though for a century and a half we have had under our eyes the races of black and of red men, they have never yet been viewed by us as subjects of natural history. I advance it, therefore, as a *suspicion only* that the blacks . . . are inferior to the whites in the endowments both of body and mind.[35] (emphasis added)

He also announced that "[i]t will be right to *make great allowances* for the difference of condition, of education, of conversation, of the sphere in which they move"[36] (emphasis added). Jefferson understood that slavery was certainly not a favorable condition in which to compare intellectual abilities. He therefore eagerly invited and even sought outside evidence to disprove what he had called his "suspicion only." Recall, too, that a decade later he had told Banneker:

Nobody wishes more than I do to see such proofs . . . that nature has given to our black brethren talents equal to those of the other colors of men, and that the appearance of a want [lack] of them is owing [due] merely to the degraded condition of their existence both in Africa and America.[37]

And on the same day that he wrote Banneker, he had told Condorcet that "I shall be delighted to see [that] . . . the want [lack] of talents observed in them is merely the effect of their degraded condition, and not proceeding from any difference in the structure of the parts on which intellect depends."[38]

Almost two decades later—and nearly four decades after he had written his two comments in his *Notes on the State of Virginia* (the same work in which he boldly argued for the emancipation of slaves)—Jefferson's enemies were still trying to denigrate him for those comments. Henri Gregoire (a Catholic priest, ardent abolitionist, and leader in the French Revolution) chided Jefferson about those comments, to which Jefferson replied:

Be assured that no person living wishes more sincerely than I do to see a complete refutation of the doubts I have myself entertained and expressed on the grade of understanding allotted to them by nature, and to find that in this respect they are on a par with ourselves. My doubts were the result of personal observation on the limited sphere of my own state, where the opportunities for the development of their genius were not favorable, and those of exercising it still less so. I expressed them therefore with great hesitation; but whatever be their degree of talent, it is no measure of their rights. Because Sir Isaac Newton was superior to others in understanding, he was not therefore lord of the person or property of others.[39]

Eight months later, he angrily bewailed to his old friend Joel Barlow, an American diplomat who had served with Jefferson during the American Revolution, about how his critics had taken his "suspicions" that he had expressed "with great hesitation" and tried to misrepresent them. Referencing his earlier letter to Gregoire, he told Barlow:

> He wrote to me also on the doubts I had expressed five or six and twenty years ago in the *Notes of Virginia* as to the grade of understanding of the Negroes. . . . It was impossible for doubt to have been more tenderly or hesitatingly expressed than that was in the *Notes of Virginia*, and nothing was or is farther from my intentions than to enlist myself as the champion of a fixed opinion where I have only expressed a doubt.[40]

For today's writers and academics to convert Jefferson's loosely held, and cautiously and rarely expressed "suspicions" into unwavering resolute racism is a blatant misrepresentation of the facts. Yet even if the critics were right about Jefferson believing that blacks were inferior to whites, recall Jefferson's statement above that just because someone such as Sir Isaac Newton was "superior to others in understanding, he was not therefore lord of the person or property of others."[41] But the critics are not right.

Consider Jefferson's lifelong record of actions and writings advocating emancipation and equality—actions and writings too often ignored today.

* * *

In *1769* when Jefferson was twenty-six, he began his political career as a member of the Virginia legislature. Upon entering that body, he approached respected senior legislator Richard Bland and proposed that the two of them undertake an "effort in that body for the permission of the emancipation of slaves."[42] Bland offered the motion and Jefferson seconded it, but it was resoundingly defeated. In fact, for even proposing that measure, Jefferson recalled that Bland was vehemently "denounced as an enemy of his country" by the other legislators "and was treated with the grossest indecorum."[43] Jefferson lamented that as long as Virginia remained a British colony, emancipation policies could expect no success.[44]

In *1770* Jefferson represented the child of a bond slave in court and argued for his freedom, explaining: "Under the law of nature, all men are born free. Everyone comes into the world with a right to his own person, which includes the liberty of moving and using it at his own will. This is what is called personal liberty, and is given him by the Author of nature."[45] Jefferson lost the case, but in *1772*, he nevertheless argued a similar case.[46]

In the early *1770*s, a number of American colonies passed various anti-slavery laws, all of which were struck down by the king,[47] thus affirming Jefferson's own apprehension that as long as America remained British colonies, anti-slavery laws would not be allowed.

In *1774* as tensions with Great Britain and America continued to escalate, Jefferson penned "A Summary View of the Rights of British America" to remind King George III that legitimate American concerns were being ignored—one of which had been the king's veto of American antislavery laws:

The abolition of domestic slavery is the great object of desire in those colonies where it was unhappily introduced in their infant state [by Britain]. But previous to the enfranchisement of the slaves we have, it is necessary to exclude all further importations from Africa. Yet our repeated attempts to effect this . . . have been hitherto defeated by His Majesty's negative [veto].[48]

In *1776* as separation from Great Britain loomed on the horizon, Jefferson wrote a draft state constitution for Virginia and included a provision that "[n]o person hereafter coming into this country [Virginia] shall be held in slavery under any pretext whatever."[49]

Later in *1776* as a member of the Continental Congress, Jefferson became the principal author of the Declaration of Independence. Among the American grievances he listed in it was that the king would not allow individual colonies to end slavery or the slave trade, even when they wished to do so:

He [King George III] has waged cruel war against human nature itself, violating its most sacred rights of life and liberty in the persons of a distant people which never offended him, captivating & carrying them into slavery in another hemisphere, or to incur miserable death in their transportation thither. . . . He has . . . determin[ed] to keep open a market where men should be bought and sold.[50]

Unfortunately, Jefferson explained that his antislavery clause was deleted from the final version of the Declaration at the demand of "South Carolina and Georgia, who had never attempted to restrain the importation of slaves, and who, on the contrary, still wished to continue it."[51]

Fortunately, however, his eloquent statement of human liberty and equality was not deleted. Slightly revised by his fellow delegates, in its final form it read: "We hold these truths to be self-evident, that all men are created equal, that they are endowed by their Creator with certain unalienable rights, that among these are life, liberty and the pursuit of happiness." These words inspired generations of Americans to combat slavery, Jim Crow legislation, and racism.[52]

Although Jefferson's forceful antislavery clause had not been included in the Declaration, the grievance was nonetheless very real. So following the separation from Great Britain, many individual states were finally able to begin abolishing slavery. Vermont did so in 1777; Pennsylvania and Massachusetts in 1780; New Hampshire in 1783; Connecticut and Rhode Island in 1784; New York in 1799; and New Jersey in 1804.[53]

After independence was declared, Jefferson held out hope that Virginia, too, would abolish slavery. Accordingly, in 1778 he introduced a bill in the Virginia legislature that he viewed as a first step: a ban on the importation of slaves from other countries into Virginia. According to Jefferson, "This passed without opposition and stopped the increase of the evil by importation, leaving to future efforts its final eradication."[54] Finally, a small first step was taken in his home state.

The following year Jefferson became state governor and undertook the next step toward what he had called "future efforts" for slavery's "final eradication." He introduced a measure to "emancipate all slaves born after passing the act,"[55] but like so many of his previous efforts, it, too, was rejected.[56] Jefferson nevertheless remained unwavering in his personal conviction that "Nothing is more certainly written in the book of fate than that these people are to be free."[57]

In *1781* Jefferson penned answers to twenty-two questions posed him by the secretary of the French delegation to America. Those responses became the already mentioned book *Notes on the State of Virginia* (1781) in which Jefferson had forcefully declared:

> The whole commerce between master and slave is . . . the most unremitting despotism on the one part, and degrading submissions on the other. . . . And with what execrations [denunciations] should the statesman be loaded who permit[s] one half the citizens thus to trample on the rights of the other. . . . And can the liberties of a nation be thought secure when we have removed their only firm basis—a conviction in the minds of the people that these liberties are of the gift of God? That they are not to be violated but with His wrath? Indeed I tremble for my country when I reflect that God is just, that His justice cannot sleep forever. . . . The Almighty has no attribute which can take side with us in such a contest. . . . [T]he way, I hope, [is] preparing under the auspices of Heaven for a total emancipation.[58]

In *1784* Jefferson returned to service in the Continental Congress where he introduced a provision to end slavery in every territory that would eventually become a state in the new nation. His proposal stated that "after the year 1800 of the Christian era, there shall be neither slavery nor involuntary servitude in any of the said states."[59]

Jefferson's law fell one vote short of passage. (Congress at that time governed itself under the Articles of Confederation.

Each state delegation was given one vote, and a majority vote required the concurrence of seven states.) He lamented:

> There were ten states present. Six voted unanimously for it, three against it, and one was divided. And seven votes being requisite to decide the proposition affirmatively [i.e., to pass the measure], it was lost. . . . Thus we see the fate of millions unborn hanging on the tongue of one man, & heaven was silent in that awful moment! But it is to be hoped it will not always be silent & that the friends to the rights of human nature will in the end prevail.[60]

In *1786*, while Jefferson was serving as American ambassador in France, he responded to an article in a French encyclopedia written by French official Louis Dominique de Meunier stating that Virginia did not allow the emancipation of slaves. Jefferson wanted de Meunier to know not only that he personally had wanted it to be otherwise but also that someday it *would* be otherwise:

> But we must await with patience the workings of an overruling Providence & hope that it is preparing the deliverance of these our suffering brethren. When the measure of their tears shall be full—when their groans shall have involved Heaven itself in darkness—doubtless a God of justice will awaken to their distress.[61]

In *1788* Jacques Pierre de Warville, a leader in the French Revolution, started an antislavery society and invited Jefferson to become a member. Jefferson declined because at that time he was in France as "a public servant" of America, therefore making it inappropriate for him to undertake something of a personal nature.[62] But he bestowed his hearty personal blessings on the society's efforts, reaffirming his own personal commitment to its goals: "You know that nobody wishes more ardently to see an abolition not only of the trade but of the condition of slavery, and certainly nobody will be more willing to encounter every sacrifice for that object."[63]

In *1787* the Confederation Congress adopted Jefferson's 1784 antislavery proposal and included it in the Northwest Ordinance of 1785.[64] The first federal Congress reaffirmed his provision when it reauthorized the Ordinance in 1789.[65] As a result of Jefferson's clause, Minnesota, Ohio, Michigan, Illinois, Indiana, and Wisconsin all entered the United States as free states.

In *1805*, after nearly forty years of efforts to end slavery, Jefferson, now serving as the president, bemoaned that it had become a task much more difficult than he had ever imagined, lamenting the national stalemate that had developed on the issue:

> I have long since given up the expectation of any early provision for the extinguishment of slavery among us. [While] there are many virtuous men who would make any sacrifices to affect it, many equally virtuous persuade themselves either that the thing is not wrong or that it cannot be remedied.[66]

In his *1806* message to Congress, President Jefferson urged the legislature to ban the slave trade as soon as was constitutionally permissible.[67] (The US Constitution contained a provision that prohibited Congress from banning the importation of slaves until "the year one thousand eight hundred and eight," Article 1, Section 9. At the time the Constitution was written and ratified, it was believed that within twenty years, the

Southern states would be ready to relinquish slavery, and this law would pave the way.)

Congress passed the ban in *1807* and Jefferson happily signed it; it went into effect on January 1, *1808*. After signing the law, he wrote to a group of Quakers, noting that:

> Whatever may have been the circumstances which influenced our forefathers to permit the introduction of personal bondage into any part of these states . . . we may rejoice that such circumstances and such a sense of them exist no longer. . . . I sincerely pray with you, my friends, that all the members of the human family may, in the time prescribed by the Father of us all, find themselves securely established in the enjoyment of life, liberty, and happiness.[68]

In *1808* he sent a message to the Reverend James Lemen, an old friend from Virginia who in 1786 had moved into the Northwest Territory at Jefferson's suggestion to work to ensure that it would remain antislavery.[69] Ohio was first organized from that region, then Indiana—both as antislavery territories. Then in *1808* when Illinois was on the verge of becoming the third official territory, President Jefferson privately contacted Lemen, who later reported:

> I received Jefferson's confidential message on October 10, 1808, suggesting . . . the organization of a church on a strictly antislavery basis for the purpose of heading a movement to finally make Illinois a free state. . . . I acted on Jefferson's plan and . . . the antislavery element formed a Baptist church . . . on an antislavery basis.[70]

In *1814* Jefferson corresponded with Edward Coles, private secretary to President Madison. Coles asked Jefferson to head a new antislavery movement, to which Jefferson responded:

> Your [antislavery letter] was duly received and was read with peculiar pleasure. . . . Mine on the subject of slavery of Negroes have long since been in possession of the public, and time has only served to give them stronger root. The love of justice and the love of country plead equally the cause of these people, and it is a moral reproach to us that they should have pleaded it so long in vain and should have produced not a single effort—nay, I fear not much serious willingness to relieve them & ourselves from our present condition of moral & political reprobation . . . [but] the hour of emancipation is advancing; in the march of time, it will come.[71]

But citing his advanced age of seventy-one, Jefferson declined to take the helm of the new antislavery movement proposed by Coles. He explained, "This enterprise is for the young—for those who can follow it up and bear it through to its consummation." But he promised he would contribute his fervent "prayers—and these are the only weapons of an old man."[72] He then encouraged Coles to take the lead:

> I hope . . . you will come forward in the public councils, become the missionary of this doctrine truly Christian, insinuate & inculcate it softly but steadily through the medium of writing and conversation, associate others in your labors, and when the phalanx [large battalion] is formed, bring on and press the proposition perseveringly until its accomplishment. . . . And you will be supported by the religious precept, "be

not weary in well doing" [Galatians 6:9]. That your success may be as speedy and complete . . . I shall as fervently and sincerely pray.[73]

In *1815* Jefferson corresponded with the Reverend David Barrow, the Virginian who had moved to Kentucky and become a cofounder of the Kentucky Abolition Society. Barrow had penned an antislavery work and sent it to Jefferson, who responded:

> The particular subject of the pamphlet you enclosed me [emancipation] was one of early and tender consideration with me; and had I continued in the councils [legislature] of my own state, it should never have been out of sight. . . . We are not in a world ungoverned by the laws and the power of a Superior Agent. Our efforts are in His hand and directed by it; and He will give them their effect in His own time. . . . That it may finally be effected and its progress hastened will be [my] last and fondest prayer.[74]

By 1820 only a little antislavery ground had been gained nationally. In 1789 Congress had banned slavery from the Northwest Territory; in 1794 it banned the exportation of slaves from America; and in 1808 it banned the importation of slaves into America. But in 1820 Congress enacted the Missouri Compromise,[75] whereby for the first time slavery was being officially expanded by the federal government.

(In 1820, Democrats, who were strongly proslavery, had gained a majority in Congress. They passed this measure in order to prevent antislavery states from gaining any further numerical advantage over the slave states. The Missouri

Compromise therefore allowed Maine to enter as a free state, but only if Missouri was permitted to enter as a slave state. Unlike the previous antislavery policy for federal territories, this Compromise opened the door for slavery in the lower part of the federal territory that had been obtained through the 1803 Louisiana Purchase.)

The Missouri Compromise was strenuously opposed by the few Founding Fathers still alive at that time. Elias Boudinot, a president of Congress during the Revolution and a framer of the Bill of Rights, warned that this new proslavery direction by Congress would bring "an end to the happiness of the United States";[76] a frail John Adams feared that lifting the slavery prohibition would destroy America;[77] and James Madison confessed that the new policy "fills me with no slight anxiety." In fact, foreseeing what would become the Civil War, Madison predicted that pitting slave states against free states would result in "awful shocks against each other."[78] But perhaps no one from that generation was as greatly distressed as the elderly seventy-seven-year-old Jefferson, who was dismayed, frustrated, and even depressed by the passage of that law and the retreat from emancipation that it represented. He confessed, "In the gloomiest moment of the Revolutionary War, I never had any apprehensions equal to what I feel from this source."[79]

Jefferson confided to a fellow political leader:

> I had for a long time ceased to read newspapers or pay any attention to public affairs, confident they were in good hands, and content to be a passenger in our bark [small ship] to the shore from which I am not distant [death]. But this momentous question, like a fire bell in the night, awakened and filled

me with terror. I considered it at once as the knell [funeral bell] of the Union. . . . I regret that I am now to die in the belief that the useless sacrifice of themselves by the generation of 1776 to acquire self-government and happiness to their country is to be thrown away by the unwise and unworthy passions of their sons. . . . [This is an] act of suicide on themselves, and of treason against the hopes of the world.[80]

He concluded with a reaffirmation of his desire to end slavery and his frustration at America not having already done so:

I can say with conscious truth that there is not a man on earth who would sacrifice more than I would to relieve us from this heavy reproach in any practicable way. The cession of that kind of "property," for so it is misnamed, is a bagatelle [an insignificant trifle] which would not cost me a second thought if in that way a general emancipation and expatriation could be effected. . . . But as it is, we have the wolf by the ears and we can neither hold him nor safely let him go.[81]

In *1825* Jefferson corresponded with Frances Wright, a young, energetic antislavery enthusiast. She first met Jefferson the previous year when the famous American hero French general Marquis de Lafayette returned to America for his farewell tour, bringing with him Frances, whom he considered an adopted daughter. When Lafayette returned to France, Frances stayed behind to become an American citizen and help fight slavery. She eventually founded Nashoba, Tennessee, as a model to illustrate Jefferson's plan of emancipation. Writing a very elderly Jefferson (who would die the next year), she asked him to help her with the effort. Jefferson replied:

At the age of eighty-two, with one foot in the grave and the other uplifted to follow it, I do not permit myself to take part in any new enterprises, even for bettering the condition of man—not even in the great one which is the subject of your letter and which has been through life that of my greatest anxieties. . . . I leave its accomplishment as the work of another generation, and I am cheered when I see that one on which it is devolved taking it up with so much good will and such minds engaged in its encouragement. The abolition of the evil is not impossible; it ought never therefore to be despaired of. Every plan should be adopted, every experiment tried, which may do something towards the ultimate object. . . . You are young, dear madam, and have powers of mind which may do much in exciting others in this arduous task. I am confident they will be so exerted, and I pray to Heaven for their success and that you may be rewarded with the blessings which such efforts merit.[82]

In *1826*, just two weeks before his death, Jefferson reiterated: "On the question of the lawfulness of slavery (that is, of the right of one man to appropriate to himself the faculties of another without his consent), I certainly retain my early opinions."[83]

With such a clear and unbroken train of words and actions against slavery and in favor of emancipation and civil rights, it is not surprising that previous generations of abolitionists regularly invoked Jefferson's words in their own civil rights efforts. For example, John Quincy Adams, called the "Hell Hound of Abolition" for his relentless pursuit of that object, told a crowd gathered before him in a famous 1837 speech:

The inconsistency of the institution of domestic slavery with the principles of the Declaration of Independence was seen and lamented by all the southern patriots of the Revolution; by no one with deeper and more unalterable conviction than by the author of the Declaration himself [Jefferson]. . . . Such was the undoubting conviction of Jefferson to his dying day. In the *Memoir of His Life*, written at the age of seventy-seven, he gave to his countrymen the solemn and emphatic warning that the day was not distant when they must hear and adopt the general emancipation of their slaves.[84]

Daniel Webster, whose efforts in the US Senate to end slavery paralleled those of John Quincy Adams in the US House, similarly invoked Jefferson. In 1845 he issued an address to the nation, reminding them:

No language can be more explicit, more emphatic, or more solemn than that in which Thomas Jefferson, from the beginning to the end of his life, uniformly declared his opposition to slavery. "I tremble for my country," said he, "when I reflect that God is just—that His justice cannot sleep forever." "The Almighty has no attribute which can take side with us in such a contest." . . . [T]o show his own view of the proper influence of the spirit of the Revolution upon slavery, he proposed the searching question: "Who can endure toil, famine, stripes, imprisonment, and death itself in vindication of his own liberty, and the next moment . . . inflict on his fellow men a bondage, one hour of which is fraught with more misery than ages of that which he rose in rebellion to oppose?"[85]

In 1854, when the Democrat-controlled Congress passed the Kansas-Nebraska Act, Abraham Lincoln cited Jefferson as part of his own crusade to end slavery and achieve civil rights and equality for blacks. Back in 1820 when Congress had first expanded the federal territories into which slavery was permitted through passage of the Missouri Compromise, they had at that time retained a ban on slavery in the Kansas-Nebraska territory (which included parts of Wyoming, Montana, Idaho, North Dakota, and South Dakota). But their passage of the 1854 Kansas-Nebraska Act changed those 1820 restrictions, allowing slavery into even more federal territory. Lincoln invoked Jefferson to condemn that act, explaining:

> Mr. Jefferson . . . conceived the idea of taking that occasion to prevent slavery ever going into the northwestern territory . . . and in the first Ordinance (which the acts of Congress were then called) for the government of the territory, provided that slavery should never be permitted therein. . . . Thus, with the author of the Declaration of Independence, the policy of prohibiting slavery in new territory originated. . . . But now [in May 1854], new light breaks upon us. Now Congress declares this [antislavery law constructed by Jefferson] ought never to have been.[86]

Black abolitionists such as Fredrick Douglass also regularly invoked Jefferson to assist their efforts. Douglass had lived in slavery until he escaped to New York, later going to work for the Massachusetts antislavery society and also serving as a Zion Methodist Church preacher. During the Civil War Douglass helped recruit the first black regiment to fight for the Union and advised Abraham Lincoln on the Emancipation Proclamation. In the decades following the war, he received presidential appointments from four Republican presidents. Concerning Jefferson, Douglass declared:

> It was the Sage of the Old Dominion [Virginia] that said— while speaking of the possibility of a conflict between the slaves and slaveholders—"God has no attribute that could take sides with the oppressor in such a contest. I tremble for my country when I reflect that God is just and that His justice cannot sleep forever." Such is the warning voice of Thomas Jefferson, and every day's experience since its utterance until now confirms its wisdom and commends its truth.[87]

At a speech in Virginia following the Civil War, Douglass declared: "I have been charged with lifelong hostility to one of the cherished institutions of Virginia [i.e., slavery]. I am not ashamed of that lifelong opposition. . . . It was, Virginia, your own Thomas Jefferson that taught me that all men are created equal."[88] And describing Jefferson's dealings with Banneker, Douglass reminded an audience, "Jefferson was not ashamed to call the black man his brother and to address him as a gentleman."[89]

On numerous other occasions Douglass similarly used Jefferson as an authority in his crusade to end slavery and achieve full equality and black civil rights.[90] Additional black civil rights advocates who likewise invoked Jefferson in a positive manner included Henry Highland Garnet,[91] Dr. Martin Luther King Jr.,[92] Colin Powell,[93] and others.

* * *

Was Jefferson impeccable on race and civil rights? Certainly not. He recognized and admitted that he had some prejudices, but he also openly acknowledged that he wanted to be proven wrong concerning those views. Yet despite his self-acknowledged weaknesses, Jefferson faithfully and consistently advocated for emancipation and civil rights throughout his long life, even when it would have been easier and better for him if he had remained silent or inactive.

Had Jefferson been free from the laws of his own state—that is, had he lived in a state such as Massachusetts, New Hampshire, or Connecticut—he likely would be hailed today as a bold civil rights leader, for his efforts and writings would certainly compare favorably with those of great civil rights advocates in the Northern states. In fact, if Jefferson had proposed his various pieces of legislation in those states, they would certainly have passed, and he would have been deemed a national civil rights hero. But his geography and circumstances doomed him to a different fate. Modern writers now refuse to recognize what previous generations openly acknowledged: Jefferson was a bold, staunch, and consistent advocate and defender of emancipation.

Thomas Jefferson Advocated a Secular Public Square through the Separation of Church and State

Many of the lies about Jefferson on subjects ranging from education to making his own Bible have been made to support one key overarching premise: Jefferson was an ardent secularist, whose overall goal was a public sphere devoid of religion and from which religious expressions had been expunged. Typical of this oft-repeated charge is the claim that "Jefferson's presidential administration was probably the most purely secular this country has ever had."[1]

But before determining whether Jefferson really was a secularist, it is important to define that term—a term that did not exist until modern times. By definition, *secularist* means:

- holding a system of political or social philosophy that rejects all forms of religious faith and worship, embracing the view that public education and other matters of civil policy should be conducted without the introduction of a religious element[2]

- having indifference to, or a rejection or exclusion of, religion and religious considerations[3]

- believing that religious considerations should be excluded from civil affairs[4]

Of what has already been presented from Jefferson's own writings and actions, it is indisputable that he was not a secularist by the first two definitions. And this chapter will demonstrate that Jefferson also did not embrace the third point.

Those who assert otherwise regularly identify Jefferson as the father of the modern separation of church and state doctrine. In fact, many today apparently believe that Jefferson personally placed the separation of church and state into the First Amendment of the Constitution:

Thomas Jefferson—the Father of the First Amendment.[5]

[T]he First Amendment was Jefferson's top priority.[6]

Jefferson can probably best be considered the founding father of separation of church and state.[7]

Jefferson . . . is responsible for the precursor to the First Amendment that is almost universally interpreted as the constitutional justification for the separation of church and state.[8]

Many modern courts also espouse this position—a claim that began in 1947 when the US Supreme Court announced:

This Court has previously recognized that the provisions of the First Amendment, in the drafting and adoption of which . . . Jefferson played such [a] leading role.[9]

The Supreme Court has even described Jefferson as "the architect of the First Amendment."[10] So firmly does the Court believe its own rhetoric in this area that in *every modern* case in which it has restricted or removed public religious, it invoked Jefferson, either directly or indirectly, as its authority.[11]

But this heavy reliance on Jefferson as the primary constitutional voice on religion and the First Amendment is a modern phenomenon, *not* a historic practice.[12] Why? Because previous generations knew American history well enough to know better than to use Jefferson in such a reckless and errant manner.

Interestingly, two centuries ago a Jefferson supporter penned a work foreshadowing modern claims by declaring Jefferson to be a leading constitutional influence. However, when Jefferson read that claim, he promptly instructed the author to correct that mistake, telling him: "One passage in the paper you enclosed me must be corrected. It is the following, 'and all say it was yourself more than any other individual, that planned and established it,' i.e., the Constitution."[13]

What did Jefferson see wrong with someone in his day stating that which is so routinely repeated today? He bluntly explained: "I was in Europe when the Constitution was planned and never saw it till after it was established."[14]

A simple fact unknown or ignored by many of today's writers is that Jefferson did *not* participate in framing the Constitution. He was not even in America when it was framed; so how could he be considered a primary influence on it? And he was likewise out of the country when the First Amendment was written. As he openly acknowledged:

> On receiving it [the Constitution while in France], I wrote strongly to Mr. Madison, urging the want of provision for the freedom of religion, freedom of the press, trial by jury, habeas corpus, the substitution of militia for a standing army, and an express reservation to the States of all rights not specifically granted to the Union. . . . *This is all the hand I had* in what related to the Constitution.[15] (emphasis added)

According to Jefferson, "all the hand" he had was to write a private letter wherein he argued for Bill of Rights.* (The lack of a bill of rights was a chief complaint not only of Jefferson but of the Anti-Federalists in general.)

Significantly, there were fifty-five individuals who framed the Constitution at the Constitutional Convention, and ninety in the first federal Congress who framed the Bill of Rights; Jefferson was among neither group. So how can he be considered the father of the First Amendment if he never saw it until months after it was finished?

Why have so many courts and modern writers made Jefferson the almost singular go-to authority on religion clauses and documents in which he had no direct involvement? Why has he been given a position of "expert" in this area that he himself properly refused?

The chief reason is that he penned a letter containing the eight-word phrase "a wall of separation between church and state." Modern secularist courts and writers have found that this

---

* Jefferson wrote additional letters to James Madison (and others) on the general topic of a Bill of Rights, but only in this one letter did he delineate a specific list of the rights that he recommended be included.

short phrase, when divorced from its historical context and the rest of Jefferson's letter, is useful in providing the appearance of historical and constitutional authority for their own efforts to secularize the public square.*

Historically speaking, however, Jefferson was actually a latecomer to the separation phrase. The famous metaphor so often attributed to him was introduced centuries earlier in the 1500s in England; and throughout the 1600s the principle it embodied was carried to America by Bible-oriented colonists who planted it deeply in the thinking of Americans. Probably the first American minister to actually use the phrase was the Rev. Roger Williams, who in 1644 wrote of "a hedge or wall of separation between the garden of the Church and the wilderness of the world."[16] All this historical usage of the phrase and principle occurred long before Jefferson ever repeated it.

So what was the historic origin of that now-famous phrase that Jefferson repeated?

The answer rests in the history of Christianity as it was taught in the Reformation and long afterwards by American ministers

---

*   While jurists and scholars often assert that the drafters of the First Amendment were influenced by Jefferson's Virginia Statute for Religious Liberty (passed in Virginia in 1786), this law was not referenced a single time in any recorded debate about the First Amendment, either in Congress or the state ratifying conventions. Furthermore, much of what it contained had already been secured in many other states prior to Virginia's passage of that act. For example, New Jersey, North Carolina, and Delaware had already given equal denominational protection well before Virginia; and New York, Pennsylvania, Georgia, and Vermont had also established religious liberty prior to the Virginia Statute. (For sources on these states, see David Barton, *Original Intent*, 2011, 208, with endnotes 24–30 on page 478, citing from *The Constitutions of the Several Independent States of America*, 1785, and *The Constitutions of the Sixteen States*, 1797.)

such as the Reverends John Wise and Joseph Priestley, who divided the history of Christianity into three periods. Jefferson was familiar with the writings of both of these ministers; their works were in his personal library, as were the writings of many other early scholars who made the same tripartite division.[17] A subject consistently examined in the discussion of these three periods was the historic relations between Church and State.

In Period I (which they called the Age of Purity), the followers of Jesus did just as He had taught them and they therefore retained Bible teachings uncorrupted. But beginning Period II (called the Age of Corruption), Roman Emperor Theodosius I made Christianity the official religion of the Empire, declaring all others illegal.[18] He commenced the practice of State leaders seizing control of the Church and its doctrines, thus assimilating the two previously separate institutions into one—a joining that persisted for well over a millennium. In Period III (the Age of Reformation), Bible-centered leaders began to loudly call for reinstating the Bible-ordained separation between the two entities.

In the Scriptures, God had placed Moses over civil affairs and Aaron over spiritual ones. The nation was one, but the jurisdictions were two, with separate leaders over each. In 2 Chronicles 26, when King Uzziah attempted to assume the duties of both State and Church, God Himself weighed in; He sovereignly and instantly struck down Uzziah, thus reaffirming the separation He had placed between the two institutions.

Period III Christian ministers understood these Biblical precedents and urged a return to the original model. As early Methodist bishop Charles Galloway affirmed:

The miter and the crown should never encircle the same brow. The crozier and the scepter should never be wielded by the same hand.[19]

Of the four items specifically mentioned—the miter, crown, crozier, and scepter—two reference the Church and two the State. Concerning the Church, the miter was the headgear worn by the high priest in Jewish times (see Exodus 28:3–4, 35–37) and later by popes, cardinals, and bishops. The crozier was the shepherd's crook carried by Church officials during special ceremonies. Pertaining to the State, the crown was the symbol of authority placed upon the heads of kings, and the scepter was held in their hand as an emblem of their extensive power (see the Bible book of Esther). Therefore, the metaphor that "the miter and the crown should never encircle the same brow" meant that the same person should not be the head of the Church and the head of the State. Galloway's declaration that "the crozier and the scepter should never be wielded by the same hand" meant that authority over the Church and authority over the State should never be given to the same individual.

Galloway's phrases not only provided clear and easily understandable visual pictures but also referenced specific historical incidents—as when Period II Roman Emperor Otto III (980–1002 AD) constructed his king's crown to fit atop the miter worn by Church officials.[20] This type of jurisdictional blending had been common in England before American colonization, as when the English Parliament passed civil laws stipulating who could take communion in church and who could be a minister of the Gospel,[21] thus governmentally controlling what should have been purely ecclesiastical matters.

It is important to note that it was not secular civil leaders who emphasized a separation of the Church from the control of the State, for it had been civil leaders who regularly took control of the Church and its doctrines, not vice versa. To the contrary, it was Bible-based ministers who issued the call for a separation. In fact, English Reformation clergyman Reverend Richard Hooker is identified as being among the first to use the phrase.

King Henry VIII had wanted a divorce, but when the Church refused to grant it, Henry simply started his own national church and gave himself a divorce under his new state-established doctrines.[22] Not only Henry VIII, but Edward VI, Mary I, and Elizabeth I after him similarly used the State to establish and enforce Church doctrines to their personal liking. Hooker found such actions reprehensible, calling for a "separation of . . . Church and Commonwealth," urging that "the walls of separation between these two must forever be upheld."[23]

Other Bible-centered ministers also spoke out against the intrusion of the State into the jurisdiction of the Church, including the Reverend John Greenwood (1556–1593), who started the church attended by many of the Pilgrims when they still lived in England. At the time, Queen Elizabeth I (daughter of Henry VIII), like so many monarchs before and after her, was head over both the State and the Church; but Greenwood asserted "that there could be but one head to the church and that head was *not* the Queen, but Christ."[24] He was eventually executed for "denying Her Majesty's ecclesiastical supremacy and attacking the existing ecclesiastical order."[25]

Then when Parliament passed a law requiring that if "any of her Majesty's subjects deny the Queen's ecclesiastical supremacy . . . they shall be committed to prison without bail,"[26] most of the

Pilgrims fled from England to Holland. From Holland they came to America where they promptly separated church and state, affirming that government had no right to "compel religion, to plant churches by power, and to force a submission to ecclesiastical government by laws and penalties."[27]

Many additional reformation-minded ministers and colonists traveling from Europe to America also openly advocated the institutional separation of State and Church, including the Reverends Roger Williams (1603–1683),[28] John Wise (1652–1725),[29] William Penn (1614–1718),[30] and others. And they often did so in language even more articulate than the original Reformers.[31]

Significantly, the entire history of the separation doctrine centered on preventing the State from taking control of the Church, meddling with or controlling its doctrines, or punishing its religious expressions. Throughout history, it had been the State that had seized and controlled the Church, not the opposite.

Furthermore, the separation doctrine had never been used to secularize the public square. As affirmed by early Quaker leader Will Wood, "The separation of Church and State does not mean the exclusion of God, righteousness, morality, from the State."[32] Early Methodist bishop Charles Galloway agreed that "the separation of the Church from the State did not mean the severance of the State from God, or of the nation from Christianity."[33]

The philosophy of keeping the State at arm's length and limited from either regulating religious practices or punishing religious expressions was planted deeply into American thinking. Eventually, it was nationally enshrined in the First Amendment, which states, "Congress shall make no law respecting an establishment of religion, or prohibiting the Free Exercise thereof . . ." The first part of this Amendment is now called the

Establishment Clause and the latter part, the Free Exercise Clause. The language of each is clear; and both clauses were pointed solely at the State, not the Church. The Establishment Clause prohibited the State from enforcing ecclesiastical conformity, and the Free Exercise Clause ensured that the *State* would protect—rather than suppress, as it currently does—citizens' rights of conscience and religious expression. Both clauses are explicit prohibitions *only* on the power of *Congress* (i.e., the government), not on religious individuals or organizations.

This was the meaning of "separation of church and state" with which Jefferson was intimately familiar; and it was this interpretation, and not the modern perversion of it, that he repeatedly reaffirmed in his own writings and practices. This is especially evident in his famous letter that invoked the separation phrase.

Consider the background of that letter and why Jefferson wrote it.

When Jefferson, the political head of those originally known as the Anti-Federalists (but subsequently known as Democratic-Republicans, or Republicans), became president in 1801, his election was particularly well received by Baptists. This political disposition was understandable, for across much of American history, the Baptists had frequently found their free exercise of religion restricted under the power of a legal alliance between the government and state-established churches.[34] Baptist ministers in various regions had often been beaten, imprisoned, fined, or banned by civic authorities who were joined to state-established churches, so it was not surprising that Baptists strongly opposed centralized government power, including at the federal level. For this reason the predominately Baptist state of Rhode Island[35] refused to send delegates to the Constitutional Convention;[36] and the Baptists were the only denomination in which a majority of its clergy across the nation voted against the ratification of the Constitution for fear of federally-consolidated powers.[37]

Jefferson's election as an anti-federalist Democratic-Republican opposed to a strong central government elated the Baptists. They were already very familiar with Jefferson's record of not only helping disestablish the official church in Virginia but also of championing the cause of religious freedom for Baptists and all other non-established denominations.[38] Not surprisingly, therefore, on his election he received numerous letters of congratulations from Baptist organizations.[39]

One of them was penned on October 7, 1801, by the Baptist Association of Danbury, Connecticut. Their letter began with an expression of gratitude to God for Jefferson's election, followed by prayers of blessing for him, to which he replied: "I reciprocate your kind prayers for the protection and blessing of the common Father and Creator of man, and tender you, for yourselves and your religious association, assurances of my high respect and esteem."[40]

The Danbury Baptists then expressed their grave concern over governmental laws that protected their free exercise. As they explained:

> Our sentiments are uniformly on the side of religious liberty—that religion is at all times and places a matter between God and individuals; that no man ought to suffer in name, person, or effects on account of his religious opinions; that the legitimate power of civil government extends no further than to punish the man who works ill to his neighbor. But sir,

our constitution of government is not specific. . . . Religion is considered as the first object of legislation and therefore what religious privileges we enjoy (as a minor part of the State) we enjoy as favors granted and not as inalienable rights.[41]

These ministers were troubled that their "religious privileges" were being guaranteed by the apparent generosity of government.

Many citizens today do not grasp their concern. Why would ministers object to the State guaranteeing their enjoyment of religious privileges? Because to the farsighted Danbury Baptists, the mere presence of governmental language protecting their free exercise of religion suggested that its exercise had become a government-granted right (and thus a right that could be taken away or regulated) rather than a God-given unalienable right (which was to be untouched by government). Fearing that the inclusion of language in governing documents securing their "religious privileges" might someday cause the government wrongly to believe that since it had "granted" the freedom of religious expression it therefore had the authority to control and restrict it, the Danbury Baptists had strenuously objected. They believed that government should not interfere with any public religious expression unless, as they told Jefferson, that religious practice caused someone to genuinely "work ill to his neighbor."[42]

The Danbury Baptists were writing to Jefferson fully understanding that he was an ally of their viewpoint, not an adversary of it. It was Jefferson's firm position that the federal government had *no* authority to interfere with, limit, regulate, or prohibit public religious expressions—a position he stated on many occasions:

[N]o power over the freedom of religion . . . [is] delegated to the United States by the Constitution [the First Amendment].[43]

In matters of religion I have considered that its free exercise is placed by the Constitution independent of the powers of the general [federal] government.[44]

[O]ur excellent Constitution . . . has not placed our religious rights under the power of any public functionary.[45]

None of these or any other statements by Jefferson contain even the slightest hint that religion should be removed from the public square, or that it should be secularized, but rather only that the government could not limit or regulate it. The possibility that the government might do so is what had troubled the Danbury Baptists. Fully understanding their concerns, Jefferson replied to them on January 1, 1802, assuring them that they had *nothing* to fear—the government would *not* meddle with their religious expressions, whether they occurred in private or in public:

Believing with you that religion is a matter which lies solely between man and his God; that he owes account to none other for his faith or his worship; that the legitimate powers of government reach actions only and not opinions; I contemplate with sovereign reverence that act of the whole American people which declared that their legislature should "make no law respecting an establishment of religion or prohibiting the free exercise thereof," thus building a wall of separation between Church and State. Adhering to this expression of the supreme will of the nation in behalf of the rights of conscience, I shall see with sincere satisfaction the progress of those sentiments which tend to restore to man all his natural rights, convinced he has no natural right in opposition to his social duties.[46]

The separation metaphor used here was not a new or original phrase originating from Jefferson; it had long been used among the often government-oppressed Baptists and their ministers. Jefferson deliberately used that phrase, already well-known to them, in order to assure them that the government would protect rather than impede their religious beliefs and expressions. As James Adams later affirmed: "Jefferson's reference to a 'wall of separation between Church and State' . . . was not formulating a secular principle to banish religion from the public arena. Rather he was trying to keep government from darkening the doors of Church."[47]

The separation metaphor so often used by courts and officials today was not used by the US Supreme Court until 1878. In that case, the Court particularly emphasized Jefferson's declaration concerning governmental limitations against interfering with religious expressions,[48] explaining:

[I]t [Jefferson's letter] may be accepted almost as an authoritative declaration of the scope and effect of the Amendment thus secured. Congress was deprived of all legislative power over mere [religious] opinion, but was left free to reach actions which were in violation of social duties or subversive of good order.[49]

The separation metaphor was invoked in the Court's decision in order to reaffirm the historical understanding that religious expressions were to be protected rather than limited.[50] In fact, to establish that there were only a narrow handful of religious expressions with which the government could legitimately interfere, the Court quoted from Jefferson's famous Virginia Statute that: "[T]he rightful purposes of civil government are for its officers to interfere when principles break out into overt acts against peace and good order. In th[is] . . . is found the true distinction between what properly belongs to the Church and what to the State."[51]

Notice that based on Jefferson's clearly stated positions, the only religious expressions that the government could hamper were acts "against peace and good order," "injurious to others," "subversive of good order," or acts by "the man who works ill to his neighbor." That Court (and others[52]) then identified a very small class of actions that, if perpetrated in the name of religion, the government did have legitimate reason to limit, including bigamy, concubinage, incest, child sacrifice, infanticide, parricide, and other similarly harmful crimes. But the government was *not* to impede traditional religious expressions in public, whether the offering of prayer, display of religious symbols, use of Scriptures, acknowledgements of God, or so forth. In short, the separation of Church and State was *not* to remove or secularize the free exercise of religion but rather to preserve and protect it, regardless of whether it occurred in private or public.

This was the universal understanding of separation of Church and State until the Supreme Court's landmark ruling in 1947 in *Everson v. Board of Education* first reversed that meaning.[53] In that case the Court cited only Jefferson's eight-word separation metaphor, completely severing it from its historical context and the rest of Jefferson's clearly worded letter, expressing for the first time that the phrase existed not to protect religion in the public square but rather to limit it.

The following year, the Court reiterated its rhetoric of the previous year, declaring: "[T]he First Amendment has erected a wall between Church and State which must be kept high and impregnable."[54] For the second time, the Court refused to reference Jefferson's full (and short) letter, using instead only his eight-word phrase, and citing it out of context and in a religiously hostile manner. The Court thus held that the First Amendment would no longer limit the government but rather would limit groups and individuals instead.

Courts have subsequently pushed this modern misinterpretation of separation increasingly outward to the point where the First Amendment's injunction that "*Congress* shall make no law respecting an establishment of religion or prohibiting the free exercise thereof" now means:

- *an individual student* may not write a research paper on a religious topic,[55] draw religious artwork in an art class,[56] or carry his personal Bible onto school grounds[57]

- *an individual student* may not say a voluntary prayer at a football game,[58] graduation,[59] or any other school event[60]

- *a school* may not place a Bible in a classroom library[61]

- *a choir* may not sing a religious song as part of a school concert[62]

- *cadets* at a state military academy may not engage in offering voluntary prayers over their meals[63]

Clearly, none of these activities involve "Congress" "making a law." The Framers of the First Amendment had designed that provision to limit government, not citizens. However, its modern misapplication now routinely results in decisions that would be egregiously untenable to the Founders as well as to every subsequent generation after them—except today. Consequently:

- A state employee in Minnesota was barred from parking his car in the state parking lot because of a religious sticker on his bumper.[64]

- A five-year-old kindergarten student in Saratoga Springs, New York, was forbidden to say a prayer over her lunch and was scolded by a teacher for doing so.[65]

- A military honor guardsman was removed from his position for saying, "God bless you and this family, and God bless the United States of America" while presenting a folded flag to a family during a military funeral—a statement that the family had requested be made at the funeral.[66]

- Senior citizens who regularly gathered at a community center in Balch Springs, Texas, were prohibited from praying over their own meals.[67]

- A library employee in Russellville, Kentucky, was barred from wearing her necklace because it had a small cross on it.[68]

- College students serving as residential assistants in Eau Claire, Wisconsin, were prohibited from holding Bible studies in their own personal dorm rooms.[69]

- A third grader in Orono, Maine, who wore a T-shirt containing the words "Jesus Christ" was required to turn the shirt inside out so the words could not be seen.[70]

- A school official in Saint Louis, Missouri, caught an elementary student praying over his lunch, lifted the student from his seat, reprimanded him in front of the other students, and took him to the principal, who ordered him to stop praying.[71]

- In cities in Texas, Indiana, Ohio, Georgia, Kansas, Michigan, Pennsylvania, California, Nebraska, and elsewhere citizens were not permitted to hand out religious literature on public sidewalks or preach in public areas, and were actually arrested or threatened with arrest for doing so.[72]

And there are literally hundreds of similar examples.[73]

But regardless of what the other Founders might have wanted regarding religious expressions and activities in the public arena, is this what Jefferson intended? Did he want to prohibit citizens from expressing their faith publically? Did he want them arrested for doing so? Was he truly a secularist who wanted a stridently religion-free public square? His words certainly do not indicate this to be his desire; but how about his actions? After all, actions speak louder than words.

Jefferson's actions in this area are completely consistent with his words. As will be seen below, he has an extremely long record of deliberately and intentionally including rather than excluding religious expressions and activities in the official public governmental square. Interestingly, most of the following actions by

Jefferson would today be challenged in court and likely even struck down on the basis of the modern perversions of his own once-clear phrase.

For example, in *1773* following the Boston Tea Party protest against oppressive British policy, Parliament retaliated with the Boston Port Bill to blockade Boston Harbor and eliminate its trade, thus hoping to financially cripple the Americans and force them into submission. The blockade was to take effect on June 1, *1774*, but upon hearing of this, Jefferson and a handful of other patriots (Richard Henry Lee, Patrick Henry, Francis Lightfoot Lee, and a few more) arranged for a measure to be introduced in the Virginia legislature calling for a public day of fasting and prayer "devoutly to implore the Divine interposition in behalf of an injured and oppressed people."[74] That measure also recommended that legislators "proceed with the Speaker and the Mace to the Church . . . and that the Reverend Mr. Price be appointed to read prayers, and the Reverend Mr. Gwatkin to preach a sermon suitable to the occasion."[75] Jefferson also wrote his local church community in Monticello urging them to arrange a parallel special day of prayer and worship at "the new church on Hardware River"[76]—a public service which Jefferson personally attended.[77]

In *1776*, while serving in the Continental Congress, Jefferson was placed on a committee of five to draft the Declaration of Independence. He was the principal author of that document, and it incorporated four explicit, open acknowledgments of God, some made by his own hand and some added by Congress. That document was actually a dual declaration: a declaration of independence from Great Britain and a declaration of dependence on God.

On July 4, *1776*, Jefferson was placed on a committee of three to draft an official seal for the new American government. His own recommendation included the Bible account of "The children of Israel in the wilderness, led by a cloud by day, and a pillar of fire by night."[78] (He certainly could have proposed a solely secular seal, but did not.)

In *1779* when Jefferson became governor of Virginia, he introduced into the state legislature a package of bills on which he and two others had been working prior to his election,[79] including:

- A Bill for Punishing Disturbers of Religious Worship and Sabbath Breakers[80]

- A Bill for Appointing Days of Public Fasting and Thanksgiving[81]

- A Bill Annulling Marriages Prohibited by the Levitical Law and Appointing the Mode of Solemnizing Lawful Marriage[82]

- A Bill for Saving the Property of the Church Heretofore by Law Established[83]

These bills contained no hint of public secularism in any of them but rather just the opposite. For example, the bill for preserving the Sabbath stipulated:

> If any person on Sunday shall himself be found laboring at his own or any other trade or calling . . . except that it be in the ordinary household offices of daily necessity or other work of necessity or charity, he shall forfeit the sum of ten shillings for every such offence.[84]

And the bill for public days of prayer declared:

> [T]he power of appointing Days of Public Fasting and Thanksgiving . . . . may . . . be exercised by the Governor. . . . Every minister of the Gospel shall, on each day so to be appointed, attend and perform Divine service and preach a sermon or discourse suited to the occasion in his church, on pain of forfeiting fifty pounds for every failure, not having a reasonable excuse.[85]

The bill for protecting marriage required:

> Marriages prohibited by the Levitical law shall be null; and persons marrying contrary to that prohibition and cohabitating as man and wife, convicted thereof in the General Court, shall be [fined] from time to time until they separate.[86]

Jefferson also helped pen and then introduce the Bill for Establishing General Courts in Virginia, which required:

> Every person so commissioned . . . [shall] take the following oath of office, to wit, "You shall swear. . . . So help you God."[87]

While helping prepare these bills prior to becoming governor, Jefferson could have opposed or altered any or all of them, but he did not. And then after becoming governor, he could have refrained from introducing them, but again, he did not. To the contrary, he personally introduced these religious activities directly into civil practice.

Then in *1780*, while still serving as governor, Jefferson ordered that an official state medal be created with the religious motto "Rebellion to Tyrants is Obedience to God."[88] This phrase, a summation of Samuel Rutherford's *Lex Rex* (1644) as well as the famous sermon preached the Rev. Dr. Jonathan Mayhew of Massachusetts in 1750,[89] had previously been proposed to Congress in 1776 as part of the new national seal.[90] By the way, Jefferson not only incorporated this phrase into official state acknowledgements but he also placed it on his own personal private seal.[91]

In *1789* Jefferson began his federal career as secretary of state to President George Washington. One of his early assignments was to oversee the layout and construction of Washington, DC.* The plan for the city was approved by Jefferson in 1791, and in 1793 construction began on permanent federal buildings such as the White House and the Capitol. Work proceeded rapidly and in *1795* newspapers happily reported:

> City of Washington, June 19. It is with much pleasure that we discover the rising consequence of our infant city. Public worship is now regularly administered at the Capitol, every Sunday morning at 11 o'clock, by the Reverend Mr. Ralph.[92]

This activity occurred under Jefferson's jurisdiction and oversight; and it was replicated in other jurisdictions under his control.

For example, from *1797* to *1801* Jefferson served as vice president of the United States under President John Adams. During this time, on November 17, *1800*, Congress moved into the new Capitol and started it first session in that location. Some

---

* Originally, the federal government met in New York City for its first year in 1789, then spent the next ten years in Philadelphia before moving in 1800 to its newly constructed its permanent home in Washington, DC.

two weeks later, on December 4, *1800*, with Theodore Sedgwick presiding over the House and Vice President Thomas Jefferson over the Senate, a plan was approved whereby Christian church services would be held each Sunday in the Hall of the House of Representatives, the largest room in the Capitol building.[93] The spiritual leadership for each Sunday's service would alternate between the chaplain of the House and the chaplain of the Senate, each of whom would either personally conduct the service or invite some other minister to preach. (The chaplains are considered "officers" of each respective body and are under the general direction of the leader of that body—Sedgwick in the House, and Jefferson in the Senate, who agreed to this alternating plan.)

It was in this most recognizable of all government buildings, the US Capitol, that Vice President Jefferson attended church[94]—a practice he also continued throughout his two terms as president.[95] In fact, US congressman Manasseh Cutler, who also attended church at the Capitol, affirmed that "He [Jefferson] and his family have constantly attended public worship in the Hall."[96] Margaret Bayard Smith, another attendee at the Capitol services, confirmed, "Mr. Jefferson, during his whole administration, was a most regular attendant."[97] She even noted that Jefferson had a designated seat at the Capitol church: "The seat he chose the first Sabbath, and the adjoining one, which his private secretary occupied, were ever afterwards by the courtesy of the congregation left for him and his secretary."[98]

(Interestingly, Throckmorton challenges the idea that Jefferson regularly attended the Capitol Church throughout his presidency. Relying on a statement made by Manasseh Cutler, he concludes that Jefferson "may not have attended services there [at the Capitol] regularly until 1802"[99]—that is, Jefferson may not have attended regularly during his first year. But in his own footnote related to that claim, Throckmorton writes, "Manasseh Cutler, after being elected in 1800, would only have begun his term in office on March 4, 1801. Even though his term began on March 4, Congress was not officially in session until December 7, 1801 (and that session concluded on May 3, 1802) and so Cutler was likely not in Washington much to observe whether or not Jefferson attended church."[100] So, Throckmorton announces I am wrong, and then undercuts his own claim—something he does multiple times in his work. And by his silence on everything past 1802, he offers no counter evidence suggesting Jefferson was not faithfully at the Capitol Church for the last seven years of his presidency—presumably because there is none that contradicts the eye-witnesses who said that he was indeed a constant and regular attendant.)

For those services Jefferson rode his horse from the White House to the Capitol,[101] a distance of 1.6 miles and a trip of about thirty minutes. He made this ride regardless of weather conditions. In fact, among Representative Cutler's entries is one noting that "[i]t was very rainy, but his [Jefferson's] ardent zeal brought him through the rain and on horseback to the Hall."[102] Other diary entries similarly confirm Jefferson's faithful attendance despite unfavorable weather.[103]

Interestingly, while Jefferson was president, the Marine Corps band, now known as the President's Own Band, played worship services at the Capitol.[104] According to attendee Margaret Bayard Smith, the band, clad in their scarlet uniforms, made a "dazzling appearance" as they played from the gallery, providing instrumental accompaniment for the singing.[105]

However, good as they were, they seemed too ostentatious for the services and "the attendance of the Marine Band was soon discontinued."[106]

Under President Jefferson, Sunday church services were also started at the War Department and the Treasury Department[107]—government buildings of the Executive Branch under Jefferson's direct control. If he thought such services were unconstitutional or improper, he certainly had the power to stop them, but he did not. Therefore, on any given Sunday, worshippers could choose between attending church at the US Capitol, the War Department, or the Treasury Department, all with the blessing of Jefferson.

Why was Jefferson such a faithful participant at the Capitol church? He once explained to a friend while they were walking to church together:

> No nation has ever yet existed or been governed without religion—nor can be. The Christian religion is the best religion that has been given to man and I, as Chief Magistrate of this nation, am bound to give it the sanction of my example.[108]

(By 1867 the church in the Capitol had become the largest church in Washington, DC.[109])

Other presidential actions of Jefferson include:

- Urging the commissioners of the District of Columbia to sell land for the construction of a Roman Catholic Church, recognizing "the advantages of every kind which it would promise" (*1801*)[110]

- Writing a letter to Constitution signer and penman Gouverneur Morris (then serving as a US senator) describing America as a Christian nation, telling him that "we are already about the 7th of the Christian nations in population, but holding a higher place in substantial abilities" (*1801*)[111]

- Signing federal acts renewing the setting aside of government lands so that missionaries might be assisted in "propagating the Gospel" among the Indians (*1802*, and again in *1803* and *1804*)[112]

- Directing the secretary of war to give federal funds to a religious school established for Cherokees in Tennessee (*1803*)[113]

- Negotiating and approving a treaty with the Kaskaskia Indians that not only directly funded a Catholic priest "to perform for the said tribe the duties of his office" but which also provided federal funding to help erect a church building in which they might worship (*1803*)[114]

- Assuring a Christian school in the newly purchased Louisiana Territory that it would enjoy "the patronage of the government" (*1804*)[115]

- Renegotiating and deleting from a lengthy clause in the 1797 United States treaty with Tripoli[116] the portion that had stated "the United States is in no sense founded on the Christian religion" (*1805*)[117]

- Signing "An Act for Establishing the Government of the Armies" in which:

- It is earnestly recommended to all officers and soldiers diligently to attend Divine service; and all officers who shall behave indecently or irreverently at any place of Divine worship shall, if commissioned officers, be brought before a general court martial, there to be publicly and severely reprimanded by the President; if noncommissioned officers or soldiers, every person so offending shall [be fined]. (*1806*)[118]

- Declaring that religion is "deemed in other countries incompatible with good government, and yet proved by our experience to be its best support" (*1807*)[119]

There are many additional examples, and they all clearly demonstrate that Jefferson has *no* record—whether as state legislator, governor, cabinet member, vice president, president, or private citizen—of attempting to secularize the public square. Furthermore, all of his religious activities at the federal level occurred after the First Amendment had been adopted, thus showing that he saw no violation of it in any of his actions. In fact, no one did—not even his enemies. No one ever raised a voice of dissent against Jefferson's federal religious practices; no one claimed that they were improper or that they violated the Constitution.

The only voice of objection ever raised was to complain that President Jefferson, unlike his predecessors George Washington and John Adams, did not issue any *national* prayer proclamations. Critics today point to this abstention by Jefferson as definitive proof of his public secularism.

For example, Supreme Court Justices William Brennan and Thurgood Marshall noted in *Marsh v. Chambers* that "Thomas

Jefferson . . . during [his] respective terms as President, refused on Establishment Clause [First Amendment] grounds to declare national days of thanksgiving or fasting."[120] And Justice Anthony Kennedy similarly remarked in *Allegheny v. ACLU*: "In keeping with his strict views of the degree of separation mandated by the Establishment Clause, Thomas Jefferson declined to follow this tradition [of issuing national proclamations]."[121]

Yet these justices are wrong. In fact, their assertions are directly repudiated by Jefferson himself. Jefferson succinctly stated that his refusal to issue national prayer proclamations was not because of any First Amendment Establishment Clause scruples about religion but rather was because of his specific views of federalism:

> I consider the government of the United States [i.e., the federal government] as interdicted [prohibited] by the Constitution from intermeddling with religious institutions, their doctrines, discipline, or exercises. This results not only from the provision that "no law shall be made respecting the establishment or free exercise of religion" [the First Amendment], but from that also which reserves to the states the powers not delegated to the United States [the Tenth Amendment]. Certainly, no power to prescribe any religious exercise or to assume authority in religious discipline has been delegated to the general [federal] government. It must then rest with the states, as far as it can be in any human authority. But it is only proposed that I should recommend, not prescribe [require] a day of fasting and prayer. . . . I am aware that the practice of my predecessors may be quoted. But I have ever believed that the example of state

executives [governors issuing prayer proclamations] led to the assumption of that authority by the general government [of the president issuing prayer proclamations] without due examination, which would have discovered that what might be a right in a state government was a violation of that right when assumed by another.[122]

Jefferson was very clear that his refusal to issue federal prayer proclamations did not spring from any concerns over public religious expressions but rather only from his view of federalism. That is, he believed that it was the Tenth Amendment and not the First Amendment that made national prayer proclamations improper.

While Jefferson refused to issue a federal call for prayer, he had certainly done so as a state leader. In addition to his 1774 efforts with Virginia's call for prayer,[123] in 1779 as state governor he issued a statewide proclamation calling his fellow Virginians to prayer, asking them to give thanks "that He [God] hath diffused the glorious light of the Gospel, whereby through the merits of our gracious Redeemer we may become the heirs of the eternal glory."[124] He also asked citizens to pray "that He would grant to His church the plentiful effusions of Divine grace and pour out his Holy Spirit on all ministers on the Gospel; that He would bless and prosper the means of education and spread the light of Christian knowledge through the remotest corners of the earth."[125] And furthermore, while governor he had also introduced the bill for "Appointing Days of Public Fasting and Thanksgiving." So Jefferson clearly was not opposed to official prayer proclamations; he simply believed that they belonged to the jurisdiction of governors, not presidents.

Jefferson may not have issued a formal prayer proclamation as president, but this certainly did not keep him from encouraging his fellow citizens to pray while he was president—as in his Second Inaugural Address:

> I shall need, too, the favor of that Being in Whose hands we are, Who led our fathers, as Israel of old, from their native land and planted them in a country flowing with all the necessaries and comforts of life; Who has covered our infancy with His providence and our riper years with His wisdom and power, and to Whose goodness I ask you to join in supplications with me that He will so enlighten the minds of your servants, guide their councils, and prosper their measures that whatsoever they do shall result in your good and shall secure to you the peace, friendship, and approbation of all nations.[126]

Jefferson did call Americans to pray, just not by issuing federal prayer proclamations. Certainly presidents before and after him did not agree with this particular view and they therefore regularly issued federal prayer proclamations, but the evidence is clear that Jefferson's refusal to participate in this single activity at the national level was not because of any notion of secularism on his part but rather because of his view of federalism.

One last point: the next time someone tells you that Jefferson's letter to the Danbury Baptists is evidence that he favored the complete separation of church and state, ask that person what Jefferson did just two days after he penned that famous letter. The answer: he attended a church service in the US Capitol building, where he heard John Leland, the great Baptist minister and opponent of established churches, preach. In fact, it is very possible that Jefferson himself had asked for Leland to preach at the Capitol church meeting on that morning.[127]

But wait! Didn't Jefferson understand the "separation" doctrine that he had just penned? Of course he did; and he understood that separation prohibited the government from *preventing* a religious expression—which is why having church in the Capitol, and having the Rev. Leland preach there was completely acceptable.

Jefferson and Leland both opposed governmentally established religion, but neither embraced anything approximating the misapplied separation of Church and State advocated today by secularist groups such as the ACLU, Freedom From Religion Foundation, Americans United for Separation of Church and State, Military Religious Freedom Foundation, and others.

Jefferson's record of including, advocating, and promoting religious activities and expressions in the public square is strong, clear, and consistent. And the institutional separation of Church and State so highly praised by today's civil libertarians did *not* originate from Jefferson, or even from secularists—nor did it have societal secularization as its object. To the contrary, it was the product of Bible teachings and Christian ministers, and its object was the protection of religious activities and expressions whether in public or private. The charge that Jefferson was "a secular humanist"[128] or any variant thereof, or that he sought in any manner to secularize the public arena, is one more of the many modern Jefferson lies that has no basis in history.

LIE #6

Thomas Jefferson Detested the Clergy

*I*n yet another attempt to portray Jefferson as holding an overall hostility to religion in general and Christianity in particular, it is claimed that Jefferson disliked Christian clergy:

> [H]e detested the entire clergy, regarding them as a worthless class living like parasites upon the labors of others.[1]

> Thomas Jefferson, in fact, was fiercely anti-cleric.[2]

> Jefferson . . . loathed institutional religion as a profane, earthly artifice that came between humanity and the heavens and kept the people sub-servient to the clergy.[3]

> "The clergy" were one of his enemies who were trying to keep him from being elected President. Surely they would have wanted a devout, God-fearing Christian to be elected! So this is one more proof of Jefferson's religious beliefs.[4]

> Some of the Framers of the Constitution were anti-clerical—Thomas Jefferson, for example.[5]

181

By now, we have covered enough original source material from Jefferson to make these claims not only incorrect but also laughable. Nevertheless, let us proceed to put the final nails in the coffin of this particular lie and lay it permanently to rest. (Of course, as noted in the last chapter, Jefferson was *not* a framer of the Constitution—despite what writers such as Austin Cline, the author of the last quotation above and a leader in prominent secularist groups, continue wrongly to assert.)

To unequivocally put to bed the charge that Jefferson was anticlerical, it is important to place him within his own time, avoiding the mistakes that occur when Modernism is applied to any historical inquiry.

Throughout the Colonial, Revolutionary, and early Federal periods, organized political parties were nonexistent. While philosophically the people divided as Whigs and Tories, Patriots and Loyalists, Monarchists and Republicans, there was no party affiliation.

This changed during the administration of President George Washington, but not at his wish or with his blessing. Widely differing viewpoints on the scope and power of the federal government emerged among his leadership. Individuals such as Secretary of Treasury Alexander Hamilton and Vice President John Adams supported increased federal authority, while others such as Secretary of State Thomas Jefferson and Attorney General Edmund Jennings Randolph sought for a reduced scope of federal power.

Those led by Adams and Hamilton coalesced into what became known as the Federalist Party, with Jefferson becoming a leader of the Anti-Federalists. (By the end of George Washington's presidency, the Anti-Federalist movement had become generally known as Democratic-Republicans, or just Republicans, and by the time of Andrew Jackson they had become the Democrats.) The Northern colonies and New England provided the strongest base of support for the Federalists, while the strength of the anti-federalist Democratic-Republicans was from Pennsylvania southward. The Federalists tended to be stronger in populous areas already accustomed to more government at numerous levels. The Democratic-Republicans were generally stronger in rural areas where people were more lightly governed.

Jefferson observed that people from the Northern regions had many good traits; they were "cool, sober, laborious, persevering . . . jealous of their own liberties and just to those of others" while those in the South had many negative traits, including being "voluptuary, indolent, unsteady, . . . zealous for their own liberties but trampling on those of others [i.e., slavery]."[6] But Jefferson saw the religious characteristics of the two regions as generally reversed: "[I]n the North they are . . . chicaning, superstitious, and hypocritical in their religion" while "in the South they are . . . candid, without attachment or pretentions to any religion but that of the heart."[7] Religion was definitely important in all regions of early America, but as Jefferson noted, there was indeed a clear difference between the way it was generally practiced in Federalist and Anti-Federalist regions.

In the more densely populated North, churches abounded, participation was convenient, and citizens were frequent and regular in their attendance. In fact, John Adams, like so many others in New England, described himself as a "church-going animal."[8] The pastors of New England therefore had frequent contact with their parishioners throughout the week and held much influence in the community. But with the sparser population southward, churches were fewer and more distant from each other, and participation often required deliberate effort. For example, for George Washington to attend church each Sunday, as was his habit,[9] was a full day commitment. It was typically a two-to three-hour ride on horseback or carriage to his church ten miles from Mt. Vernon. A two-hour service was common, and the return ride home took another few hours, thus consuming the entire day. So while ministers in the South were just as important as in the North, they had fewer opportunities to influence and interact with their parishioners. These very real religious nuances between the two regions directly influenced the politics of each.

The presidential election of 1800 was America's first real partisan political contest, pitting Thomas Jefferson the Democratic-Republican against John Adams the Federalist. New Englanders were fiercely loyal to their Federalist hero, Adams, while those southward strongly supported their champion, Jefferson. The campaign was vicious—probably the most venomous in American history, with the Federalists taking a much nastier approach in their attacks against Jefferson than the Democratic-Republicans did against Adams.

For example, Jefferson was accused by his Federalist critics not only of being anti-Christian but also of being a murderer, an atheist, a thief, and a cohort of foreign convicts. It was reported that he was secretly plotting the destruction and overthrow of the Constitution. He was accused of defrauding a widow and her children, and the nation was alerted that he planned to abolish the navy and starve the farmers.[10] Citizens were warned that if Jefferson were elected, he would confiscate and burn every Bible in America. (When he won the election, some New Englanders actually buried their Bibles so he could not find and destroy them.[11])

Since one of the quickest ways to vilify and ostracize a person in religion-conscious New England was to claim that he was antireligious or lacked morals, Federalist ministers regularly accused Jefferson of both. Some of the most contemptible attacks against him came from such ministers, who preached sermons about him—sermons often containing blatant lies, gross distortions, and vile misrepresentations.

But John Adams was not exempted from similarly ill-intentioned attacks; he also was maligned and misrepresented by his Republican opponents. Years later he recounted the maltreatment he had suffered to his close friend and fellow signer of the Declaration, Benjamin Rush: "If I am to judge by the newspapers and pamphlets that have been printed in America for twenty years past, I should think that both parties believed me the meanest villain in the world."[12]

But however fierce may have been the attacks on Adams, those on Jefferson were definitely much more despicable. Regardless of what Jefferson said or did concerning religion, no matter how innocent or honest his actions or words may have been, they were spun negatively and used against him by his enemies, especially Federalist clergymen.

The Reverend Cotton Mather Smith of Connecticut provides an excellent example. Smith had served as a military chaplain during the American Revolution and delivered over four thousand sermons and messages in his lengthy career.[13] On one occasion he was visited by a friend of Jefferson, who was offended and appalled by what Reverend Smith told him. Afterwards, he repeated that conversation to Jefferson:

I called on and dined with the Reverend Cotton Mather
Smith of Sharon. . . . I found him an engaged federal politi-
cian. He soon found that my political feelings were not in
unison with his and asked whether my good wishes would
really extend Mr. Jefferson to the Presidential Chair [in the
election of 1800]. I answered in the affirmative—on which,
accompanied with much other malicious invective [vicious
attack] and in presence of five men and two women, he
said that you, Sir, "had obtained your property by fraud
and robbery, and that in one instance you had defrauded
and robbed a widow and fatherless children of an estate
to which you were executor." . . . I told him with some
warmth that I did not believe it. He said that "it was true"
and that "it could be proved." . . . I thought it my duty, sir,
to communicate the assertion.[14]

Upon hearing that accusation, Jefferson replied to his friend:

Every tittle of it is fable [i.e., a lie]. . . . I never was executor
but in two instances. . . . In one of the cases only were there
a widow and children: she was my sister. She retained and
managed the estate in her own hands, and no part of it was
ever in mine. . . . If Mr. Smith, therefore, thinks the precepts
of the Gospel [are] intended for those who preach them as
well as for others, he will doubtless someday feel the duties
of repentance and of acknowledgment in such forms as to
correct the wrong he has done.[15]

Despite Smith's blatant lie that Jefferson obtained his
belongings by defrauding widows and orphans, the charge
nevertheless roared across New England.

Similarly false charges were made against Jefferson by the Reverend William Linn of New York, who pastored several churches, served as a military chaplain during the Revolution, became the first chaplain of the House of Representatives, and then a university president. Linn, a staunch Federalist and close friend of Federalist leader Alexander Hamilton, was thus a mortal political enemy of Jefferson.

Linn penned *Serious Considerations on the Election of a President* in which he warned that if Jefferson won the 1800 election, "The effects would be to destroy religion, introduce immorality, and loosen all the bonds of society."[16] He concluded his pamphlet by telling the country that "Jefferson's opponent," John Adams, was "irreproachable," bluntly cautioning Americans that "it would be more acceptable to God and beneficial to the interests of your country to throw away your votes" than to vote for Jefferson.[17]

The Reverend John Mason, another New York Federalist pastor, also detested Jefferson. He, too, was a close friend of Alexander Hamilton and actually attended Hamilton at his death after he was shot down in the famous duel with Aaron Burr. Mason authored *The Voice of Warning to Christians on the Ensuing Election* to warn Americans that Jefferson was a "confirmed" and "a hardened infidel" and one "who writes against the truth of God's Word; who makes not even a profession of Christianity; who is without Sabbaths, without the sanctuary, without so much as a decent external respect for the faith and the worship of Christians."[18]

Of course, as has already been shown, Jefferson had done exactly the opposite of what Mason claimed with each of these charges, including having helped write and sponsor the civil law in Virginia that punished violators of the Sabbath. Nevertheless, Mason solemnly warned voters:

> If therefore an infidel [Jefferson] preside over our country, it will be YOUR fault, Christians, and YOUR act—and YOU shall answer it! And for aiding and abetting such a design, I charge upon your consciences the SIN of striking hands in a covenant of friendship with the enemies of your Master's glory.[19]

The Reverend Nathanael Emmons of Massachusetts similarly lifted a strident voice against Jefferson. He had been an ardent patriot during the Revolution, later establishing several missionary and theological societies, with two hundred of his sermons being published and widely distributed.

A devoted Federalist, Emmons worked actively against Jefferson; but despite his best efforts, Jefferson was elected. In a famous sermon preached afterwards, Emmons asserted that Jefferson was the American Jeroboam.

(In the Bible, Jeroboam was the wicked leader who divided Israel following the death of Solomon. Taking ten of Israel's twelve tribes, Jeroboam became their king and led them away from God, ordaining pagan priests and pagan places of worship throughout the land, thus causing the ten tribes to eventually be conquered and destroyed.)

In Emmons' two-hour sermon he compared the wise and Godly leader Solomon (whom he likened to John Adams) with the wicked and nefarious leader Jeroboam (whom he asserted was Thomas Jefferson). He then chastised voters for having chosen Jefferson, telling them:

Solomon [John Adams] did a great deal to promote the temporal and eternal interests of his subjects; but Jeroboam [Jefferson] did as much to ruin his subjects both in time and eternity. . . . It is more than possible that our nation may find themselves in the hand of a Jeroboam who will drive them from following the Lord; and whenever they do, they will rue the day and detest the folly, delusion, and intrigue which raised him to the head of the United States.[20]

Years later, during the War of 1812 (and several years after Jefferson had retired from his two terms as president) Emmons still couldn't let go of his personal obsession of and hatred for Jefferson. In fact, he directly blamed Jefferson for the war, even though the war had occurred years *after* his presidency. In an 1813 sermon, he continued the odious tone of his sermon from more than a decade earlier, still chiding voters with a denunciation of their stupidity for having chosen the "wicked" Jefferson:

[W]hen [the nation] neglected their best men and chose the worst [Jefferson], their glory departed and their calamities began. Against the solemn warning voice of some of the best patriots in the Union, they committed the supreme power into the hands of Mr. Jefferson, who had publicly condemned the federal Constitution. This they did with their eyes wide open. . . . We deserved to be punished.[21]

Publicly condemned the Constitution? Jefferson? The War of 1812 was America's "punishment" for electing Jefferson? Such was the loathsome tone of sermons and publications of that era, and such was the caliber of lies issued against Jefferson by leading Federalist ministers. Of their relentlessly brutal attacks, Jefferson acknowledged:

> [F]rom the [Federalist] clergy I expect no mercy. They crucified their Savior, Who preached that their kingdom was not of this world [John 18:36]; and all who practice on that precept must expect the extreme of their wrath. The laws of the present day withhold their hands from blood, but lies and slander still remain to them.[22]

Early Jefferson historian Claude G. Bowers affirmed:

> [I]n New England States, where the greater part of the ministers were militant Federalists, he was hated with an unholy hate. More false witness had been borne by the ministers of New England and New York against Jefferson than had ever been borne against any other American publicist.[23]

Political historian Saul Padover agreed.

> They accused Jefferson of everything. If the sermons of the clergy were to be believed, there was no crime in the calendar of which Jefferson was not guilty and no unspeakable evil which he had not committed.[24]

With these types of reprehensible charges coming from Federalist clergy, it should not be surprising that comments Jefferson made about these specific Federalist ministers might indeed seem anti-clergy. But the modern errant conclusion that imputes his comments against Federalist clergy to all clergy can be reached only through Minimalism (ignoring complex situations in order to present an exaggeratedly simplistic conclusion). Regrettably, Minimalists, Secularists, and Negativists routinely ignore Jefferson's scores of letters praising other clergymen. They also universally dismiss the countless Democratic-Republican ministers and clergy who praised and championed Jefferson with a zeal and fervor equal to that of the hatred shown him by Federalist ministers. As Harvard historian Alan Heimert acknowledged:

> The "Republican [Jeffersonian] Revival" of 1800–1801 is one of the most neglected significant episodes in American intellectual and political development. . . . There were many preachers—many more than historians allow—who avidly and vocally supported the Republican party, and did so in the conviction that Republicanism embodied the first principles of evangelical Christianity. . . . Jefferson's animus against establishments was known and understood among Dissenters.[25]

One of those Evangelical ministers who vociferously supported Jefferson was the Reverend John Leland of Massachusetts. Before the American Revolution Leland moved to Virginia where he pastored Baptist churches and became a good friend of Jefferson, working closely with him to disestablish the Anglican Church in the state. In 1788 Leland was selected as a Virginia delegate to ratify the US Constitution. In 1791 he moved back to Massachusetts, and in 1800 became a leader in organizing the Evangelicals in New England to support Jefferson for president.[26]

Following Jefferson's successful election, Leland preached a sermon in which he effused:

> Heaven above looked down and awakened the American genius. . . . This exertion of the American genius has brought forth the *Man of the People*, the defender of the rights of

man and the rights of conscience to fill the chair of state. . . . Pardon me, my hearers, if I am overwarm. I lived in Virginia fourteen years. The beneficent influence of my hero was too generally felt to leave me a stoic. . . . Let us then adore that God Who has been so favorable to our land and nation.[27]

Leland even made a special trip from Massachusetts to the White House to bring his friend Jefferson a special gift: a giant cheese. As related by early political biographers:

> Leland proposed that his flock should celebrate [Jefferson's] victory by making for the new Chief Magistrate the biggest cheese the world had ever seen. Every man and woman who owned a cow was to give for this cheese all the milk yielded on a certain day—only no federal cow must contribute a drop. A huge cider-press was fitted up to make it in, and on the appointed day, the whole country turned out with pails and tubs of curd, the girls and women in their best gowns and ribbons, and the men in their Sunday coats and clean shirt-collars. The cheese was put to press with prayer, and hymn-singing, and great solemnity. When it was well dried, it weighed 1,600 pounds. It was placed on a sleigh, and Elder John Leland drove with it all the way to Washington. It was a journey of three weeks. All the country had heard of the big cheese, and came out to look at it as the Elder drove along.[28]

The massive cheese had Jefferson's favorite motto etched into it: "Rebellion to Tyrants is Obedience to God."[29] Jefferson and Leland went inside the White House where Leland spoke in the East Room, declaring: "We believe the Supreme Ruler of the Universe, Who raises up men to achieve great events, has raised up a Jefferson at this critical day to defend republicanism."[30]

Leland's visit to the White House occurred on Friday, January 1, 1802—the same day that Jefferson wrote his famous separation letter to Leland's fellow Baptists in Danbury, Connecticut, assuring them that because of "a wall of separation between church and state," they had nothing to fear from government interfering with their religious practices or expressions. And (as noted earlier) two days later, on Sunday, January 3, Leland preached the sermon at the Capitol church, with Jefferson in attendance.[31]

Members of Congress such as the Reverend Manasseh Cutler, a Federalist minister from Massachusetts, attended that church service. Cutler was disgusted by his fellow minister, the Anti-Federalist Leland, and complained:

> Last Sunday, Leland the cheesemonger, a poor, ignorant, illiterate, clownish preacher (who was the conductor of this monument of human weakness and folly [the Republican cheese] to the place of its destination), was introduced as the preacher to both Houses of Congress.[32]

Cutler not only loathed Leland but was also revolted by his sermon, whose text was:

> "And behold a greater than Solomon is here" [Matthew 12:42]. The design of the preacher was principally to apply the allusion not to the person intended in the text [i.e., Jesus], but to him who was then present [i.e., Jefferson]. . . . Such an outrage upon religion, the Sabbath, and common decency was extremely painful to every sober thinking person present.[33]

Federalist ministers clearly did not like Democratic-Republican ministers doing to Jefferson the opposite of what they had inflicted upon him. But Jefferson was so moved by Leland's visit that when Leland left Washington to return to Massachusetts, Jefferson "gave Rev. Mr. Leland, bearer of the cheese, $200"[34]—one of the largest contributions Jefferson ever made to any person or cause.[35]

Jefferson personally arranged for other Christian ministers to preach at the Capitol, including the Reverend James O'Kelly, another of his strong supporters. Originally a Methodist, O'Kelly later founded a movement known as the "Republican Methodists" because of the common beliefs they shared with Jefferson's political movement. He twice visited Jefferson at the White House, and Jefferson twice arranged for him to preach in the church at the Capitol.[36]

Another Democratic-Republican evangelical minister with whom Jefferson was very close was his own pastor, the Reverend Charles Clay, who was an Anglican minister at St. Anne's parish in Fredericksville before and during the American War for Independence. Jefferson attended his church during that time.

Clay had been greatly influenced by the religious revival known as the Great Awakening and was a thoroughly energetic and evangelical preacher. He was also a strong patriot, ministering during the Revolution both to the American forces from the area and to the captured British forces imprisoned nearby. Clay was a neighbor of Jefferson, became a justice of the peace, and even acted as Jefferson's attorney.

By 1777 the board of Reverend Clay's church had stopped paying his salary—apparently because of either his overt patriotism or his fervent evangelical tendencies, both of which were not common among traditional Anglican churches. After being unable to secure the back pay for Clay, Jefferson worked with a group of citizens to start a new church that the Reverend Clay would pastor—the Calvinistic Reformed Church, which Jefferson called the Protestant Episcopal Church. Jefferson explained that they started that church for "deriving to ourselves . . . the benefits of Gospel knowledge and religious improvement" and for "supporting those . . . qualifying themselves by regular education for explaining the Holy Scriptures."[37]

Jefferson and the associated group personally pledged the financial support necessary for the Reverend Clay and the new church. In fact, Jefferson himself drafted the public announcement setting forth the reason they were supporting Clay, and how they financially planned to do so:

> Whereas by a late act of General Assembly, freedom of religious opinion and worship is restored to all, and it is left to the members of each religious society to employ such teachers as they think fit for their own spiritual comfort and instruction and to maintain the same by their free and voluntary contributions. . . . [A]pproving highly the political conduct of Revd. Charles Clay, who early rejecting the tyrant and tyranny of Britain, proved his religion genuine by its harmony with the liberties of mankind, and conforming his public prayers to the spirit and injured rights of his country, ever addressed the God of battles for victory to our arms (while others impiously prayed that our enemies might vanquish and overcome us), do hereby oblige ourselves, our heirs, executors, and administrators to pay to the said Charles Clay of Albemarle, his executors, or administrators the several sums affixed to our respective names.[38]

Of the many who signed that financial pledge, Jefferson was by far among the most generous contributors.[39]

Jefferson also wrote a public letter of commendation for the Reverend Clay in case he should ever seek employment at another church, publicly testifying:

> The Reverend Charles Clay has been many years rector of this parish and has been particularly known to me. During the whole course of that time, his deportment has been exemplary, as became a divine, and his attention to parochial duties unexceptionable. . . . As he has some thought of leaving us, I feel myself obliged, in compliance with the common duty of bearing witness to the truth when called on, to give this testimonial of his merit that it may not be altogether unknown to those with whom he may propose to take up his residence.[40]

Jefferson wrote similar letters for other ministers he knew, including the Reverend James Fontaine, recommending him for the position of chaplain in the state government.[41] He also penned a letter of enthusiastic praise for the Rev. Mr. Glendye, who was moving to Baltimore.[42]

Furthermore, Jefferson closely attended many sermons of his republican clergy friends, and those sermons helped directly shape his political philosophy. For example, because Jefferson was a close follower of the Reverend Clay's sermons, it is therefore not surprising to find that Jefferson's political language paralleled the language of Clay's sermons. As one student of Jefferson noted:

Given the close friendship and identification that Jefferson publicly made with Clay and his sermons, the language therefore that is found in these sermons is important because of its similarities with much of Jefferson's terminology in his public writings. The phrase "Providence" or "Divine Providence," used 34 times in [Clay's] sermon on *The Governor Among the Nations*, is similar to the closing phrase in the Declaration of Independence. . . . Clay also referred to "God as the Author of Nature," "God the Supreme ruler," "God the Fountain of All power," "the Supreme Governor of the World," "the Supreme Universal King and Lord," "the Governor among the Nations," and the "Great Governor of the World, the King of Nations." These terms were common to the sermons of the day, and to the common prayer books, and therefore if Jefferson used such language in his writings, it would not be accurate to assume that he derived it from enlightenment or deistic sources.[43]

Writers today regularly ignore the fact that the religious terms Jefferson used in his political writings were commonly used by many evangelical ministers.[44] They wrongly claim that Jefferson's use of such terms proves he was a deist,[45] but if this is true, then that same language similarly proves that many evangelical ministers of the day were also deists—clearly an untenable position. Such logic is a product of Modernism, which wrongly insists that since the words Jefferson used two centuries ago are not the words Evangelicals use today then Jefferson must have been irreligious.

Another minister who strongly supported Jefferson was the Reverend Lorenzo Dow, one of the best known figures of the national revival known as the Second Great Awakening. Dow was originally associated with the Methodists; and in 1794 he began traveling on horseback and preaching, often up to twenty times a week. Like the Reverend George Whitefield, he traversed the vast expanse of the nation preaching everywhere he went, including even journeying to countries abroad to preach the Gospel.

On one occasion while speaking at a Baptist church near Jefferson's home, Dow praised Jefferson for disestablishing the Anglican Church in Virginia. He also asserted that Jefferson's overall willingness to everywhere disestablish what he termed "law religion" (which is the state establishment by law of a particular denomination) was the real reason that Federalists so fiercely opposed Jefferson and called him an "infidel." (During the time that Jefferson was working for religious freedom and the disestablishment of official state-established denominations, nearly every New England Federalist state had its own state-established denomination.) Dow explained:

> Jefferson, seeing the evil of law religion, &c., had those barbarous laws . . . repealed. . . . These things procured the epithet [abusive label] "Infidel!" for a mark of distinguishment. . . . But religious venom of all things is the worst! From those circumstances arose the prejudice of the clergy of different societies who would be fond of a law religion as the ground of their animosity and ambition against him, because their hopes of gain are stagnated by it.[46]

Jefferson, too, believed that his efforts to disestablish a state-church were the reason for most of the Federalist attacks against him. As he confided to his close friend Benjamin Rush during the venomous presidential election:

[T]hey [the Federalist clergy] believe that any portion of power confided to me will be exerted in opposition to their schemes—and they believe rightly, for I have sworn upon the altar of God eternal hostility against every form of tyranny over the mind of man. But this is all they have to fear from me; and enough, too, in their opinion. And this is the cause of their printing lying pamphlets against me. . . . But enough of this. It is more than I have before committed to paper on the subject of all the lies which have been preached and printed against me.[47]

Years later Jefferson remained convinced that his opposition to official state-established denominations and his support for placing all Christian denominations on the same equal legal footing had been the primary source of the religious attacks against him, affirming:

[T]he priests indeed have heretofore thought proper to ascribe to me religious, or rather anti-religious sentiments of their own fabric, but such as soothed their resentments against the act of Virginia for establishing religious freedom. They wished him to be thought atheist, deist, or devil, who could advocate freedom from their [state-established] religious dictations.[48]

In addition to the Bible-centered Evangelicals already mentioned, numerous others strongly supported Jefferson, including the Reverend Samuel Knox, a Presbyterian minister from Maryland and a vocal anti-Unitarian who not only wrote *A Vindication of the Religion of Mr. Jefferson* in 1800 but who also worked for the Democratic-Republican cause.[49] Others among

Jefferson's strong supporters were the Reverend Samuel Miller, a Presbyterian minister from New York and New Jersey;[50] the Reverend Elias Smith, a Baptist minister in New Hampshire;[51] and many more, including those who had worked hand-in-hand with him to introduce and pass religious liberty legislation in the Virginia legislature (such as the Reverends John Todd, William Irvin, Billy Woods, Jeremiah Moore, and others[52]).

A further indication of Jefferson's strong overall support for churches and ministers is seen in his own financial records. He gave generously not only to churches he attended but also to many other churches as well, including the "German church," "Gloria Dei Church" (a local black church), the "Revd. Mr. Chambers' . . . church," a Methodist church, an Episcopal church at the Navy Yard in Washington, and others.[53] And he also contributed freely to the construction of several new churches, including three Baptist, two Presbyterian, two Episcopalian, a church in Louisiana, and so on.[54] Furthermore, he financially supported missionaries[55] and contributed liberally to the support of many ministers, including the Reverends W. Coutts, Matthew Maury, John Leland, David Austin, Stephen Balch, Thomas Cavender, Jacob Eyerman, Andrew McCormick, John Bausman, and others.[56]

Clearly, Jefferson was very close to and supportive of many ministers. But if one reads only his letters in which (1) he fired back with contempt against those ministers who viciously attacked him, or (2) he denounced the clergy of Period II and Period III who wanted to preserve state religious establishments, then one could wrongly conclude that Jefferson was anti-clergy.[57]

In fact, Jefferson's opposition to state-established clergy was one of the reasons that he connected so well with Anti-Federalist

Democratic-Republican ministers: they had common goals in jointly opposing "priest-craft" and "law religion." Yet pains were taken to make clear that the term *priestcraft* (a term used by Jefferson on many occasions) did not encompass all clergy but rather only certain types. As the Reverend Leland explained:

By *Priest-Craft*, no contempt is designed to be cast upon any of the Lord's priest's, from Melchizedeck to Zacharias, nor upon any of the ministers of Christ, either those who have been remarkably endowed with power from on high to work miracles, &c. or those of ordinary endowments who have been governed by supreme love to the Savior and benevolence to mankind. These, to the world, have been like the stars of night. But by priest-craft is intended the rushing into the sacred work for the sake of ease, wealth, honor, and ecclesiastical dignity. Whether they plead lineal succession or Divine impulse, their course is directed for self-advantage. By good words and fair speeches, they deceive the simple and [use] solemn threatening of fines, gibbets [means of execution], or the flames of Hell to those who do not adhere to their institutes.[58]

(Concerning this latter category, there were actually clergy during the American Revolution who threatened their parishioners with Hell if they helped the patriots.[59] Recall, too, that Jefferson had specifically denounced these types of ministers in the very same letter in which he declared his enthusiastic support for the Reverend Clay.)

Those who generally fit the category of "priest-craft" as described by the Reverend Leland and despised by Jefferson were largely based in New England. As Jefferson affirmed to his friend and fellow-signer of the Declaration Elbridge Gerry, one of Jefferson's few supporters in Massachusetts: "In your corner alone [i.e., in New England], priestcraft and lawcraft are still able to throw dust into the eyes of the people."[60]

It is vital to recognize that when Jefferson was speaking of what he considered to be destructive religious leaders, he regularly used the terms *priests, priest-ridden*, or those who practice *priest-craft*[61] as distinguished from terms such as *ministers, pastors,* or *clergy*. For example, in a letter to his friend Horatio Spafford, the father of the man who authored the classic Christian hymn "It Is Well with My Soul," Jefferson declared:

> I join in your reprobation [disapproval] of our merchants, priests, and lawyers for their adherence to England and monarchy in preference to their own country and its constitution. . . . In every country and in every age, the priest has been hostile to liberty; he is always in alliance with the despot, abetting his abuses in return for protection to his own. . . . [T]hey have perverted the purest religion ever preached to man into mystery and jargon unintelligible to all mankind.[62]

Jefferson's context is clear: he was referencing only those clergy who had an "adherence to England and monarchy in preference to their own country and its constitution." Yet secularists brazenly lift a single line from this very letter to claim that Jefferson was an opponent of all ministers. For example, Farrell Till, atheist editor of the *Skeptical Review*, writes:

> Thomas Jefferson, in fact, was fiercely anti-cleric. In a letter to Horatio Spafford in 1814, Jefferson said, "In every country and every age, the priest has been hostile to liberty. He is

always in alliance with the despot, abetting his abuses in return for protection to his own."[63]

Clearly, that was not the context of Jefferson's letter. Note also that Jefferson is describing priests that sided with England and monarchy. But as we have seen, he was well aware that many clergy in America were patriots. He obviously did not mean to include these men (some of whom were personal friends) in this condemnation. Ripped out of its context, the sentence quoted by Till does make it seem that Jefferson was anticlerical. That is why historical context is so very important.

A final proof that Jefferson was not opposed to all clergy can found in his discussions concerning the 1776 Virginia constitution, which contained a prohibition against ministers serving in the legislature.[64] Jefferson explained why he originally supported this provision:

> The clergy are excluded because if admitted into the legislature at all, the probability is that they would form its majority, for they are dispersed through every county in the state; they have influence with the people and great opportunities of persuading them to elect them into the legislature. This body, though shattered, is still formidable, still forms a *corps*, and is still actuated by the *esprit de corps*. The nature of that spirit has been severely felt by mankind, and has filled the history of ten or twelve centuries [i.e., throughout Period II and the early part of Period III] with too many atrocities not to merit a proscription from meddling with government.[65]

Recall that this was the early constitution of a state that for the previous century and a half had an official state-established denomination (i.e., the Anglicans). Jefferson believed that what had occurred in those 150 years when Anglican Virginia had persecuted ministers from other denominations might still continue in the new independent state, and he wanted that possibility precluded.

Years later, however, when the power of the state-established church in Virginia had been fully broken and a proven record of all Christian denominations being treated equally under the law had been fully demonstrated, Jefferson no longer supported that original clause, explaining to the Reverend Jeremiah Moore:

> I observe . . . an abridgment of the right of being elected, which after 17 years more of experience and reflection, I do not approve: it is the incapacitation of a clergyman from being elected. . . . Even in 1783, we doubted the stability of our recent measures for reducing them [the clergy] to the footing of other useful callings [but i]t now appears that our means were effectual. The clergy here seem to have relinquished all pretension to privilege and to stand on a footing with lawyers, physicians &c., They ought therefore to possess the same rights.[66]

Jefferson therefore approved of ministers running for office. In fact, after telling his good friend, the Reverend Charles Clay, that "I understand you are a candidate for the representation of your district in Congress," he then wished him "every prosperity in this and in all your other undertakings."[67] And Jefferson himself even personally recruited the Rev. William Woods, a local Baptist pastor, to run for a seat in the state legislature.[68]

In summary, Jefferson was definitely not anti-clergy. Many of Jefferson's writings openly praise clergymen and their important work; clergy were among his closest friends, and he regularly opened his pocketbook and exerted his influence to help them. The modern claim that Jefferson was anti-clerical is another one of the many Jefferson lies that must be shaken off.

LIE #7

Thomas Jefferson Was an Atheist and Anti-Christian

*P*erhaps the most prevalent falsehood about Jefferson is that he was anti-religious in general and anti-Christian in particular. Is this true? For many modern writers the answer is simple:

> Jefferson hated religion. . . . [Professor Joseph] Ellis claims that "like Voltaire, Jefferson longed for the day when the last king would be strangled with the entrails of the last priest."[1]

> Several of our founding fathers were deist and even hated Christianity . . . [including] Thomas Jefferson.[2]

> Jefferson hated organized religion.[3]

> Jefferson. . . . It's very likely he was an atheist.[4]

> [His] writings clearly prove that he was not a Christian but a Freethinker.[5]

The term *Freethinker* may be unfamiliar to some. Atheist groups assert that it is merely another name for atheism,[6] and although the *Merriam-Webster Dictionary* does define an atheist as a freethinker,[7] many scholars disagree that the two terms are interchangeable.[8] But regardless, it is not necessary to spend much time on the question of whether Jefferson was an atheist. As we have seen, he clearly believed that God existed, and his writings make clear that many of his endeavors were inspired by a strong belief in God and in His first principles. So Jefferson definitely was not an atheist Freethinker; but was he a Christian?

Modern writers often want to put Jefferson into a neat, tidy box. This is a mistake. He was a very complex person, and his views on some issues clearly changed over time. Such was certainly the case with his religious convictions. But many scholars and popular authors alike regularly assert that Jefferson was a deist who rejected traditional Christianity,[9] especially citing as proof letters he wrote toward the end of his long life. While these letters must be considered by any serious student of Jefferson's faith, they are not the whole story. It is important to understand that while late in life Jefferson came to reject some elements of orthodox Christianity, there are good reasons to believe that he was a more traditional Christian throughout his earlier years. Moreover, there never was a time when he questioned the overall value of Christianity to individuals or to a nation, or a time when he was anti-Jesus or rejected Christianity as a whole. Consider, then, something of his long faith journey.

Jefferson, born in 1743, was baptized into the Anglican Church. Records of his religious beliefs and church attendance as a young man are sparse, but we do know that he grew up being trained in Anglican religious schools before entering William and Mary, an Anglican college, in 1760. In 1768, he became a vestryman (a leader of his local Anglican church), and in accepting the office, he pledged "to conform to the Doctrine and Discipline of the Church of England."[10] Although most contemporary Anglican churches in America (sometimes called Episcopal churches) have become quite doctrinally liberal, in the 18th century the denomination was Biblically orthodox in terms of its "Doctrines and Discipline"—that is, its doctrinal statements, prayer book, articles of faith, and so forth.

In 1772, Jefferson married Martha Wayles Skelton, who was described by those who knew her as "saintly."[11] At the time of their wedding, America was four decades deep into the national revival known as the Great Awakening. Martha and Thomas were influenced in a positive manner by these revivals.

In 1776, Jefferson penned a piece that provided significant insight into his religious beliefs at that time. America had just separated from Great Britain, and Jefferson was preparing to deliver a major speech in the state legislature, arguing for disestablishing the Anglican Church as the official state denomination in Virginia. He titled his thoughts for that speech "Notes on Religion," and in it he invoked literally dozens of Scripture, often citing specific chapter and verse to make his arguments.

From the founding of Virginia, the Anglican Church had been the colony's established church. While non-Anglicans were generally tolerated, they often faced numerous disabilities and hurdles. Jefferson witnessed and was directly involved with numerous legal conflicts involving Christian doctrinal disputes over those official disabilities. Although he was a dedicated life-long Anglican, he often became an advocate for other Christian denominations whose followers had been fined, imprisoned, or punished by state authorities for preaching or conducting religious services without proper state or Anglican permission. From those experiences, as well as his own study of the history of Christianity in Europe over previous centuries, Jefferson concluded that such conflicts generally arose not from what Jesus Himself had said in the Gospels but rather from some doctrinal point subsequently made by His disciples in the Epistles.

In making this distinction, in his notes for his speech he observed:

> The fundamentals of Xty [Christianity] as found in the Gospels are: (1) Faith; (2) Repentance. That faith is everywhere explained to be a belief that Jesus was the Messiah Who had been promised. Repentance was to be proved sincerely by good works.[12]

He then noted:

> The Epistles were written to persons already Christians. A person might be a Xn [Christian], then, before they [the Epistles] were written. Consequently, the fundamentals of Christianity were to be found in the preaching of our Savior, which is related in the Gospels. These fundamentals are to be found in the Epistles, dropped here and there and promiscuously [randomly] mixed with other truths; but these other truths are not to be made fundamentals. They serve for edification indeed, and explaining to us matters in worship and morality. . . . But yet every sentence in them (though the writers were inspired) must not be taken up and made a fundamental, without assent to which a man is not to be admitted a member of the Xn [Christian] church here, or to His kingdom hereafter. The Apostles Creed was by them taken to contain all things necessary to salvation, and consequently to a communion.[13]

Notice several important points here: Jefferson called Jesus "*our* Savior," using an inclusive pronoun that personally included himself in that group. Next, he noted that in the Epistles, their "writers were inspired"—an acknowledgment of the Divine inspiration of the Scriptures. He also said that the teachings of the Epistles were not to supersede the things Christ set forth in the Gospels, and that the Gospels and the Apostles Creed "contain all things necessary to salvation."

The Apostles Creed, originating in the early church and summarizing the core teachings of Christianity, was regularly memorized by students as part of their education in the Founding Era.[14] It had also been thoroughly inculcated throughout the Anglican education that Jefferson had received for so many years in his youth.[15] That Creed, as taught in the Anglican Church (of which Jefferson was a member), declared:

> I believe in God the Father Almighty, maker of heaven and earth; and in Jesus Christ His only Son, our Lord, Who was conceived by the Holy Ghost, born of the Virgin Mary, suffered under Pontius Pilate, was crucified, dead, and buried; He descended into hell; the third day He rose again from the dead; He ascended into heaven; and sitteth on the right hand of God the Father Almighty; from thence He shall come to judge the quick and the dead. I believe in the Holy Ghost, the holy catholic Church, the communion of saints, the forgiveness of sins, the resurrection of the body, and the life everlasting.[16]

According to Jefferson, the doctrines in this Creed are the summation of the Gospels and "contain all things necessary to salvation."[17]

Jefferson believed that what made denominations distinctive

was not their disagreement on the interpretation of the Gospels but rather their differing emphases on various points within the Epistles. To illustrate this, he pointed to a prominent characteristic of Anglicans: a Bishop as an officer of the church. Jefferson noted that this church office had not been established by Jesus in the Gospels but rather was instituted as a result of teachings in the Epistles. As he explained: "The epistles of Paul to Timothy and Titus are relied on (together with tradition) for the Apostolic institution of bishops."[18]

Indeed, bishops were not mentioned in the Gospels but only in the Epistles (such as 1 Timothy 3:1–2, Titus 1:7, and Philippians 1:1); therefore, not all denominations agreed about how churches should be governed. In fact, Congregationalist ministers vehemently rejected the idea of bishops, and fiercely resisted the appointment of any Anglican bishop for America.[19] But because these Congregational Christians did not approve of the office of a bishop as found in the Epistles did not mean that they were less Christian than the Anglicans, or that they rejected the tenets of salvation set forth in the Gospels.

Jefferson then offered a second example, pointing out that under the teachings of Jesus, every individual Christian was to be a minister of God; but subsequent denominations, invoking teachings from the Epistles, taught that ministers were to be only a narrow, specially called group.[20]

Other similar areas of distinction, and thus of Christian controversy, included infant baptism, predestination, eschatology, form of church government, mode of celebrating sacraments, and so forth. Jefferson believed that such contentions came not from the simplicity of what Christ had taught in the Gospels but rather from what was found in the Epistles.

Prior to the American Revolution, civil governments, including that in Virginia, had been guilty of passing coercive civil laws on issues raised only in the Epistles. To such laws, Jefferson strenuously objected:

> Why require those things in order to [receive] ecclesiastical communion which Christ does not require in order to [receive] life eternal? How can that be the church of Christ which excludes such persons from its communion as He will one day receive into the kingdom of heaven?[21]

Significantly, on multiple occasions throughout this lengthy piece, Jefferson included himself in the group of Christ-centered Christians, invoked literally dozens of Scriptures to prove his point, and used rhetoric rarely found from him in his later years.

Some argue that the religious content in Jefferson's 1776 "Notes on Religion" is insignificant or dispositive. They view this piece no differently than his letter to Peter Carr in which his "question with boldness even the existence of a God" statement was simply setting forth both sides of an issue rather than indicating his own personal views. Yet several things within the 1776 piece do make it quite different.

For example, when invoking religious arguments in his later writings (whether against slavery, for religious conscience, against government coercion in religious expressions, or for other reasons), or when writing lengthy epistles on religious topics (such as to Joseph Priestley, William Short, John Adams, et al), rarely does he give specificity of Scriptures, providing precise chapter and verse. But in this 1776 work, he does, and the sheer quantity of Scriptures he cites here far surpasses anything from late in life. He also repeatedly uses terms here that later in life he used only infrequently (such as "salvation," "Holy Spirit," "Holy Ghost," and "Godhead"). Also, this work contains comments that from a theological standpoint were gratuitous and not necessary to the argument he was making—such as when he states that the Scriptures are inspired, or that the Apostles Creed contains everything necessary to salvation. There were doctrinal points that Jefferson did not need to make in order to argue for his primary objective: state disestablishment. Additionally, when presenting several doctrines, he uses first-person, inclusive personal pronouns in this piece, whereas in later writings, he uses third-person and indefinite pronouns such as "some believe." So this 1776 work contains several elements that make it quite different from his later works, especially since all of these elements appear together at the same time in the same work.

So, during the Great Awakening and throughout the time of his marriage to Martha, the preponderance of evidence from that period suggests that Jefferson was a traditional Anglican Christian gentleman.*

Most people know someone whose religious faith was shaken by a tragedy. Such may have been the case with Jefferson. There is no question that he loved and adored his wife Martha and their six children (five daughters and one son). Martha was his constant companion and closest friend, and they were deeply devoted to each other. In fact, the children openly spoke of the sweet and precious relationship between the two, including Martha's "passionate attachment to him, and her

---

* During this time, there are a very few of his many letters in which he appears to question some points of traditional orthodoxy, but these are definitely the exception rather than the rule, which is a marked reversal from later in his life.

exalted opinion of him."[22] But the two also shared much loss and grief over their dear children. Of the six, only two lived to adulthood; Martha saw three of her children die, and Thomas saw five of them buried.

After only ten years of blissful marriage, Martha died, never physically recovering after the birth of their final child.[23] Her death was a stunning blow to Jefferson, and he was emotionally devastated. Presidential biographer William Stoddard writes that Jefferson "was utterly absorbed in sorrow and took no note of what was going on around him. His dream of life had been shattered, and it seemed as if life itself had lost its claim upon him, for no faith or hope of his reached onward and inward to any other."[24]

Jefferson's eldest daughter, Martha, named for her mother, was with him at the time of his wife's death, and she was her father's "constant companion" during "the first month of desolation which followed."[25] She recounted Jefferson's frame of mind during that tragic period, recalling:

> For four months that she lingered, he was never out of calling; when not at her bedside, he was writing in a small room which opened immediately at the head of her bed. A moment before the closing scene, he was led from the room almost in a state of insensibility by his sister Mrs. Carr, who with great difficulty got him into his library where he fainted and remained so long insensible that they feared he never would revive. The scene that followed I did not witness; but the violence of his emotion when, almost by stealth, I entered his room at night, to this day I dare not trust myself to describe. He kept [never left] his room three weeks, and I was never a moment from his

side. He walked almost incessantly night and day, only lying down occasionally, when nature was completely exhausted, on a pallet that had been brought in during his long fainting-fit. My aunts remained constantly with him for some weeks—I do not remember how many. When at last he left his room, he rode out, and from that time he was incessantly on horseback, rambling about the mountain in the least frequented roads, and just as often through the woods.[26]

Not long after Martha's death, Jefferson was sent by the Continental Congress as a diplomat to France. During those years, with the deep impact and clear remembrances and grief over Martha still so real to him, many questions remained unanswered and his faith was shaken. But by the time he became president, he had returned to a more stable faith position, albeit voicing more religious doubts than in earlier years.

One indication of his return toward more traditional beliefs was evident only four years into his presidency when he faced another personal tragedy. In 1804 his twenty-five-year-old daughter, Mary (Polly), was in poor health after giving birth to her third child. Her husband, a congressman, was away in Washington with President Jefferson, so Polly moved into Monticello where she could receive constant attention. As soon as the legislative session was over, Jefferson rushed home to help care for her, but just a few short weeks after he returned, his beloved Polly died. This left only his eldest daughter, Martha, and himself as the two remaining from the family of eight.

Martha's daughter (Jefferson's granddaughter) reported his reaction to the death of Polly:

My mother [Martha] has told me that on the day of her sister's death, she left her father alone for some hours. He then sent for her, and she found him with the Bible in his hands. He who has been so often and so harshly accused of unbelief, he, in his hour of intense affliction, sought and found consolation in the Sacred Volume.[27]

While such events impacted Jefferson's faith, it certainly appears that the greatest influence on his personal religious views, especially in his later years when he embraced and expressed so much unorthodoxy, was the religious disposition of the community around him. In many ways Jefferson seemed to be a mirror that accurately reflected the spiritual condition of his cherished central Virginia region around Charlottesville, the area in which he grew up and lived, and to which he retired after his presidency. Consider the changes in the Charlottesville area across the decades of Jefferson's life and how closely he seemed to reflect those community changes in his own spiritual beliefs.

Let's begin with the Great Awakening, which lasted approximately from 1730 to 1770 in the nation (but somewhat later in Virginia). While Virginia was officially Anglican in that time, the revival caused the rapid growth of Presbyterians, Baptists, and Methodists in the state. Many ministers moved easily between denominations—such as the Reverend Devereaux Jarratt, whom Bishop Francis Asbury credited with converting more people to Christianity than any other minister in the state.[28] Jarratt was trained as a Presbyterian but became an Anglican priest and spoke regularly in Methodist churches. Even the area's devout laymen were often active in multiple denominations, such as Jefferson's good friend and neighbor Henry Fry, who served with Jefferson on the board of Anglican churches but worked actively in Methodist churches.

This type of unprecedented interdenominational cooperation had been an emphasis of leading ministers during the Great Awakening, who accentuated the vital areas of the Scriptures on which nearly all Christians agreed rather than the areas about which they vigorously disagreed. Under the influence of such cooperation, even the state-established Anglican Church in Virginia softened its long-standing policy. As affirmed by Virginia historian William H. B. Thomas, "[T]he necessity of attending an Anglican church was relaxed—provided every man attend some church regularly."[29]

These ministers also directly addressed issues of personal piety. They presented a practical Christianity that touched daily behavior and provided relevant Biblical teaching with social applications, speaking not only of one's individual relationship with God but also of personal moral issues such as integrity, courage, drunkenness, profanity, and immorality.[30]

And many sermons addressed legislative policies of the day, contrasting existing or proposed public policies with Biblical positions on those issues, including taxation, good government, gambling, and slavery.[31] In fact, when Quaker leader John Woolman visited Virginia during this period and witnessed Southern slavery for the first time, he began advocating vigorously in behalf of emancipation.[32] This eventually resulted in the Quakers becoming a leading national voice against slavery.

The Great Awakening likewise promoted the concepts of individualism and inalienable rights (such as personal liberty, religious expression, freedom of conscience, and so on) and held that it was the duty of government to protect those rights.

It was during this time that many of the Dissenting (that is, non-Anglican) churches and ministers became active in politics, working to end preferential treatment of Anglicanism and to keep the government from interfering with their religious expressions and activities.

Another characteristic of the Great Awakenings was that blacks were very active and involved. National black evangelists such as Harry Hoosier and John Early spent time preaching to both black and white groups across central Virginia. The Reverend John Leland reported:

> The poor slaves, under all their hardships, discover as great inclination for religion as the free-born do. When they engage in the service of God, they spare no pains. It is nothing strange for them to walk twenty miles on Sunday morning to meeting, and back again at night. . . . [T]hey are remarkably fond of meeting together to sing, pray, and exhort, and sometimes preach. . . . When they attempt to preach, they seldom fail of being very zealous.[33]

In the Charlottesville region during this time, most ministers could probably be described as evangelical, regardless of their denominations or backgrounds. And Jefferson was close friends and maintained a strong personal relationship with many of them, including the Reverends Charles Clay, John Leland, James O'Kelly, and others.

Significantly, many of the practices common in Charlottesville during this time became lifelong established features of Jefferson's personal views. For example, he developed an enduring affinity for interdenominational cooperation, and emphasizing the doctrinal majors uniting Christians rather than the things dividing them—that is, stressing the simple unadorned teachings of the Gospels more than those of the Epistles. He also focused on protecting God-given inalienable rights, opposing state religious establishments, preserving the freedom of conscience, emancipating slaves, and so on—all features of the Great Awakening.

The First Great Awakening had barely ended in Virginia before the Second Great Awakening began, which lasted approximately from 1800 to 1840 across the nation. But by 1810 while the new revival was still going strong in other parts of the country, the spiritual condition of the Charlottesville area had turned in a very unsatisfactory direction, rejecting several traditional core Christian beliefs, a change that also became directly mirrored in Jefferson's religious views.

Addressing the unfortunate Charlottesville situation, evangelical minister John Holt Rice, who later helped Jefferson when he founded the University of Virginia, reported:

> Presbyterian congregations are decreasing every year and appear as if they would dwindle into nothing. The Baptists and Methodists are at a stand. A strange apathy has seized the people. . . . The people feel about nothing but money. As to religion, the very stillness of death reigns amongst us. I can find no resemblance to this part of the country but in Ezekiel's valley of dry bones [Ezekiel 37: 1–14].[34]

Holt further affirmed that the Methodists were not just "at a stand," but that "Mr. O'Kelly, the chief of the Christian Methodists . . . is nearly deserted by his followers."[35] And as pastors died off or retired during that time, many Charlottesville churches could find no replacements and simply closed their doors; in other cases, the pulpit might have remained unfilled for more than a decade.[36]

Simultaneous with these gloomy developments in Virginia, a new spiritual movement began in other parts of the country that eventually took deep root in Charlottesville. It was characterized by a radical call for a return to what it considered the simplest and most primitive form of Christianity, decrying many practices and doctrines of the modern Christian church that it deemed corrupt. Ironically, in seeking to revive a so-called earlier and purer version of Christianity, it actually introduced doctrinal heresy.[37] This movement became known as Christian Primitivism, or the Restoration Movement, and it had developed around four primary leaders.

One was Presbyterian minister Barton Stone of Kentucky, who led the famous Cane Ridge revival. (Stone had grown up Anglican but had also been a Baptist, Methodist, and Presbyterian.) He called for an end to denominations and argued that Christians should have "No creed but Christ, no book but the Bible."[38] He used only the simple descriptive title "Christian" for his congregations.

Another Restoration leader was Thomas Campbell (formerly a Presbyterian minister in Pennsylvania). He held many of the same beliefs as Stone, and his son Alexander advocated those positions in the western parts of Virginia. Their followers likewise embraced the unpretentious designation of "Christian."

A third principal figure was the Reverend Elias Smith of New Hampshire, who left the Baptist denomination to begin a new group that "agreed to consider ourselves Christians, without the addition of any unscriptural name."[39]

A fourth was Jefferson's friend, the Reverend James O'Kelly

of Virginia, who had actually started the primitivism trend well before any of the other three,[40] changing the name of his group from its original "Republican Methodists" to simply "Christians."

The followers of Stone, Smith, and O'Kelly came together in 1810, calling themselves "Christian Connection" (sometimes "Christian Connexion"). Campbell's group, while philosophically aligned with the other three, did not join them until years later, but in 1811 it did take the name "Christian Association."

Ministers embracing the teachings of these four groups became spiritual leaders in the Charlottesville area and had great influence there, with the number of their adherents growing rapidly over the next decade. But in their fervor to restore primitive Christianity and return to what they deemed to be the Bible's simplicity, they rejected many of Christendom's historic creeds, including the doctrine of the Trinity. As bluntly explained by the Reverend Barton Stone, "The word Trinity is not found in the Bible";[41] they therefore considered it a false doctrine of men, not of God.

Of the four major leaders, only O'Kelly openly embraced Trinitarianism;[42] Smith and Stone rejected it; and since Thomas Campbell took no position,[43] his followers included those from both Trinitarian and Anti-Trinitarian positions. It is interesting to note that none of the four groups rejected Jesus as the son of God or as the means of salvation but only as a part of the Trinity. Of course, as O'Kelly pointed out: "To me it appears that to deny Jesus Christ as being equal Deity is a destructive idea and in fact is, at least in effect, denying the Atonement."[44]

But with this view he was in the definite minority. The opposite position was openly expounded by leading ministers in Charlottesville for the last fifteen years of Jefferson's life—the time in which he had finally returned home, having at last permanently retired from public office.

Because Restorationists (Primitivists) claimed that the Bible was their only guidebook, they also rejected what they deemed to be several other "corrupt" traditions of Christianity. As the Reverend Elias Smith explained:

> In all the glorious things said of Christ, there is no mention of his Divinity, his being God-man, his incarnation, the human and the Divine nature, the human soul of Christ, his being God the Creator and yet the son of the Creator; these things are inventions of men and ought to be rejected.[45]

He therefore thundered:

> I am a Christian . . . holding as abominable in the sight of God, everything . . . such as Calvinism, Arminianism, Freewillism, Universalism, Reverends, Parsons, Chaplains, Doctors of Divinity, Clergy, Bands, Surplices, Notes, Creeds, Covenants, and Platforms.[46]

A review of writings associated with the Restoration Movement identifies distinct religious tenets that came to characterize it, including:

- A rejection of denominationalism and all denominational titles except that of "Christian"

- A stress on Christian unity

- An emphasis on the Gospels rather than the Epistles—on getting back to the teachings of Jesus, which therefore meant a de-emphasis on the Epistles and the Old Testament

- A rejection of church hierarchal structure: each church was local and to be locally controlled

- Anti-Trinitarianism, with an emphasis on using only explicit Bible language and Bible terms

- Anti-Calvinism, to the point of complete loathing of any of its doctrines

In fact, concerning the last point, the movement's hatred for Calvinism was so great that part of the reason Restorationists rejected the Trinity was simply because Calvin had embraced it. As Alexander Campbell affirmed, "I object to the *Calvinistic* doctrine of the Trinity."[47] He then attempted to defend his own concept of the Trinity, but his effort was so convoluted that the Reverend Stone rebuked him, claiming that by his attempt to defend Trinitarianism, he was actually embracing the Calvinism they all claimed to deplore.[48]

So strong was their hatred of Calvin and his doctrines that the Reverend Elias Smith even characterized Calvinism as part of ungodliness, declaring, "my mind was delivered from Calvinism, universalism, and deism—three doctrines of men which people love who do not love holiness."[49]

Sadly, the Restoration and Christian Primitivist Movement was the dominant religious force in Charlottesville in Jefferson's later years, and he openly embraced and promoted the same views held by so many of the professing Christians and ministers in his own community.

It is possible that Jefferson had earlier developed these same beliefs before they were espoused by the Primitivists, for in his library he owned books from both America and

Europe expressing those theological views.[50] Or perhaps he had held Primitivist beliefs but did not articulate them until he retired from public office and become associated with ministers boldly proclaiming the same views. Or perhaps he did develop these views as a result of his later active involvement with the Primitivist and Restoration Movement.

Regardless of the reason, whether the proverbial chicken or the egg came first, the result was that Jefferson's writings throughout this later time are by far the most unorthodox of his life. They routinely reflect the major tenets of Christian Primitivism and Restorationism and use almost the exact tenor and words as those of the Restoration minsters surrounding him.

Consider some of Jefferson's declarations from late in life that reflected and affirmed the major beliefs of the Movement.

ON PRIMITIVISM AND RESTORATION

In his later years Jefferson repeatedly wrote of the need to return to primitive Christianity and restore it to the time of Jesus. Notice how frequently in these years he used the terms restoration and primitivism or variants thereof—terms he rarely used in earlier writings:

> [T]he genuine and simple religion of Jesus will one day be restored such as it was preached and practiced by Himself. . . . I hope that the day of restoration is to come.[51]

> Happy in the prospect of a restoration of primitive Christianity, I must leave to younger athletes to encounter and lop off the false branches which have been engrafted into it by the mythologists of the middle and modern ages.[52]

I . . . express my gratification with your efforts for the revival of primitive Christianity in your quarter.[53]

[I]t is only by . . . getting back to the plain and unsophisticated precepts of Christ that we become real Christians.[54]

Had the doctrines of Jesus been preached always as pure as they came from His lips, the whole civilized world would now have been Christian.[55]

ON CHRISTIAN UNITY AND COOPERATION

Jefferson first embraced Christian nonpreferentialism and interdenominational cooperation during the Great Awakening. Recall that his 1779 Statute for Religious Freedom (finally passed in 1786) ensured that the state would no longer favor the Anglican denomination; and in 1800 he had helped institute the policy whereby ministers from all denominations were invited to preach in the church at the Capitol. Even late in life when he seemed less favorable to orthodox Christianity, he still invited all denominations to establish seminaries (or what he termed "a professorship of their own tenets"[56]) at his beloved University of Virginia. Recall, too, that Jefferson had regularly given money to many different ministers and denominations and helped them build new churches.

Jefferson also openly celebrated those parts of the country wherein the various denominations "condescend to interchange with . . . the civilities of preaching freely and frequently in each other's meeting-houses,"[57] and he specifically praised the locations in Charlottesville (such as the "union building" and the county courthouse) where the various denominations would rotate the preaching responsibilities among themselves. As he extolled to a friend:

In our village of Charlottesville . . . [w]e have four sects, but
without either church or meeting-house. The court house is
the common temple, one Sunday in the month to each. Here,
Episcopalian and Presbyterian, Methodist and Baptist meet
together, join in hymning their Maker, listen with attention
and devotion to each other's preachers, and all mix in society
with perfect harmony.[58]

Jefferson believed strongly that the teachings of Jesus
brought unity but that the teachings of denominations brought
disunity and conflict. As he explained to John Adams at the
height of the Restoration Movement:

No doctrines of His lead to schism. It is the speculations of
crazy theologists which have made a Babel of a religion the
most moral and sublime ever preached to man, and calculated to heal and not to create differences. These religious ani-
mosities I impute to those who call themselves His ministers
and who engraft their casuistries [personal interpretations]
on the stock of His simple precepts. I am sometimes more
angry with them than is authorized by the blessed charities
which He preached.[59]

ON EMPHASIZING THE GOSPELS AND DE-EMPHASIZING THE EPISTLES AND OLD TESTAMENT

Jefferson had always drawn a clear distinction between the
simple words of Jesus found in the Gospels and those found
in the rest of the Bible—the point he had made strongly in his
1776 Notes on Religion. But during the Restoration Movement,
that distinction took on a new fervor, leading not only to a near
wholesale rejection of anything not found in the four Gospels

but sometimes even of things found in them if he suspected those portions had been added as part of what he believed were the corrupted teachings introduced by the Apostles. For example, in those later years, he declared:

> In the New Testament, there is internal evidence that parts of it have proceeded from an extraordinary man, and that other parts are of the fabric of very inferior minds. It is as easy to separate those parts as to pick out diamonds from dunghills.[60]

> Among the sayings and discourses imputed to Him [Jesus] by His biographers [in the four Gospels], I find many passages of fine imagination, correct morality, and of the most lovely benevolence; and others again, of so much ignorance, so much absurdity, so much untruth, charlatanism and imposture as to pronounce it impossible that such contradictions should have proceeded from the same Being. I separate, therefore, the gold from the dross; restore to Him the former and leave the latter to the stupidity of some, and roguery of others of His disciples. Of this band of dupes and impostors, Paul was the great Coryphaeus [leader and spokesperson] and first corruptor of the doctrines of Jesus.[61]

Another non-Gospel text against which Jefferson took a strong stand was the book of Revelation. In 1825 General Alexander Smyth, a military officer from the War of 1812 and a longtime Virginia legislator, sought Jefferson's opinion about a work he had prepared on the end times and the book of Revelation. Jefferson responded, telling Smyth:

> [Y]ou must be so good as to excuse me, because I make it an invariable rule to decline ever giving [public] opinions on

new publications in any case whatever. No man on earth has less taste or talent for criticism than myself, and least and last of all should I undertake to criticize works on the Apocalypse. It is between fifty and sixty years since I read it, and I then considered it as merely the ravings of a maniac, no more worthy nor capable of explanation than the incoherencies of our own nightly dreams.[62]

But this negative opinion about the book of Revelation did not mean that Jefferson had no opinion on the end times, for much earlier in life he had addressed this issue. Jesus had specifically addressed this subject in the Gospels, and so in 1783 Jefferson had instructed his daughter Martha:

I hope you will have good sense enough to disregard these foolish predictions that the world is to be at an end soon. The Almighty has never made known to anybody at what time He created it, nor will He tell anybody when He means to put an end to it [Matthew 24:36]—if ever He means to do it. As to preparations for that event, the best way is for you to be always prepared for it [Matthew 24:42–44]. The only way to be so is never to do nor say anything amiss or to do anything wrong. If ever you are about to say anything amiss or to do anything wrong, consider beforehand; you will feel something within you which will tell you it is wrong and ought not to be said or done; this is your conscience, and be sure to obey it. Our Maker has given us all this faithful internal monitor, and if you always obey it you will always be prepared for the end of the world, or for a much more certain event, which is death.[63]

Just as Jefferson had come to deprecate the Epistles, so, too, did he the Old Testament. For example, during the Restoration Movement and late in his life he wrote a lengthy letter to William Short, whom he considered an adopted son, extolling what Jesus taught in the Gospels but deriding what had been taught in the Old Testament:

> That sect [the Jews] had presented for the object of their worship a Being of terrific character: cruel, vindictive, capricious, and unjust. Jesus, taking for His type the best qualities of the human head and heart (wisdom, justice, goodness) and adding to them power, ascribed all of these (but in infinite perfection) to the Supreme Being, and formed Him really worthy of their adoration.[64]

In the same letter, Jefferson also denounced the Old Testament tendency toward continual fighting between nations, contrasting that practice with what Jesus had taught, claiming that "The one [Moses] instilled into his people the most anti-social spirit towards other nations; the other [Jesus] preached philanthropy and universal charity and benevolence."[65]

Jefferson disapproved the Old Testament position of "an eye for an eye, a tooth for a tooth"[66] and disagreed with Old Testament theology "which supposes the God of infinite justice to punish the sins of the fathers upon their children, unto the 3rd and 4th generation."[67] In short, in late life, Jefferson, just like the ministers of the Christian Primitivism Movement, focused almost exclusively on the Gospels, openly criticizing both the Epistles and the Old Testament.

ANTI-CALVINISTIC

Throughout most of his life, Jefferson had viewed Presbyterians (the denomination most closely associated with Calvinism) as allies, declaring that "the Presbyterian spirit is known to be so congenial with friendly liberty."[68] Recall, too, that in 1777 he had even been a primary founder of the Calvinistic Reformed Church of Charlottesville,[69] a theologically close cousin of Calvinism. And one of the largest personal contributions he made was to help build a new Presbyterian church.[70] But with the Restoration Movement's hatred of Calvinist theology and its strident rejection of Reformed theology, Presbyterians became an object of Jefferson's denunciation:

> The Presbyterian clergy are loudest, the most intolerant of all sects,* the most tyrannical and ambitious—ready at the word of the lawgiver (if such a word could be now obtained) to put the torch to the pile and to rekindle in this virgin

---

* According to some scholars, another reason that Jefferson came to dislike Presbyterians was their opposition to the professorship of Thomas Cooper at the University of Virginia after it became known that Cooper held Unitarian beliefs. Because Jefferson feared that their opposition might be turned against the university in general, Cooper was disinvited from teaching, thus angering Jefferson. (Recall from Lie #2 that Jefferson inquired only into the qualifications of character and knowledge for his University faculty, not their religious beliefs, and he did not appreciate others doing so.) While this is perhaps correct, Jefferson forthrightly told Cooper that "the real ground of our decision was that our funds were, in fact, hypothecated [pledged in payment] for five or six years to redeem the loan we had reluctantly made" (letter to Dr. Thomas Cooper on August 14, 1820). So possibly for the type of interference and opposition exhibited by Presbyterians in the Cooper affair, but especially because of their adherence to the doctrines of Calvin, Jefferson came to loathe them in his later years. He also seemed to have been drawn to denominations that embraced more democratic forms of church government (such as the Baptists), generally more openly criticizing those with hierarchical church government.

hemisphere the flames in which their oracle Calvin consumed the poor Servetus [a leader in the Reformation whom Calvin permitted to be burned at the stake for heresy regarding Trinitarianism], because he could not find in his Euclid the proposition which has demonstrated that three are one and one is three, nor subscribe to that of Calvin that magistrates have a right to exterminate all heretics to Calvinistic creed. They pant to reestablish by law that holy inquisition which they can now only infuse into public opinion.[71]

Jefferson further declared that "[m]y fundamental principle would be the reverse of Calvin's"[72] and that "Calvinism has introduced into the Christian religion more new absurdities than its leader had purged it of old ones" during the Reformation.[73] Jefferson even listed several specific teachings of Calvin with which he vehemently disagreed, including Calvin's claim "that God, from the beginning, elected certain individuals to be saved and certain others to be damned; and that no crimes of the former can damn them, no virtues of the latter save."[74] He also denounced Calvin's teaching "that good works, or the love of our neighbor, are nothing" and "that reason in religion is of unlawful use."[75]

Jefferson, reflecting what became his personal detestation of Calvin, pointedly told John Adams:

I can never join Calvin in addressing his God. He was indeed an atheist (which I can never be), or rather his religion was daemonism [worship of an evil god]. If ever man worshipped a false god, he did. The being described in his five points is not the God Whom you and I acknowledge and adore—the Creator and Benevolent Governor of the world, but a demon of malignant spirit. It would be more pardonable to believe in no God at all than to blaspheme Him by the atrocious attributes of Calvin.[76]

BIBLE SPECIFIC LANGUAGE AND ANTI-TRINITARIANISM

As noted earlier, Restorationists and Christian Primitivists thought that if a term was not in the Bible, then it should not be in Christianity. This is why the Reverend Stone had said that the doctrine of the trinity should be rejected. In the later years of Jefferson's life, he openly embraced the same view. Like the Reverend Elias Smith, he, too, delineated what he considered to be non-Biblical beliefs that should be rejected, including the "immaculate conception of Jesus, his deification, the creation of the world by him [instead of God], his miraculous powers, his resurrection and visible ascension, his corporeal presence in the Eucharist, the Trinity; original sin, atonement, regeneration, election, orders of hierarchy, &c."[77] He also predicted, wrongly:

> [T]he day will come when the mystical generation [i.e., the conception] of Jesus by the Supreme Being as his father, in the womb of a virgin, will be classed with the fable of the generation of Minerva [the Roman virgin goddess] in the brain of Jupiter.[78]

Are such statements heretical by the standards of orthodox Christianity? Absolutely. But unfortunately, this is what was being preached and advocated by religious leaders in central Virginia who were leading what titled major Christian movements of that day. Jefferson attended their churches and heard this message directly from them.* It should be remembered, however, that the Restoration Movement also had many sound doctrines (that Jesus was the Savior, baptism and communion were important, the teachings of Jesus were to be diligently studied and followed, and so forth), but they clearly held several errant ones. It is Jefferson's writings in this latter category—writings primarily from his declining years—that understandably cause so much consternation among traditional Christians.

UNITARIANISM

The Primitivist emphasis on Christian unity and Anti-Trinitarianism provided the seedbed in which Unitarianism flourished. But it is important to note that Unitarianism in Jefferson's day was not what it is has become today.

There is some debate as to when Unitarianism (which at that time meant an acceptance of the Christian God but a rejection of the Trinity) first appeared in America. It is generally agreed that William Ellery Channing offered a clear account of its doctrines in 1819, and no one disputes that the American Unitarian Association was formed in 1825.[79] Unitarianism had definite theological problems, but even then it was still considered a Christian denomination.[80] Indeed, observers in that day reported, "several of the ablest defenders of Christianity against

---

*   That Jefferson did so is yet another affirmation of the spiritual transformation that he had undergone in his later years. Thirty years earlier, some of his closest friends and correspondents had been evangelical ministers such as Charles Clay, John Leland, James O'Kelly, and others who openly embraced traditional orthodox Christianity and Trinitarianism. But in his later years this changed, and his close associates and correspondents became Anti-Trinitarians such as Joseph Priestly, William Short, John Adams, and others.

the attacks of infidels have been Unitarians."[81] But in 1838 it underwent a radical change when Ralph Waldo Emerson began slowly reshaping Channing's 1819 teachings, which were still largely Christian-professing, into . . .

> a Transcendentalist version of the ethical theism of Plato, the Stoics and Kant, coordinated with the nascent evolutionist science of the day and the newly explored mysticism of the ancient East. This new religious philosophy, as construed and applied by the Boston preacher Theodore Parker and other disciples of Emerson, included the other great ethnic faiths with Christianity in a universal religion of Humanity and through its intellectual hospitality operated to open Unitarian fellowship to evolutionists, monists, pragmatists, and humanists.[82]

Many of today's ultra-heretical Unitarian doctrines did not exist at the time of Jefferson. This includes the modern Unitarian beliefs that: education and character development is the only way to salvation; hell is not real and there is no penalty for sin; everyone will go to heaven; the worship of self is superior to the worship of God; none of the Scripture are inspired; and so forth.[83] At Jefferson's time, the primary heterodox doctrine was a rejection of the Trinity and the idea that Jesus was the son of God but not God Himself.

In addition to Jefferson's connection with Christian Primitivism, there were at least four additional societal reasons why he could be comfortable with Unitarianism.

First, perhaps more than any other religious group in that day, the Unitarians placed a very strong emphasis on teaching morals. Recall Jefferson's keen interest in this subject with his personal and diligent study of the moral teachings of leaders from the previous three millennia. In fact, the Unitarians' emphasis on morality was so strong that it was the reason that President John Quincy Adams (who held Biblically orthodox positions) attended a Unitarian Church in Washington, DC. After openly acknowledging that "I did not subscribe to many of his [the minister's] doctrines, particularly not to the fundamental one of his Unitarian creed,"[84] Adams then explained that he attended the church because the minister's "moral discourses were always good, and . . . I listened to them with pleasure and profit."[85] Jefferson likewise found Unitarian moral teachings to be very appealing, for its ministers at that time laid great stress on the practical day-to-day application of the moral teachings of Jesus and the Bible; so did Jefferson.

Second, Unitarians took a strong position against slavery and for emancipation. Although abolition advocates reported that "the Unitarians, next to the Quakers, seem to have acted with more zeal in behalf of the Negroes,"[86] some Unitarians disputed that, arguing that they had done even more than the Quakers. As Unitarian minister Samuel May explained, "We Unitarians have given to the antislavery cause more preachers, writers, lecturers, agents, poets, than any other denomination."[87] Emancipation was obviously a position that Jefferson had advocated throughout his life, so it was another reason he felt at home among Unitarians.

Third, Unitarians emphasized the interdenominational cooperation that, as has already been demonstrated, was a lifelong hallmark of Jefferson's personal beliefs.

Fourth, while other denominations confined their membership to only those Christians who embraced their specific doctrines, the Unitarians welcomed all who called themselves Christian. This type of open Christian acceptance was particularly attractive to Jefferson, for he had been continually attacked and vilified by specific denominations of Christians, even during the times when he was publicly expressing orthodox Christian beliefs. But among Unitarians he found acceptance and a personal peace—a relief from unrelenting attacks and controversies. (He seemed to forget, however, that many of the Federalists who attacked him during his campaigns had been New England Unitarians; but at that time he was probably more cognizant of their Federalist political affiliation than their Unitarian religious one.)

Perhaps as a result of the vicious attacks he had suffered, Jefferson became generally loath to talk about his personal faith with others unless they were among a handful of his very close personal friends.[*] And even with these, he would still ask them to return his letter after they had read it[88] or else burn, destroy, or keep it secret[89] so that its contents would not become fodder for his enemies.

In fact, two decades earlier, at a time when his publicly-expressed Christian beliefs still appeared generally orthodox, Jefferson told his attorney general, Levi Lincoln, that if content from his private letters about religion should "get into print," the effect would be that he "would become the butt of every set of disquisitions which every priest would undertake to write on every tenet it expresses. Their object is not truth, but matter whereon to write against."[90]

---

[*] Including Benjamin Rush, Charles Clay, John Adams, William Short, and Thomas Cooper.

Lengthy experience had taught Jefferson to let nothing about his religious views become public. He therefore largely adopted a live-and-let-live approach to this subject. As he explained to one inquirer:

> I take no part in controversies, religious or political. At the age of eighty, tranquility is the greatest good of life; and the strongest of our desires, that of dying in the good will of all mankind. And with the assurances of all my good will to Unitarian and Trinitarian, to Whig and Tory, accept for yourself that of my entire respect.[91]

Perhaps it was because Jefferson was so drawn to the cooperation and acceptance of Restoration and Primitivism that he also accepted so many of their other Unitarian beliefs. But whatever the reason, he found early Unitarianism to be personally satisfying and wanted it to sweep the country, optimistically declaring late in life, "I confidently expect that the present generation will see Unitarianism become the general religion of the United States."[92] He hopefully expressed, "I trust that there is not a young man now living in the United States who will not die an Unitarian."[93]

But in this, Jefferson was wrong. By the time he died four years later, the trend was already swinging back; the effect of the Second Great Awakening was substantially slowing Unitarianism across the nation. O'Kelly, one of the Founders of the Restoration Movement and the only clear Trinitarian among its four major leaders, wrote in 1824: "The Arians [those who do not believe that the Godhead is equal], or Unitarians, in this state [North Carolina] perhaps are fading fast; some of their preachers, I hope, may be convinced of their dangerous error and return to the Christian Church."[94]

Regrettably, Jefferson did not live long enough to experience the spiritual reversal that eventually occurred in his central Virginia valley. And given the pattern of his life, it is certainly possible that had time permitted, he might well have changed his position and come back to more traditional Christian beliefs.

So what conclusions can be made about Jefferson's spiritual condition and the question of whether or not he was a Christian? Well, Jefferson definitely called himself a Christian. For example, during the Restoration Movement he told his old friend Charles Thomson, "I am a real Christian, that is to say, a disciple of the doctrines of Jesus."[95] And well before that, he had similarly told Benjamin Rush: "To the corruptions of Christianity I am indeed opposed; but not to the genuine precepts of Jesus Himself. I am a Christian in the only sense in which He wished any one to be: sincerely attached to His doctrines in preference to all others."[96]

But such unequivocal declarations are not the end of the story, for many of the declarations made by Jefferson during the period of the Restoration Movement, although they are consistent with Christian Primitivism, definitely do not comport with an orthodox understanding of what it means to be a Christian. Apparently, Jefferson himself recognized this, and in 1819 he acknowledged to the Reverend Ezra Stiles, "I am of a sect by myself, as far as I know."[97]

Dumas Malone, the Pulitzer Prize–winning biographer of Thomas Jefferson, understood the difficulty of analyzing of Jefferson's faith. He acknowledged that on the one hand, "This apostle of spiritual freedom regarded himself as a Christian, and unquestionably he was one in his ethical standards."[98] But on the other hand, when one references the statements he made especially during his latter years, "Jefferson did not refer to the Messiah, the Savior, or the Christ," although he did continue to have "unbounded admiration for Jesus."[99]

Significantly, for many of the Christian doctrines that Jefferson called into question in his last fifteen or so years, somewhere across his earlier sixty-eight years there had been occasions in which he had directly or indirectly embraced that same doctrine.* For example, only a decade before Jefferson entered the Restoration Movement, he personally assured Dr. Benjamin Rush that "he believed in the Divine mission of the Savior of the World," "in the Divine institution of the Sabbath," and "likewise in the resurrection, and a future state of rewards and punishments."[100] After conversing with Jefferson on his personal religious views of Christianity, Rush, an outspoken Christian leader, confessed to Jefferson that "you are by no means so heterodox as you have been supposed to be by your enemies,"[101] although acknowledging that there were still some theological differences between himself and Jefferson.[102] So Jefferson did undergo changes of his spiritual views across the years.

And Jefferson's life also seemed to demonstrate what still occurs too frequently today. If someone is personally wounded and deeply hurt by those who openly profess themselves to be representatives of Jesus Christ (as had been the case with the ministers who viciously lied about and unscrupulously

---

* Specifically concerning the Divinity of Christ, in his earlier years, Jefferson, on sparse and limited occasions, had expressed uncertainties about and struggled over that subject, but in later years his writings on the subject turned from uncertainly to a certainty that Jesus was not Divine, and from a sparseness to a frequency in expressing that belief.

attacked Jefferson in the presidential campaign of 1800), then the aggrieved person often turns against and rejects the beliefs professed by those who injured him. This response, while understandable, is still not excusable from an eternal viewpoint. Nevertheless, it may well have been a significant contributing factor to push Jefferson in an unorthodox direction. Certainly, his writings about Christianity and many of its doctrines took on a different tone after his presidency than they had before it.

No human can know whether or not Jefferson finished his life as a Christian in good standing with God through Jesus Christ; only God knows. Perhaps Jefferson, having once had a traditional Anglican Christian faith which later became contaminated and weak, fits into the category of 1 Corinthians 3:15 that "if anyone's work is burned up, he will suffer loss, though he himself will be saved, but only as through fire."

But while Jefferson's ultimate condition as a Christian is uncertain, several things are definitely certain, including the unequivocal fact that Jefferson was *not* anti-religion or an atheist. As he affirmed to John Adams during the time of his greatest unorthodoxy, "[A]n atheist . . . I can never be."[103]

Likewise, Jefferson was definitely not a deist. A deist believes in an impersonal God uninvolved with mankind, and embraces the "clockmaker theory" that there was once a God Who made the universe and wound it up like a clock but that it now runs of its own volition; the clockmaker is gone, so prayer is therefore unavailing because the clockmaker no longer intervenes in the affairs of men.[104] It is clear that none of Jefferson's religious writings from any period of his life reveal anything less than his strong conviction in a personal God[105] Who answers prayers and interposes in the affairs of mankind[106] and before Whom every individual will stand to be judged.[107]

And not only was Jefferson definitely neither an atheist nor a deist, he also was not a secularist—nor was he irreligious. To the contrary, he strongly promoted religion in general and Christian values in particular. In fact, after Jefferson's death when his grandson was queried about Jefferson's religious opinions and beliefs, he reported:

> [I] never heard from him the expression of one thought, feeling, or sentiment inconsistent with the highest moral standard or the purest Christian charity in its most enlarged sense. His moral character was of the highest order, founded upon the purest and sternest models of antiquity, softened, chastened and developed by the influences of the all-pervading benevolence of the doctrines of Christ, which he had intensely and admiringly studied. . . . In his contemplative moments, his mind turned to religion, which he studied thoroughly. He had seen and read much of the abuses and perversions of Christianity; he abhorred those abuses and their authors and denounced them without reserve. He was regular in his attendance on church, taking his prayer-book with him. He drew the plan of the Episcopal Church in Charlottesville, was one of the largest contributors to its erection, and contributed regularly to the support of its minister. I paid, after his death, his subscription of $200 to the erection of the Presbyterian Church in the same village. A gentleman of some distinction calling on him, and expressing his disbelief in the truths of the Bible, his reply was, "Then, sir, you have studied it to little purpose." He was guilty of no profanity himself and did not tolerate it in

others—he detested impiety, and his favorite quotation for his young friends as a basis for their morals was the XVth Psalm of David.[108]

Jefferson experienced a definite gradual drift in his spiritual life, and late in life rejected some key tenets of orthodox Christianity, including those regarding the Divinity of Christ. Nevertheless, throughout his long life he always identified himself as a Christian, was steadfastly pro-Jesus, and was consistently pro-Christian in his public demeanor and public endeavors.

Thomas Jefferson:
An American Hero

ur examination of historical primary source documents has proven that the picture of Jefferson's faith and morals painted by critics today is often wrong:

1. DNA evidence has not proved that Jefferson fathered any children outside of his marriage to Martha. His moral reputation was attacked two centuries ago by enemies making what they knew were vindictive but groundless charges, attempting to besmirch him during a presidential election. Jefferson, acknowledging that God knew the truth, regularly appealed to Him as his judge on this issue. He longed for the time when the Great Judge would clear him of any moral wrong-doing and prove the accusations false.

2. Jefferson enjoyed a traditional religious education and was not responsible for instituting secular, religion-free education in any educational endeavor in which he was involved. As part of his work to disestablish an official state denomination and to institute denominational

nonpreferentialism, he founded America's first major trans- or nondenominational university. He invited multiple Christian denominations be an active part of university life and personally directed that religious instruction and activities occur on campus.

3. Jefferson did not write a Bible of any kind. He did create two religious works about Jesus that were what he titled them. The first was an abridgment of the New Testament for the use of Indians and the second was a compilation of the moral teachings of Jesus for his own personal study. In both he included multiple references to the metaphysical—that is, the supernatural and miraculous. Furthermore, Jefferson also owned a number of Bibles that he personally used and studied, was a member of the Virginia Bible Society, financially supported the printing of Bibles, and gave Bibles to younger family members. And the Bible was also used in educational institutions he helped start or direct, from Washington's public schools to the University of Virginia.

4. Jefferson was not a racist who hated blacks and opposed civil rights, but rather was a lifelong advocate of emancipation. His efforts were largely unsuccessful because of the state in which he lived. If he had been born in a northern state and had undertaken the same efforts, he would have succeeded and would be heralded today as one of America's greatest civil rights advocates. Even so, he was regularly praised by subsequent generations for his civil rights efforts and was favorably invoked by numerous civil rights leaders, both black and white.

Jefferson referenced religious beliefs and teachings as the basis of his views on emancipation and equality, repeatedly declaring that God was just and that He would eventually bring slavery in America to an end, one way or another.

5. Jefferson repeatedly incorporated religious activities directly into public settings. In fact, he invoked the "wall of separation" between church and state metaphor only once, and then only to affirm the historic understanding that government had no authority to regulate or prohibit religious activities or expressions. Throughout his political career he called for days of prayer, introduced religious bills in the state legislature, signed numerous federal acts supporting religious groups and activities, and facilitated official churches inside government buildings. Were Jefferson alive today, he would likely be one of the firmest voices in denouncing a secularized public square.

6. Jefferson was not anticlerical. He did repeatedly denounce clergy who participated in the unholy alliance of "kingcraft and priestcraft." He also opposed those who supported the legally-enforced state establishments of religions that favored one denomination over another. Such clergy viewed Jefferson as their enemy (and he they), but ministers who sought legal equality and non-preferentialism were his outspoken supporters. Jefferson praised many such clergy, wrote letters of recommendation for them, gave generously to their churches, and recruited them to run for political office. He was the

hero of countless ministers and remained close friends with many throughout his life.

7. Jefferson was not a secularist or an atheist. He believed that God intervened in the affairs of men and nations. He thus regularly prayed, believing that God would answer his prayers for his family, his country, the unity of the Christian church, and the end of slavery. And while he always called himself a Christian, he ended his life as a Christian Primitivist, being in personal disagreement with some historic tenets of orthodox Christianity while still holding fast to other traditionally sound beliefs. Yet throughout his long and winding spiritual journey there was never a time when he was anything other than pro-Jesus.

Jefferson was a complex person who lived a long and public life. It is possible to find (or concoct) isolated evidence that supports any of the falsehoods told about him by many modern scholars and popular authors, but a careful examination of the totality of Jefferson's own words and deeds, along with other primary source evidence, definitely refutes modern lies about him.

The reason that such an investigation became necessary is because of the general historical illiteracy that has engulfed the nation over the past half-century. Much of this adverse change has been facilitated by six historical malpractices now present in far too many classrooms and curriculums:

1. *Historical Negativism*, which pours out a steady flow of demeaning portrayals of traditional heroes, values, and institutions. It rarely mentions the positive and

frequently presents the negative as if it were the whole story. Consequently, even though Jefferson was venerated and honored for generations, today he is often attacked, belittled, and dismissed with epithets such as "atheist," "rapist," "deadbeat dad," "vindictive racist," "slave-owning, serial slave, sex addict," and similar pejoratives.

2. *Historical Relativism*, which rejects absolutes and transcendent principles in history, religion, culture, and law. Assessments against irrefutable facts or fixed standards are avoided, whether comparing legal systems, political philosophy, or morals. Hence, students are taught that all forms of governments are good; all religions are profitable; all economic systems are workable; and values are merely personal preferences, with demonstrable differences deemed either inconsequential or simply ignored. And since individuals are to interpret events for themselves, subjectivity and feelings prevail over objectivity, truth, and facts. Hence, because some individuals personally dislike the fact that specific Virginia laws directly impeded Jefferson from releasing his slaves, as he personally desired to do, they instead accuse him of being an "aggressive and vindictive" racist – a "creepy, brutal hypocrite" who was "a patron saint for white supremacists;" this may be their personal opinion, but it is not supported by objective facts. So, too, do many other accusations made against Jefferson by relativistts reflect their own personal views rather than historical reality.

3. *Antinationalism*, which rejects traditional national unifying values and institutions and often encourages loyalty to things larger or smaller than the nation, such as a global awareness or an emphasis on one's subgroup. This deemphasis on the nation, combined with an overemphasis on negatives about it, has weakened a veneration and respect for those things that make the nation unique and distinctive, including our Constitution, republican form of government, religious faith, and common morality, as well as traditional heroes such as Thomas Jefferson.

4. *Modernism*, which examines historical incidents and persons as if they lived today rather than in the past, thereby separating history from its context and producing flawed conclusions. For example, because for decades no state university has included religious activities and classes for all its students, the assumption is that it was probably the same in Jefferson's day, so his views on education must have been secular, and evidence to the contrary is simply ignored as implausible. And because for decades religious expressions have been expunged from the public square, it is simply accepted that it was also the same two centuries ago; thus any Jefferson actions otherwise are simply dismissed out of hand as being inaccurate.

5. *Minimalism*, which often reduces complicated situations and individuals to simplistic characterizations. Hence, comments Jefferson made that rejected some tenets of orthodox Christianity, particularly late in life, become the basis for portraying him as a lifelong secularist who

opposed Christianity. There is no consideration given to the possibility that Jefferson had a complicated spiritual journey, and no notice is taken of the adverse effects of Christian Primitivism and Restorationism upon him. Similarly, modern scholars and writers often extrapolate from his statements criticizing specific ministers who were his political enemies or who supported tyrannical state-established institutions and practices to the conclusion that he was completely anticlerical. While Minimalism, or missing the major point, can occur through oversimplification, it can also transpire through overcomplication—that is, not seeing the forest for the trees. (Examples of how academics sometimes fixate on the minor to the exclusion of the major were presented in the Preface.)

6. *A Rigid or Unrelenting Secularism*, which ignores or misportrays religious influences, motivations, and persons. This can occur through deliberate omission, or by the selective presentation of facts. For example, many who write on religion and the Founders focus on the few whose religious views and practices are not as clearly orthodox as most Founders. They then generalize from this unrepresentative group of Founders to the entire Founding generation. Or more commonly, they just remain silent about the important role faith played in the lives of virtually all Americans at that time. (As we have seen even with respect to Jefferson, although he came to reject some specific tenets of orthodox Christianity, overall religious faith remained important

to him throughout his entire life.) This particular malpractice is one of the more pernicious and difficult to detect, for one has to already be familiar with major parts of history in order to recognize what is being distorted or left out. Therefore exploiting what most citizens do not know about Jefferson and his faith, secularist writers can thus take his directive to "Question with boldness even the existence of a God" and successfully assert that he is encouraging a disbelief in God when actually he was encouraging good apologetics. Or they can present his statement that "it does me no injury for my neighbor to say there are twenty gods or no god" and assert his ambivalence to religious beliefs when in reality he is passionately arguing against any right of government to interfere with the sacred rights of religious conscience. But unless a reader is already familiar with the full context of such quotes, secularist writers can use them as compelling "evidence" that Jefferson himself was a rigid secularist.

The malpractices discussed above do horrible damage to history, but the problems don't stop there. They also lead to bad policy. For instance, in *Everson v. Board of Education*, Justice Wiley Rutledge observed that "No provision of the Constitution is more closely tied to or given content by its generating history than the religious clause of the First Amendment. It is at once the refined product and the terse summation of that history."[1] Fair enough. But the problem is that he then went on to argue that the Founders intended to erect a high wall of separation between church and state that required a secularization of the public square. As we have seen, this was not true even for Thomas Jefferson; and it certainly was not the case for the Founders who actually drafted and ratified the First Amendment. Yet court after court has restricted religious liberty and expression in the name of this poor historical analysis, even regularly substituting Jefferson's metaphor in place of the First Amendment's actual language.[2] (Fortunately, some Justices and courts do have a far better grasp of history. Realizing that the religion clauses of the First Amendment were intended to protect religion and religious expressions, they are now beginning to correctly acknowledge that Jefferson's "wall of separation" is an "extra-constitution" and "tiresome" metaphor, and are returning to upholding rather than prohibiting public religious expressions.[3])

In the words of former US Supreme Court Chief Justice William Rehnquist:

> [T]he greatest injury of the "wall" notion is its mischie-vous diversion of judges from the actual intentions of the drafters of the Bill of Rights . . . no amount of repetition of historical errors in judicial opinions can make the errors true. The "wall of separation between church and State" is a metaphor based on bad history. . . . It should be frankly and explicitly abandoned.[4]

To avoid bad history and thus the bad public policies that result from it, we must learn to recognize and avoid these six historical malpractices. Perhaps the best means for doing so is given in Romans 12:21, which instructs us to defeat the evil with the good—to emphasize the antithesis. So what are the antidotes for the six poisons so often injected into American history today?

The effects and influences of *Historical Negativism* can be overcome by remembering that whenever any negative historical story is presented, check and see if there is a second view, or if there were any positive aspects that were omitted from the account. Negatives will always be easy to find and emphasize (such as the witch trials), but identifying the positives (such as the numerous contributions of the Puritans to our successful civil institutions and practices) will take deliberate effort.

Thomas Jefferson understood how easily negatives could become the sole focus; he therefore made deliberate efforts to bring out the positives. His grandson recalled learning this lesson directly from him:

> He [my grandfather] spoke only of the good qualities of men, which induced the belief that he knew little of them; but no one knew them better. I had formed this opinion, and on hearing him speak very favorably of men with defects known to myself, stated them to him. When he asked if I supposed he had not observed them (adding others not noted by me, and evincing [demonstrating] much more accurate knowledge of the individual character than I possessed), observing, "My habit is to speak only of men's good qualities."[5]*

In today's Negativist-dominated environment, it requires intentional effort to identify the positives that have been ignored. One of the best ways to do this with an individual such as

---

* This was Jefferson's practice in public, when speaking of individuals in front of others. In such settings, he maintained public civility, decorum, and decency. But there were some private occasions when he did write candidly to intimate friends of his personal feelings of dislike for a few individuals, but this was not his public practice.

Jefferson is to become acquainted with a general overview of his life, events, and writings. Ideally, this requires diving deeply into primary sources (e.g. Jefferson's presidential papers, letters, etc.), but most of us do not have the time to do this. As such, a good antidote to negativism is to read good, balanced, biographies written by those who have done extensive work with these primary sources. (I list a number of such works at www. wallbuilders.com.)

The remedy for *Historical Relativism* is always to look for absolute, established, irrefutable facts about the subject. It really doesn't matter how someone "feels" about Jefferson, or whether or not they like or agree with him. Either he did or did not promote emancipation, encourage public religious expressions, include religion in education, and so forth, regardless of whether someone personally agrees or disagrees with him on those issues.

Similar to the means for overcoming Negativism, reading a good biography or sound historical overview helps establish a baseline for identifying truth and objective facts. (Make sure that the author provides not just snippet quotations from historical sources but that he provides enough content to establish the context of quotes, and that he also provides citations to primary sources for the quotations and factual claims made in the book, as I have done throughout this work, but which, as noted earlier, writers such as Professors Isaac Kramnick and Laurence Moore do not do in *The Godless Constitution*.) Such an overview provides general basic knowledge by which it becomes easier to identify which aspects of a modern writer's story are merely opinions, as well as any aspects he might be ignoring or exaggerating in order to reflect his own personal views.

Truth is transcendent and immutable, not individually constructed; and establishing truth should always be the objective of any study or reading. As James Madison affirmed, "For what is the object of our discussion? Truth, sir—to draw a true and just conclusion."[6]

The remedy for *Antinationalism* begins with acknowledging that America actually is unique, and that its prosperity, freedom, and stability did not occur by accident but were the consequence of both our ancestors' commitment to certain ideas and God's Providence. With respect to the former, it is worth taking time to identify the specific ideas that produced the positive results we have so long enjoyed. Many of these ideas are brilliantly encapsulated in the 155 words drafted by Jefferson at the beginning of the Declaration, including the affirmation of our official national belief that: (1) there is a Creator; (2) the Creator gives certain inalienable rights to every individual; (3) government exists primarily to secure these inalienable rights to every individual; (4) there is a fixed and absolute moral law ("the laws of nature and of nature's God"); (5) below the level of inalienable rights and fixed moral law, decisions are made by the majority—i.e., by "the consent of the governed"; and (6) if government does not secure these previous five elements, then the people have a right to alter or change their government.

Of course these six principles are universal and apply to all people, not just Americans; and far too many individuals across the world do not enjoy these rights or experience the exercise of these principles that were implemented in America. As Jefferson observed, "the comparisons of our governments with those of Europe are like a comparison of heaven and hell,"[7] and today many countries still have governments that are repressive and arbitrary.

We must reject the relativism and antinationalism of modern writers who do not recognize that some political philosophies and systems are superior to others. As well, we should always remember that our God-given inalienable rights belong to every man and woman, not to any particular group. The rights of due process, religious expression, freedom of speech, and self-protection come not because one belongs to the majority or the minority, is black or Latino, male or young, rich or poor, but rather because such rights are bestowed on every individual by our Creator.

Recognizing individuality is the approach that God takes; and good history also focuses on examining the person—on examining Jefferson as an individual rather than part of a group of racists, secularists, slaveholders, Freethinkers, or any other group to which modern writers may attempt to attach him.

The antidote to *Modernism* is to develop a broad general knowledge of the past, not just the present. Because our current educational system now graduates students lacking even minimal historical knowledge, citizens are misled by outlandish charges Modernists make about not only Jefferson but also other Founders as well as traditionally venerated historical events.

If rudimentary historical literacy is to be achieved today, it must be individually secured, for it is no longer possible to rely on public schools (and even many private schools) for this once elementary knowledge. Fortunately, Americans are now seeking to educate themselves about our own history, and are even willing to pay to learn what used to be common at school.

It is not unusual, for instance, for a book about American history (especially the American Founding or an American Founder) to be on the *New York Times* bestseller list. Many of these books are solid, balanced accounts of their subjects, including David McCullough's *John Adams* and *1776*, Glenn Beck's *Being George Washington*, Newt Gingrich's *Valley Forge* and *Victory at Yorktown*, this book, and others. Of course many excellent books do not end up on this list, which is why I provide a far more extensive list of good historical books at www.wallbuilders.com.

There are two significant factors that further exacerbate our current historical illiteracy. One is contemporary educational law, the other educational philosophy.

Federal laws such as No Child Left Behind and Race to the Top as well as comparable state laws require student account-ability testing in schools, but that testing typically covers only reading, math, and science, not history. Because test results are connected to funding, many schools instruct their educators to focus on teaching the subject matter to be covered in the testing. History thus receives only minimal attention, and the little it does receive is often extremely negative.[8]

Concerning the second factor, educational philosophy, in the past students would study American history in every grade, K-12. Today, however, many states now require American history to be taught in only three grades. Often, elementary students (usually fifth grade) study from Columbus to the Stamp Act; Junior High students (usually eighth grade) from the American Revolution to the end of the nineteenth century; and High School students (often ninth grade) generally learn only what happened from 1900 forward.[9]

Yet it would seem that high school students—young adults

on the verge of entering active national citizenship—should study the Founding Fathers, Declaration of Independence, Constitution, and Bill of Rights along with responsible civics and participatory constitutional government, but in many states these topics are covered in fifth-grade history, or sometimes in junior high. But what eleven or thirteen-year-old really cares about habeas corpus, trial by jury, the rights of religious conscience, judicial tyranny, or taxation without representation? Most don't, but high schoolers should. Yet we teach this history primarily only in lower grades.

And the presentation of American history today is too often reduced to a succession of often-sterile facts, dates, and places interspersed with outlandishly negative criticisms of men and women who were highly venerated in the past. But previous generations of Americans learned history by the addition of biographies—by studying the lives and experiences of those who made it. We thus learned about the principles of liberty and the American Revolution by reading biographies of George Washington, Abigail Adams, James Otis, and James Armistead; we learned about the progress of science by studying Benjamin Franklin, David Rittenhouse, George Washington Carver, and Thomas Edison; we studied the Civil War and the fight for civil rights by learning about the life and struggles of Abraham Lincoln, Robert E. Lee, Robert Small, and Harriet Tubman; and so forth.

This long-established custom of learning history by studying the lives of its heroes has fallen into disfavor over the past half-century, but it is this practice that best overcomes Modernism. Fortunately, many excellent biographies are available, and I list a number of them at www.wallbuilders.com. Biographies help develop a broader individual macroknowledge of historical persons, events, customs, and beliefs rather than what has too often become just the modern microview.

The remedy for the fifth malpractice, *Minimalism*, is to establish context. Begin with the assumption that things are usually not as simple as they seem. Certainly our own personal experience routinely affirms this to be the case, and it is no less so throughout history. Always look for the context of what is being said; don't separate something from its historical setting. Thus, when critics, as they often do, simply lift a single line from a letter—such as Jefferson's "wall of separation" metaphor or his "question with boldness even the existence of a God" statement—then go back and read the whole letter. And whenever a word or phrase you don't understand appears in a quote, stop and look it up so that you can grasp its meaning and thus understand its context. Don't necessarily accept that something is as easy or conclusive as a writer makes it appear unless you have personally checked enough facts presented by that writer to know if his portrayals and conclusions are indeed accurate and can be trusted.

The solution for *Rigid Secularism* is to recognize that religious faith has always had a tremendous influence in American history both on individuals and events. As Dr. Paul C. Vitz, a professor at New York University who analyzed numerous textbooks, accurately observed:

> [T]he facts are clear: religion, especially Christianity, has played and continues to play a central role in American life. To neglect to report this is simply to fail to carry out the major duty of any textbook writer – the duty to tell the truth.[10]

He wisely noted:

Over and over, we have seen that liberal and secular bias is primarily accomplished by exclusion—by leaving out the opposing position. Such a bias is much harder to observe than a positive vilification or direct criticism, but it is the essence of censorship.[11]

Thus, always assume that religious principles or motivations are involved somewhere in the story, then investigate accordingly. Of course people are influenced by a variety of concerns and ideas, but at least prior to the mid-twentieth century it is pure foolishness to discount the impact of Christianity on Americans from all walks of life.

For early educators, historians, and political leaders, their default position was that virtually everything was somehow related to God and/or religious faith:

[T]he longer I live, the more convincing proofs I see of this truth: that God governs in the affairs of men.[12]

— STATESMAN BENJAMIN FRANKLIN (1706–1790)

To record the progress of human affairs as directed by the Providence of God—to exhibit the connection of events, showing how an immense series is produced as cause and effect—to display the character of man and of God—is the interesting office of a historian.[13]

—HISTORIAN JEDIDIAH MORSE (1761–1826)

History is God's providence in human affairs.[14]

—JUSTICE JAMES MOORE WAYNE (1790–1867)

That God rules in the affairs of men is as certain as any truth of physical science. . . . nothing is by chance, though men in their ignorance of causes may think so.[15] [T]he fortunes of a nation are not under the control of blind destiny [but] follow the steps by which a favoring Providence, calling our institutions into being, has conducted the country to its present happiness and glory.[16]

—GEORGE BANCROFT, "FATHER OF AMERICAN HISTORY" (1800–1891)

[Y]ou will notice that while the oppressors have carried out their plans and had things their own way, there were other forces silently at work which in time undermined their plans, as if a Divine Hand were directing the counter-plan. Whoever peruses the "Story of Liberty" without recognizing this feature will fail of fully comprehending the meaning of history.[17]

—HISTORIAN CHARLES COFFIN (1823–1896)

Numerous others also held that it was unusual for historical events and accounts not to be in some way related, either directly or indirectly, to a religious perspective or influence. So take the time to do a little research, gather the evidence, and then reach an independent conclusion warranted by the actual facts, not just by a secularist presentation of them.

By adopting these practices, the effects of the six modern historical malpractices can be minimized. And since biographical history contributes so much to these objectives, it is worth closing this work with some glimpses into the personal life of Jefferson, showing something of his heart, faith, and character.

Jefferson was one of the rare men who became a hero in his

own lifetime. And unlike many others who attain such a distinction, he always remained humble and unpretentious, living and acting as the common person for whom he had sacrificed so much. As a result, people would often converse with him without recognizing who he was. Jefferson's granddaughter related one such account:

> On one occasion while traveling, he stopped at a country inn. A stranger who did not know who he was entered into conversation with this plainly dressed and unassuming traveler. He [the stranger] introduced one subject after another into the conversation, and found him [Jefferson] perfectly acquainted with each. Filled with wonder, he seized the first opportunity to inquire of the landlord who his guest was, saying that when he spoke of the law, he thought he was a lawyer; then turning the conversation on medicine, felt sure he was a physician; but having touched on theology, he became convinced he was a clergyman. "Oh," replied the landlord, "why I thought you knew the Squire." The stranger was then astonished to hear that the traveler whom he had found so affable and simple in his manners was Jefferson.[18]

On another occasion, Jefferson was going from Washington, DC back home to Charlottesville, riding in a group with others on horseback. As they approached a stream that had no bridge, they saw a traveler on foot standing and waiting at the edge of the water, hoping to hitch a ride across. The man silently watched the others pass and ford the stream, but upon seeing Jefferson (and not knowing who he was) he stopped him and asked if he could mount behind him and ride to the other side. Jefferson graciously agreed, and after putting the traveler down across the stream, Jefferson rode on to catch up with the rest of his party. A man who had witnessed the scene approached the traveler and asked why he had not asked any of the others to carry him across the stream. The traveler replied, "From their looks, I did not like to ask them; the old gentleman looked as if he would do it, and I asked him."[19] He was shocked to learn that the man who had carried him across the stream was the president of the United States, but such was the character of Jefferson.

Whenever he had the opportunity to show kindness or help others, he did so, especially to the poor and needy. Yet he often had to overcome his own internal resistance to do so. His dilemma was similar to that described in the Bible in Romans 7—that for "the inner being" to do what is right, one often has to "wage war against the law of my mind." On one occasion, Jefferson wrote about this conflict, letting his heart talk to his head (in this letter, his heart speaks in the first person, his head in the third person):

> [A] desire to do what is right has sometimes induced me [i.e., the heart] to conform to your [my head's] counsels. A few facts, however, which I can readily recall to your memory, will suffice to prove to you that nature has not organized you [my head] for our moral direction. When the poor wearied soldier, whom we overtook at Chickahominy with his pack on his back, begged us to let him get up behind our chariot [carriage], you [my mind] began to calculate that the road was full of soldiers and that if all should be taken up, our horses would fail in their journey. We drove on therefore, but soon becoming sensible you had made me [the heart] do wrong—that though we cannot relieve all the distressed,

we should relieve as many as we can—I turned about to take up the soldier, but he had entered a bypath and was no more to be found; and from that moment to this, I could never find him out to ask his forgiveness. Again, when the poor woman came to ask a charity in Philadelphia, you [my mind] whispered that she looked like a drunkard, and that half a dollar was enough to give her for the ale-house. Those who want the dispositions [who lack the resolve] to give, easily find reasons why they ought not to give. When I sought her out afterwards and did what I should have done at first, you know that she employed the money immediately towards placing her child at school. If our country, when pressed with wrongs at the point of the bayonet, had been governed by its heads instead of its hearts, where should we have been now? Hanging on a gallows as high as Haman's [Esther 7:10].[20]

Jefferson's account books affirm his generosity to the poor and needy, recording the frequent charity he bestowed (usually secretly or anonymously) on those he saw in need, regardless of when or where he found them.

Jefferson was also humble, unassuming, and good natured; and his manners never deserted him—even to those who opposed him. On one occasion while returning on horseback to Washington, he greeted a passing pedestrian. The stranger did not recognize President Jefferson, but the two began a friendly conversation that soon turned to politics. The man began to attack and deride the president (not realizing that he was talking to him), even repeating several of the lies that had been spread about him. Jefferson was amused, and "he asked the man if he knew the President personally? 'No,' was the reply, 'nor do I wish to.' 'But do you think it fair,' asked Jefferson, 'to repeat such stories about a man and condemn one you dare not face?' 'I will never shrink from meeting Mr. Jefferson should he ever come in my way' replied the stranger."[21]

Jefferson then promised the man that if he would come to the White House at a certain time the next day, that he would personally introduce him to the president. The next day the stranger appeared for the meeting and was taken to meet President Jefferson. The man was immediately embarrassed and began to apologize, but Jefferson, with a grin on his face, laughed off the apology and extended his hand in a warm welcome greeting. The two then spent several hours in delightful conversation, and when the man rose to depart, Jefferson prevailed on him to stay for dinner.[22] Jefferson was truly an amiable, pleasant, and polite individual.

Jefferson also maintained a lifelong passion for accuracy and truth that was apparent on many occasions, including while serving America overseas in France. On one occasion he was engaged in a discussion with the famous French naturalist Georges Comte de Buffon, who had penned a massive thirty-six-volume encyclopedia on natural history. Jefferson, himself a noted naturalist, had examined that enormous work and found inaccuracies relating to some American animals, specifically the American moose. He pointed out these mistakes to Buffon, who disagreed that he had made any errors. Jefferson secretly wrote his old friend, Revolutionary General John Sullivan, then serving as the governor of New Hampshire, and asked him to send a moose skeleton. The general was surprised by the unusual request but arranged a hunting party, bagged a moose, and sent its frame to Jefferson in Paris. Jefferson then arranged for a dinner with Buffon and during the meal produced the moose skeleton.

> Buffon immediately acknowledged his error and expressed his great admiration for Mr. Jefferson's energetic determination to establish the truth. "I should have consulted you, monsieur," he said with usual French civility, "before publishing my book on natural history, and then I should have been sure of my facts."[23]

Although a famous public figure, Jefferson loved and cherished his private life, especially time with his family. He had lost so many of his own precious children, and he loved his grandchildren as if they were his own children.[24] Jefferson's granddaughter Ellen recalled:

> From him seemed to flow all the pleasures of my life. To him I owed all the small blessings and joyful surprises of my childish and girlish years. . . . When about fifteen years old, I began to think of a watch, but knew the state of my father's finances promised no such indulgence. . . . [But my grandfather gave me] an elegant lady's watch with chain and seals, [which] was in my hand, which trembled for very joy. My Bible came from him, my Shakespeare, my first writing-table, my first handsome writing-desk, my first Leghorn hat [a fancy hat adorned with ribbons], my first silk dress. What, in short, of all my small treasures did not come from him? . . . Our grandfather seemed to read our hearts, to see our invisible wishes, to be our good genie to wave the fairy wand to brighten our young lives by his goodness and his gifts.[25]

But Thomas did not spoil his grandchildren with his generous gifts; he trained and shaped their character, just as he had with his own children. His granddaughter recalled:

> He reproved without wounding us, and commended without making us vain. He took pains to correct our errors and false ideas, checked the bold, encouraged the timid, and tried to teach us to reason soundly and feel rightly. Our smaller follies he treated with good-humored raillery [teasing], our graver ones with kind and serious admonition. He was watchful over our manners, and called our attention to every violation of propriety [politeness and decorum].[26]

Jefferson also had a genuine sense of humor and would offer tongue-in-cheek comments that his grandchildren described as playful or "sportive."[27] Some targets for humor never seem to change, such as lawyers and doctors, and according to one of the original professors at the University of Virginia, Jefferson joked openly about the latter:

> [H]e would speak jocularly [jokingly], especially to the unprofessional, of medical practice; and on one occasion . . . [i]n the presence of Dr. Everett . . . he remarked that whenever he saw three physicians together, he looked up to discover whether there was not a turkey-buzzard in the neighborhood. The annoyance of the doctor, I am told, was manifest.[28]

Jefferson was truly a remarkable man. He had some faults, probably much fewer than many other great leaders, but he had numerous virtues worthy of study and emulation. He was unquestionably used as an instrument of God; and all races and generations of Americans have benefited from the blessings he helped secure for this nation and its posterity.

What was once said about George Washington by President Calvin Coolidge can equally be said of Thomas Jefferson:

> We cannot yet estimate him. We can only indicate our reverence for him and thank the Divine Providence which sent him to serve and inspire his fellow men.[29]

ABOUT THE AUTHOR

David Barton is the founder and president of WallBuilders, a national profamily organization that presents America's forgotten history and heroes with an emphasis on our moral, religious, and constitutional heritage. He is the author of many best-selling books, including *Original Intent, U-Turn, The Bulletproof George Washington, American History in Black and White, The Question of Freemasonry and the Founding Fathers*, and many others. He addresses hundreds of groups each year. David and his wife, Cheryl, have three grown children.

Barton was named by *Time* magazine as one of America's twenty-five most influential evangelicals, and he has received numerous national and international awards, including Who's Who in Education and DAR's highest award, the George Washington Honor Medal.

NOTES

PREFACE

1. Marvin Olasky, "A message to WORLD readers on the David Barton controversy," *World* magazine, August 16, 2012 (at: http://online.worldmag.com/2012/08/16/a-message-to-world-readers-on-the-david-barton-controversy/).

2. The publisher of another of my works, *The Founders Bible*, released after *The Jefferson Lies*, reported to me some unexpected and unsolicited contacts he had with Warren Throckmorton, explaining: "About a month ago, I started to get hounded by Throckmorton via email and on our website. He even called my former publishing partner and ended up issuing a warning and a threat. Warren 'warned' that he had assembled a coalition of people, supposed conservative Christians, who were mounting a campaign against David. If we intended to publish *The Founders' Bible*, anyone associated with Barton was likely to suffer financially, because they were going to come against him. Sort of hit me blindside." I received this email from the publisher of *The Founders Bible* on August 16, 2012.

3. Thomas Kidd, "The David Barton controversy," *World* magazine, August 25, 2012 (at: http://www.worldmag.com/2012/08/the_david_barton_controversy).

4. Thomas S. Kidd, "The Barton Controversy," *World* magazine, August 7, 2021 (at: http://www.worldmag.com/2012/08/the_david_barton_controversy).

5. *Debates and Proceedings in the Congress of the United States* (Washington, DC: Gales and Seaton, 1851), 6th Cong., 797, December 4, 1800.

6. John Quincy Adams, *Memoirs of John Quincy Adams, Charles Francis Adams*, editor (Philadelphia: J. B. Lippincott & Co., 1874), Vol. I, 265, diary entry for October 23, 1803, and Vol. I, 268, diary entry for October 30, 1803; *National Intelligencer*, December 9, 1820, 3; *National Intelligencer*, December 30, 1820, 3. See also James Hutson, *Religion and the Founding of the American Republic* (Washington, DC: Library of Congress, 1998), 89.

7. Bishop Claggett's letter of February 18, 1801, attests that while Vice President, Jefferson attended church services in the House. Available in the Maryland Diocesan Archives.

8. Margaret Smith, *The First Forty Years of Washington Society* (New York: Charles Scribner's Sons, 1906), 13; James Hutson, *Religion and the Founding of the American Republic*, 84.

9. Thomas Jefferson, *The Papers of Thomas Jefferson*, Julian Boyd, editor (Princeton: Princeton University Press, 1950), Vol. I, 495, from "Report on a Seal for the United States, with Related Papers," August 20, 1776. See also John Adams, *Letters of John Adams*, Charles Francis Adams, editor (Boston: Charles C. Little and James Brown, 1841), Vol. I, 152, to Abigail Adams on August 14, 1776.

10. Thomas Jefferson, *The Works of Thomas Jefferson*, Paul Ford, editor (New York: G. Putnam's Sons, 1904), Vol. II, 42, "Notice of Fast to the Inhabitants of the Parish of Saint Anne," June 1774.

11. Jefferson, *The Papers of Thomas Jefferson* (1950), Vol. 1, 116, to the Inhabitants of the Parish of St. Anne before July 23, 1774.

12. Ibid., Vol. 4, 35–36, "Robert Scot's Invoice for Executing Indian Medal, with Jefferson's Memoranda."

13. See, for example, Ibid., Vol. II, 555, "A Bill for Punishing Disturbers of Religious Worship and Sabbath Breakers"; Vol. II, 555, "A Bill for Appointing Days of Public Fasting and Thanksgiving"; Vol. I, 556, "A Bill Annulling the Marriages Prohibited by the Levitical Law, and Appointing the Mode of Solemnizing Lawful Marriage"; Vol. I, 553, "A Bill for Saving the Property of the Church Heretofore by Law Established"; Vol. 1, 621, a "Bill for Establishing a General Court"; etc.

14. *Official Letters of the Governors of the State of Virginia*, H. R. McIlwaine, editor (Richmond: Virginia State Library, 1928), Vol. II, 65, Thomas Jefferson, "Proclamation," November 11, 1779; Jefferson, *The Papers of Thomas Jefferson*, Vol. 3, 178, "Proclamation Appointing a Day of Thanksgiving and Prayer," November 11, 1779.

15. David Barton, *The Jefferson Lies: Exposing the Myths You've Always Believed about Thomas Jefferson*, (Nashville: Thomas Nelson, 2011), 135.

16. Rev. John Holmes, *Historical Sketches of the Missions of the United Brethren for Propagating the Gospel among the Heathen, From Their Commencement to the Year 1817* (London: Printed for the Author, 1827), 143.

17. Ibid., 179–180.

18. Ibid., 180–181.

19. Ibid., 186.

20. Ibid., 186–187. For further discussion, see George Henry Loskiel, *History of the Mission of the United Brethren Among the Indians in North America. In Three Parts* (London: The Brethren's Society, 1794) and John Heckenealder, *A Narrative of the Mission of the United Brethren among the Delaware and Mohigan Indians, &c. by John Heckenealder, who was many years in the service of that Mission* (Philadelphia, 1820).

21. Throckmorton and Coulter, *Getting Jefferson Right: Fact Checking Claims about Our Third President* (Grove City, PA: Salem Grove Press, 2012), 12.

22. Ibid., 11.

23. Ibid, 17.

24. Ibid.

25. *Journals of the Continental Congress* (Washington: Government Printing Office, 1905), Vol. III, 350–351, November 11, 1775

26. Ibid., Vol. VII, 72–73, January 30, 1777.

27. Ibid., Vol. XV, 1181–1182, October 16, 1779.

28. Ibid., Vol. XXVII, 659–660, December 3, 1784.

29. Ibid., Vol. III, 433–434, December 16, 1775.

30. Ibid., Vol. IV, 111, February 5, 1776.

31. Ibid., Vol. IV, 111, February 5, 1776.

32. Ibid., Vol. IV, 267, April 10, 1776; (1904);(1933), Vol. XXVIII, 306-307, April 26, 1785; Vol. XXVIII, 399, May 27, 1785; Vol. XXVIII, 407–408, 417, June 1 & 2, 1785; (1937); etc.

33. Ibid., Vol. IV, 267, April 10, 1776.

34. George Washington, *The Writings of George Washington*, John C. Fitzpatrick, editor (Washington: U.S. Government Printing Office, 1936), Vol. XV, 55, from his speech to the Delaware Indian Chiefs on May 12, 1779. Some object that this speech was written by an aide. This may be the case, but aides routinely draft letters, speeches, addresses, etc. This does not keep historians from attributing these texts to the presidents who send or deliver them. We speak, for instance, of George Washington's Farewell Address, even though Alexander Hamilton played a major role in drafting it.

35. Ibid., Vol. XVII, 283, to the President of Congress on December 17, 1779.

36. *Journals of the Continental Congress* (1933), Vol. XXVIII, 381, May 20, 1785.

37. Ibid., Vol. XXVIII, 399, May 27, 1785.

38. Ibid., Vol. V, 785, September 19, 1776.

39. John Hancock, "A Brief," dated June 20, 1788, from an original broadside in our possession (at: http://www.wallbuilders.com/LIBissuesArticles.asp?id=132083).

40. George Washington, *The Writings of George Washington*, Vol. 29, 489, to the Reverend John Ettwein on May 12, 1788.

41. Ibid., Vol. 30, 354–355, n. The original of his letter to the Society of United Brethren for Propagating the Gospel among the Heathen can be found in the collection of the Moravian Archives in Bethlehem, PA (at: http://bdhp.moravian.edu/personal_papers/letters/1789fromgw.html).

42. *American State Papers: Documents, Legislative and Executive of the Congress of the United States, Walter Lowrie & Matthew St. Claire Clarke*, editors (Washington, DC: Gales and Seaton 1832), Vol. IV, 546, "A Treaty between the United States of America and the Oneida, Tuscarora, and Stockbridge Indians, dwelling in the country of the Oneidas," treaty done on December 2, 1794. See also *Journal of the Executive Proceedings of the Senate of the United States of America* (Washington: Duff Green, 1828), Vol. I, 170, January 9, 1795.

43. *American State Papers* (1832), Vol. IV, 687, "The Kaskaskia and Other Tribes," treaty signed August 13, 1803; reported by Thomas Jefferson to the Senate on October 31, 1803.

44. See, for example, *Debates and Proceedings* (Washington: Gales and Seaton, 1851), Vol. 11, 1332, "An Act in Addition to an Act, Entitled, 'An Act in Addition to an Act Regulating the Grants of Land Appropriated for Military Services, and for the Society of the United Brethren for Propagating the Gospel Among the Heathen'," April 26, 1802; *Debates and Proceedings* (1851), Vol. 12, 1602, "An Act to Revive and Continue in Force An Act in Addition to an Act, Entitled, 'An Act in Addition to an Act Regulating the Grants of Land Appropriated for Military Services, and for the Society of the United Brethren for Propagating the Gospel Among the Heathen,' and for Other Purposes," March 3, 1803; *Debates and Proceedings* (1852), Vol. 13, 1279, "An Act Granting Further Time for Locating Military Land Warrants, and for Other Purposes," March 19, 1804.

45. *The Public Statutes at Large of the United States of America*, Richard Peters, editor (Boston: Charles C. Little and James Brown, 1846), Vol. VII, 166, Art. 16, "Articles of a Treaty Made and Concluded at the foot of the Rapids of the Miami of Lake Erie," treaty dated September 29, 1817, proclamation for the treaty dated January 4, 1819.

46. *American State Papers* (1834), Vol. VII, 242-243, Art. 10, "Treaty with the Great and Little Osages," treaty dated June 2, 1825, reported by John Quincy Adams to the Senate on December 14, 1825.

47. Theodore Roosevelt, "Proclamation 526—Opening of Sioux Lands of the Rosebud Reservation, South Dakota," *The American Presidency Project*, May 13, 1904 (at: http://www.presidency.ucsb.edu/ws/?pid=69471); Theodore Roosevelt, "Proclamation 521 – Disposal of Sioux Lands," *The American Presidency Project*, March 30, 1904 (at: http://www.presidency.ucsb.edu/ws/?pid=69465); Theodore Roosevelt, "Executive Order – Cancellation of Lands Set Apart in Utah," *The American Presidency Project*, February 5, 1906 (at: http://www.presidency.ucsb.edu/ws/?pid=76705).

48. *Report of the Secretary of the Interior for the Fiscal Year Ending June 30, 1887* (Washington: Government Printing Office, 1887), Vol. II, 976, Rev. Charles W. Shelton quoting President Cleveland; Charles B. Galloway, *Christianity and the American Commonwealth* (Nashville: Publishing House Methodist Episcopal Church, 1898), 177.

49. *Letters of Delegates to Congress*, Paul H. Smith, editor (Washington, DC: Library of Congress, 1991) Vol. 18, 448-449n, letter from Charles Thomson to William Moore on April 9, 1782.

50. Throckmorton and Coulter, *Getting Jefferson Right*, 17.

51. Ibid., 11.

52. *Journals of the Continental Congress* (1937), Vol. XXXIV, 485-487, September 3, 1788.

53. Throckmorton and Coulter, *Getting Jefferson Right*, 11–12.

54. See, for example, Rev. John Holmes, *Historical Sketches of the Missions of the United Brethren*, 201, passim.

55. Throckmorton and Coulter, *Getting Jefferson Right*, 16.

56. See, for example, Rev. John Holmes, *Historical Sketches of the Missions of the United Brethren*, 202, 214, etc.

57. Ibid., 201–202, 208–209.

58. Throckmorton and Coulter, *Getting Jefferson Right*, 15.

59. Ibid., 16.

60. Ibid., 18.

61. Rev. John Holmes, *Historical Sketches of the Missions of the United Brethren*, 201.

62. Ibid., 128.

63. Throckmorton and Coulter, *Getting Jefferson Right*, 9.

64. *History of American Mission to the Heathen, From Their Commencement to the Present Time* (Worcester: Spooner & Howland, 1840), 21.

65. Rev. John Holmes, *Historical Sketches of the Missions of the United Brethren*, 189.

66. *History of American Mission to the Heathen*, 21.

67. Ibid., 21.

68. See, for example, Rev. John Holmes, *Historical Sketches of the Missions of the United Brethren*, 210, "With a view to execute their horrid purpose, the young Indians got together, chose the most ferocious to be their leaders, deposed all the old Chiefs, and guarded the whole Indian assembly, as if they were prisoners of war, especially the aged of both sexes. The venerable old Chief Tettepachsit was the first whom, they accused of possession poison, and having destroyed many Indians by his art. When the poor old man would not confess, they fastened with cords to two posts, and began to roast him at a slow fire."; 210–211, "During this torture, he [Chief Tettepachsit] said, that he kept poison in the house of our Indian brother Joshua. Nothing was more welcome to the savages than this accusation, for they wished to deprive us of the assistance of this man, who was the only Christian Indian residing with us at that time....We knew nothing of these horrible events, until the evening of the 16th, when a message was brought, that the savages had burned an old woman to death, who had been baptized by the Brethren in former times, and also that our poor Joshua was kept close prisoner."; 139, "Their external troubles, however, did not yet terminate. They had not only a kind of tax imposed upon them, to show their dependence on the Iroquois , but the following very singular message was sent them: "The great head, i.e. the Council in Onondago, speak the truth and lie not: they rejoice that some of the believing Indians have moved to Wayomik, but now they lift up the remaining Mahikans and Delawares, and set them down also in Wayomik; for there a fire is kindled for them, and there they may plant and think on God: but if they will not hear, the great head will come and clean their ears with a red-hot iron (meaning they would set their houses on fire) and shoot them through the head with musquet-balls."

69. Throckmorton and Coulter, *Getting Jefferson Right*, 79.

70. Ibid., 80.

71. Thomas Jefferson, *The Papers of Thomas Jefferson Second Series: Jefferson's Extracts from the Gospels*. "The Philosophy of Jesus" and "The Life and Morals of Jesus," Dickinson W. Adams, editor (Princeton: Princeton University Press, 1983), 50, "The Reconstruction of 'The Philosophy of Jesus'."

72. Ibid.

73. Ibid.

74. Mark Beliles, *Thomas Jefferson's Abridgement of the Words of Jesus of Nazareth* (Charlottesville, VA: Mark Beliles, 1993), 16–17.

75. David Barton, *The Jefferson Lies*, 68.

76. Throckmorton and Coulter, *Getting Jefferson Right*, 66.

77. The Eighth Report of the Bible Society of Philadelphia; Read before the Society, May 1, 1816 (Philadelphia: Printed by Order of the Society; William Fry, Printer, 1816), 44–52.

78. "The Thomas Jefferson Papers," *Library of Congress*, Samuel Greenhow to Thomas Jefferson on November 11, 1813 (at: http://memory.loc.gov/master/mss/mtj/mtj1/046/1300/1325.jpg and http://memory.loc.gov/master/mss/mtj/mtj1/046/1300/1326.jpg).

79. Thomas Jefferson, *The Writings of Thomas Jefferson* (Washington, DC: Taylor & Maury, 1854), Vol. VI, 308-309, to Samuel Greenhow on January 31, 1814.

80. *Address of the Managers of the Bible Society of Virginia to the Public* (Richmond: Samuel Pleasants, 1814), 7, "Constitution of the Bible Society of Virginia," 1813, Shaw # 30910.

81. Throckmorton and Coulter, *Getting Jefferson Right*, 63.

82. *Address of the Managers of the Bible Society of Virginia to the Public* (1814), 8, "Constitution of the Bible Society of Virginia," 1813, Shaw # 30910.

83. William Maxwell, *A Memoir of the Rev. John H. Rice* (Philadelphia: J. Whetham, 1835), 127, letter from Rev. John H. Rice to William Maxwell on April 10, 1816.

84. Throckmorton and Coulter, *Getting Jefferson Right*, 64.

85. Thomas Buckley, *Establishing Religious Freedom: Jefferson's Statute in Virginia* (University of Virginia Press, 2013), 157.

86. Throckmorton and Coulter, *Getting Jefferson Right*, 128–135.

87. Ibid., 129.

88. Ibid., 130.

89. Thomas Jefferson, *The Papers of Thomas Jefferson, Second Series: Jefferson's Memorandum Books* (Princeton: Princeton University Press, 1997), Vol. II, 1403, March 8, 1824.

90. Ibid., 1154, May 15, 1805.

91. Ibid., 1196, January 6, 1807.

92. Ibid., 1177, April 18, 1806.

93. Noah Webster, *An American Dictionary of the English Language* (New York: S. Converse, 1828), Vol. II, "subscription," and "subscriber."

94. See, for example, "Art by the Book," *The Age*, July 22, 2006 (at: http://www.theage.com.au/news/arts/art-by-the-book/2006/07/20/1153166519892.html?page=fullpage#contentSwap1); "Phillis Wheatley," Answers.com (at: http://www.answers.com/topic/phillis-wheatley) (accessed on January 21, 2013); Richard Gray, *A History of American Literature* (West Sussex: Blackwell Publishers, 2012), 155; "A Pair of Albums, Each Titled 'Sketches of Custome by Coke Smyth,' Containing Original Watercolours," AbeBooks.com, book description for John Richard Coke Smyth, *A Pair of Albums,*

Each Titled Sketches of Costume, 1835 (at: http://www.abebooks.com/servlet/BookDet
ailsPL?bi=1269415985&searchurl=pics%3Don%26sortby%3D1%26tn%3Dsketches)
(accessed on January 21, 2013); "William Hogarth Biography," Hogarth Biography (at:
http://mcdragon19.tripod.com/id58.html) (accessed on January 21, 2013); and many
others.

95. See, for example, Thomas Jefferson, *The Papers of Thomas Jefferson, Second Series,* Vol.
II, 814, April 7, 1791, and Vol. II, 1376, June 25, 1821.

96. Throckmorton and Coulter, *Getting Jefferson Right,* 132.

97. "Thomas Jefferson's Library," *Library of Congress* (at: http://myloc.gov/Exhibitions/
jeffersonslibrary/Pages/Overview.aspx) (accessed on January 21, 2013).

98. Thomas Jefferson, *The Papers of Thomas Jefferson, Second Series* (1997), Vol. I, 689,
December 27, 1787; 759, June 23, 1790; Vol. II, 811, February 19, 1791; 814, April 7,
1791; 874, July 7, 1792; 915, May 12, 1794; 979, February 26, 1798; 1005, September 6,
1799; 1013, January 25, 1800; 1016, April 25, 1800; 1017, May 5, 1800; 1028, October
23, 1800 [additional money towards the book mentioned on September 6, 1799]; 1127,
May 17, 1804 [additional money towards the book mentioned on February 27, 1798];
1174, February 22, 1806; 1181, June 9, 1806; 1191, October 13, 1806; 1195, December
21 & 27, 1807 [2 subscriptions mentioned]; 1274, March 15, 1812; 1280, June 17, 1812;
1319, February 29, 1816; 1364, April 15, 1820; 1376, June 25, 1821; and 1390, October
22, 1822.

99. Ibid., Vol. II, 1195, December 21, 1807.

100. Thomas Jefferson, *The Works of Thomas Jefferson* (1905), Vol. XI, 6, to Charles Thomson
on January 11, 1808.

101. Ibid.

102. Throckmorton and Coulter, *Getting Jefferson Right,* 127.

103. Henry S. Randall, *The Life of Thomas Jefferson* (New York: Derby & Jackson, 1858),
Vol. III, 654.

104. Throckmorton and Coulter, *Getting Jefferson Right,* 72.

105. *The Life and Morals of Jesus of Nazareth, Extracted Textually from the Gospels in Greek,
Latin, French, and English,* Thomas Jefferson, editor (Washington, DC: Government
Printing Office, 1904).

106. See Billy Hallowell, "David Barton vs. His Critics: The Blaze's Extensive Analysis of
Their Claims & Thomas Jefferson's Faith," *The Blaze,* August 15, 2012 (at: http://www.
theblaze.com/stories/davidbarton-vs-his-critics-theblazes-extensive-analysis-of-their-
claims-thomas-jeffersons-faith/).

107. Matthew 5:1-10, 19–48; Matthew 6:1–34; Matthew 7:1–29; Matthew 8:1, 11; Matthew
10:5–31, [34–41], 42; Matthew 11:[2–9], 28–30; Matthew 12:1–5, 11–12, 33–37,
41–44, 46–50; Matthew 13:1–9, 18–33,[34], 36–43, 44, [45–51], 52; Matthew 15:1–20;
Matthew 18:1–6, 10–11, [12–14], 15–17; Matthew 19:3–24, 29–30; Matthew 20:1–16;
Matthew 21:28–31, 33–41; Matthew 22:1–32, 35–40; Matthew 23:1–33; Matthew
25:1–46; Matthew 26:49–50, 55, 57, 59–62; Matthew 27:[1], 26, 46; [Matthew 36:55];

Mark 2:15–17; Mark 14:[61–62], 63–64; Luke 2:1–7, 21–22, 39–49, 51–52; Luke 3:23–38; [Luke 6:12–16]; Luke 7:36–47; Luke 10:25–37; Luke 11:37–48, 52; Luke 12:13–21, 35–48; Luke 13:1–9; Luke 14:1–14, [25], 26–33; Luke 15:[1–2], 32; Luke 16:1–13, 19–31; Luke 17:7–10; Luke 18:1–8; Luke 22:24–27, 67–68, 70; Luke 23:1–25, 33–34; John 4:24; John 8:1–11; John 10:1–16; John 12:24–25; John 13:4–17, 34–35; John 18:1–5, 8, 12, 19–23, 36; and John 19:16, [17], 25–30. (The verses in brackets are those excluded in earlier works but included in subsequent reconstructions of Jefferson's 1804 work, already covered in the section above on Jefferson and miracles.)

108. Matthew 3:4–6, 13; Matthew 4:12; Matthew 5:1–47; Matthew 6:1–34; Matthew 7:1–20, 24–29; Matthew 8:1; Matthew 9:36; Matthew 10: 5–6, 9–18, 23, 26–31; Matthew 11:28–30; Matthew 12:1–5, 9–12, 14–15, 35–37; Matthew 13:1–9, 18–30, 36–57; Matthew 18:1–4, 7–9, 12–17, 21–35; Matthew 19:1–26; Matthew 20:1–16; Matthew 21:1–3, 6–8, 10, 17, 28–31, 33, 45, 46; Matthew 22:1–33, 40; Matthew 23:1–33; Matthew 24:1–2, 16–21, 29, 32, 33, 36–51; Matthew 25:1–46; Matthew 26:14–20, 31, 33, 35–45, 48–52, 55–57, 75; Matthew 27:3–8, 13, 15–23, 26–27, 29–31, 39–43, 46–50, 55–56, 60; Mark 1:4, 21–22; Mark 2:15–17, 27; Mark 3:31–35; Mark 4:10, 21–23, 26–34; Mark 6:6–7, 12, 30, 17–28; Mark 7:1–5, 14–24; Mark 11:12, 15–19, 27; Mark 12:1–9, 28–31, 32–33, 41–44; Mark 14:1–8, 51–52, 53, 55–61, 63–65; Luke 2:1–7, 21, 39–40, 42–48, 51–52; Luke 3:1–2, 23; Luke 5:27–29, 36–38; Luke 6:12–17, 24–26, 34–36, 38; Luke 7:36–46; Luke 9:57–62; Luke 10:1–8, 10–12, 25–42; Luke 11:1–13, 37–46, 52–54; Luke 12:1–7, 13–48, 54–59; Luke 13:1–9; Luke 14:1–24, 28–32; Luke 15:1–32; Luke 16:1–15, 18–31; Luke 17:1–4, 7–10, 20, 26–36; Luke 18:1–14; Luke 19:1–28; Luke 21:34–36; Luke 22:24–27, 33–34, 67–68, 70; Luke 23:5–16, 26–32, 34, 39–41; John 2:12–16; John 3:22; John 7:1–16, 19–26, 32, 43–53; John 8:1–11; John 9: 1–3; John 10:1–5, 11–14, 16; John 12:19–24; John 13:2, 4–17, 21–26, 31, 34–35; John 18:1–8, 15–18, 19–23, 25–31, 33–38; and John 19:17–27, 31–34, 38–42.

109. Matthew 5:1–10, 19–47; Matthew 6:1–34; Matthew 7:1–20, 24–29; Matthew 8:1; Matthew 10:5–6, 9–18, 23, 26–31; Matthew 11:28–30; Matthew 12:1–5, 11–12, 35–37; Matthew 13:1–9, 18–30, 36–43, 44, [45–51], 52; Matthew 18:1–4, 7–9, [12–14], 15–17; Matthew 19:3–24; Matthew 20:1–16; Matthew 21:28–31, 33; Matthew 22:1–32, 40; Matthew 23:1–33; Matthew 25:1–46; Matthew 26:49–50, 55, 57; Matthew 27:26, 46; Mark 2:15–17; Mark 14:[61], 63–64; Luke 2:1–7, 21, 39–40, 42–48, 51–52; Luke 3:23; [Luke 6:12–16]; Luke 7:36–46; Luke 10:25–37; Luke 11:37–46, 52; Luke 12:13–21, 35–48; Luke 13:1–9; Luke 14:1–14, 28–32; Luke 15:[1–2], 32; Luke 16:1–13, 19–31; Luke 17:7–10; Luke 18:1–8; Luke 22:24–27, 67–68, 70; Luke 23:5–16, 34; John 8:1–11; John 10:1–5, 11–14, 16; John 12:24; John 13:4–17, 34–35; John 18:1–5, 8, 12, 19–23, 36; and John 19:[17], 25–27. (The verses in brackets are those excluded in earlier works but included in subsequent reconstructions of Jefferson's 1804 work, already covered in the section above on Jefferson and miracles.)

110. Matthew 3:4–6, 13; Matthew 4:12; Matthew 5:11–18; Matthew 9:36; Matthew

12:9–10, 14–15; Matthew 13:53–57; Matthew 18: 7–9, 21–35; Matthew 19:1–2, 25; Matthew 23:1–3, 6–8, 10, 17, 45, 46; Matthew 22:33; Matthew 24:1–2, 16–21, 29, 32, 33, 36–51; Matthew 26:14–20, 31, 33, 35–45, 48, 51–52, 56, 75; Matthew 27:3–8, 13, 15–23, 27, 29–31, 39–43, 47–50, 55–56, 60; Mark 1:4, 21–22; Mark 2:27; Mark 3:31–35; Mark 4:10, 21–23, 26–34; Mark 6:6–7, 12, 30, 17–28; Mark 7:1–5, 14–24; Mark 11:12, 15–19, 27; Mark 12:1–9, 28–31, 32–33, 41–44; Mark 14:1–8, 51–52, 53, 55–60, 65; Luke 3:1–2; Luke 5:27–29, 36–38; Luke 6:17, 24–26, 34–36, 38; Luke 9:57–62; Luke 10:1–8, 10–12, 38–42; Luke 11:1–13, 53–54; Luke 12:1–7, 22–34, 54–59; Luke 14:15–24; Luke 15:3–31; Luke 16:14–15, 18; Luke 17:1–4, 20, 26–36; Luke 18:9–14; Luke 19:1–28; Luke 21:34–36; Luke 22:33–34; Luke 23:26–32, 39–41; John 2:12–16; John 3:22; John 7:1–16, 19–26, 32, 43–53; John 9: 1–3; John 12:19–23; John 13:2, 21–26, 31; John 18:6–7, 15–18, 25–31, 33–35; and John 19:18–27, 31–34, 38–42.

111. Matthew 5:48; Matthew 7:21–23; Matthew 8:11; Matthew 10:7–8, 19–22, 24–31, [34–41], 42; Matthew 11:[2–9]; Matthew 12:41–44, 46–50; Matthew 13:33, [34], 35; Matthew 15:1–20; Matthew 18:5–6, 10–11; Matthew 19:27–30; Matthew 23:32–41; Matthew 22:35–39; Matthew 26:59–62; Matthew 27: [1]; [Matthew 36:55]; Mark 14:[62]; Luke 2:22, 41–49; Luke 3:24–38; Luke 7:47; Luke 11:47–48; Luke 14:[25], 26–27, 33; Luke 23:1–4, 17–25, 33; John 4:24; John 10:6–10, 15; John 12:25; and John 19:16, 30. (The verses in brackets are those excluded in earlier works but included in subsequent reconstructions of Jefferson's 1804 work, already covered in the section above on Jefferson and miracles.)

112. *The Statutes at Large: Being a Collection of All the Laws of Virginia, from the First Session of the Legislature, in 1619,* William Waller Hening, editor (Richmond, VA: George Cochran, 1823), Vol. XI, 39, "ChaXXI: An Act to Authorize the Manumission of Slaves."

113. Ibid.

114. Thomas Jefferson, *The Works of Thomas Jefferson* (1905), Vol. XI, 419, to Edward Coles on August 25, 1814. See also E. B. Washburne, Sketch of Edward Coles (Chicago: Jansen, McClurg & Company, 1882), 27, to Edward Coles on August 25, 1814.

115. *The Statues at Large; Being A Collection of all the Laws of Virginia,* Vol. IX, 184–187, "An act for the appointment of naval officers and ascertain their fees" October, 1776; 267–279, "An act for regulating and disciplining the Militia," May, 1777; 471–472, "An act for preventing the farther importation of Slaves," October, 1778; (1822), Vol. X, 113, "An act for the manumission of a certain slave," May, 1779; 211, "An act for manumission of certain Slaves," October, 1779; 307–308, "An act to authorize the citizens of South Carolina and Georgia to remove their slaves into this state," May, 1780; 371, "An act for restoring certain slaves to George Harmer," October, 1780; 372, "An act for the manumission of certain Slaves," October, 1780; (1823), Vol. XI, 23–25, "An act for the recovery of slaves, horses, and other property, lost during the war," May, 1782; 39–40, "An act to authorize the manumission of slaves," May, 1782; 59, "An

act concerning Slaves," May, 1782; 308–309, "An act directing the emancipation of certain slaves who have served as soldiers in this state, and for the emancipation of the slave Aberdeen," October, 1783; 435, "An act to amend and reduce the several acts for appropriating the public revenue, into one act," October, 1784; (1823), Vol. XII, 145, "An act concerning wills," October, 1785; 182–183, "An act concerning slaves," October, 1785; 192–193, "An act for apprehending and securing runaways," October, 1785; 327, "An act to amend and condense into one act, the several laws for appropriating the public revenue," October, 1786; 345, "An act directing the method of trying Slaves charged with treason or felony," October, 1786; 380–381, "An act to emancipate James, a negro slave, the property of William Armistead, gentleman," October, 1786; 505–506, "An act to explain and amend the acts for preventing fraudulent gifts of slaves," passed December 31, 1787; 613–616, "An act to confirm the freedom of certain negroes late the property of Chareles Moorman, deceased," passed December 12, 1787; 681, "An act to repeal part of an act, directing the trial of slaves committing capital crimes, and for the more effectual punishing conspiracies and insurrections of them, and for the better government of negroes, mulattoes, or Indians, bond or free," passed November 21, 1788; 713–714, "An act concerning the importation of slaves, into the district of Kentucky," passed December 26, 1788; (1823), Vol. XIII, 30, "An act concerning the Benefit of Clergy," passed November 27, 1789, Sec. 8; 104–105, "An act appointing trustees for the purpose of purchasing certain slaves for the use and benefit of the children of James Bullock, deceased," passed December 1, 1789; 136–138, "An act for the better securing certain debts within mentioned, due and owing to the Commonwealth," passed December 25, 1790; 619, "An act for the manumission of a Negro named Saul," passed November 13, 1792; 619–620, "An act authorizing the emancipation of Abraham, a Negro Slave, late the property of Benjamin Temple," passed November 16, 1792; etc.; and *The Revised Code of the Laws of Virginia* (Ritchie, 1819), Vol. I, 421–444, "C. 111. An act reducing into one, the several acts concerning Slaves, Free Negroes and Mulattoes," passed March 2, 1819, footnotes for this act provide listing of law relating to slavery passed in the state and mention laws from 1794, 1797, 1803 and many others.

116. *The Revised Code of the Laws of Virginia* (Ritchie, 1819), Vol. I, 434, "An Act Reducing into One, the Several Acts Concerning Slaves, Free Negroes and Mulattoes," 1792.

117. Dumas Malone, *Jefferson and His Time: The Sage of Monticello* (Boston: Little, Brown and Company, 1981), Vol. Six, 511, Appendix II, "Jefferson's Financial Affairs."

118. Ibid., 489.

119. Paul Johnson, *A History of the American People* (New York: Harper Perennial, 1997), 244.

120. Dumas Malone, *Jefferson and His Time*, Vol. Six, 511–512.

121. Andrew Levy, *The First Emancipator: The Forgotten Story of Robert Carter the Founding Father Who Freed His Slaves* (New York: Random House, 2005), 169. See also "Robert 'Councilor' Carter III," Nomini Hall (at: http://rllint.people.wm.edu/robert.html) (accessed on August 30, 2012); "Robert Carter (1728–1804)," *Encyclopedia Virginia*, 2010 (at: http://www.encyclopediavirginia.org/Carter_Robert_1728-1804).

122. Throckmorton and Coulter, *Getting Jefferson Right*, 19.

123. Ibid.

INTRODUCTION

1. See, for example, *Thomas G. West, Vindicating the Founders: Race, Sex, Class, and Justice in the Origins of America* (New York: Rowman & Littlefield Publishers, 1997), 1–32; W. E. Burghardt DuBois, *The Suppression of the African Slave-Trade to the United States of America 1638–1870* (New York: Longmans, Green, and Co., 1896), 39–92; David Brion Davis, *The Problem of Slavery in the Age of Revolution 1770–1823* (Ithaca: Cornell University Press, 1975), 164–183.

2. Robert G. Parkinson, "First from the Right: Massive Resistance and the Image of Thomas Jefferson in the 1950s," *Virginia Magazine of History and Biography*, Vol. 112, No. 1, abstract (at: http://www.vahistorical.org/publications/abstract_parkinson.htm) (accessed on December 20, 2012).

3. John Leland, *The Writings of the Late Elder John Leland, Including Some Events in His Life, Written by Himself, With Additional Sketches*, L. F. Greene, editor (New York: G. W. Wood, 1845), 255, "A Blow at the Root: Being a Fashionable Fast-Day Sermon, Delivered at Cheshire, April 9, 1801."

4. Edwin A. Alderman, *Classics Old and New; A Series of School Readers; A Fifth Reader* (New York: American Book Company, 1907), 99.

5. Moses Jacob Ezekiel, "Thomas Jefferson," United States Senate (at: http://www.senate.gov/artandhistory/art/artifact/Sculpture_22_00002.htm) (accessed on December 20, 2012).

6. John Leland, *The Writings of the Late Elder John Leland*, 255, "A Blow at the Root: Being a Fashionable Fast-Day Sermon, Delivered at Cheshire, April 9, 1801."

7. Dumas Malone, *Jefferson and His Time: The Sage of Monticello* (Boston: Little, Brown and Company, 1981), Vol. Six, see title.

8. Thomas Marshall Green, *Historic Families of Kentucky* (Cincinnati: Robert Clarke Co., 1889), 73.

9. Jefferson has been featured on seventeen US postage stamps, as compared to 105 for Washington and 34 for Franklin. And he is one of three Americans to be featured simultaneously on paper currency and a coin (the two dollar bill and the nickel). However, reflecting the negative attitude that has developed toward Jefferson in recent years, only two of the postage stamps honoring him were issued in the past 45 years. (Stamps honoring Jefferson were issued in 1851, 1856, 1857, 1861, 1867, 1870, 1890, 1894, 1895, 1903, 1904, 1922, 1934, 1938, 1952, 1954, 1968, 1986, and 1993; and by the Confederacy in 1861 & 1862. At: http://sammler.com/stamps/president_stamps.htm.)

10. Thomas Jefferson, *The Papers of Thomas Jefferson*, Julian P. Boyd, editor (Princeton: Princeton University Press, 1953), Vol. 7, 586, written by Chelier de Chastellux on December 27, 1784, translated in a 1787 London manuscript.

11. Benjamin Rush, *Letters of Benjamin Rush*, L. H. Butterfield, editor (Philadelphia: American Philosophical Society, 1951), Vol. II, 779, to James Currie on July 26, 1796.

12. Ezra Stiles, *The Literary Diary of Ezra Stiles*, Franklin Bowditch Dexter, editor (New York: Charles Scribner's and Sons, 1901), Vol. III, 125, diary entry for June 8, 1784.

13. John Quincy Adams, *Diary of John Quincy Adams*, David Grayson Allen, editor (Cambridge: Harvard University Press, 1981), Vol. 1, 233, diary entry for March 11, 1785.

14. George Washington, *The Papers of George Washington*, W. W. Abbott, editor (Charlottesville: University Press of Virginia, 1997), Vol. 6, 294, to George Washington on May 25, 1788.

15. Alexis De Tocqueville, *Democracy in America*, Henry Reeve, translator (New York: George Dearborn & Co. & Adlard and Saunders, 1838), Vol. II, 186.

16. John Kennedy, "Remarks at a Dinner Honoring Nobel Prize Winners of the Western Hemisphere," The American Presidency Project, April 29, 1962 (at: http://www.presidency.ucsb.edu/ws/?pid=8623).

17. Leilani Corpus, "Tiananmen Square Massacre," *Forerunner*, June, 1989 (at: http://www.forerunner.com/forerunner/X0092_Tiananmen.html).

18. Esther B. Fein, "Clamor in the East; Unshackled Czech Workers Declare Their Independence," *New York Times*, November 28, 1989 (at: http://www.nytimes.com/1989/11/28/world/clamor-in-the-east-unshackled-czech-workers-declare-their-independence.html).

19. Thomas L. Friedman, "Upheaval in the East; Havel's 'Paradoxical' Plea: Help Soviets," *New York Times*, February 22, 1990 (at: http://www.nytimes.com/1990/02/22/world/upheaval-in-the-east-havel-s-paradoxical-plea-help-soviets.html?scp=2&sq=Thomas+Jefferson&st=nyt&pagewanted=all).

20. Ethan Schwartz, "Kosinski's Literary Homecoming: 'Painted Bird' to Be Published in Poland," *Washington Post*, April 5, 1989, 1.

21. Mikhail Gorbachev, "Notable Comments on Jefferson (20th Century)," Monticello, April 13, 1993 (at: http://www.monticello.org/site/jefferson/notable-comments-jefferson-20th-century).

22. David Remnick, "Ukraine Split on Independence as Republic Awaits Bush Visit," *Washington Post*, August 1, 1991, 1.

23. Margaret Thatcher, "Lady Margaret Thatcher at Monticello, on the Occasion of the 253rd Anniversary of the Birth of Thomas Jefferson and the Presentation of the First Thomas Jefferson Medal for Statesmanship," Monticello, April 13, 1996 (at: http://www.monticello.org/site/jefferson/notable-comments-jefferson-20th-century).

24. B. J. Lossing, *Biographical Sketches of the Signers of the Declaration of American Independence* (New York: George F. Cooledge & Brother, 1848), 174.

25. George Bancroft, *History of the United States of America, from the Discovery of the American Continent* (Boston: Little, Brown, & Company, 1864), Vol. VIII, 462–463.

26. Richard Frothingham, *The Rise of the Republic of the United States* (Boston: Little, Brown, and Company, 1872), 235.

27. John Fiske, *The American Revolution* (Boston: Houghton, Mifflin and Company, 1897), Vol. I, 193.

28. Edward S. Ellis, *Great Americans of History: Thomas Jefferson, a Character Sketch* (Chicago: Union School Furnishing Company, 1898), 38, 47.

29. William Eleroy Curtis, *The True Thomas Jefferson* (Philadelphia: J. B. Lippincott Company, 1901), 388.

30. Henry William Elson, *History of the United States of America* (New York: The Macmillan Company, 1914), 405.

31. Ken Burns, "Notable Comments on Jefferson (20th Century)," Monticello, June 7, 1996 (at: http://www.monticello.org/site/jefferson/notable-comments-jefferson-20th-century).

32. See, for example, *National Assessment of Education Progress at Grades 4, 8, and 12, The Nation's Report Card: U.S. History 2010* (U.S. Department of Education, 2011), 37; Intercollegiate Studies Institute American Civic Literacy Program, "Summary," 2008, 1–4; as well as numerous other periodic studies done by the National Endowment for the Humanities, the Colonial Williamsburg Charter Society, the US Capitol Historical Society, the American Council of Trustees and Alumni, the US Department of Education, the American School Board Journal, and others.

33. Report on NAEP nationwide testing, More than one-fifth of the students could not identify George Washington as the commander of the colonial forces during the Revolution. Seventy-four percent could not identify the purpose of the Emancipation Proclamation. And nearly half failed to recognize Patrick Henry as the man who said "Give me liberty or give me death." Anne D. Neal and Jerry L. Martin, *Restoring America's Legacy* (American Council of Trustees and Alumni, 2002), "Appendix A: Center for Survey Research & Analysis, Elite College History Survey. Conducted for the American Council of Trustees and Alumni," report from 1999, 4, concerning "Give me liberty or give me death" quote 66 percent correctly identified Patrick Henry, concerning the purpose of the Emancipation Proclamation 26 percent correctly identified what was proclaimed in it, concerning the American General at Yorktown 34 percent identified George Washington versus 37 percent identified Ulysses S. Grant.

34. Anne D. Neal and Jerry L. Martin, *Restoring America's Legacy* (American Council of Trustees and Alumni, 2002), "Appendix A: Center for Survey Research & Analysis, Elite College History Survey. Conducted for the American Council of Trustees and Alumni," report from 1999, 3.

35. Americans Failing Citizenship Test Again," American Enterprise Institute for Public Policy Research, April 30, 2012 (at: http://www.citizenship-aei.org/2012/04/americans-failing-citizenship-test-again/), says that 82% of Americans could not name two rights in the Declaration.

36. "Take the Quiz: What We Don't Know," Newsweek.com, March 20, 2011 (at: http://www.newsweek.com/2011/03/20/take-the-quiz-what-we-don-t-know.html).

37. See, for example, Lion Calandera, "Why do Americans get the Constitution so wrong?" The *Christian Science Monitor*, September 17, 2010 (at: http://www.csmonitor.com/

Commentary/Opinion/2010/0917/Why-do-Americans-get-the-Constitution-so-wrong); Brit Hume, "Poll: Most Americans Can Name Three Stooges, but Not Three Branches of Government," FoxNews, August 15, 2006 (at: http://www.foxnews.com/story/0,2933,208577,00.html#ixzz2E1kq5uZS).

38. "Americans Failing Citizenship Test Again," American Enterprise Institute for Public Policy Research, April 30, 2012 (at: http://www.citizenship-aei.org/2012/04/americans-failing-citizenship-test-again/), says that 75 percent incorrectly answered "What does the judiciary branch do?"

39. "Take the Quiz: What We Don't Know," Newsweek.com, March 20, 2011 (at: http://www.newsweek.com/2011/03/20/take-the-quiz-what-we-don-t-know.html).

40. Take the Quiz: What We Don't know," U.S. News, March 20, 2011 (at: http://www.thedailybeast.com/newsweek/2011/03/20/take-the-quiz-what-we-don-t-know.item-4.html).

41. "Americans Failing Citizenship Test Again," American Enterprise Institute for Public Policy Research, April 30, 2012 (at: http://www.citizenship-aei.org/2012/04/americans-failing-citizenship-test-again/),"; "Take the Quiz: What We Don't know," U.S. News, March 20, 2011 (at: http://www.thedailybeast.com/newsweek/2011/03/20/take-the-quiz-what-we-don-t-know.item-32.html).

42. Francie Grace, "Simpsons Outpace U.S. Constitution," CBS News, March 1, 2006 (at: http://www.cbsnews.com/news/simpsons-outpace-us-constitution/).

43. Ibid.

44. Of the twenty-seven, fourteen women and five men were tried, found guilty and hanged; another man was tortured to death by crushing because he refused to cooperate with the court by not answering their questions. To persuade him to talk they took him to a field and put a board on him with rocks, they increased the number of rocks until he would cooperate but he continued to refuse and was crushed to death. He was therefore never convicted but is considered the twentieth victim as he was on trial for being a wizard. And seven individuals died in prison awaiting trial; one was a baby in prison with her mother, who was awaiting trial as a witch. "The Salem Witch Trials of 1692," Salem Witch Museum, January 13, 2011 (at: http://www.salemwitchmuseum.com/education/index.shtml) per the museum's Department of Education.

45. William Warren Sweet, The Story of Religion in America (New York: Harper & Brothers, 1950), 61.

46. Charles B. Galloway, Christianity and the American Commonwealth (Nashville: Publishing House Methodist Episcopal Church, 1898), 110. Lower numbers are calculated by Brian P. Levack, The Witch-Hunt in Early Modern Europe, (New York: Longmans, 1987), 20–28, but still surpass 100,000. See also Ann Llewellyn Barstow, Witchcraze: A New History of the European Witch Hunts (San Francisco: Pandora, 1994), 179–181.

47. Charles B. Galloway, Christianity and the American Commonwealth, 110.

48. *Dictionary of American Biography*, Allen Johnson, editor (New York: Charles Scribber's Sons, 1929), s.v. "John Wise," "Increase Mather," and "Thomas Brattle." See also Mark Gribbean, "Salem Witch Trials: Reason Returns," Court TV: Crime Library (at: http://www.crimelibrary.com/notorious_murders/not_guilty/salem_witches/12.html?sect=12) (accessed on February 28, 2013); David D. Hall, *Witch-Hunting in Seventeenth-Century New England* (Boston: Northeastern University Press, 1991), 350, 354 fn25; and Jonathan Kirsch, *The Grand Inquisitor's Manual* (New York: HarperOne, 2008), 245.

49. John Fiske, *Civil Government in the United States Considered with some Reference to its Origins* (Boston: Houghton, Mifflin, and Company, 1890), 147–148, 198; David D. Hall, *A Reforming People: Puritanism and the Transformation of Public Life in New England* (New York: Alfred A. Knopf, 2011), passim; Francis J. Bremer, *The Puritan Experiment* (Lebanon, NH: University Press of New England, 1995), 62; Daniel L. Dreisbach and Mark David Hall, *The Sacred Rights of Conscience: Selected Readings on Religious Liberty an Church-State Relations in the American Founding* (Indianapolis: Liberty Fund Press, 2009), 86–102.

50. John Fiske, *Civil Government in the United States*, 147–148.

51. Ibid., 192.

52. Francis J. Bremer, *The Puritan Experiment* (Lebanon, NH: University Press of New England, 1995), 62; Francis C. Gray, *Remarks on the Early Laws of Massachusetts Bay; With the Code Adopted in the Year 1641 and Called The Body of Liberties, Now First Printed* (Boston: Charles C. Little and James Brown, 1843), 28–49, "A Copie of the Liberties of the Massachusetts Collonie in New England" (usually called the "Massachusetts Body of Liberties"), 1641 (online at: http://catalog.hathitrust.org/Record/010447674).

53. Concerning widespread education, see *The Code of 1650, Being a Compilation of the Earliest Laws and Orders of the General Court of Connecticut* (Hartford: Silus Andrus, 1822), 92–94, "Schooles" commonly called the "Old Deluder Satan Law." Concerning the high literacy rate, see, for example, John Adams, *The Works of John Adams*, Charles Francis Adams, editor (Boston: Charles C. Little and James Brown, 1851), Vol. III, 456, "A Dissertation on the Canon and Feudal Law," 1765 ("A native of America who cannot read and write is as rare as an appearance as a Jacobite or a Roman Catholic, that is, as rare as a comet or an earthquake"); Kenneth A. Lockridge, *Literacy in Colonial New England* (New York: W.W. Norton, 1974), 98, 13 (calculating that 60 percent of males in New England were literate in 1660, and that 85 percent were literate in 1760). See also Lawrence A. Cremin, *American Education: The Colonial Experience 1607–1783* (New York: Harper & Row, 1970, 546, which gives the literacy rate of England ranging from 48% in the rural areas to 74% in the towns vs. American literacy rates of 70–100% in the 1750's. Cf. Samuel Eliot Morison, *The Intellectual Life of Colonial New England* (New York: New York University Press, 1936), 82–85.

54. See, for example, *The Crossing* movie by A&E from 2000.

55. See, for example, *The Crossing* movie by A&E from 2000; *Secrets of the Founding Fathers* movie by the History Channel from 2009; *George Washington* movie by NBC (not yet released, January 2013), see information about this movie at: http://www.theblaze.com/stories/2012/11/15/nbc-is-developing-new-george-washington-drama/.

56. Megan Rolland, "Oklahoma City district pushes pause on hip-hop curriculum," NewsOK, October 1, 2010 (at: http://newsok.com/oklahoma-city-district-pushes-pause-on-hip-hop-curriculum/article/3500154?custom_click=masthead_toptenhttp://newsok.com/oklahoma-city-district-pushes-pause-on-hip-hop-curriculum/article/3500154?custom_click=masthead_topten)

57. See, for example, Simon Adams, *Propaganda in War & Peace: Manipulating the Truth* (Chicago: Heinemann Library, 2006), 23–24; Randall Huff, *American Popular Culture Through History: The Revolutionary War Era* (Westport, CT: Greenwood Press, 2004), 168–169; *Encyclopedia of Media and Propaganda in Wartime America*, Martin J. Manning and Clarence R. Wyatt, editors (ABC-CLIO, 2011), 76–77; *Readings in Propaganda and Persuasion: New and Classic Essays*, Garth S. Jowett and Victoria O'Donnell, editors (CA: Sage Publications, 2006), 76–78.

58. "M. Shahid Alam," DiscovertheNetworks (at: http://www.discoverthenetworks.org/individualProfile.asp?indid=2160) (accessed on December 19, 2012); "The Boston Tea Party Terrorism? Texas Schools are Teaching Just That (And More)," the *Blaze*, November 20, 2012 (at: http://www.theblaze.com/stories/was-the-boston-tea-party-terrorism-texas-schools-are-teaching-just-that-and-more/) – the curriculum mentioned "CSCOPE" is used in about 70 percent of Texas school districts (at: http://www.cscope.us/faq.html), but under public pressure, this claim was finally removed in 2012.

59. Dan Gainor, "Thanksgiving Celebrates Our 'Original Sin,' 'Views Virtually Identical To Nazis,' Journalism Prof Preaches," CNS News, November 22, 2012 (at: http://cnsnews.com/blog/dan-gainor/thanksgiving-celebrates-our-original-sin-views-virtually-identical-nazis-journalism); Megan Rolland, "Oklahoma City district pushes pause on hip-hop curriculum," NewsOK, October 1, 2010 (at: http://newsok.com/oklahoma-city-district-pushes-pause-on-hip-hop-curriculum/article/3500154?custom_click=masthead_topten) – the curriculum mentioned in this article is called "Flocabulary," and is used in over 15,000 schools according to the curriculum's website (at: http://flocabulary.com/what-is-flocabulary/).

60. Sanford Levinson, "Our Imbecilic Constitution," *New York Times*, May 28, 2012 (at: http://campaignstops.blogs.nytimes.com/2012/05/28/our-imbecilic-constitution/)

61. Charles Evans Hughes, *The Autobiographical Notes of Charles Evans Hughes*, David J. Danelski and Joseph S. Tulchin, editors (Cambridge: Harvard University Press, 1973), 144, speech at Elmira, May 3, 1907.

62. See, for example, the Ninth Circuit held in *Eklund v. Byron Unified Sch. Dist.*, No. C 02-3004 PJH (N.D. Cal. 2003), aff'd,154 Fed.Appx. 648 (9th Cir. 2005) (unpublished), cert. denied, 2006 WL 1522671 (Oct. 2, 2006) that students must be taught Islam, but then held in *Newdow v. U.S. Congress*, 292 F.3d 597 (9th Cir. 2002) that those same

students may not be exposed to the phrase "under God" in the Pledge of Allegiance, thus preferring Islam above Judeo-Christianity; Kamran Karimi, *In Allah They Trust* (Tulsa, OK: Harrison House, 2011), 18–23, foreword; Bob Unruh, "Muslim Religion Taught Under Guise of History," WND.com September 20, 2007 (at: http://www.wnd. com/2007/09/43621/); "Furor over Islam taught at US public school," AFP, April 16, 2008 (at: http://afp.google.com/article/ALeqM5hZ1Teh3JilpIBlmHrV58PvRRU09Q); Sabrina Ford, "Arabic mandatory at city public school," *New York Post*, May 24, 2012 (at: http://www.nypost.com/p/news/local/manhattan/arabic_mandatory_at_city_ public_UdLomjOOnZNfjDfs6YQrUN); Todd Starnes, "School Apologizes After Students Pray to Allah on Field Trip to Mosque," Fox News, September 17, 2010 (at: http://www.foxnews.com/us/2010/09/17/school-apologizes-students-pray-allah-field-trip-mosque/); Aryeh Weinberg, "Alone on the Quad: Understanding Jewish Student Isolation on Campus," Institute for Jewish & Community Research, December, 2011 (at: http://www.jewishresearch.org/quad/12-11/alone-quad.html); "Executive Summary: The Trouble with Textbooks: Distorting history and Religion," Institute for Jewish & Community Research (at: http://troublewithtextbooks.org/) (accessed on January 18, 2013).

63. John Witherspoon, *The Works of John Witherspoon* (Philadelphia: William W. Woodward, 1800), Vol. I, 306–307, "The Trial of Religious Truth by Its Moral Influence. A Sermon Preached at the Opening of the Synod of Glasgow and Air, October 9, 1759."

64. "2011 Population Data Sheet," Population Reference Bureau (at: http://www.prb.org/ Publications/Datasheets/2011/world-population-data-sheet/world-map.aspx#/map/ population/northern_america), numbers for 2011: 7 billion worldwide, 311.7 million for the U.S. for a percentage of 4.45; "United States GDP," *Trading Economics* (at: http:// www.tradingeconomics.com/united-states/gdp), numbers for 2011: "The GDP value of the United States represents 24.35 percent of the world economy."

65. See, for example, Daniel Luzer, "Professors Object to Texas Textbook Standards," *Washington Monthly*, April 17, 2010 (at: http://www.washingtonmonthly.com/college_ guide/blog/professors_object_to_texas_tex_1.php).

66. "Les Constitutions de la France," Conseil Constitutionnel (at: http://www.conseil-constitutionnel.fr/conseil-constitutionnel/francais/la-constitution/les-constitutions-de-la-france/les-constitutions-de-la-france.5080.html) (accessed on December 20, 2012). See also "French Legal Research," Georgetown Law Library (at: http://www. law.georgetown.edu/library/research/guides/frenchlegalresearch.cfm) (accessed on December 20, 2012).

67. "Brazil Index," International Constitutional Law (at: http://www.servat.unibe.ch/icl/ br__indx.html) (accessed on December 20, 2012); "Political Database of the Americas: Federative Republic of Brazil," Georgetown University (at http://pdba.georgetown.edu/ Constitutions/Brazil/brazil.html) (accessed on December 20, 2012).

68. "Info Poland: Constitutional History," University of Buffalo (at: http://info-poland. buffalo.edu/web/history/constitution/index.shtml) (accessed on December 20, 2012).

69. "History," (at: http://www.afghan-web.com/history/) (accessed on December 20, 2012).

70. "Russian History: Chronology Through 1990," Bucknell University (at: http://www.bucknell.edu/x20139.xmlhttp://www.bucknell.edu/x20139.xml) (accessed on December 20, 2012); "Russian History: Chronology Through Present," Bucknell University (at: http://www.bucknell.edu/x20140.xmlhttp://www.bucknell.edu/x20140.xml) (accessed on December 20, 2012).

71. Johan Kwantes, "The Idea Behind the Constitution: an Interview with Chaihark Hahm," Netherland Institutes for Advanced study in the Humanities and Social Sciences: 43, 10–14, (at: http://www.hiil.org/data/sitemanagement/media/The_confused_Korean_Constitutional_Identity-article_in_NIAS_newsletter_2_.pdf).

72. "Social Studies TEKS, Second Review: David Barton," Texas Education Agency, September 2009, 8 (at: http://www.tea.state.tx.us/index2.aspx?id=6184).

73. Ibid, 10, 12.

74. When the Matthew Shepard and James Byrd, Jr. Hate Crimes Prevention Act of 2009 was being marked up in the Judiciary Committee, ReLouis Gohmert introduced an amendment that the law also include the military and seniors under its protections, but it was voted down. Special protection was thus expanded to victims of crimes based on sexual orientation but not victims of crimes from other groups. See, for example, Louie Gohmert, "Hate Crimes Bill Infringes First Amendment Rights," *Texas Insider*, April 27, 2009 (at: http://www.texasinsider.org/hate-crimes-bill-infringes-first-amendment-rights/); "H.R. 1913: All Actions," Library of Congress: THOMAS, 2009 (at: http://thomas.loc.gov/cgi-bin/bdquery/z?d111:HR01913:@@@X).

75. Herbert M. Beck, *Aliens' Text Book on Citizenship* (Camden: Sinnickson Chew & Sons Co., 1919, 1941), 7–8.

76. Moni Basu, "Navajo man wants the nation to hear its officials apology," CNN, December 19, 2012 (at: http://inamerica.blogs.cnn.com/2012/12/19/native-american-apology/); "Five Times Obama Has Apologized for America," *Washington Free Beacon*, August 31, 2012 (at: http://freebeacon.com/five-times-obama-has-apologized-for-america/); Nile Gardiner and Morgan Lorraine Roach, "Barack Obama's Top 10 Apologies: How the President Has Humiliated a Superpower," The Heritage Foundation, June 2, 2009 (at: http://www.heritage.org/research/reports/2009/06/barack-obamas-top-10-apologies-how-the-president-has-humiliated-a-superpower); Elizabeth Harrington, "Michael Moore: 'Calm Down, White People, and Put Away Your Guns," CNSNews, December 26, 2012 (at: http://cnsnews.com/news/article/michael-moore-calm-down-white-people-and-put-away-your-guns); Louis Michael Seidman, "Let's Give Up on the Constitution," the *New York Times*, December 30, 2012 (at: www.nytimes.com/2012/12/31/opinion/lets-give-up-on-the-constitution.html?pagewanted=all&_r=4&); etc.

77. "Student Campaigns to Restore Pledge of Allegiance," *WND*, September 26, 2010 (at: http://www.wnd.com/2010/09/204669/).

78. See, for example, John Morton Blum, *Liberty, Justice, Order* (New York: W. W. Norton & Company, 1993), 26–27; Conor Cruise O'Brien, *The Long Affair. Thomas Jefferson and the French Revolution, 1785–1800* (Chicago: University of Chicago Press, 1996), 319; etc.

79. Variations of this argument are made by Mark Noll, Nathan Hatch, and George Marsden, *The Search for Christian America* (Westchester. Crossway Books, 1983), passim and es97-100; and John Fea, *Was America Founded as a Christian Nation?: A Historical Introduction* (Louisville: Westminster John Knox Press, 2011), 153–54.

80. See, for example, James Gillespie Birney, *The American Churches, The Bulwarks of American Slavery* (Newburyport: Charles Whipple, 1842; reprinted New York: Arno Press, 1969), 14–41. Additionally, in 1845, pro-slavery Baptists ministers and congregations split from their denomination to form the Southern Baptists; in 1850, the Southern Methodists also split and formed their own denomination over the slavery issue; and in 1861, pro-slavery Presbyterians similarly split to form their own denomination.

81. See, for example, James Gillespie Birney, *The American Churches*, 14–41.

82. See, for example, the *Los Angeles Times*, August 3, 1995, "America's Unchristian Beginnings" Steven Morris, B-9 (at: http://articles.latimes.com/print/1995-08-03/local/me-30974_1_jesus-christ). This article was picked up on wire services and appeared in newspapers across the nation; James Watkins, "Were United States Founding Fathers Christians?" *Hope and Humor* (at: http://www.jameswatkins.com/foundingfathers.htmhttp://www.jameswatkins.com/foundingfathers.htm) (accessed December 20, 2012); George Washington, *Maxims of George Washington* (Mount Vernon: The Mount Vernon Ladies' Association, 1989), 164; George Washington Remembers: *Reflections on the French and Indian War*, Fred Anderson, editor (Maryland: Rowman & Littlefield, 2004), 129; David L. Holmes, "The Founding Fathers, Deism, and Christianity," *Encyclopedia Britannica* (at: http://www.britannica.com/EBchecked/topic/1272214/The-Founding-Fathers-Deism-and-Christianity#908190.hook) (accessed on January 18, 2013); James Breig, "Deism: One Nation Under a Clockwork God?" Colonial Williamsburg, Spring 2009 (at: http://www.history.org/foundation/journal/spring09/deism.cfm); etc.

83. See, for example, Howard W. Allen and Jerome M. Clubb, *Race, Class, and the Death Penalty. Capital Punishment in American History* (New York: State University of New York Press, 2008), 21–23; Stuart Banner, *The Death Penalty: An American History* (Cambridge: Harvard University Press, 2002), 4–7.

84. Daniel Dorchester, *Christianity in the United States from the First Settlement Down to the Present Time* (New York: Phillips & Hunt, 1888), 121–122.

85. Ibid., 123–124.

86. See, for instance, *American Archives: Fourth Series. Containing A Documentary History of the English Colonies in North America, from the King's Message to Parliament on March 7, 1774 to the Declaration of Independence by the United States* (Washington: St.

Clair Clarke and Peter Force, 1837), Vol. I, 910–911, "Rights and Grievances of these Colonies," October 14, 1774; Vol. I, 917–921, "The Address to the People of Great Britain," October 21, 1774.

87. Henry Adams, *History of the United States During the First Administration of Thomas Jefferson* (New York: Scribners, 1889), Vol. 1, 277.

88. See, for example, Dr. D. James Kennedy, "Jefferson: Deist or Christian?" WND.com, June 19, 2002 (at: http://www.wnd.com/2002/06/14285/), which describes Jefferson as "a nominal Christian" but not "a genuine Christian"; "The Religious Affiliation of Third U.S. President Thomas Jefferson," adherents.com, July, 2005 (at: http://www.adherents.com/people/pj/Thomas_Jefferson.html), which describes Jefferson as holding "many clearly Christian, Deist, and Unitarian beliefs, but was not a member of any congregation or denomination"; Jim Walker, "Thomas Jefferson on Christianity & Religion," Free Republic (at: http://www.freerepublic.com/focus/news/745447/posts) (accessed on January 18, 2013), which describes Jefferson as believing "in a Creator" but "his concept of it resembled that of the god of deism"; "Thomas Jefferson and Religion," Wikipedia (at: http://en.wikipedia.org/wiki/Thomas_Jefferson_and_religion) (accessed on January 18, 2013), which describes Jefferson as being "most closely connected with Unitarianism and the religious philosophy of Christian deism"; etc.

89. For multiple examples of this phenomenon, see *The Forgotten Founders on Religion and Public Life*, Daniel L. Dreisbach, Mark David Hall, and Jeffry H. Morrison, editors (Notre Dame: University of Notre Dame Press, 2009), xiii–xxi, who describe this tendency. For specific examples, see Vincent Phillip Munoz, *God and the Founders: Madison, Washington, and Jefferson* (University of Notre Dame: Cambridge University Press, 2009); *The Founding Fathers and the Debate Over Religion in Revolutionary America: A History in Documents*, Matthew L. Harris and Thomas S. Kidd, editors (Oxford: Oxford University Press, 2012), "Table of Contents: The Founding Fathers' Own Views on Religion" which lists only Jefferson, John & Samuel Adams, Franklin, Thomas Paine, Patrick Henry, Roger Sherman, William Livingston and Elias Boudinot; Edwin S. Gaustad, *Faith of Our Fathers: Religion and the New Nation* (San Francisco: Harper & Row, 1987), "Contents" which lists Jefferson, Madison, Franklin, Washington, and John Adams; Frank Lambert, *The Founding Fathers and the Place of Religion in America* (Princeton: Princeton University Press, 2003), 173–177, 188, 210–211, 231, 236, 254, talking about Franklin, Jefferson, Paine, William Livingston, John Adams, Madison, William Williams, and Ezra Stiles; John Meacham, *American Gospel: God, the Founding Fathers, and the Making of a Nation* (New York: Random House, 2006), 3–95.

90. Thomas McKean, "The Following is a Copy Verbatim of the Sentence of the Court Upon John Roberts, Pronounced by His Honour the Chief Justice," *Pennsylvania Packet*, November 7, 1778; reprinted in William B. Reed, *Life and Correspondence of Joseph Reed* (Philadelphia: Lindsay and Blakiston, 1847), Vol. II, 36–37.

91. John Hancock, "A Proclamation for a Day of Fasting and Prayer," *Independent Chronicle and the Universal Advertiser*, March 26, 1789, 1; John Hancock, "A Proclamation for a Day of Fasting, Humiliation and Prayer," April 25, 1782, Evans #17593; John Hancock, "A Proclamation for a Day of Public Fasting and Prayer," May 15, 1783, Evans #18024; John Hancock, "A Proclamation for a Day of Humiliation, Fasting, and Prayer," April 17, 1788, Evans #21236; John Hancock, "A Proclamation for a Day of Fasting and Prayer," March 31, 1797, Evans #23549; John Hancock, "A Proclamation for a Day of Fasting, Humiliation, and Prayer," March 29, 1792, Evans #24519; John Hancock, "A Proclamation for a Day of Public Fasting, Humiliation and Prayer," April 11, 1793, from a Broadside in the General Editor's possession. See a complete list of the 22 calls to prayer in: William DeLoss Love, *The Fast and Thanksgiving Days of New England* (Boston: Houghton, Mifflin and Company, 1895), 505–508, "Calendar."

92. *The First Report of the Bible Society Established at Philadelphia; Read Before the Society at Their Annual Meeting, May 1, 1809* (Philadelphia: Printed by Order of Society; Fry and Kammerer, 1809), 31.

93. See, for example, *Cyclopedia of New Jersey Biography* (New York: American Historical Society, 1921), Vol. I, 33,"Hopkinson, Francis"; *The Pennsylvania Magazine of History and Biography* (Philadelphia: The Historical Society of Pennsylvania, 1882), Vol. VI, 124.

94. *Dictionary of American Biography*, 682, "Paine, Robert Treat."

95. John Sanderson, *Biography of the Signers to the Declaration of Independence* (Philadelphia: J. Maxwell, 1823), Vol. III, 202, 292; Charles A. Goodrich, *Lives of the Signers to the Declaration of Independence* (New York: Thomas Mather, 1840), 166–167.

96. See, for example, *Appleton's Cyclopedia of American Biography*, James Grant Wilson and John Fiske, editors (New York: D. Appleton and Company, 1889), Vol. VI, 584–585, "Witherspoon, John"; John Sanderson, *Biography of the Signers to the Declaration of Independence*, Vol. V, 104.

97. Kenneth C. Davis, *Don't Know Much About History* (New York: Avon Books, 1990), 61.

98. William Wirt, *Sketches of the Life and Character of Patrick Henry* (Philadelphia: James Webster, 1817), 123.

99. Kenneth C. Davis, *Don't Know Much About History*, 21.

100. Ebenezer Hazard, *Historical Collections; Consisting of State Papers, and Other Authentic documents; Intended as Materials for an History of the United States of America* (Philadelphia: T. Dobson, 1792) 119, "Agreement between the Settlers at New-Plymouth, November 11th, 1620."

101. George Washington, *Maxims of George Washington* (1989).

102. George Washington, *Maxims of Washington; Political, Social, Moral and Religious*, John F. Schroeder, editor (New York: D. Appleton and Company, 1855).

103. George Washington, *Maxims of George Washington* (1989), 164.

104. George Washington, *Maxims of Washington* (1855), 367.

105. Isaac Kramnick and Laurence Moore, *The Godless Constitution* (New York: W. W. Norton & Company, 1996), 12, 22, 27, passim.

106. Ibid., 179.

LIE #1

1. Eugene A. Foster et al., "Jefferson Fathered Slave's Last Child," *Nature*, November 5, 1998, Vol. 396, 27–28.

2. Eric Lander and Joseph Ellis, "Founding Father," *Nature*, November 5, 1998, Vol. 396, 1.

3. Christopher Hitchens, "What do Jefferson and Clinton have in common (besides randiness)?" *Ivory Tower*, quoting Joseph Ellis, November 18, 1998 (at: http://www.salon.com/it/feature/1998/11/cov_18featureb.html).

4. Dr. David N. Mayer, "The Thomas Jefferson-Sally Hemings Myth and the Politicization of American History," John M. Ashbrook Center for Public Affairs, April 9, 2001 (at: http://www.ashbrook.org/articles/mayer-hemings.html).

5. Henry Gee, "The Sex Life of President Thomas Jefferson," *Nature*, November 12, 1998 (at: http://www.nature.com/news/1998/981112/full/new981112-1.html).

6. Dr. David N. Mayer, "The Thomas Jefferson-Sally Hemings Myth and the Politicization of American History," John M. Ashbrook Center for Public Affairs, April 9, 2001 (at: http://www.ashbrook.org/articles/mayer-hemings.html).

7. See, for example, Andrea Dworkin, *Woman Hating* (New York: E. P. Dutton & Co., Inc., 1974), 184; Gloria Steinem, *Revolution from Within: A Book of Self-Esteem* (Boston: Little, Brown and Company,1992), 259–261; Marilyn French, *The War Against Women* (New York: Summit Books, 1992), 182; Robin Morgan, *The Word of a Woman* (New York: W. W. Norton & Company, 1992), 84; Catharine A. MacKinnon, *Feminism Unmodified* (Cambridge: Harvard University Press, 1987), 88; Naomi Wolf, *The Beauty Myth* (New York: William Morrow and Company, Inc., 1991), 138; Andrea Dworkin, *Our Blood* (New York: Harper & Row, 1976), 20; Andrea Dworkin, *Letters from a War Zone: Writings 1976–1989* (New York: E. P. Dutton, 1988), 14, 118–119; and Christina Hoff Sommers, *Who Stole Feminism? How Women Have Betrayed Women* (New York: Simon & Schuster, 1994), 44–46, 220, 222, assessing the statements of numerous feminists on this subject.

8. Peter S. Onuf, "Every Generation is an 'Independent Nation': Colonization, Miscegenation, and the Fate of Jefferson's Children," *The William and Mary Quarterly*, January 2000, Third Series, Vol. LVII, No. 1, 157.

9. See, for example, Gloria Sonnen, "The Enslaved American Woman: Her Unique Plight," Bowdoin College, History/Africana Studies, November 15, 1999, 4 "Master-Slave Relations" (at: http://www.bowdoin.edu/~prael/projects/gsonnen/page4.html); "Enslavement: 6. Master/ Slave," National Humanities Center (at: http://nationalhumanitiescenter.org/pds/maai/enslavement/text6/text6read.htm) (accessed on January 23, 2013); etc.

10. Fawn M. Brodie, *Thomas Jefferson, An Intimate History* (New York: W. W. Norton & Co., 1974); Barbara Chase-Riboud, *Sally Hemings: A Novel* (New York: St. Martin's Press, 1979); Annette Gordon-Reed, *Thomas Jefferson and Sally Hemings: An American Controversy* (Charlottesville: The University Press of Virginia, 1997).

11. Jan Ellen Lewis and Peter S. Onuf, *Sally Hemings and Thomas Jefferson: History, Memory, and Civic Culture,* (University of Virginia: University of Virginia Press, 1999), 104 105, 107; Paul R. Abramson, et. al., *Sexual Rights in America: the Ninth Amendment and the Pursuit of Happiness* (New York: New York University Press, 2003), 9; *Writings African American Women: An Encyclopedia of Literature By and About Women of Color,* Elizabeth Ann Beulieu, editor (Westport, CT: Greenwood Press, 2006), Vol. 2, 796, "Slave Narrative"; Margaret L. Anderson and Howard F. Taylor, *Sociology: Understanding a Diverse Society.* Fourth Edition (CA: Thomason Learning Inc., 2008), 345–346; etc.

12. Although the portrayal if often made that white slaveowner sexual abuse of black female slaves was common and widespread, numerous historical studies indicate that sexual relations between white masters and black slaves actually occurred only in a small minority of cases and that the overwhelming majority of white masters did not exercise a sexual prerogative over their female slaves. For example, by 1850 the American population had grown to a burgeoning 23.2 million; the slave population was 3.2 million, or 13.8 percent of the total population. Among the black population over the sixty years since the first census in 1790, census numbers show a maximum of 11.2 percent of the 1850 population to be mulatto, which represents only 1.55 percent of the total America population. See, for example, J. D. B. DeBow, *Statistical View of the United States, Embracing its Territory, Population – White, Free Colored, and Slave – Moral and Social Condition, Industry, Property, and Revenue; the Detailed Statistics of Cities, Towns, and Counties; Being a Compendium of the Seventh Census* (Washington, DC: Beverley Tucker, 1854), 39, 63, 82; Department of Commerce Bureau of the Census, William J. Harris, director, *Negroes in the United States* (Washington, DC: Government Printing Office, 1915), Bulletin 129, 15. See also Edward Byron Reuter, *The Mulatto in the United States* (Boston: The Gorham Press, 1918), 116, etc. Yet despite the clear statistical facts and the numerous studies, see writers such as Peter S. Onuf, "Every Generation Is an 'Independent Nation': Colonization, Miscegenation, and the Fate of Jefferson's Children," the *William and Mary Quarterly,* January 2000, Third Series, Vol. LVII, No. 1, wherein he uniformly stereotypes all Anglos by decrying the "whites' despotic power over their . . . female slaves' bodies," 157; "the despotic power of white masters over the bodies of black female slaves," 158; "white men exploited black women," 160; "White slave owners exploited their slave women," 160; passim.

13. Faye Z. Belgrave and Kevin W. Allison, *African American Psychology: From Africa to America.* Second Edition (CA: Sage Publications, 2010), 437–438; Catherine Fisher Collins, *The Imprisonment of African American Women: Causes, Experiences and Effects.* Second Edition (Jefferson, NC: McFarland & Company, Inc., 2010), 42–43.

14. See, for example, Michelle Chen, "Bill to Study Slavery Reparations Still Facing Resistance," *New Standard*, March 7, 2007 (at: http://newstandardnews.net/content/index.cfm/items/4449); Paul Shepard, "U.S. Slavery Reparations: Hope that a race will be compensated gains momentum," *Seattle Times*, February 11, 2011 (at: http://community.seattletimes.nwsource.com/archive/?date=20010211&slug=reparation11); *Reparations for Slavery: A Reader*, Ronald P. Salzberger and Mary C. Truck, editors (Maryland: Rowman & Littlefield Publishers, 2004); Raymond Winbush, *Should America Pay? Slavery and Raging Debate on Reparations* (Harper Collins, 2010); etc.

15. Eugene A. Foster, et. al, "Reply: The Thomas Jefferson Paternity Case," *Nature*, January 7, 1999, Vol. 397, 32 (at: http://www.nature.com/nature/journal/v397/n6714/full/397032c0.html).

16. Thomas Jefferson, *The Papers of Thomas Jefferson,* Barbara B. Oberg, editor (Princeton: Princeton University Press, 2004), Vol. 31, 274, to John Wales Eppes on December 21, 1799.

17. See, for example, Jone Johnson Lewis, "Sally Hemings: Mistress of Thomas Jefferson?" About.com (at: http://womenshistory.about.com/od/hemingssally/a/sally_hemings.htm) (accessed on January 23, 2013); Annette Gordon-Reed, *Thomas Jefferson and Sally Hemings*, 1, 172; Fawn M. Brodie, Thomas Jefferson, An Intimate History, 228–232.

18. The children generally agreed upon by most scholars include Thomas (born in 1790), Harriet I (apparently died in infancy), Beverly (son, born 1798), Harriet II (1801), Madison (1805), and Eston (1808). However, authorities from Monticello, where Hemings was a slave, indicate that she had six children. However, other modern writers have placed the number of Hemings' children at anywhere from four to seven – or more. For example: four children – "Sally Hemings," *New York Times* (at: http://topics.nytimes.com/top/reference/timestopics/people/h/sally_hemings/index.html) (accessed on January 23, 2013); five children – McKenzie Wallenborn, "Dr. Wallenborn's Minority Report," Monticello, March 23, 2000 (at: http://www.monticello.org/site/plantation-and-slavery/minority-report-monticello-research-committee-thomas-jefferson-and-sally); six children – "Thomas Jefferson and Sally Hemings: A Brief Account," Monticello (at: http://www.monticello.org/plantation/hemingscontro/hemings-jefferson_contro.html) (accessed on January 23, 2013); Jone Johnson Lewis, "Sally Hemings: Mistress of Thomas Jefferson?" About.com (at: http://womenshistory.about.com/od/hemingssally/a/sally_hemings.htm) (accessed on February 24, 2011); R. F. Holznagel and Paul Hehn, "Who2.com profile of Sally Hemings," Who2.com (at: http://www.who2.com/sallyhemings.html) (accessed on January 23, 2013); and seven children – Glenn Speark, "'The Hemingses of Monticello' by Annette Gordon-Reed: A look at the third president, his slave mistress and the antebellum South," *Los Angeles Times*, November 14, 2008 (at: http://articles.latimes.com/2008/nov/14/entertainment/et-book14); and other varying numbers – Patrick Mullins, "Scholars Overturn Case for Thomas Jefferson's Relationship with Slave Sally Hemings," *Capitalism Magazine*, June 2, 2001 (at: http://www.tjheritage.org/documents/CapitalismMagazine.pdf); "Thomas

Jefferson and Sally Hemings: Case Closed?" Claremont Institute, August 30, 2001 (at: http://www.claremont.org/publications/crb/id.1015/article_detail.asp); Annette Gordon-Reed, "Thomas Jefferson and Sally Hemings: An American Controversy," review by Harry Hellenbrand, H-Net Reviews, February, 1998 (at: www.h-net.msu.edu/reviews/showpdf.cgi?path=8812887909950).

19. See, for example, the forum published in the *William and Mary Quarterly*, January 2000, Third Series, Vol. LVII, No. 1 (January 2000), 121–210, with the opinions of Jan Lewis, Joseph J. Ellis, Lucia Stanton, Peter S. Onuf, Annette Gordon-Reed, Andrew Burstein, and Fraser D. Neiman.

20. Eric Lander and Joseph Ellis, "Founding Father," *Nature*, November 5, 1998, Vol. 396, 1.

21. Joseph J. Ellis, "Jefferson: Post-DNA," the *William and Mary Quarterly*, Third Series, Vol. LVII, No. 1 (January 2000), 136, n14.

22. Dennis Cauchon, "Jefferson Affair No Longer Rumor," *USA Today*, November 2, 1998.

23. Barbra Murray and Brian Duffy, "Jefferson's Secret Life," *U.S. News* Online, November 9, 1998 (at: http://www.usnews.com/usnews/culture/articles/981109/archive_005152.htm).

24. Donna Britt, "A Slaveholder's Hypocrisy was Inevitable," *Washington Post*, November 6, 1998, B01.

25. Dinitia Smith and Nicholas Wade, "DNA Tests Offer Evidence that Jefferson Fathered a Child With His Slave," *New York Times*, November 1, 1998.

26. Clarence Page, "New Disclosures Show Two Thomas Jeffersons," *Chicago Tribune*, November 5, 1998, 1.

27. Ibid., 2.

28. Christopher Hitchens, "What do Jefferson and Clinton have in common (besides randiness)?" *Ivory Tower*, November 18, 1998, 3–4 (at: http://www.salon.com/it/feature/1998/11/cov_18featureb.html).

29. Richard Cohen, "Grand Illusion," *Washington Post*, December 13, 1998, W10.

30. Clarence Page, "New Disclosures," 2.

31. Dinitia Smith and Nicholas Wade, "DNA Tests Offer Evidence that Jefferson Fathered a Child with His Slave," *New York Times*, November 1, 1998.

32. Dr. David N. Mayer "The Thomas Jefferson-Sally Hemings Myth and the Politicization of American History," John M. Ashbrook Center for Public Affairs, April 9, 2001 (at: http://www.ashbrook.org/articles/mayer-hemings.html), quoting Prof. Annette Gordon-Reed, "The All Too Human Jefferson," *Wall Street Journal*, November 24, 1998, Letter to the Editor.

33. Joseph J. Ellis, "Jefferson: Post-DNA," the *William and Mary Quarterly*, Third Series, Vol. LVII, No. 1 (January 2000), 130. See also Michael Lind, *The Next American Nation: The New Nationalism and the Fourth American Revolution* (New York: The Free Press, 1995), 369–371; Conor Cruise O'Brien, *The Long Affair*, 306–307.

34. Eugene A. Foster, et. al, "Jefferson Fathered Slave's Last Child," *Nature*, November 5, 1998, Vol. 396, 27–28.

35. Eugene A. Foster, et. al, "Reply: The Thomas Jefferson Paternity Case," *Nature*, January 7, 1999, Vol. 396, 32 (at: http://www.nature.com/nature/journal/v397/n6714/full/397032c0.html).

36. For a list of the professors and the schools they're associated with, see this link: http://www.tjheritage.org/scholars.html.

37. The Jefferson-Hemings Scholars Commission, "Final Report," Thomas Jefferson Heritage Society, 19, April 12, 2011 (at: http://www.tjheritage.org/documents/SCReport1.pdf).

38. The Jefferson-Hemings Scholars Commission, "Final Report," Thomas Jefferson Heritage Society, 13, April 12, 2001 (at: http://www.tjheritage.org/documents/SCreport.pdf).

39. Gene Edward Veith, "Founder's DNA Revisited," *World*, February 20, 1999, 24.

40. Mona Charen, "Was Jefferson Libeled by DNA?" *Jewish World Review*, January 19, 1999 (at: http://jewishworldreview.com/cols/charen011999.asp).

41. Herbert Barger, "The Jefferson-Hemings DNA Study," Angel Fire, released February 12, 1999, revised August 30, 2000 (at: http://www.angelfire.com/va/TJTruth/background.html).

42. The Jefferson-Hemings Scholars Commission, "Final Report," Thomas Jefferson Heritage Society, 9, April 12, 2001 (at: www.tjheritage.org/documents/SCReport1.pdf).

43. The Jefferson-Hemings Scholars Commission, "Final Report," Thomas Jefferson Heritage Society, 28–30, April 12, 2001 (at: http://www.tjheritage.org/documents/SCreport.pdf).

44. Eugene Foster, et. al., "Reply: The Thomas Jefferson Paternity Case," *Nature*, January 7, 1999, Vol. 396, 32 (at: http://www.nature.com/nature/journal/v397/n6714/full/397032c0.html).

45. Jefferson family genealogist reports that he provided this information to these outlets but that it was ignored by them. See Herbert Barger, "Letters to the Editor: Rushing to Rescue TJ," *C-ville Weekly*, November, 2005. See also Jan Ellen Lewis and Peter S. Onuf, "Sally Hemings and Thomas Jefferson: History, Memory and Civic Culture," Thomas Jefferson Heritage Society, book review by Herbert Barger (at: http://www.tjheritage.org/books.html) (accessed on January 24, 2013).

46. See, for example, John Marshall, "Ellis doesn't want to revisit his own past," *Seattle Post-Intelligencer*, December 6, 2004 (at: http://www.seattlepi.com/ae/books/article/Ellis-doesn-t-want-to-revisit-his-own-past-1161328.php); Bonnie Goodman, "Has Scandal Taken Its Toll on Joseph Ellis?" History News Network, June 29, 2005 (at: http://hnn.us/articles/8656.html); Ana Marie Cox, "In Wake of the Scandal Over Joseph Ellis, Scholars Ask 'Why?' and 'What Now?'," *Chronicle of Higher Education*, July 13, 2001 (at: http://www.wellesley.edu/Polisci/wj/227/Ellis/44a01001.htm); Dennis Loy Johnson, "The History Lesson of Joseph Ellis," Mobylives.com, June 20, 2001 (at: http://www.mobylives.com/Joseph_Ellis.html).

47. Dennis Loy Johnson, "The History Lesson of Joseph Ellis," Mobylives.com, June 20, 2001 (at: http://www.mobylives.com/Joseph_Ellis.html).

48. "Review & Outlook: Founding Fatherhood," *Wall Street Journal*, February 26, 1999, Sec. W, 15.

49. Gene Edward Veith, "Founder's DNA Revisited," *World*, February 20, 1999, 24.

50. Mona Charen, "Was Jefferson Libeled by DNA?" *Jewish World Review*, January 19, 1999 (at: http://jewishworldreview.com/cols/charen011999.asp).

51. "DNA Test Fails to Link Jefferson, Monticello Slave Descendant," *Washington Post*, March 23, 2000. Additionally, on March 20, 2000, our WallBuilders office personally spoke with Dr. Eugene Foster, who had conducted the testing, to affirm that his most recent testing had again proved that Thomas Jefferson was not the father of Thomas Woodson; Dr. Foster confirmed that such was the case.

52. Madison Hemings, "Life Among the Lowly," Pike County (Ohio) *Republican*, March 13, 1873, reprinted by Annette Gordon-Reed, *Thomas Jefferson and Sally Hemings*, 246, Appendix B.

53. Ibid. See also Dumas Malone, *Jefferson and His Time: Jefferson the Virginian* (Boston: Little, Brown and Company, 1948), Vol. One, 384; Dumas Malone, *Jefferson and His Time: The Sage of Monticello* (Boston: Little, Brown and Company, 1981), Vol. Six, xv, 146.

54. Annette Gordon-Reed, *Thomas Jefferson and Sally Hemings*, 259, Appendix E.

55. Letter from Ellen Randolph Coolidge to Joseph Coolidge on October 26, 1858, original on file at the University of Virginia Library; David N. Myer, "The Thomas Jefferson–Sally Hemings Myth and the Politicization of American History," Ashbrook Center, April 9, 2001 (at: http://www.ashbrook.org/articles/mayer-hemings.html).

56. Jan Lewis, "Introduction," *William and Mary Quarterly*, January, 2000, Third Series, Vol. VII, No. 1, 122.; "What's Next for 'Genius Grant' Winner Gordon Reed," NPR, September 28, 2010 (at: http://www.npr.org/templates/story/story.php?storyId=130180642).

57. Joseph J. Ellis, "Jefferson: Post-DNA," the *William and Mary Quarterly*, January 2000, Third Series, Vol. LVII, No. 1, 136–137, n15.

58. *Dictionary of American Biography*, Allen Johnson, editor (New York: Charles Scribner's Sons, 1929), s.v. "James Thomson Callender."

59. Thomas Jefferson, *The Papers of Thomas Jefferson*, Barbara B. Oberg, editor (Princeton: Princeton University Press, 2003), Vol. 30, 583, James Callender to Thomas Jefferson on November 19, 1798.

60. These numbers are based on searches through the published *Papers of Thomas Jefferson* and the Library of Congress' online collection of the same. See, for example, "The Thomas Jefferson Papers" collection from the *Library of Congress* (at: http://www.loc.gov/collections/thomas-jefferson-papers/?q=Callender). The three letters that Jefferson wrote to James Callender are dated October 11, 1798, September 6, 1799, and October 6, 1799.

61. James Madison, *The Papers of James Madison*. Secretary of State Series, Robert J. Brugger, editor (Charlottesville: University Press of Virginia, 1986), Vol. I, 117, James Callender to James Madison on April 27, 1801, after Jefferson failed to respond to a letter from Callender on April 12, 1801; Thomas Jefferson, *The Papers of Thomas Jefferson*, Vol. 33, 573–574, James Callender to Thomas Jefferson on April 12, 1801.

62. Thomas Jefferson, *Memoir, Correspondence, and Miscellanies*, Thomas Jefferson Randolph, editor (Charlottesville: F. Carr, and Co., 1829), Vol. IV, 23, to Mrs. John Adams on July 22, 1804.

63. James Madison, *Letters and Other Writings of James Madison* (Philadelphia: J. P. Lippincott & Co., 1865), Vol. II, 172, to James Monroe on May 6, 1801.

64. Thomas Jefferson, *The Writings of Thomas Jefferson*, Andrew A. Lipscomb, editor (Washington, DC: The Thomas Jefferson Memorial Association, 1903), Vol. X, 332, letter to James Monroe on July 15, 1802, where Jefferson says, "Soon after I was elected to the government, Callender came on here, wishing to be made postmaster at Richmond. I knew him to be totally unfit for it; and however ready I was to aid him with my own charities (and I then gave him fifty dollars,) I did not think the public offices confided to me to give away as charities."

65. Thomas Jefferson, *The Writings of Thomas Jefferson* (1903), Vol. X, 332, letter to James Monroe on July 15, 1802 and James Madison, *Letters and Other Writings*, Vol. II, 173, letter to James Monroe on June 1, 1801.

66. Thomas Jefferson, *The Works of Thomas Jefferson*, Paul Leicester Ford, editor (New York: G. P. Putnam's Sons, 1900), Vol. IX, 260, to James Monroe on May 26, 1801.

67. Ibid., Vol. IX, 262–263, to James Monroe on May 29, 1801.

68. James Monroe, *The Writings of James Monroe*, Stanislaus Murray Hamilton, editor (New York: G. P. Putnam's Sons, 1900), Vol. III, 289, to Thomas Jefferson on June 1, 1801.

69. James Madison, *Letters and Other Writings*, Vol. II, 173, to James Monroe on June 1, 1801.

70. Ibid.

71. James Monroe, *The Writings of James Monroe*, Vol. III, 290, to James Madison on June 6, 1801.

72. James Madison, *The Papers of James Madison*, Robert J. Brugger, editor (Charlottesville: University Press of Virginia, 1986), Vol. I, 117, James T. Callender to James Madison on April 27, 1801.

73. Ibid., Vol. I, 118, James T. Callender to James Madison on April 27, 1801.

74. *Dictionary of American Biography*, s.v. "James Thomson Callender."

75. Dumas Malone, *Jefferson the President, First Term, 1801–1805* (Boston: Little, Brown and Company, 1970), Vol. Four, 220, n43, quoting from *N.Y. Evening Post* on February 27, 1805.

76. See, for example, *Dictionary of American Biography*, s.v. "James Callender"; PBS: *American Experience* (at: http://www.pbs.org/wgbh/amex/adams/peopleevents/p_callender.html) (accessed on July 26, 2013); *George Morgan, The Life of James Monroe* (Boston: Small, Maynard and Company, 1921), 211; and many others.

77. Dumas Malone, *Jefferson the President, First Term*, Vol. Four, 208, quoting the *Richmond Recorder* on May 28, 1803.

78. J. T. Callender, "The President Again," *The Recorder; Or, Lady's and Gentleman's Miscellany* (Richmond), September 1, 1802.

79. Ibid.

80. Ibid., December 8, 1802.

81. Thomas Jefferson Memorial Foundation, "Report of the Research Committee on Thomas Jefferson and Sally Hemings," Monticello, January, 2000 (at: http://www. monticello.org/sites/default/files/inline-pdfs/jefferson-hemings_report.pdf).

82. J. T. Callender, "More About Sally and the President," *The Recorder; Or, Lady's and Gentleman's Miscellany* (Richmond), September 22, 1802.

83. Thomas Jefferson Memorial Foundation, "Report of the Research Committee on Thomas Jefferson and Sally Hemings," Monticello, January, 2000, quoting from the Richmond Recorder on December 1, 1802 (at: http://www.monticello.org/sites/default/files/inline-pdfs/jefferson-hemings_report.pdf).

84. Ibid.

85. *The Boston Gazette, Commercial and Political* (Boston: 1802), 2, "Jefferson and Sally," September 16, 1802.

86. J. T. Callender, *The Prospect Before Us* (Richmond: 1800), Vol. 1, 27, 34, passim.

87. Ibid., Vol. 1, 4, 9, 18, 22, 24, 26–28, 32, 34, and passim.

88. Dumas Malone, *Jefferson the President, First Term*, Vol. Four, 207.

89. James Truslow Adams, *The Living Jefferson* (New York: Charles Scribner's Sons, 1936), 315.

90. Virginius Dabney, *The Jefferson Scandals: A Rebuttal* (New York: Dodd, Mead, & Company, 1981), 15.

91. Dumas Malone, *Jefferson the President, First Term*, Vol. Four, 212.

92. John Chester Miller, *The Wolf by the Ears: Thomas Jefferson and Slavery* (New York: The Free Press, 1977), 153.

93. Ibid., 154.

94. Benjamin Ellis Martin, "Transition Period of the American Press," *Magazine of American History*, Martha J. Lamb, editor (New York City: A. S. Barnes & Company, 1887), Vol. XVII, No. 4, 285, April 1887.

95. Ibid., 285–286.

96. Thomas Jefferson, *The Works of Thomas Jefferson* (1905), Vol. X, 368 to Thomas Seymour on February 11, 1807. See also *Thomas Jefferson, Memoir, Correspondence, and Miscellanies*, Vol. IV, 129, to Wilson C. Nicholas on June 13, 1809.

97. Charles Warren, *Odd Byways in American History* (Cambridge: Harvard University Press, 1942), 127. See also Dumas Malone, *Jefferson and the Ordeal of Liberty* (Boston: Little, Brown and Company, 1962), Vol. Three, 479.

98. Dumas Malone, *Jefferson the President, First Term*, Vol. Four, 206.

99. Thomas Jefferson, *The Works of Thomas Jefferson* (1905), Vol. XI, 366, to Dr. George Logan on June 20, 1816.

100. Thomas Jefferson, *The Writings of Thomas Jefferson*, Vol. XI, 155, to Thomas Seymour on February 11, 1807.

101. Thomas Jefferson, *Memoir, Correspondence, and Miscellanies*, Vol. IV, 129, to Wilson C. Nicholas on June 13, 1809.

102. Ibid., Vol. III, 439, to Uriah McGregory on August 13, 1800.

103. Kenneth Chang, "DNA Tests Sheds Light On Old Scandal: Jefferson Fathered Slave Son," ABC News, November 5, 1998.

104. Thomas Jefferson, *Memoir, Correspondence, and Miscellanies,* Vol. III, 494–495, to Governor James Monroe on July 15, 1802.

105. Thomas Jefferson, *Memoir, Correspondence, and Miscellanies*, Thomas Jefferson Randolph, editor (Charlottesville: F. Carr, and Co., 1829), Vol. IV, 24, to Mrs. John Adams on July 22, 1804.

106. Thomas Jefferson, *Memoir, Correspondence, and Miscellanies*, Thomas Jefferson Randolph, editor (Boston: Gray and Bowen, 1830) Vol. IV, 129, to William Duane on March 22, 1806; Thomas Jefferson, *Thomas Jefferson Correspondence: Printed from the Originals in the Collections of William K. Bixby*, Worthington Chauncey Ford, editor (Boston: Plimpton Press, 1916), 115, to Robert Smith on July 1, 1805.

107. Fawn M. Brodie, *Thomas Jefferson: An Intimate History* (New York: W. W. Norton & Company, Inc., 1974), 229.

108. Ibid.

109. Jedidiah Morse, *The American Geography* (London: John Stockdale, 1792), 447.

110. University of Texas/Texas State Historical Association, "Southwestern Historical Quarterly: A. W. Moore, A Reconnaissance in Texas in 1846," University of Texas, Vol. 30, July 1926–April 1927 (at: http://texashistory.unt.edu/ark:/67531/metapth117142/m1/278/).

111. Alfred Theodore Andreas, *A. T. Andreas Illustrated Historical Atlas of the State of Iowa* (Andreas Atlas Co., 1875), 468.

112. James V. Drake, *An Historical Sketch of Wilson County, Tennessee, From Its First Settlement to the Present Time* (Nashville: Tavel, Eastman & Howell, 1879), 10.

113. Alfred Theodore Andreas, *History of the State of Kansas,* William C. Cutler, editor (Chicago: A. T. Andreas, 1883), 486.

114. *Biographical and Historical Memoirs of Fulton County, Arkansas* (originally published 1889, reprinted Higginsville, MO: Hearthstone Legacy Publications, 2004), 261.

115. Willard Sterne Randall, *Thomas Jefferson: A Life* (New York: Henry Holt and Co., 1994), 476.

116. Garry Wills, "Uncle Thomas's Cabin," the *New York Review of Books*, book review of Fawn Brodie's *Thomas Jefferson: An Intimate History*, April 18, 1974.

LIE #2

1. Dr. Daryl Cornett, David Barton, William Henard, and John Sassi, *Christian America? Perspectives on Our Religious Heritage* (Nashville: Broadman & Holman, 2011), 289–290.

2. Anita Vickers, *New Nation* (Westport, CT: Greenwood Press, 2002), 74.

3. Leonard Levy, *Jefferson and Civil Liberties: The Darker Side* (Cambridge: The Belknap Press of Harvard University Press, 1989), 15.

4. John S. Brubacher & Willis Rudy, *Higher Education in Transition: A History of American Colleges and Universities*. Fourth Edition (New Brunswick, NJ: Transaction Books, 2004), 147–148.

5. Thomas Jefferson, *Memoir, Correspondence, and Miscellanies*, Thomas Jefferson Randolph, editor (Charlottesville: F. Carr and Co., 1829), Vol. I, 39, "Autobiography"; *The History of the College of William and Mary From its Foundation, 1693 to 1870* (Baltimore: John Murphy & Co., 1870), 157. The College of William & Mary was a part of the Church of England, or the Anglican Church, when Jefferson entered the college in 1760. Students were required to attend daily prayers, which were taken from the *Book of Common Prayer*. To see the Scriptural and religious content of those daily activities at that time, see *The Book of Common Prayer, and Administration of the Sacraments, and Other Rites and Ceremonies of the Church, According to the Use of the Church of England* (Cambridge: Joseph Bentham, 1760), with its "The Calendar; with the Table of Lessons" for the daily Scripture readings.

6. Thomas Jefferson, *The Works of Thomas Jefferson*, Henry A. Washington, editor (New York: Townsend Mac Coun., 1884), Vol. I, 2, "Autobiography Draft Fragment, January 6, 1821."

7. George Marsden, *The Soul of the American University* (New York: Oxford University Press, 1994), 59.

8. Gaillard Hunt, *The Life of James Madison* (New York: Doubleday, Page and Co., 1902), 13.

9. *Selections from the Scottish Philosophy of Common Sense*, G. A. Johnston, editor (Chicago: Open Court Publishing Company, 1911), 149, 180, 183, 186, 217.

10. Paul Starobin, *After America; Narratives for the Next Global Age* (London: Penguin Books, 2009), no page numbers.

11. *Thomas Jefferson: A Free Mind*, Lowell B. Catlett, editor (Canada: Trafford Publishing, 2004), 29.

12. Henry Sage, "The Enlightenment in America," *Academic American*, 2007 (at: http://www.academicamerican.com/colonial/topics/enlighten.htm).

13. Thomas Jefferson, *The Writings of Thomas Jefferson*, Henry Augustine Washington, editor (Washington, DC: Taylor & Maury, 1854), Vol. VII, 305, to James Madison on August 30, 1823.

14. Ibid., Vol. VII, 407, to Henry Lee on May 8, 1825.

15. Thomas Jefferson, *Memoir, Correspondence, and Miscellanies*, Vol. II, 221, to Joseph Jones on August 14, 1787.

16. As an aside, it is worth noting that the Bible was the most frequently-cited source in the political literature of the Founding Era, being invoked more often than all Enlightenment Era thinkers combined, thus demonstrating that religious teachings

were indeed an important (but now often ignored) influence that shaped the Founders' political philosophy. (See Donald S. Lutz, The Origins of American Constitutionalism (Baton Rouge: Louisiana State University Press, 1988), 141.) Some today attack Lutz's findings, complaining that he included Founding Era sermons within the political literature he surveyed (see, for example, http://americanvision.org/9760/christian-american-friends-please-stop-citing-lutz-study/), but it would be a display of overt secularist bias, if not historical recklessness, to exclude such works from consideration. Here are three reasons (among many others) why such literature cannot be dismissed as irrelevant.

1. Famous Cornell University historian Clinton Rossiter, in his award-winning book Seedtime of the Republic, identified six individuals who most directly "contributed to the rise of political liberty" in America. Of the six, two were civil leaders: Benjamin Franklin and Richard Bland; the other four were ministers: the Revs. Thomas Hooker, Roger Williams, Jonathan Mayhew, and John Wise. Rossiter demonstrates that the contributions of such ministers and their writings were indispensable to America's civil liberties. (Clinton Rossiter, Seedtime of the Republic (New York: Harcourt, Brace and Co., 1953), 2.)

2. In 1772, as the storm cloud of Revolution loomed on the horizon, leading patriots and the famous Sons of Liberty reprinted and widely distributed two religious writings by the Rev. John Wise. Why? Because as early as 1687, Wise was already teaching that "taxation without representation is tyranny," that the "consent of the governed" was the foundation of government, and that all men were created equal. (See http://www.americanheritage.com/articles/magazine/ah/2001/2/2001_2_50.shtml; and Rossiter, 219; and http://www.founding.com/library/lbody.cfm?id=506&parent=501 "The Inspiration of the Declaration, Speech at Philadelphia, Pennsylvania, on the One Hundred and Fiftieth Anniversary of the Declaration of Independence, Calvin Coolidge, July 5, 1926.") Thus the Founders believed Wise's writings to be important in helping shape American civic thinking in the years leading up to American Independence – an historical fact recognized by subsequent generations. For example, in 1864, historian Benjamin Morris affirmed: "Some of the most glittering sentences in the immortal Declaration of Independence are almost literal quotations from this [1772 reprinted] essay of John Wise. . . . It was used as a political textbook in the great struggle for freedom." (B.F. Morris, *Christian Life and Character of the Civil Institutions of the United States, Developed in the Official and Historical Annals of the Republic* (Philadelphia: George W. Childs, 1864), 341.) And in his famous 1926 speech in Philadelphia on the 150th anniversary of the Declaration of Independence, President Calvin Coolidge similarly acknowledged: "The thoughts [in the Declaration] can very largely be traced back to what John Wise was writing." (http://www.founding.com/library/lbody.cfm?id=506&parent=501 "The Inspiration of the Declaration, Speech at Philadelphia, Pennsylvania, on the One Hundred and Fiftieth Anniversary of the Declaration of Independence, Calvin Coolidge, July 5, 1926.")

3. Ministers, through their writings and sermons (such as their annual Election Sermons and countless others on the principles of government), were instrumental in laying the intellectual basis for American Independence. In fact, historian Alice Baldwin affirms: "There is not a right asserted in the Declaration of Independence which had not been discussed by the New England clergy before 1763. (Alice M. Baldwin, *The New England Clergy and the American Revolution* (New York: Frederick Ungar, 1958), 170.) Many of these sermons were actually printed and distributed at state expense – a fact openly acknowledged by the state on the cover page of many such sermons.

Numerous other such facts can be provided, but this book is not focused on acknowledging the significant intellectual and philosophical influence of the clergy in the American Founding, other than to point out that criticizing Lutz's work because it included sermons and other religious literature is misguided and reflects a lack of knowledge of actual political literature of the Founding Era.

17. Donald S. Lutz, *The Origins of American Constitutionalism* (Baton Rouge: Louisiana State University Press, 1988), 143.

18. John Adams, *Diary and Autobiography of John Adams*, L. H. Butterfield, editor (Cambridge: Belknap Press, 1962), Vol. 2, 391, diary entry on June 23, 1779.

19. James Madison, *Letters and Other Writings of James Madison* (New York: R. Worthington, 1884), Vol. IV, 58, to N. P. Trist on February 1830.

20. John Quincy Adams, *An Oration Addressed to the Citizens of the Town of Quincy, on the Fourth of July, 1831* (Boston: Richardson, Lord & Holbrook, 1831), 15.

21. John Witherspoon, *The Works of John Witherspoon* (Edinburgh: J. Ogle, 1815), Vol. V, 242, from "The Absolute Necessity of Salvation Through Christ," January 2, 1758.

22. Benjamin Rush, *Letters of Benjamin Rush*, L. H. Butterfield, editor (New Jersey: Princeton University Press, 1951), Vol. II, 748, to James Kidd on May 13, 1794.

23. William Wirt, *Sketches of the Life and Character of Patrick Henry* (Philadelphia. James Webster, 1817), 386–387, to Betsy Aylett on August 20, 1796.

24. James Wilson, *The Works of the Honourable James Wilson*, Bird Wilson, editor (Philadelphia: Lorenzo Press, 1804), Vol. I, 276–277, "Of Man, As An Individual."

25. Thomas Jefferson, *Memoir, Correspondence, and Miscellanies*, Vol. IV, 80, to John Norvell on June 11, 1807.

26. Thomas Jefferson, *The Writings of Thomas Jefferson*, Vol. XII, 405, to Col. William Duane on August 12, 1810.

27. Thomas Jefferson, *The Works of Thomas Jefferson* (1904), Vol. V, 181, to John Adams on August 27, 1786.

28. Thomas Jefferson, *The Works of Thomas Jefferson* (1904), Vol. V, 171, to Charles Gysbert, Count Van Hogendorp, on August 25, 1786.

29. Thomas Jefferson, *The Works of Thomas Jefferson* (1905), Vol. XI, 168, to Dr. Benjamin Rush on January 16, 1811.

30. *The Works of Francis Bacon*, James Spedding, editor (London: Spottiswoode & Co., 1857), Vol. III, 509, "Preface to the De Interpretatione Naturae Prooemium"; John

Timbs, *Stories of Inventors and Discoverers in Science and the Useful Arts* (London: Kent and Co., 1860), 91, "Lord Bacon's 'New Philosophy'"; David C. Innes, "The Novelty and Genius of Francis Bacon," Piety and Humanity (at: http://pietyandhumanity. blogspot.com/2010/02/novelty-and-genius-of-francis-bacon.html) (accessed on January 28, 2013). Bacon was also called the "Father of the Scientific Method": Dr. Peter Hammond, "How the Reformation Changed the World," Frontline Fellowship (at: http://www.frontline.org.za/articles/howreformation_changedworld.htm) (accessed on January 28, 2013).

31. *A Short Biographical Dictionary of English Literature*, John William Cousins, editor (New York: E. P. Dutton & Co., 1910), s.v. "Sir Francis Bacon" (at: http://www.luminarium. org/sevenlit/bacon/bio.php).

32. Sir Francis Bacon, "Essays of Francis Bacon: Of Atheism," Public Domain Books (at: http://www.authorama.com/essays-of-francis-bacon-17.html) (accessed on January 28, 2013).

33. Charles E. Hummell, "The Faith Behind the Famous: Isaac Newton," Christian History, April 1, 1991 (at: http://www.ctlibrary.com/ch/1991/issue30/3038.html). See also Mitch Stokes, *Isaac Newton* (Nashville: Thomas Nelson, 2010), 82–84.

34. See, for example, Sir Isaac Newton, *Newton's Principia, the Mathematical Principles of Natural Philosophy* (originally published in 1687; reprinted New York: Daniel Adee, 1848), 504.

35. John Locke, The *Works of John Locke* (London: T. Davison, 1801), Vol. X, p.175, "The Fundamental Constitutions of Carolina," 1669.

36. See, for example, *Concise Oxford Dictionary of World Religions*, John Bowker, editor (Oxford: Oxford University Press, 2000), 151; James A. Herrick, *The Radical Rhetoric of the English Deists: The Discourse of Skepticism, 1680–1750* (Columbia: University of South Carolina Press, 1997), 15; Kerry S. Walters, *Rational Infidels: The American Deists* (Durango, CO: Longwood Academic, 1992), 24, 210; Kerry S. Walters, *The American Deists: Voices of Reason and Dissent in the Early Republic* (Lawrence: University Press of Kansas, 1992), 6–7; John W. Yolton, *John Locke and the Way of Ideas* (Oxford: Oxford University Press, 1956), 25, 115; etc.

37. John Locke, *The Works of John Locke* (London: Awnsham & Churchill, 1722), Vol. III, 113–143, "A Paraphrase and Notes on St. Paul's Epistle to the Galatians" (originally published in 1705); 145–212, "A Paraphrase and Notes on St. Paul's First Epistle to the Corinthians" (originally published in 1706); 213–250, "A Paraphrase and Notes on St. Paul's Second Epistle to the Corinthians" (originally published in 1706); 251–341, "A Paraphrase and Notes on St. Paul's Epistle to the Romans" (originally published in 1707); and 343–384, "A Paraphrase and Notes on St. Paul's Epistle to the Ephesians" (originally published in 1707).

38. John Locke, *A Common Place-Book to the Holy Bible: or, the Scripture's Sufficiency Practically Demonstrated* (London: Awnsham & Churchill, 1697).

39. John Adams, *The Works of John Adams*, Charles Francis Adams, editor (Boston: Little, Brown and Company, 1856), Vol. X, 311, to William Tudor on April 5, 1818, and Vol. IV, 82–83, from his article "Novanglus," circa 1775, and Vol. I, 53–54, to Jonathan Sewell on February 1760; Benjamin Franklin, *The Papers of Benjamin Franklin*, William B. Willcox, editor (New Haven: Yale University Press, 1973), Vol. 17, 6, from "The Colonist's Advocate," on January 4, 1770, and Vol. 4, 107, from Franklin's "Idea of the English School"; Thomas Jefferson, *The Writings of Thomas Jefferson* (1895), Vol. V, 173, to Thomas Mann Randolph on May 30, 1790, and Vol. XI, 71, to John Norvell on June 14, 1807; Thomas Jefferson, *The Works of Thomas Jefferson* (1905), Vol. XII, 307, to James Madison on August 30, 1823, "Richard Henry Lee charged it as copied from Locke's Two Treatise on government"; Benjamin Rush, *The Selected Writings of Benjamin Rush*, Dagobert D. Runes, editor (New York: The Philosophical Library, Inc., 1947), 78, "Observations on the Government of Pennsylvania"; Benjamin Rush, *Medical Inquiries and Observations* (Philadelphia: T. & G. Palmer, 1805), Vol. I, 402, "Duties of a Physician"; and Benjamin Rush, *Medical Inquiries and Observations*, Vol. II, 19, from his "The Influence of Physical Causes Upon the Moral Faculty"; John Quincy Adams, *The Jubilee of the Constitution* (New York: Samuel Colman, 1839), 40–41; James Wilson, *The Works of the Honourable James Wilson*, Vol. I, 67–68, "Of the General Principles of Law and Obligation."

40. John Locke, Two Treatises of Government (London: Awnsham & Churchill, 1689), passim; the number of verses was documented by the author's staff, in individually identifying and counting the Bible verses in this work.

41. Thomas Jefferson, *The Writings of Thomas Jefferson*, Vol. II, 93–94, "Notes on Religion," October, 1776.

42. See, for example, *Thomas Jefferson, Memoirs, Correspondence, and Miscellanies*, Vol. III, 515–517, "Syllabus of an estimate of the merit of the doctrines of Jesus, compared with those of others"; Vol. IV, 222–226, to John Adams on October 13, 1813; *Thomas Jefferson, The Writings of Thomas Jefferson*, Vol. XV, 1–3, to F. A. Van Der Kemp on April 25, 1816; Vol. VII, 252–253, to Dr. Benjamin Waterhouse on June 26, 1822; Vol. VI, 518, to Charles Thompson on January 9, 1816; etc.

43. Thomas Jefferson, *The Papers of Thomas Jefferson*, Julian P. Boyd, editor (Princeton: Princeton University Press, 1952), Vol. 6, 432, to Wilson Cary Nicholas on December 31, 1783.

44. Ibid., Vol. 23, 271, to John Witherspoon on March 12, 1792.

45. John Witherspoon, *The Works of John Witherspoon* (Philadelphia: William W. Woodward, 1802), Vol. III, 42, "The Dominion of Providence Over the Passions of Men," May 17, 1776.

46. Thomas Jefferson, *The Works of Thomas Jefferson* (1904), Vol. VIII, 153–154, to Wilson Carey Nicholas on November 22, 1794.

47. Williston Walker, *John Calvin: The Organiser of Reformed Protestantism: 1509–1564* (New York: G. P. Putnam's Sons, 1906), 363.

48. Idib., 367.
49. Dorothy C. Bass, "Gideon Blackburn's Mission to the Cherokees" Christianization and Civilization," *Journal of Presbyterian History* (1974) Vol. 52, 209–210 which cites Henry Dearborn to R.J. Meigs, National Archives Microfilm, M-15, "Records of the Secretary of War, Letters Sent, Indian Affairs," 1 July 1803.
50. "Thomas Jefferson to the Nuns of the Order of St. Ursula on May 15, 1804," original on file with the New Orleans Parish (at: http://dauthazbeechphagein.blogspot.com/2010/08/thomas-jeffersons-letter-to-sister.html).
51. Thomas Jefferson, "The Thomas Jefferson Papers," Library of Congress, to Robert Brent on August 14, 1805 (at: http://hdl.loc.gov/loc.mss/mtj.mtjbib015028).
52. Ibid.
53. *Records of the Columbia Historical Society* (Washington, DC: Columbia Historical Society, 1895), Vol. 1, 122–123.
54. Ibid., Vol. 1, 127, from the report by Mr. Henry Ould on February 10, 1813. See also *National Intelligencer* (Washington: 1817), March 20, 1817, 2, "Lancastrian School" report by Robert Ould dated November 18, 1816, which says "41 besides the above number read in the Old and New Testament, and are able to spell words of from three to five syllables. 26 are learning to read Dr. Watt's Divine Songs and spell words of two syllables."
55. Some object that Jefferson, in his Notes of the State of Virginia (1781), resisted "putting the Bible and Testament into the hands of the children at an age when their judgments are not sufficiently matured for religious inquiries" (*Thomas Jefferson, Notes on the State of Virginia* (Philadelphia: Matthew Carey, 1794, second edition; first edition 1781), 245). However, in his day, learning to read from the Scriptures and becoming familiar with their general teachings was quite different from the "religious inquiries" common to youth catechisms at that time. See *The New England Primer* for an example of "religious enquiries" built around specific doctrines rather than just general principles. While I believe (as did Founding Fathers such as Benjamin Rush, Noah Webster, and others) that such "religious inquiries" for children are actually useful and beneficial, Jefferson did not hold this view. Nevertheless, these "religious inquiries" of which he spoke fell into a different category than that of children learning to read by using the Bible, as was being done in the public schools of Washington DC when Jefferson served on its Board of Trustees. The early US Supreme Court expressed a similar view concerning a city-run school for youth in Philadelphia when it declared, "Why may not the Bible, and especially the New Testament, without note or comment, be read and taught as a Divine revelation in the [school]—its general precepts expounded, its evidences explained and its glorious principles of morality inculcated?" (Vidal v. Girard's Executors, 43 U.S. 126, 200 (1844). As John Quincy Adams affirmed, "To a man of liberal education . . . with regard to the history contained in the Bible . . . it is not so much praiseworthy to be acquainted with as it is shameful to be ignorant of it" (John Quincy Adams, *Letters of John Quincy Adams to His Son on the Bible and Its Teachings* [Auburn: Derby, Miller, &

Co. 1848], 34). In short, in Jefferson's day, simply reading the Bible did not constitute the "religious inquiries" for youth to which he objected.

56. Samuel Yorke, *History of the Public Schools of Washington City, D.C.* (Washington, DC: Gill & Witherow, 1876), 1–6; *Centennial History of the City of Washington, DC* (Dayton, OH: United Brethren Publishing House, 1892), 484–486.

57. *Records of the Columbia Historical Society*, Vol. 8, 62.

58. Samuel Knox, *Essay on the Best System of Liberal Education* (Baltimore: Warner and Hanna, 1799), 78–79, Evans # 35690.

59. Thomas Jefferson, *The Writings of Thomas Jefferson* (1904), Vol. XIX, 365–366, "Board of Visitors, Minutes, Charlottesville, July 28, 1817."

60. Ibid., Vol. XIX, 367, "Board of Visitors, Minutes, Charlottesville, October 7, 1817."

61. Leonard Levy, *Jefferson and Civil Liberties: The Darker Side*, 8.

62. Thomas Jefferson, *The Writings of Thomas Jefferson* (1853), Vol. 1, 69–70, from his Autobiography.

63. Thomas Jefferson, *The Writings of Thomas Jefferson* (1903), Vol. 1, p. 71, from his Autobiography.

64. Thomas Jefferson, *The Works of Thomas Jefferson* (1904), Vol. II, 434, "A Bill for Amending the Constitution of the College of William and Mary."

65. Thomas Jefferson, "Report of the Commissioners for the University of Virginia," The University of Virginia, August 4, 1818 (at: http://nersp.osg.ufl.edu/~lombardi/edudocs/jefferson_uva_1818.html).

66. Ibid.

67. Thomas Jefferson, *The Writings of Thomas Jefferson* (1904), Vol. XV, 405–406, to Dr. Thomas Cooper on November 2, 1822.

68. Ibid., Vol. XIX, 414, "Board of Visitors, Minutes, October 7, 1822."

69. Ibid., Vol. XV, 405–406, to Dr. Thomas Cooper on November 2, 1822.

70. Ibid., Vol. XIX, 414, "Board of Visitors, Minutes, October 7, 1822."

71. William Henry Foote, *Sketches of Virginia, Historical and Biographical* (Philadelphia: J. B. Lippincott & Co., 1855), 325.

72. See, for example, his articles expressing his strong support in his own *Virginia Evangelical and Literary Magazine*, such as that In Vol. I, 548, January, 1818; Philip Alexander Bruce, *History of the University of Virginia, 1819–1919* (New York: The MacMillian Company, 1920), Vol. I, 204. See also Robert P. Davis, et al, *Virginia Presbyterians in American Life: Hanover Presbytery 1755–1980* (Richmond: Hanover Presbytery, 1892), 66, 72.

73. *The Virginia Evangelical and Literary Magazine*, John Holt Rice, editor (Richmond: William W. Gray, 1818), Vol. I, 548.

74. Alexander Garrett, "Outline of Cornerstone Ceremonies," The University of Virginia, October 6, 1817 (at: http://etext.virginia.edu/etcbin/toccer-new2?id=Jef1Gri.sgm&images=images/modeng&data=/texts/english/modeng/parsed&tag=public&part=47&division=div1).

75. Thomas Jefferson, "Report of the Commissioners for the University of Virginia," The University of Virginia, August 4, 1818 (at: http://etext.virginia.edu/etcbin/toccer-new2?id=JefRock.sgm&images=images/modeng&data=/texts/english/modeng/parse d&tag=public&part=1&division=div1).

76. See, for example, Cornett, Barton, Henard, and Sassi, *Christian America? Perspectives on Our Religious Heritage*, 289–290.

77. *The New York Review* (New York: George Dearborn & Co., 1837), Vol. I, No. I, March 1837, 19, review of George Tucker's 1837 two volume *The Life of Thomas Jefferson*.

78. Thomas Jefferson, *The Writings of Thomas Jefferson* (1903), Vol. XV, 267–269, to Dr. Thomas Cooper on August 14, 1820.

79. Henry S. Randall, *The Life of Thomas Jefferson* (New York: Derby & Jackson, 1858), Vol. III, 467–468, from Robley Dunglison to Henry S. Randall on June 1, 1856.

80. Ibid., Vol. III, 467, from George Tucker to Henry S. Randall on May 28, 1856.

81. Thomas Jefferson, *The Writings of Thomas Jefferson* (1904), Vol. XI, 413, to Benjamin Rush on January 3, 1808.

82. Ibid., Vol. XIX, 367, "Board of Visitors, Minutes, Charlottesville, October 7, 1817."

83. Ibid., Vol. XIX, 389, "Board of Visitors, Minutes, October 2–3, 1820."

84. Roy Honeywell, *The Educational Work of Thomas Jefferson* (Cambridge: Harvard University Press, 1931), Vol. 16, 92.

85. Thomas Jefferson, "Report to the President and Directors of the Literary Fund," The Avalon Project, October 7, 1822 (at: http://avalon.law.yale.edu/19th_century/jeffrep3.asp).

86. Thomas Jefferson, "*The Papers of Thomas Jefferson*," Library of Congress, to James Madison on August 8, 1824 (at: http://memory.loc.gov/cgi-bin/ampage?collId=m tj1&fileName=mtj1page054.db&recNum=725&itemLink=/ammem/collections/jefferson_papers/mtjser1.html&linkText=7&tempFile=./temp/~ammem_kF9i&filec ode=mtj&itemnum=1&ndocs=1).

87. James Madison, *The Writings of James Madison*, Gaillard Hunt, editor (New York: G. P. Putnam's Sons, 1910), Vol. IX, 203–207, to Thomas Jefferson on September 10, 1824.

88. Thomas Jefferson, *The Writings of Thomas Jefferson* (1904), Vol. XVI, 19, to Judge Augustus B. Woodward, March 24, 1824.

89. Thomas Jefferson, "Report of the Commissioners for the University of Virginia," The University of Virginia, August 4, 1818 (at: http://etext.virginia.edu/etcbin/toccer-new2?id=JefRock.sgm&images=images/modeng&data=/texts/english/modeng/pars ed&tag=public&part=1&division=div1). See also Thomas Jefferson, *The Writings of Thomas Jefferson* (1904), Vol. XIX, 394, "Board of Visitors, Minutes, October 2–3, 1820"; Vol. XIX, 411–412, "Board of Visitors, Minutes, October 7, 1822"; Vol. XIX, 449–450, "Board of Visitors, Minutes, October 4, 1824."

90. Thomas Jefferson, *The Writings of Thomas Jefferson* (1904), Vol. XIX, 449–450, "A Meeting of the Visitors of the University of Virginia on Monday the 4th of October, 1824."

91. Ibid., Vol. XIX, 449, "A Meeting of the Visitors of the University of Virginia on Monday the 4th of October, 1824."

92. Thomas Jefferson, *Memoir, Correspondence, and Miscellanies*, (1830) Vol. II, 216, to Peter Carr on August 10, 1787.

93. Ibid., Vol. I, 286, to Peter Carr on August 19, 1785.

94. Ibid., Vol. I, 287, to Peter Carr on August 19, 1785.

95. *The History of Legal Education in the United States: Commentaries and Primary Sources*, Steve Sheppard, editor (Pasadena: Salem Press Inc., 1999), Part I, Section A, 156.

96. Thomas Jefferson, *Memoir, Correspondence, and Miscellanies*, Vol. II, 215, to Peter Carr on August 10, 1787.

97. Ibid., Vol. II, 216, to Peter Carr on August 10, 1787.

98. See, for example, Rufus K. Noyes, *Views of Religion* (Boston: L. K. Washburn, 1906), 197; Jim Walker, "Thomas Jefferson," No Beliefs (at: http://nobeliefs.com/jefferson.htm) (accessed on January 30, 2013); Robin Morigan, "Fighting Words for a Secular America," *Ms.* magazine, Fall 2004 (at: http://www.msmagazine.com/fall2004/fightingwords.asp); Gary Leupp, "On Jefferson, Diderot and the Political Use of God," The China Rose (at: http://chinarose.wordpress.com/2010/01/09/denis-diderot-humanist-avant-lettrist-philosopher-polymath/) (accessed on January 30, 2013), and many others.

99. Apologetics," Apologetics Index (at: http://www.apologeticsindex.org/a13.html) (accessed on January 30, 2013); "Apologetics," *Merriam-Webster* (at: http://www.merriam-webster.com/dictionary/apologetics) (accessed on January 30, 2013); "Apologetics," *The Free Dictionary* (at: http://www.thefreedictionary.com/apologetics) (accessed on January 30, 2013); "Apologetics," Oxford Dictionaries (at: http://oxforddictionaries.com/definition/american_english/apologetics) (accessed on January 30, 2013).

100. Elias Boudinot, *The Age of Revelation, or the Age of Reason Shewn to be an Age of Infidelity* (Philadelphia: Asbury Dickins, 1801), iii–iv, "Dedication," to his daughter, Susan Bradford.

101. Ibid., vi.

102. John Witherspoon, *Lectures on Moral Philosophy* (Philadelphia: Williams W. Woodward, 1822), 5, 38.

103. Ezra Stiles, *The United States Elevated To Glory And Honor; A Sermon, At the Anniversary Election, May 8th, 1783* (New Haven: Thomas & Samuel Green, 1783), 56.

104. Thomas Jefferson, *Memoirs, Correspondence, and Miscellanies*, Vol. IV, 363–364, to John Adams on April 11, 1823.

105. Ibid., Vol. IV, 363–364, to John Adams on April 11, 1823.

106. Ibid., Vol. II, 216–218, to Peter Carr on August 10, 1787.

107. See, for example, *Worcester v. Georgia*, 31 U.S. 515 (1832); *City of Charleston v Benjamin*, 2 Strob. 508 (SuCt. S.C. 1846); etc.

108. Noah Webster, *An American Dictionary of the English Language* (New York: S. Converse, 1828), Vol. I, s.v. "Evangelist."

109. *The Encyclopedia Britannica. A Dictionary of Arts, Sciences, Literature, and General Information* (New York: Encyclopedia Britannica, Inc., 1910), Vol. 3, s.v. "Bible"; Brooke Foss Westcott, *A General Survey of the History of the Canon of the New Testament* (London: Macmillan and Co., 1866), 390–391; and Edward Reuss, *History of the Canon of the Holy Scriptures in the Christian Church*, trans. David Hunter (Edinburgh: James Gemmell, 1884), 205–206.

110. Thomas Jefferson, *Memoir, Correspondence, and Miscellanies*, Vol. II, 216–218, to Peter Carr on August 10, 1787.

111. Mark A. Beliles, *Religion and Republicanism in Jefferson's Virginia*, doctrinal dissertation for Whitfield Theological Seminary school, 1993, 102–103.

112. Robert M. Healey, *Jefferson on Religion in Public Education* (Hamden, CT: Archon Books, 1970), 27.

113. Thomas Jefferson, *Memoir, Correspondence, and Miscellanies*, Vol. II, 216, to Peter Carr on August 10, 1787.

114. Ibid., Vol. IV, 364, to John Adams on April 11, 1823.

115. See, for example, books by Josh McDowell: *The New Evidence That Demands A Verdict Fully Updated To Answer The Questions Challenging Christians Today* (Nashville: Thomas Nelson, 1999), *A Ready Defence: the Best of Josh McDowell* (Nashville, TN: Thomas Nelson, 1992), *Evidence for Christianity* (Nashville: Thomas Nelson, 2006); Ray Comfort: *God doesn't believe in Atheists* (FL: Bridge-Logos Publishers, 1993); Lee Strobel: *The Case for Christ: A Journalist's Personal Investigation of the Evidence for Jesus* (Grand Rapids: Zondervan, 1998); Ravi Zacharias: *A Shattered Visage: The Real Face of Atheism* (Wolgemuth & Hyatt, 1990), *The Real Face of Atheism, Can Man Live without God* (Nashville: Thomas Nelson, 2004), *Jesus Among Other Gods: The Absolute Claims of the Christian Message* (Nashville: W Publishing Group, 2002), *The End of Reason: A Response to the New Atheists* (Grand Rapids: Zondervan, 2008), *Beyond Opinion: Living the Faith we Defend* (Nashville: Thomas Nelson, 2008), *Why Jesus? Rediscovering His Truth in an Age of Mass Marketed Spirituality* (Nashville: Faith Words, 2012).

LIE # 3

1. Craig Cabaniss, Bob Kauflin, Dave Harvey, and Jeff Purswell, *Worldliness: Resisting the Seduction of a Fallen World*, C. J. Mahaney, editor (Wheaton: Crossway Books, 2008), 15.

2. Robert S. Alley, "The Real Jefferson on Religion," secularhumanism.org (at: http://www.secularhumanism.org/library/fi/alley_18_4.html) (accessed on February 8, 2011).

3. Jim Walker, "Thomas Jefferson on Christianity & Religion," nobeliefs.com (at: http://www.nobeliefs.com/jefferson.htm) (accessed on May 23, 2011).

4. Don Landis, "Jonah and the Great Fish," Answers in Genesis, September 5, 2006 (at: http://www.answersingenesis.org/articles/am/v1/n1/great-fish).

5.   See, for example, Steve Waldman, *Founding Faith: Providence, Politics, and the Birth of Religious Freedom in America* (New York: Random House, 2008), 72; Stephen J. Nichols, *Jesus; Made in America: A Cultural History from the Puritans to the Passion of the Christ* (Downers Grove: IVP Academic, 2008), 55; Rev. Peter Edward Lanzillotta, "Insights from Jefferson's Bible," interfaithservicesofthelowcountry.com, June 28, 2010 (at: http://interfaithservicesofthelowcountry.com/for-july-4th-insights-into-jeffersons-bible/); *Encyclopedia of Religious Controversies in the United States*, George H. Shriver & Bill J. Leonard, editors (Westport: Greenwood Press, 1997), 238; *Dictionary of Christianity in America*, Daniel G. Reid, editor (Downers Grove: InterVarsity Press, 1990), 590, s.v. "Thomas Jefferson"; Winford Claiborne, "Revised Version of Christianity," gosepelhour.net (at: http://www.gospelhour.net/2211.html) (accessed on February 8, 2011); "American Enlightenment," Wikipedia.com (at: http://en.wikipedia.org/wiki/American_Enlightenmemt) (accessed on May 23, 2011); Mark A. Noll, George M. Marsden, Nathan O. Hatch, *The Search for Christian America* (Colorado Springs: Helmers & Howard, 1989), 75; "An Interview with Mikey Weinstein of Military Religious Freedom Foundation," *Pagan + Politics*, February 26, 2010 (at: http://www.facebook.com/note.php?note_id=360240177811); etc.

6.   Thomas Jefferson, *Memoir, Correspondence, and Miscellanies*, Thomas Jefferson Randolph, editor (Charlottesville: F. Carr, and Co., 1829), Vol. IV, 23, to Mrs. John Adams on July 22, 1804, Vol. IV, 228, to John Adams on October 28, 1813, and Vol. II, 48–50, to Mrs. Cosway on October 12, 1786; Thomas Jefferson, *The Works of Thomas Jefferson*, Paul Leicester Ford, editor (New York: G. P. Putnam's Sons, 1904), Vol. II, 253–254, "Notes on Religion," October 1776, Thomas Jefferson, *The Writings of Thomas Jefferson* (Washington, DC: The Thomas Jefferson Memorial Association, 1904), Vol. XIV, 71–73, to John Adams on January 24, 1814; etc.

7.   Ellen Coolidge, *The Domestic Life of Thomas Jefferson*, Sarah N. Randolph, editor (New York: Harper & Brothers, 1871), 345, Ellen Coolidge to Henry S. Randall.

8.   Dumas Malone, *Jefferson and His Time: The Sage of Monticello* (Boston: Little, Brown and Company 1981), Vol. 6, 122.

9.   Thomas Jefferson, *The Writings of Thomas Jefferson* (1904), Vol. IX, 485–488, to Samuel H. Smith on September 21, 1814. See also Dumas Malone, *Jefferson and His Time: The Sage of Monticello*, Vol. 6, 123.

10. William Maxwell, *A Memoir of the Rev. John H. Rice* (Philadelphia: J. Whetham, 1835), 127, from Rev. John H. Rice to William Maxwell on April 10, 1816; Thomas Jefferson, *The Writings of Thomas Jefferson* (1904), Vol. XIV, 81, to Samuel Greenhow on January 31, 1814.

11. *The Holy Bible, Containing the Old and New Testaments: Together with the Apocrypha; Translated out of the Original Tongues and with the Former Translations, Diligently Compared and Revised* (Philadelphia: John Thomason & Abraham Small, 1798), Vol. I, "Subscribers' Names."

12. See, for example, "Framed Bible Pages," Houston Baptist University (at: http://www.hbu.edu/hbu/Framed_Bible_pages_.asp?SnID=2) (accessed on December 2, 2010); "Thomas Jefferson and the Bible: Publications He Owned," Thomas Jefferson Foundation, January, 2007 (at: http://www.monticello.org/library/exhibits/images/biblepublications.pdf).

13. *The Holy Bible, Containing the Old and New Testaments: Together with the Apocrypha; Translated out of the Original Tongues and with the Former Translations, Diligently Compared and Revised* (Philadelphia: John Thomason & Abraham Small, 1798), Vol. I, "Subscribers' Names." Some 1,269 of his fellow Americans joined Jefferson in subscribing to this work, including Declaration signers John Hancock and Samuel Chase, Constitution signers Gunning Bedford, George Read, James Wilson, John Dickinson, Jared Ingersoll, Thomas Mifflin, and Alexander Hamilton, Constitutional Convention delegate John Lansing, Chief Justice and author of the Federalist Papers John Jay, and Revolutionary General and Secretary of State Timothy Pickering. This list of subscribers helps show how important the Bible was to many Americans—including political leaders— in this era. On the latter point see Daniel L. Dreisbach, "The Bible in the Political Rhetoric of the American Founding," *Politics and Religion* 4 (December 2011), 401–427.

14. Thomas Jefferson, *The Works of Thomas Jefferson* (1905), Vol. XI, 6, to Charles Thomson on January 11, 1808.

15. Ibid., Vol. XI, 84, to Charles Thomson on December 25, 1808.

16. "Thomas Jefferson and the Bible: Publications He Owned," Thomas Jefferson Foundation, January, 2007 (at: http://www.monticello.org/library/exhibits/images/biblepublications.pdf).

17. Daniel Webster, *The Writings and Speeches of Daniel Webster Hitherto Uncollected* (Boston: Little, Brown, & Company, 1903), Vol. IV, 657, to Professor Pease on June 15, 1852.

18. Henry S. Randall, *The Life of Thomas Jefferson* (New York: Derby & Jackson, 1858), Vol. III, 654.

19. Thomas Jefferson, *Memoir, Correspondence, and Miscellanies* (1830), Vol. IV, 14, to Dr. Joseph Priestly on January 29, 1804.

20. See, for example, Thomas Jefferson, *The Papers of Thomas Jefferson*, Barbara B. Oberg, editor (Princeton: Princeton University Press, 2003), Vol. 30, 238, to William Linn on April 2, 1798; Thomas Jefferson, *The Works of Thomas Jefferson* (1905), Vol. 12, 222, to Jedidiah Morse on March 6, 1822; Vol. 1, 219–227, Autobiography, "Notes of a conversation with Mr. [George] Hammond [a British diplomat], June 3, 1792"; Vol. 9, 123–126, to Benjamin Hawkins [U.S. Senator and Indian agent] on March 14, 1800; etc.

21. *The Public Statutes at Large of the United States of America*, Richard Peters, editor (Boston: Charles C. Little and James Brown, 1845), Vol. II, 155, "An Act in Addition to an Act Entitled 'An Act, in Addition to an Act Regulating the Grants of Land

Appropriated for Military Services, and for the Society of the United Brethren, for Propagating the Gospel Among the Heathen',", April 26, 1802.

22. The Rev. William Bennet, *The Excellence of Christian Morality, A Sermon Preached before the Society in Scotland for Propagating Christian Knowledge, at their Anniversary Meeting, Thursday, 6th June 1799* (Edinburgh: 1800).

23. Ibid., 12.

24. *Thomas Jefferson's Abridgement of The Words of Jesus of Nazareth* (Charlottesville: Mark Beliles, 1993), 13–14, quoting a letter from Edward Dowse to Thomas Jefferson on April 5, 1803.

25. Thomas Jefferson, *The Writings of Thomas Jefferson* (1904), Vol. X, 376–377, to Edward Dowse on April 19, 1803.

26. *Thomas Jefferson's Abridgement*, 14.

27. *The Debates and Proceedings in the Congress of the United States*, (Washington: Gales and Seaton, 1851), 7th Cong., 2nd Sess., 1602, "An Act to Revive and Continue in Force An Act in Addition to an Act, Entitled, 'An Act in Addition to an Act Regulating the Grants of Land Appropriated for Military Services, and for the Society of the United Brethren for Propagating the Gospel Among the Heathen,' and for Other Purposes," March 3, 1803.

28. *American State Papers: Documents, Legislative and Executive of the Congress of the United States*, Walter Lowrie and Matthew St. Claire Clarke, editors (Washington, DC: Gales and Seaton, 1832), Vol. IV, 687, "The Kaskaskia and Other Tribes," October 31, 1803.

29. *Wallace v. Jaffree*, 472 U.S. 38, 103, n. 5 (1983), (Rehnquist, J. dissenting).

30. *The Public Statutes at Large of the United States of America*, (1845), Vol. II, 271–272, "An Act Granting Further Time for Locating Military Land Warrants, and for Other Purposes," March 19, 1804.

31. Thomas Jefferson, *The Writings of Thomas Jefferson* (1904), Vol. XVI, 289, to Thomas, Ellicot, and Others on November 13, 1807.

32. Thomas Jefferson, *The Writings of Thomas Jefferson* (1904), Vol. XII, 270–271, to Governor James Jay on April 7, 1809. See also Thomas Jefferson, *The Papers of Thomas Jefferson Retirement Series*, J. Jefferson Looney, editor (Princeton: Princeton University Press, 2011), Vol. VII, 281, to Benjamin Smith Barton, April 3, 1814.

33. Thomas Jefferson, *Memoir, Correspondence, and Miscellanies* (1830), Vol. IV, 14, to Dr. Joseph Priestly on January 29, 1804.

34. See, for example, Michael Hinton, *The 100 Minute Bible* (Canterbury: The 100-Minute Press, 2007); Lee Cantelon, *The Words: Jesus of Nazareth* (Grand Rapids: Credo House Publishers, 2007); Phillip Law, *The Abridged Bible – from Adam to Apocalypse* (London: Continuum, 2006); J. Talboys Wheeler, *A Popular Abridgement of New Testament History, For Schools, Families, and General Reading* (London: Arthur Hall, Virtue & Co., 1854); and Henricus Oort, Isaac Hooykaas, Abraham Kuenen, Philip Henry Wicksted, *The Bible For Learners* (Boston: Roberts Brothers, 1898), Vol. III, "The Narratives of the New Testament"; Caroline Maxwell, *The History of the Holy Bible; an Abridgment*

of the Old and New Testament (London: Harvey and Darton, 1827); Isaiah Thomas and Alexander Thomas, *The Holy Bible Abridged: or, the History of the Old and New Testament* (Worcester, MA: Thomas, Son & Thomas, 1796); *Annotations of the Four Gospels, Compiled and Abridged for the Use of Students*. In Two Volumes (London: J. Davis, 1799).

35. Dickinson W. Adams, *Jefferson's Extracts from the Gospels* (Princeton: Princeton University Press, 1983), 28.

36. Charles B. Sanford, *The Religious Life of Thomas Jefferson* (Charlottesville: University Press of Virginia, 1984).

37. *Thomas Jefferson's Abridgement.*

38. *Jefferson's "Bible" The Life and Morals of Jesus of Nazareth*, Judd Patton, editor (Grove City: American Book Distributors, 1996), xiv, summarizing the 1983 Dickinson W. Adams, *Jefferson's Extracts from the Gospels*, which was a reconstruction of Jefferson's *Philosophy of Jesus*.

39. Charles B. Sanford, *The Religious Life of Thomas Jefferson*, 189.

40. See, for example, Henry S. Randall, *The Life of Thomas Jefferson*, Vol. III, 654–655, "Appendix No. XXX"; *The Selected Religious Letters and Papers of Thomas Jefferson*, Mark A. Beliles, editor (Charlottesville, VA: America Publications, 2013), 397–428; *Thomas Jefferson's Abridgement*, 25–71.

41. Thomas Jefferson, *The Writings of Thomas Jefferson* (1904), Vol. XV, 2, to F. A. Van Der Kemp on April 25, 1816.

42. Dumas Malone, *Jefferson the President, First Term 1801–1805* (Boston: Little Brown & Co., 1970), Vol. Four, 205.

43. *The Papers of Thomas Jefferson: Second Series. Jefferson's Extracts from the Gospels*, Dickinson W. Adams, editor (Princeton: Princeton University Press, 1983), 28n, "Introduction."

44. Throckmorton and Coulter, *Getting Jefferson Right*, 100–103.

45. Thomas Jefferson, *The Writings of Thomas Jefferson*, H. A. Washington, editor (New York: Riker, Throne, & Co., 1854), Vol. IX, 475–476, "Notes on a Draught for a second Inaugural Address,"

46. Mark A. Beliles and Jerry Newcombe, *Doubting Thomas? The Religious Life and Legacy of Thomas Jefferson* (New York: Morgan James Publishing, 2015), 297n.

47. Henry S. Randall, *The Life of Thomas Jefferson* (New York: Derby & Jackson, 1858), Vol. III, 452, n.

48. Thomas Jefferson, *Memoir, Correspondence, and Miscellanies*(1830), Vol. 4, 13–14, to Doctor Priestly on January 29, 1804; Vol. 4, 223–224, to John Adams on October 13, 1813; Thomas Jefferson, *The Writings of Thomas Jefferson* (1903),Vol. 14, 232–233, to Charles Clay on January 29, 1815; Vol. 14, 385–386, to Charles Thompson on January 9, 1816.

49. Thomas Jefferson, *The Writings of Thomas Jefferson*, H. A. Washington, editor (New York: John C. Riker, 1854), Vol. IV, 475–476, letter to Dr. Priestley on April 9, 1803.

50. Thomas Jefferson, *The Writings of Thomas Jefferson*, H. A. Washington, editor (New York: John C. Riker, 1854), Vol. IV, 482–483, "Syllabus of an Estimate of the Merit of the Doctrines of Jesus, compared with those of others" send with a letter to Benjamin Rush on April 21, 1803. Thomas Jefferson also sent this syllabus to William Short: Thomas Jefferson, *Memoirs, Correspondence, and Private Papers of Thomas Jefferson*, Thomas Jefferson Randolph, editor (London: Henry Colburn and Richard Bentley, 1829), Vol. III, 329, letter to William Short on April 13, 1820.

51. See, for example, Thomas Jefferson, *The Writings of Thomas Jefferson*, H. A. Washington, editor (New York: John C. Riker, 1854), Vol. IV, 475, to Dr. Priestley on April 9, 1803; Thomas Jefferson, *Memoir, Correspondence, and Miscellanies* (1830), Vol. III, 506–509, to Benjamin Rush on April 21, 1803; "Thomas Jefferson to William Canby, 18 September 1813," *National Archives* (at: http://founders.archives.gov/documents/Jefferson/03-06-02-0395).

52. Thomas Jefferson, *Memoir, Correspondence, and Miscellanies* (1830), Vol. III, 509, from his "Syllabus of an Estimate of the Merits of the Doctrines of Jesus, Compared with Those of Others," sent with a letter to Benjamin Rush on April 21, 1803.

53. John Maclean, *History of the College of New Jersey, From its Origin in 1746 to the Commencement of 1854* (Philadelphia: J. B. Lippincott & Co., 1877), Vol. I, 364–365.

54. John Witherspoon, *The Works of John Witherspoon* (Philadelphia: William W. Woodward, 1802), Vol. III, 367–475, "Lectures on Moral Philosophy."

55. *Quinquennial Catalogue of the Officers and Graduates of Harvard University, 1636–1895* (Cambridge: Harvard University, 1895), 41, "Officers of Government and Instruction: Instructors."

56. Ibid., 22, "Officers of Government and Instruction: Professors."

57. *An Account of Washington College in the State of Maryland* (Philadelphia: Joseph Crukshank, 1784), 42, Evans No. 18785.

58. *The History of the College of William and Mary From its Foundation, 1660, to 1874* (Richmond: J. W. Randolph & English, 1874), 81, "Catalogue of Alumni: Faculty."

59. Herbert Baxter Adams, *Thomas Jefferson and the University of Virginia* (Washington, DC: Government Printing Office, 1888), Issues 1–3, 158; Henry S. Randall, *The Life of Thomas Jefferson*, Vol. III, 467–468, from Robley Dunglison to Henry S. Randall on June 1, 1856.

60. See, for example, *The History of the College of William and Mary*, 153–162, "Extracts from the Laws of the College of William and Mary"; *The Laws of Yale College, in New Haven, in Connecticut, Enacted by the President and Fellows, The Sixth Day of October, A.D. 1795* (New Haven: T & S Green, 1795), 13–14; etc.

61. Adam Smith, *The Theory of Moral Sentiments* (London: A. Millar, 1759).

62. Richard Price, *A Review of the Principal Questions and Difficulties in Morals* (London: T. Cadall, 1757).

63. See, for example, Benjamin Rush, *Essays: Literary, Moral, and Philosophical* (Philadelphia: Thomas & Samuel Bradford, 1798), 114–124, "An Address to the Ministers of the

Gospel of Every Denomination in the United States upon Subjects Interesting to Morals," 1788; 263–274, "Observations upon the Influence of the Habitual Use of Tobacco upon Health, Morals, and Property," 1798; Benjamin Rush, *An Inquiry into the Effects of Ardent Spirits Upon the Human Body and Mind, with an Account of the Means of Preventing, and of the Remedies for Curing Them* (New York: 1811); an illustration titled "A Moral and Physical Thermometer: Or, a Scale of the Progress of Temperance and Intemperance"; Benjamin Rush, *An Inquiry into the Physical Causes upon the Moral Faculty Delivered Before a Meeting of the American Philosophical Society, Held at Philadelphia, on the Twenty-Seventh of February, 1796* (Philadelphia: Haswell, Barrington,and Haswell, 1839); John Witherspoon, *The Works of the Rev. John Witherspoon* (Philadelphia: William W. Woodward, 1802), Vol. III, 367–475, "Lectures on Moral Philosophy"; Noah Webster, *A Collection of Papers on Political, Literary, and Moral Subjects* (New York: Webster & Clark, 1843); etc.

64. See, for example, Gouverneur Morris, *A Diary of the French Revolution* (Boston: Houghton Mifflin Co., 1939), Vol. II, 172, diary entry for April 29, 1791, and Vol. II, 452, to Lord George Gordon on June 28, 1792; David Ramsay, *The History of the American Revolution* (Dublin: William Jones, 1795), Vol. II, 452; *The Documentary History of the Supreme Court of the United States, 1789–1800*, Maeva Marcus, editor (New York: Columbia University Press, 1988), Vol. III, 436, quoting Judge William Paterson in the *United States Oracle* (New Hampshire), May 24, 1800; Richard Henry Lee, *The Letters of Richard Henry Lee*, James Curtis Ballagh, editor (New York: The MacMillan Company, 1914), Vol. II, 411, to Colonel Martin Pickett on March 5, 1786; John Adams, *The Works of John Adams*, Charles Francis Adams, editor (Boston: Little, Brown, and Company, 1854), Vol. IX, 636, to Benjamin Rush on August 28, 1811; Joseph Story, *Vidal v. Girard's Executors*, 43 U.S. 127, 200 (1844); *Independent Chronicle* (Boston), February 22, 1787, Fisher Ames writing as Camillus, Fisher Ames, *The Works of Fisher Ames*, Seth Ames, editor (Boston: Little, Brown and Company, 1854), Vol. I, 67, to George Richards Minot, August 12, 1789; *The Speeches of the Different Governors of the Legislature of the State of New York, Commencing with Those of George Clinton and Continued Down to the Present Time* (Albany: J. B. Van Steenbergh, 1825), 108, Governor Daniel Tompkins on January 30, 1810; John Adams, John Hancock, Samuel Adams, et. al., *A Constitution or Frame of Government Agreed Upon by the Delegates of the People for the State of Massachusetts* (Boston: Benjamin Edes & Sons, 1780), 7, "Declaration of Rights," Part the First, Article III; John Sanderson, *Biography of the Signers to the Declaration of Independence* (Philadelphia; R. W. Pomeroy, 1824), Vol. IX, 333, Thomas Stone to his son in October, 1787; (James McHenry) Bernard C. Steiner, *One Hundred and Ten Years of Bible Society Work in Maryland, 1810–1920* (Baltimore: The Maryland Bible Society, 1921), 14; Daniel Webster, *The Works of Daniel Webster* (Boston: Little, Brown and Company, 1853), Vol. II, 107–108, "Remarks to the Ladies of Richmond," October 5, 1840; and many similar quotes.

65. See, for example, virtually any state code of laws in the era. Some of many possible examples include: *Acts and Laws of the State of Connecticut, in America* (New London, Timothy Green, 1784), 213–14, 21–22, 157–60, 235–37, 258–59, 182–87, 196–97, 101, 8, 41, 43, 87, 89, 97, 67; *The Laws of the State of New Hampshire, The Constitution of the State of New Hampshire and the Constitution of the United States with its Proposed Amendments* (Portsmouth: John Melcher, 1797), 279, 285; *Constitution and Laws of the State of New Hampshire; Together with the Constitution of the United States* (Dover: Samuel Bragg, 1805), 267, 275, 278–279, 286, 374; *Laws of the State of New York, Comprising the Constitution and Acts of the Legislature Since the Revolution from the First to the Twentieth Session, Inclusive* (New York: Thomas Greenleaf, 1798), Vol. I, 57–60, 336–338, 428; John Haywood, *A Manual of the Laws of North Carolina, Arranger Under Distinct Heads in Alphabetical Order* (Raleigh: J. Gales, 1814), 65, 264–265, 267; Collinson Read, *An Abridgment of the Laws of Pennsylvania, Being a Complete Digest of All Such Acts of Assembly, as Concern the Commonwealth at Large* (Philadelphia: 1801), 31, 175, 286, 379, 382; *Laws of the Commonwealth of Pennsylvania* (Philadelphia: John Bioren, 1810), Vol. I, 26–27, 29, 113; *The Public Laws of the State of Rhode Island and Providence Plantations, as Revised by a Committee and Finally Enacted by the Honourable General Assembly at their Session in January, 1798* (Providence: Carter and Wilkinson, 1798), 585–586, 594–595; *Statutes of the State of Vermont* (Bennington: Anthony Haswell, 1791), 17–18, 50, 155, 265; *The Revised Code of the Laws of Virginia; Being a Collection of All Such Acts of the General Assembly, of a Public and Permanent nature, as are Now in Force* (Richmond: Thomas Ritchie, 1819), Vol. I, 585–586; etc.

66. Thomas Jefferson, *The Writings of Thomas Jefferson*, Vol. X, 374–375, to Joseph Priestly on April 9, 1803.

67. Thomas Jefferson, *Memoir, Correspondence, and Miscellanies* (1830), Vol. IV, 223, to John Adams on October 13, 1813.

68. Thomas Jefferson, *The Writings of Thomas Jefferson* (1904), Vol. X, 376–377, to Edward Dowse on April 19, 180, Vol. XII, 315, to James Fishback on September 27, 1809, Vol. XIII, 377–378, to William Canby on September 18, 1813, and Vol. XIV, 232–233, to the Rev. Charles Clay on January 29, 18153; Thomas Jefferson, *Memoir, Correspondence, and Miscellanies*, (1830), Vol. III, 506–507, to Benjamin Rush on April 21, 1803, and Vol. IV, 222–226, to John Adams on October 13, 1813; Thomas Jefferson, *The Works of Thomas Jefferson*, Paul Leicester Ford, editor (New York: G. P. Putnam's Sons, 1905), Vol. XII, 241, to Benjamin Waterhouse on June 26, 1822; etc.

69. Thomas Jefferson, *Memoir, Correspondence, and Miscellanies*, (1830), Vol. IV, 13–14, to Joseph Priestley on January 29, 1804, and Vol. III, 509, to Benjamin Rush on April 21, 1803, to which is attached a "Syllabus of an Estimate of the Merit of the Doctrines of Jesus, Compared with Those of Others."

70. Thomas Jefferson, *Memoir, Correspondence, and Miscellanies*, (1830), Vol. IV, 223–224, to John Adams on October 13, 1813.

71. Thomas Jefferson, *The Writings of Thomas Jefferson*, (1904), Vol. XIV, 232–233, to the Rev. Charles Clay on January 29, 1815.
72. Ibid., Vol. XIV, 385, to Charles Thompson on January 9, 1816.
73. Ibid., Vol. XIV, 386, to Charles Thompson on January 9, 1816.
74. Ibid., Vol. XIX, 246, to Joseph Delaplaine on April 12, 1817. See also Marie Kimball, *Jefferson: The Road to Glory, 1743 to 1776* (New York: Coward-McCann, 1943), 106–109.
75. *The Life and Morals of Jesus of Nazareth, Extracted Textually from the Gospels in Greek, Latin, French, and English*, Thomas Jefferson, editor (Washington, DC: Government Printing Office, 1904), Index, where he numbers eighty-one teachings with multiple Scripture verses for many teachings.
76. See, for example, *The Life and Morals of Jesus of Nazareth*, (1904), "A Table of the Texts"; Henry S. Randall, *The Life of Thomas Jefferson* (New York: Derby & Jackson, 1858), Vol. III, 654–655, "Appendix No. XXX"; and *The Selected Religious Letters and Papers of Thomas Jefferson*, Mark A. Beliles, editor (Charlottesville, VA: America Publications, 2013), 428–429.
77. Henry S. Randall, *The Life of Thomas Jefferson*, Vol. III, 671–672, Thomas Jefferson Randolph to Henry S. Randall.
78. See, for example, *Congressional Record: Containing the Proceedings and Debates of the Fifty-Seventh Congress, First Session; Also Special Session of the Senate* (Washington, DC: Government Printing Office, 1902), Vol. XXXV, 5272–5273, May 10, 1902, and Vol. XXXV, 5783–5784, May 21, 1902.
79. Ibid., Vol. XXV, 5273, May 10, 1902.
80. Ibid., Vol. XXV, 5272, May 10, 1902.
81. *The Life and Morals of Jesus of Nazareth* (1904), 19, introduction by Cyrus Adler, librarian at the Smithsonian Institute.
82. *Thomas Jefferson, Jefferson's "Bible"* (1996), xv, Introduction.
83. Ibid.

LIE # 4

1. See, for example, John Quincy Adams: Josiah Quincy, *Memoir of the Life of John Quincy Adams* (Boston: Crosby, Nichols, Lee and Company, 1860), 177–178; William H. Seward, *Life and Public Services of John Quincy Adams* (Auburn: Derby, Miller and Company, 1849), 291–293; *Address of John Quincy Adams, to His Constituents of the Twelfth Congressional District, at Braintree, September 17th, 1842* (Boston: J. H. Eastburn, 1842), 25; Daniel Webster: Daniel Webster, *The Writings and Speeches of Daniel Webster*, Edward Everett, editor (Boston: Little, Brown and Company, 1903), Vol. 15, 205, "Address on the Annexation of Texas" on January 29, 1845; Abraham Lincoln: Abraham Lincoln, *The Collected Works of Abraham Lincoln*, Roy P. Basler, editor (New Brunswick, NJ: Rutgers University Press, 1953), Vol. II, 249–250, speech at Peoria, Illinois on October 16, 1854; Frederick Douglass: *Frederick Douglass: Selected*

Speeches and Writings, Philip S. Foner, editor (Chicago: Lawrence Hill Books, 1999), 27, 30, letter to Horace Greeley, April 15, 1846; 314, "The Anti-Slavery Movement," speech delivered on March 19, 1855; 347, "The Dred Scott Decision," speech delivered on May 14, 1857; 356, "The Dred Scott Decision," speech delivered on May 14, 1857; Henry Highland Garnet: Henry Highland Garnet, *Memorial Discourse* (Philadelphia: Joseph M. Wilson, 1865), 80–81; Martin Luther King, Jr: Martin Luther King, Jr., "Letter from a Birmingham Jail," Bates College, April 16, 1963 (http://abacus.bates. edu/admin/offices/dos/mlk/letter.html); Colin Powell: Colin Powell, "Acceptance Speech," National Constitution Center, July 4, 2002 (at: http://constitutioncenter.org/ libertymedal/recipient_2002_speech.html); and others.

2. Conor Cruise O'Brien, "Thomas Jefferson: Radical and Racist," *Atlantic Monthly*, October 1997 (at: http://www.theatlantic.com/past/docs/issues/96oct/obrien/obrien. htm).

3. Stephen E. Ambrose, *To America: Personal Reflections of an Historian* (New York: Simon & Schuster, 2002), 2.

4. Professor Paul Finkelman (Duke University and Albany Law School),"The Monster of Monticello," *New York Times*, November 30, 2012 (at: http://www.nytimes. com/2012/12/01/opinion/the-real-thomas-jefferson.html?_r=0).

5. Thomas Jefferson's Dark Side," *Abolitionist*, February 12, 1997 (at: http://afgen.com/ jeffersn.html).

6. *Dred Scott v. Sanford*, 60 U.S. 393, 572–573 (1856) (Curtis, J., dissenting); John Hancock, *Essays on the Elective Franchise; or, Who Has the Right to Vote?* (Philadelphia: Merrihew & Son, 1865), 22–23.

7. Thomas Jefferson, *The Papers of Thomas Jefferson*, Julian P. Boyd, editor (Princeton: Princeton University Press, 1953), Vol. 8, 258–259, from Dr. Richard Price on July 2, 1785.

8. Thomas Jefferson, *Memoir, Correspondence, and Miscellanies*, Thomas Jefferson Randolph, editor (Charlottesville: F. Carr & Co., 1829), Vol. I, 268, to Dr. Richard Price on August 7, 1785.

9. Ibid., Vol. I, 268–269, to Dr. Richard Price on August 7, 1785.

10. Ibid., Vol. I, 269, to Dr. Richard Price on August 7, 1785.

11. Thomas Jefferson, *The Works of Thomas Jefferson*, Paul Leicester Ford, editor (New York: G. P. Putnam's Sons, 1905), Vol. XI, 264, to David Barrow on May 1, 1815.

12. W. O. Blake, *The History of Slavery and the Slave Trade; Ancient and Modern* (Ohio: J. & H. Miller, 1857), 374.

13. Ibid., 386.

14. George M. Stroud, *A Sketch of the Laws Relating to Slavery in the Several States of the United States of America* (Philadelphia: Henry Longstreth, 1856), 150.

15. *The Revised Code of the Laws of Virginia* (Richmond: Thomas Ritcher, 1819), Vol. 1, 434.

16. Ibid., Vol. 1, 435.

17. Ibid., Vol. 1, 436. See also George M. Stroud, *A Sketch of the Laws Relating to Slavery*, 150–151.

18. Dumas Malone, *Jefferson and His Time: The Sage of Monticello* (Boston: Little Brown and Company, 1981), Vol. Six, 319.

19. Thomas Jefferson, *The Works of Thomas Jefferson*, Paul Leicester Ford, editor (New York: G. P. Putnam's Sons, 1898), Vol. XI, 197, to Thomas Jefferson Randolph on November 8, 1808.

20. Dumas Malone, *Jefferson and His Times: Jefferson the Virginian* (Boston: Little, Brown and Company, 1948), Vol. 1, 441.

21. Edward Ellis, *Thomas Jefferson, A Character Sketch* (Chicago: The University Association, 1898), 45–46.

22. Henry S. Randall, *The Life of Thomas Jefferson* (New York: Derby & Jackson, 1858), Vol. III, 676, Appendix XXXVI: from Thomas Jefferson Randolph to Henry Randall.

23. Jefferson and Slavery," Monticello (at: http://www.monticello.org/site/jefferson/jefferson-and-slavery) (accessed on January 29, 2013).

24. Thomas Jefferson, *The Works of Thomas Jefferson* (1905), Vol. XI, 238, to Edward Coles on August 25, 1814.

25. Thomas Jefferson, *The Papers of Thomas Jefferson*, Charles T. Cullen, editor (Princeton: Princeton University Press, 1986), Vol. 22, 49, from Benjamin Banneker on August 19, 1791.

26. Thomas Jefferson, *The Papers of Thomas Jefferson* (1986), Vol. 22, 49–50, from Benjamin Banneker on August 19, 1791.

27. Ibid., 51–52.

28. Ibid., 97–98.

29. Ibid., 98–99.

30. Franziska Massner, *Thomas Jefferson and Slavery – Was He Really an Opponent of the Institution?* (Norderstedt: Druck and Bindung, 2005), 7.

31. Oscar Reiss, *Blacks in Colonial America* (Jefferson, NC: McFarland & Company, 1997), 173.

32. Garry Wills, *Augustine's Confessions* (Princeton: Princeton University Press, 2011), 7.

33. Joseph M. Hentz, *The Real Thomas Paine* (Bloomington: iUniverse, 2010), 67.

34. Thomas Jefferson, *Notes on the State of Virginia* (Philadelphia: Matthew Carey, 1794, second edition; first edition 1781), 232, 239, "Query XIV The Administration of Justice and Description of the Laws?"

35. Ibid., 239.

36. Ibid., 232.

37. Thomas Jefferson, *The Papers of Thomas Jefferson* (1986), Vol. 22, 97–98, to Benjamin Banneker on August 30, 1791.

38. Ibid., 98–99, to Marquis de Condorcet on August 30, 1791.

39. Thomas Jefferson, *The Works of Thomas Jefferson* (1905), Vol. XI, 99–100, to Henri Gregoire on February 25, 1809.

40. Ibid., 121, to Joel Barlow on October 8, 1809.

41. Ibid., 99–100, to Henri Gregoire on February 25, 1809.

42. Thomas Jefferson, *The Writings of Thomas Jefferson* (1903), Vol. I, 4, from his Autobiography.

43. Thomas Jefferson, *The Works of Thomas Jefferson* (1905), Vol. XI, 417, to Edward Coles on August 25, 1814.

44. Thomas Jefferson, *The Writings of Thomas Jefferson* (1903), Vol. I, 4, from his Autobiography.

45. Thomas Jefferson, *The Works of Thomas Jefferson* (1904), Vol. I, 474, "Argument in the case of Howell v. Netherland."

46. Thomas Jefferson, *The Thomas Jefferson Papers: Jefferson's Memorandum Books,* James Bear and Lucia Stanton, editors (Princeton: Princeton University Press, 1997), Vol. I, 271.

47. See, for example, Benjamin Franklin, *The Works of Benjamin Franklin*, Jared Sparks, editor (Boston: Tappan, Whittemore, and Mason, 1839), Vol. VIII, 42, to the Rev. Dean Woodward on April 10, 1773.

48. Thomas Jefferson, *The Papers of Thomas Jefferson* (1950), Vol. I, 130, "A Summary View of the Rights of British America," 1774.

49. Ibid., Vol. I, 353, draft of the "Virginia Constitution," written before June 13, 1776.

50. Thomas Jefferson, "Rough Draft of the Declaration of Independence," ushistory.org (at: http://www.ushistory.org/declaration/document/rough.htm) (accessed on January 29, 2013).

51. Thomas Jefferson, *Memoir, Correspondence, and Miscellanies* (1829), Vol. I, 16, from his Autobiography.

52. Alexander Tsesis, *For Liberty and Equality: The Life and Times of the Declaration of Independence* (New York: Oxford University Press, 2012), passim.

53. *A Constitution or Form of Government Agreed Upon by the Delegates of the People of the State of Massachusetts-Bay* (Boston: Benjamin Edes and Sons, 1780), 7, Art. I, "Declaration of Rights"; *An Abridgment of the Laws of Pennsylvania*, Collinson Read, editor (Philadelphia: 1801), 264–266, Act of March 1, 780; *The Public Statute Laws of the State of Connecticut* (Hartford: Hudson and Goodwin, 1808), Book I, 623–625, Act passed in October, 1777; *Rhode Island Session Laws* (Providence: Wheeler, 1784), 7–8, Act of February 27, 1784; *The Constitutions of the Sixteen States* (Boston: Manning and Loring, 1797), 279, Vermont Constitution, 1786, Art. I, "Declaration of Rights"; 50, New Hampshire Constitution, 1792, Art. I, "Bill of Rights"; *Laws of the State of New York, Passed at the Twenty-Second Session, Second Meeting of the Legislature* (Albany: Loring Andrew, 1799), 721–723, Act of March 29, 1799; *Laws of the State of New Jersey*, Compiled and Published Under the Authority of the Legislature, Joseph Bloomfield, editor (Trenton: James J. Wilson, 1811), 103–105, Act of February 15, 1804. See also the *Dictionary of African American Slavery*, Randall Miller and John Smith, editors (Westport: Praeger Publishers, 1997), 394, 820–821, *The Federal and*

State Constitutions, Francis Newton Thorpe (Washington D.C.: Government Printing Office, 1909), Vol. VI, 3739–3740, "Constitution of Vermont, 1777, A Declaration of the Rights of the Inhabitants of the State of Vermont;" and "State Constitution, Bill of Rights," *New Hampshire Government*, October 31, 1783 (at: http://www.nh.gov/constitution/billofrights.html).

54. Thomas Jefferson, *The Writings of Thomas Jefferson* (1853), Vol. I, 38, from his Autobiography.

55. Thomas Jefferson, Notes on the State of Virginia(1794), 228, "Query XIV The Administration of Justice and Description of the Laws?"

56. Thomas Jefferson, *Memoir, Correspondence, and Miscellanies*, (1829), Vol. I, 41–42, from his Autobiography.

57. Ibid.

58. Thomas Jefferson, *Notes on the State of Virginia* (1794), 270–272, "Query XVIII The Particular Customs and Manners that may Happen to be Received in that State?"

59. *Journals of the Continental Congress*, Gaillard Hunt, editor (Washington, DC: Government Printing Office, 1928), Vol. XXVI, 118–119, March 1, 1784; Thomas Jefferson, *The Writings of Thomas Jefferson* (1894), Vol. III, 432, "Report of Government for the Western Territory;" Northwest Ordinance.

60. Thomas Jefferson, *The Works of Thomas Jefferson* (1904), Vol. V, 65, "Observations on the Article Etats-Unis Prepared for the Encyclopedie" to Monsieur de Meusnier on June 22, 1786.

61. Ibid., Vol. V, 71–72, "Observations on the Article Etats-Unis Prepared for the Encyclopedie" to Monsieur de Meusnier on June 22, 1786.

62. Thomas Ibid., Vol. V, 388, to Jean Pierre Brissot de Warville on February 11, 1788.

63. Ibid., Vol. V, 388, to Jean Pierre Brissot de Warville on February 11, 1788.

64. Thomas Jefferson, *The Writings of Thomas Jefferson* (1894), Vol. III, 432, "Report of Government for the Western Territory;" Northwest Ordinance; The Laws of the United States of America (Philadelphia: Richard Folwell, 1796), Vol. II, 567, "An Ordinance for the Government of the Territory of the United States North-west of the River Ohio," Art. VI, July 13, 1787.

65. *Acts Passed at a Congress of the United States of America Begun and Held at the City of New-York, on Wednesday the Fourth of March, in the Year 1789* (Harford: Hudson & Goodwin, 1791), 178–179, May 26, 1790.

66. Thomas Jefferson, *The Works of Thomas Jefferson* (1904), Vol. X, 126, to William A. Burwell on January 28, 1805.

67. Thomas Jefferson, *The Writings of Thomas Jefferson* (1897), Vol. VIII, 492–493, "Sixth Annual Message," December 2, 1806.

68. Ibid., Vol. XVI, 290, to Messrs. Thomas, Ellicot, and others on November 13, 1807.

69. Willard Carey MacNaul, *The Jefferson-Lemen Compact* (Chicago: The University of Chicago Press, 1915), 10, Lemen's records on December 11, 1782 and May, 1784, show Jefferson's encouragement to Lemen to go to Illinois and Lemen's decision to go.

70. Ibid., 30, Jefferson to Lemen on January 10, 1809.

71. Thomas Jefferson, *The Works of Thomas Jefferson* (1905), Vol. XI, 416–418, to Edward Coles on August 25, 1814.

72. Ibid., Vol. XI, 419, to Edward Coles on August 25, 1814.

73. Ibid., Vol. XI, 419–420, to Edward Coles on August 25, 1814.

74. Ibid., Vol. XI, 470–471, to David Barrow on May 1, 1815

75. "Missouri Compromise," *Teaching American History*, March 6, 1820 (at: http://teachingamericanhistory.org/library/index.asp?document=841).

76. George Adams Boyd, *Elias Boudinot* (Princeton: Princeton University Press, 1952), 290, Elias Boudinot to his nephew Elias E. Boudinot on November 27, 1819.

77. John Adams, *The Works of John Adams*, Charles Francis Adams, editor (Boston: Little, Brown and Company, 1856), Vol. X, 386, to Thomas Jefferson on December 18, 1819.

78. James Madison, *The Writings of James Madison*, Gaillard Hunt, editor (New York: G. P. Putnam's Sons, 1910), Vol. IX, 12, to Robert Walsh on November 27, 1819.

79. Thomas Jefferson, *The Works of Thomas Jefferson* (1905), Vol. XII, 157, to Hugh Nelson on February 7, 1820.

80. Thomas Jefferson, *Memoir, Correspondence, and Miscellanies* (1829), Vol. IV, 323–324, to John Holmes on April 22, 1820.

81. Ibid., Vol. IV, 324, to John Holmes on April 22, 1820.

82. Thomas Jefferson, *The Writings of Thomas Jefferson* (1904), Vol. XVI, 119–120, to Frances Wright on August 7, 1825.

83. Ibid., Vol. XVI, 162–163, to the Hon. Edward Everett on April 8, 1826.

84. John Quincy Adams, *An Oration Delivered Before The Inhabitants Of The Town Of Newburyport at Their Request on the Sixty-First Anniversary of the Declaration of Independence, July 4, 1837* (Newburyport: Charles Whipple, 1837), 50.

85. Daniel Webster, *The Writings and Speeches of Daniel Webster*, Edward Everett, editor (Boston: Little, Brown and Company, 1903), Vol. 15, 205, "Address on the Annexation of Texas" on January 29, 1845.

86. Abraham Lincoln, *The Collected Works of Abraham Lincoln* (1953), Vol. II, 249–250, speech at Peoria, Illinois on October 16, 1854.

87. Fredrick Douglass, *My Bondage and My Freedom* (New York: Miller, Orton & Mulligan, 1855), 440, "Inhumanity of Slavery. Extract from a Lecture on Slavery at Rochester, December 8, 1850."

88. Frederick Douglas, *The Frederick Douglass Papers, Series One, Speeches, Debates, and Interviews*, John W. Blassingame and John McKivigan, editors (New Haven: Yale University Press, 1992), Vol. 4, 307, "Address in Baltimore," November 17, 1864.

89. Frederick Douglass, *Frederick Douglass: A Critical Reader*, Bill Lawson and Frank Kirkland, editors (Malden, MA: Blackwell Publishers, 1999), 237, "Address to the Indian Industrial School," March, 1893.

90. Frederick Douglass, "Letter to Horace Greeley," The Gilder Lehrman Center for the Study of Slavery, Resistance, & Abolition, April 15, 1846 (at: http://www.yale.edu/glc/

archive/1096.htm); Frederick Douglas, *The Frederick Douglass Papers* (1985), Vol. 3, 21, "The Anti-Slavery Movement," speech delivered on March 19, 1855; 180, "The Dred Scott Decision," speech delivered on May 14, 1857; etc.

91. Henry Highland Garnet, *Memorial Discourse* (1865), 80–81.

92. Martin Luther King, Jr., "Letter from a Birmingham Jail," Bates College, April 16, 1963 (http://abacus.bates.edu/admin/offices/dos/mlk/letter.html), accessed June 2, 2011.

93. Colin Powell, "Acceptance Speech," National Constitution Center, July 4, 2002, (at: http://constitutioncenter.org/libertymedal/recipient_2002_speech.html).

LIE # 5

1. John E. Remsburg, *Six Historic Americans* (New York: The Truth Seeker Company, 1906), 81.

2. *Random House Webster's Unabridged Dictionary* (New York: Random House Inc., 2013), s.v. "secularism."

3. *Merriam-Webster Unabridged Dictionary* (Merriam-Webster Inc., 2013), s.v. "secularism."

4. *The American Heritage Dictionary of the English Language* (Boston: Houghton Mifflin Company, 2009), s.v. "secularism."

5. *Proposed Restriction of Immigration: Hearing before the Committee on Immigration and Naturalization. House of Representatives, Sixty-Sixth Congress Second Session on H.R. 12320* (Washington, DC: Government Printing Office, 1921), 57, "A Brief in Opposition to the Exclusion of Foreign Language Newspapers from Second-Class Mailing Privileges," April 22, 1920. See also "A few words from the father of the First Amendment," KintaLake Blog (at: http://kintlake.blogspot.com/2010/03/few-words-from-author-of-first.html) (accessed on January 17, 2013).

6. Tom Head, "The First Amendment: Text, Origins, and Meaning," About.com (at: http://civilliberty.about.com/od/firstamendment/tp/First-Amendment.htm) (accessed on May 10, 2011).

7. Deuce, "Our Religious Forefathers II," *Modern Ghana*, November 15, 2007 (at: http://www.modernghana.com/blogs/147715/31/our-religious-forefathers-ii.html).

8. Sembj, "Humanism, Thomas Jefferson and the Constitution," Hub Pages (at: http://hubpages.com/hub/Humanism-Thomas-Jefferson-and-The-Constitution) (accessed on April 18, 2011).

9. *Everson v. Bd. of Educ.* 330 U.S. 1, 13 (1947).

10. See, for example, *Abington Sch. Dist. v. Schempp*, 374 U.S. 203, 214, 234–235 (1963), *McDaniel v. Paty*, 435 U.S. 618, 629, n9 (1978).

11. Forty-seven major decisions on religion have been delivered since 1947, and Jefferson was *cited authoritatively* in seventeen: *Everson v. Bd. of Educ.* 330 U.S. 1, 13, 16 (1947); *McCollum v. Bd. of Educ.* 333 U.S. 203, 211 (1948); *McGowan v. Maryland*, 366 U.S. 420, 443 (1961); *Torcaso v. Watkins*, 367 U.S. 488, 493 (1961); *Engel v. Vitale*, 370 U.S. 421, 425 (1962); *Sch. Dist. of Abington TP. v. Schempp*, 374 U.S. 203, 234–235 (1963)

(Brennan, J., concurring); *Bd. of Educ. v. Allen,* 392 U.S. 236, 251 (1968) (Black, J., dissenting); *Epperson v. Arkansas,* 393 U.S. 97, 106 (1968); *Comm. for Pub. Educ. v. Nyquist,* 413 U.S. 756, 760–761, 771 (1973); *Larkin v. Grende's Den, Inc.,* 459 U.S. 116, 122–123 (1982); *Marsh v. Chambers,* 463 U.S. 783, 802 (1983) (Marshall & Brennan, JJ., dissenting); *Lynch v. Donnelly,* 465 U.S. 668, 673 (1984), *Lee v. Weisman,* 505 U.S. 577, 600–601 (1992) (Blackmun & Stevens & O'Connor, JJ. concurring); *Capitol Square Rev. & Advisory Bd. v. Pinette,* 515 U.S. 753 (1995), (Stevens, J., dissenting); *Mitchell v. Helms,* 530 U.S. 793, 873 (2000) (Souter & Stevens & Ginsburg, JJ., dissenting); *Zelman v. Simmons-Harris,* 536 U.S. 639, 711 122 S. Ct. 2460, 2485 (2002) (Souter, J., dissenting); and *Van Orden v. Perry,* 545 U.S. 677, (2005) (Stevens & Ginsburg, JJ., dissenting). *Jefferson's "wall of separation between Church and State" metaphor* (or some slight modification thereof) was cited in an additional twelve: *Zorach v. Clauson,* 343 U.S. 306, 317 (1952), (Black, J., dissenting); *Lemon v. Kurtzman,* 403 U.S. 602, 614 (1971); *Roemer v. Maryland Pub. Works Bd.* 426 U.S. 736, 768 (1976); *Wolman v. Walter,* 433 U.S. 229, 236, 257 (1977); *Comm. for Pub. Educ. v. Regan,* 444 U.S. 646, 671 (1980) (Stevens, J., dissenting); *Aguilar v. Felton,* 473 U.S. 402, 420 (1985) (Burger, J., dissenting); *Bowen v. Kendrick,* 487 U.S. 589, 617–618, 638 (1988) (majority opinion & Blackmun, J., dissenting); *Texas Monthly, Inc. v. Bullock,* 489 U.S. 1, 1, 43 (1989); *Allegheny County v. Greater Pittsburgh ACLU,* 492 U.S. 573, 636–637, 650–651, 657–658 (1989) (Brennan & Marshall & Stevens, JJ., concurring in part and dissenting in part) (Stevens & Brennan & Marshall, JJ., concurring in part and dissenting in part) (Kennedy & Rehnquist & White & Scalia, JJ., concurring in part and dissenting in part); *Seminole Tribe of Fla. v. Florida,* 517 U.S. 44, 96 (1996) (Stevens, JJ., dissenting); *Santa Fe IndeSch. Dist. v. Doe,* 530 U.S. 290, 323 (2000) (Rehnquist & Scalia & Thomas, JJ., dissenting); and *Pleasant Grove City v Summum,* 555 U.S. 460 (2009) (Scalia & Thomas, JJ., concurring). Of the remaining eighteen cases, all of them *relied on a case in which Jefferson had already been invoked* by the Court as a primary authority in reaching its decision to restrict or remove religious expressions: *Walz v. Tax Comm'n,* 397 U.S. 664 (1970) (Brennan, J., concurring); *Tilton v. Richardson,* 403 U.S. 672 (1971); *Lemon v. Kurtzman,* 411 U.S. 192 (1973); *Levitt v. Comm. for Pub. Educ.,* 413 U.S. 472 (1973); *Sloan v. Lemon,* 413 U.S. 825 (1973), *Norwood v. Harrison,* 413 U.S. 455 (1973); *Wheeler v. Barrera,* 417 U.S. 402 (1974); *Meek v. Pittenger,* 421 U.S. 349 (1975); *Stone v. Graham,* 449 U.S. 39 (1980); *Larson v. Valente,* 456 U.S. 228 (1982); *Wallace v. Jaffree,* 472 U.S. 38 (1985) (Powell, J., concurring); *Sch. Dist. of the City of Grand Rapids v. Ball,* 473 U.S. 373 (1985); *Estate of Thornton v. Caldor, Inc.* 472 U.S. 703 (1985); *Edwards v. Aguillard,* 482 U.S. 578 (1987); *Zobrest v. Catalina Foothills Sch. Dist.,* 509 U.S. 1 (1993); *Bd. of Educ. Kiryas Joel v. Grumet,* 512 U.S. 687 (1994); and *Agostini v. Felton,* 521 U.S. 203 (1997); and *McCreary County, Kentucky, et al. Petitioners v. American Civil Liberties Union of Kentucky et al.,* 545 U.S. 844 (2005). *Therefore, Jefferson has been invoked either directly or indirectly as the Constitutional authority in all forty-seven major Supreme Court cases on religion.*

12. See the documentation of this trend by Professor Mark David Hall, "Jeffersonian Wall and Madisonian Lines: The Supreme Court's Use of History and Religion Clauses Cases," *Oregon Law Review* 85 (2006), 563–614.

13. Thomas Jefferson, *The Writings of Thomas Jefferson*, Andrew A. Lipscomb, editor (Washington, DC: The Thomas Jefferson Memorial Association, 1904), Vol. X, 325, to Dr. Joseph Priestly on June 19, 1802.

14. Ibid.

15. Ibid.

16. Roger Williams, *The Bloudy Tenent of Persecution for Cause of Conscience Discussed; and Mr. Cotton's Letter Examined and Answered* (London: J. Haddon, 1848), 435, "Mr. Cotton's Letter Examined and Answered."

17. See, for example, *The Nation: A Weekly Journal Devoted to Politics, Literature, Science & Art* (New York: *The Evening Post* Publishing Company, 1888), Vol. XLVI, No. 1196, 450, "The Veto Power," May 31, 1888, Thomas Jefferson, "The Thomas Jefferson Papers," Library of Congress, to Martha Jefferson on April 25, 1803 (at: http://hdl.loc. gov/loc.mss/mtj.mtjbib012345), Catalog of the Library of Thomas Jefferson (Library of Congress, 1815), mentioning several works by Priestley throughout.

18. *Documents of the Christian Church*, Henry Bettenson, editor (London: Oxford University Press, 1943), 31, Theodosian Code XVI.1.2.

19. Charles B. Galloway, *Christianity and the American Commonwealth* (Nashville: Publishing House Methodist Episcopal Church, 1898), 144.

20. "The Legitimization of Authority," Shelton Hall University (at: http://pirate.shu. edu/~wisterro/coronation.htm) (accessed on May 16, 2011).

21. See, for example, *An Ordinance of the Lords and Commons Assembled in Parliament. Together with Rules and Directions concerning Suspension from the Sacrament of the Lords Supper in Cases of Ignorance and Scandal. Also the Names of Such Ministers and Others That are Appointed Triers and Judges of the Ability of Elders in the Twelve Classes Within the Province of London* (London: John Wright, October 21, 1645); *A Declaration of the Commons Assembled in Parliament Against all Such Persons as Shall Take Upon Them to Preach or Expound the Scriptures in any Church or Chapel, or any other Public Place, Except They be Ordained Either Here or in Some Other Reformed Church* (London: Edward Husband, January 2, 1646); etc.

22. "Anglicanism," *Catholic Encyclopedia* (at: http://www.newadvent.org/cathen/01498a. htm) (accessed on March 1, 2013).

23. Richard Hooker, *The Works of the Learned and Judicious Divine*, Mr. Richard Hooker (Oxford: University Press, 1845), Vol. II, 484, 486.

24. Frederick Greenwood, *Greenwood Genealogies, 1154–1914* (New York: The Lyons Genealogical Company, 1914), 30, "The Execution of John Greenwood."

25. Ibid., 34.

26. Ibid., 35.

27. Claude H. Van Tyne, *The Causes of the War of Independence* (Boston: Houghton Mifflin Company, 1922), 3.

28. Roger Williams, *The Bloudy Tenent*, 1–2, 171.

29. John Wise, *A Vindication of the Government of New-England Churches. And the Churches Quarrel Espoused, or a Reply to Certain Proposals* (Boston: John Boyles, 1772), Chapter II, 35.

30. Thomas Clarkson, *Memoirs of the Private and Public Life of William Penn* (London: Richard Taylor and Co., 1813), 240–244, "An Address to the Protestants of All Persuasions Upon the Present Conjuncture, More Especially to the Magistracy and Clergy for the Promotion of Virtue and Charity," 1679.

31. See, for example, John Wise, *A Vindication of the Government of New-England Churches*, 47–48; Reverend Isaac Backus, *An Appeal to the Public for Religious Liberty Against the Oppressions of the Present Day* (Boston: John Boyle, 1773), 19, 26; *The Americana, A Universal Reference Library*, Frederick Converse Beach, editor (New York: Scientific American Compiling Department, 1908), Vol. 12, "Pennsylvania"; Bishop Charles Galloway, *Christianity and the American Commonwealth*, 179; John Leland, *The Writings of the Late Elder John Leland, Including Some Events in His Life, Written by Himself, with Additional Sketches*, L. F. Greene, editor (New York: G. W. Wood, 1845), 579–580, "Short Saying of Times, Men, Measures, and Religion, Exhibited in an Address, Delivered at Cheshire, July 5, 1830"; Roger Williams, *The Bloudy Tenent*, 1–2, 171; etc.

32. Will C. Wood, *Five Problems of State and Religion* (Boston: Henry Hoyt, 1877), 92.

33. Charles B. Galloway, *Christianity and the American Commonwealth*, 143.

34. William Cathcart, *Baptist Patriots in the American Revolution* (Philadelphia: S. A. George & Co., 1876), 12–18; Isaac Backus, *A History of New England, With Particular Reference to the Denomination of Christians Called Baptists* (Newton, MA: Backus Historical Society, 1871), Vol. II, 97–98; George Bancroft, *A History of the United States of America* (Boston: Little, Brown, and Company, 1858), Vol. 1, 449–450; Sanford Hoadley Cobb, *The Rise of Religious Liberty in America Republicanism in Jefferson's Virginia* (New York: MacMillan, 1902), 112; Bruce Gourley, *Baptist Index*, "An outline of Baptist Persecution in America" (at: http://www.brucegourley.com/baptists/persecutionoutline.htm) (accessed January 18, 2013). Lewis Peyton Little, *Imprisoned Preachers and Religious Liberty in Virginia* (Lynchburg, VA: J. P. Bell Co., Inc., 1938), xiii; etc.

35. "Another reason for denominating this country a land of Baptists is, that they have always been more numerous than any other sect of Christians which dwell therein; two-fifths of the inhabitants at least are reputed Baptists. . . . Their governors, deputy-governors, judges, assemblymen, justices, and officers (civil and military) have been chiefly of that denomination." Morgan Edwards, *Collections of the Rhode Island Historical Society* (1867) Vol. VI, 304. Morgan Edwards (1722–1795) was a Baptist minister, called "The First American Baptist Historian," and the founder of Rhode Island College, now known as Brown University.

36. Benson John Lossing, *Harper's Encyclopedia of United States History: From 458 A.D. to 1915* (New York: Harper & Brothers, 1915), Vol. VII, s.v. "Rhode Island."

37. See, for example, John Eidsmoe, *Christianity and the Constitution* (Michigan: Baker Book House, 1987), 353. Eidsmoe compiled the figures from a dissertation by James Hutchinson Smylie, *American Clergyman and the Constitution of the United States of America* (Princeton: 1954).

38. B. L. Rayner, *Life of Thomas Jefferson* (Boston: Lilly, Wait, Colman, & Holden, 1834), 113–119; Henry S. Randall, *The Life of Thomas Jefferson* (New York: Derby & Jackson, 1858), Vol. I, 203; John T. Morse, Jr., *Thomas Jefferson* (Boston: Houghton, Mifflin and Company, 1898), 41; Samuel M. Schmucker, *The Life of Thomas Jefferson* (New York: A. L. Burt Company, 1903), 67–71. See also Thomas Jefferson, *The Works of Thomas Jefferson* (1904), Vol. 1, 61–64, "A Declaration by the Representatives of the United States of America, in General Congress Assembled."

39. See, for example, Thomas Jefferson, "Thomas Jefferson Papers," *Library of Congress*, from Ketocton Baptist Association on August 18, 1808 (at: http://hdl.loc.gov/loc.mss/mtj.mtjbib018945); from Baltimore Baptist Association on October 15, 1808 (at: http://hdl.loc.gov/loc.mss/mtj.mtjbib019174); Thomas Jefferson, *The Papers of Thomas Jefferson Retirement Series*, J. Jefferson Looney, editor (Princeton: Princeton University Press, 2004), Vol. 1, 63, from Albemarle Buckmountain Baptist Church on March 17, 1809; etc.

40. Thomas Jefferson, *The Writings of Thomas Jefferson* (1904), Vol. XVI, 281–282, to Messrs. Nehemiah Dodge, Ephraim Robbins, and Stephen S. Nelson: A Committee of the Danbury Baptist Association in the State of Connecticut on January 1, 1802.

41. Thomas Jefferson, *The Papers of Thomas Jefferson*, Barbara B. Oberg, editor (Princeton: Princeton University Press, 2008), Vol. 35, 407–408, from the Danbury Baptist Association to Thomas Jefferson on October 7, 1801.

42. Ibid., 408, from the Danbury Baptist Association to Thomas Jefferson on October 7, 1801.

43. *Debate in the Several State Conventions, on the Adoption of the Federal Constitution, as Recommended by the General Convention at Philadelphia in 1787,* Jonathan Elliot, editor (Washington, DC: Printed for the Editor, 1836), Vol. IV, 540, "Kentucky Resolutions of 1798 and 1799. [The Original Draft Prepared by Thomas Jefferson]," November, 1798.

44. James D. Richardson, *A Compilation of the Messages and Papers of the Presidents, 1789–1897* (Washington, DC: Published by the Authority of Congress, 1899), Vol. I, 379, Thomas Jefferson, "Second Inaugural Address," March 4, 1805.

45. Thomas Jefferson, *The Writings of Thomas Jefferson* (1903), Vol. XVI, 325, to the Society of the Methodist Episcopal Church on December 9, 1808.

46. Ibid., 281–282, to Messrs. Nehemiah Dodge, Ephraim Robbins, and Stephen S. Nelson: A Committee of the Danbury Baptist Association in the State of Connecticut on January 1, 1802.

47. James L. Adams, *Yankee Doodle Went to Church: The Righteous Revolution of 1776* (Old Tappan, NJ: Fleming H. Revell Company, 1989), 12–13.

48. Daniel L. Dreisbach, *Thomas Jefferson and the Wall of Separation between Church and State* (New York: New York University Press, 2002), 98, 102; *The Wall between Church and State*, Dallin H. Oaks, editor (Chicago: University of Chicago Press, 1963), 17, Robert M. Hutchins, "Future of the Wall"; *DePaul Law Review* (1992), Vol. 42, 3–5, Craig B. Mousin, "Confronting the Wall of Separation: A New Dialogue between Law and Religion on the Meaning of the First Amendment."

49. *Reynolds v. U.S.*, 98 U.S. 145, 162–164 (1878).

50. Ibid., 164 (1878).

51. Ibid., 163 (1878).

52. See, for example, *Commonwealth v. Nesbit*, 84 Pa. 398 (Pa. SuCt. 1859); *Lindenmuller v. People*, 33 Barb 548 (SuCt. N.Y. 1861); and others.

53. *Everson v. Bd. of Educ.*, 330 U.S. 1, 18 (1947).

54. *McCollum v. Bd. of Educ.*, 333 U.S. 203, 212 (1948).

55. *Brittney Kaye Settle v. Dickson County Sch. Bd.*, 53 F. 3d 152 (6th Cir. 1995).

56. Cicely Gosier, "Student Penalized Over Religious Artwork," Christian Broadcast Network, April 6, 2008 (at: http://www.cbn.com/cbnnews/us/2008/April/Student-Penalized-Over-Religious-Artwork-/).

57. "Student Files Suit to Defend his Right to Bring Bible to School," Standard News Wire (at: http://www.standardnewswire.com/news/224236110.html) (accessed on June 29, 2011); Harvey Rice, "Suit Claims Students Not Allowed to Carry Bibles," *Houston Chronicle*, May 23, 2000 (at: http://www.chron.com/CDA/archives/archive.mpl?id=2000_3216815).

58. *Doe v. Santa Fe IndeSch,*. 530 U.S. 290 (1999).

59. *Graham v. C. Cmty. Sch. Dist. of Decatur County*, 608 F. Su531 (D. Iowa 1985); *Kay v. Douglas Sch. Dist.*, 719 P.2d 875 (Or. A1986); *Lee v. Weisman*, 505 U.S. 577 (1992); *Gearon v. Loudon County Sch. Bd.*, 844 F. Su1097 (E.D. Va. 1993); *Deveney v. Bd. of Educ., Kanawha County*, 231 F. Su2d 483 (S.D. W. Va. 2002).

60. *Chandler v. James*, 180 F.3d 1254 (11th Cir. 1999); *Doe v. Santa Fe IndeSch.*, 530 U.S. 290 (1999).

61. *Roberts v. Madigan*, 921 F.2d 1047, 59 USLW 2415, 19 Fed.R.Serv.3d 530, 64 Ed. Law Re1038 (1989).

62. Doug Huntington, "Graduation Choir Wants to Sing 'Lord's Prayer' in Honor of Deceased," *Christian Post*, May 28, 2007 (at: http://www.christianpost.com/news/graduation-choir-wants-to-sing-lords-prayer-in-honor-of-deceased-27653/).

63. Patrick Buchanan, "The de-Christianization of VMI," WND.com, January 29, 2002 (at: http://www.wnd.com/index.php?pageId=12556).

64. Conrad deFiebre, "Suit Claims Man's Religious Freedom is Being Thwarted; A Revenue Employee Says He's Not Allowed to Display Signs on His Car or Cubicle," *Star Tribune*, July 2, 2004.

65. *Broadus v. Saratoga Springs City Sch. Dist.*, 02-cv-0136 (N.D.N.Y. 2002); Ellen Sorokin, "Deal Reached on Praying Toddler," *Washington Times*, June 12, 2002.

66. Diane Lynne, "Petition posted to defend 'God Bless America!'" WND.com, January 31, 2003 (at: http://www.wnd.com/?pageId=16879); "'God bless' spells trouble for Guardsman," WND.com, August 22, 2003 (at: http://www.wnd.com/news/article.asp?ARTICLE_ID=34213).

67. "Seniors Sue After City Stifles Sermons at Community Center," Associated Press, October 31, 2003 (at: http://www.firstamendmentcenter.org/seniors-sue-after-city-stifles-sermons-at-community-center); Terry Eastland, "Understanding the First Amendment," *Weekly Standard*, January 15, 2004 (at: http://www.weeklystandard.com/Content/Public/Articles/000/000/003/599kpgpv.asp); "Dallas Suburb, Senior Citizens Settle Religious-Rights Case," Associated Press, January 9, 2004 (at: http://www.firstamendmentcenter.org/dallas-suburb-senior-citizens-settle-religious-rights-case); "Testimony at U.S. Senate Hearing," Senate, Testimony of Mr. Barney Clark, June 8, 2004 (at: http://judiciary.senate.gov/testimony.cfm? =1218&wit_id=3522); Robert Longley, "Texas Seniors Win Religious Speech Battle," About.com (at: http://usgovinfo.about.com/cs/usconstitution/a/seniorswin.htm) (accessed on May 16, 2011); issue decided in *J. B. Barton, et al. v. City of Balch Springs*, et al, No. 3:03-CV-2258-G (N.D. Tex. 2004).

68. *Draper v. Logan County Pub. Lib.,* 403 F. Su2d 608 (W.D. Ky. Aug. 29, 2003).

69. Carrie Antlfinger, "UW-Eau Claire is reviewing legalities of Bible study ban," Associated Press, November 3, 2005 (at: http://thefire.org/article/6399.html); Michael Gendall, "Campus dorm policy under review," *Badger Herald*, November 10, 2005 (at: http://badgerherald.com/news/2005/11/10/campus_dorm_policy_u.php); settled in *Steiger v. Lord-Larson,* No. 05-C-0700-S (W.D. Wis. Mar. 2006).

70. Susan Jones, "'Jesus Christ' Sweatshirt Ends Up Offending Everyone," Cybercast News Service, March 6, 2001 (at: http://cnsnews.com/news/article/jesus-christ-sweatshirt-ends-offending-everyone).

71. Laurie Goodstein, "Disciplining of Student is Defended; Gingrich Said Prayer Brought Punishment," *Washington Post*, December 6, 1994.

72. The following cases and articles detail the facts surrounding the refusal of officials to permit handing out religious literature or preaching on public sidewalks: *Colston v. Crowley IndeSch. Dist.,* No. 4:06-CV-00097 (N.D. Tex. June 20, 2006); *Hodges v. City of Lebanon,* No. 1:03-cv-00596 (S.D. Ind. 2003); *Parks v. Finan,* 385 F.3d 694 (6th Cir. 2004); *Baumann v. City of Cumming,* 2:07-CV-0095 (N.D. Ga. Feb. 27, 2008); and *Pulver v. City of Hastings,* 4:07-cv-03006 (D. Neb. Feb. 4, 2008); "Blind Justice: Free speech prohibited on sidewalk outside Calif. courthouse," Alliance Defense Fund, February 9, 2010 (at: http://www.adfmedia.org/News/PRDetail/3731); "Christian arrested for reading the Bible in public" Christian Newswire, February 2, 2011 (at: http://www.christiannewswire.com/news/8717116846.html); "Black Preacher arrested for preaching on public right of way," Christian Newswire, July 17, 2011 (at: http://www.

christiannewswire.com/news/2704114444.html); Andrea Phillips "Religious Freedom sought in public school," Worldwide Religious News, August 27, 2011 (at: http://wwrn.org/articles/4074/?&section=church-state); "One man is not a parade," Alliance Defense Fund (at: http://www.alliancedefensefund.org/Home/ADFContent?cid=4213) (accessed on May 26, 2011); Bob Unruh, "Mall to Christians: God talk banned," WND.com, January 30, 2010 (at: http://www.wnd.com/?pageId=123535); "Men jailed for being on the public sidewalk," WND.com, February 8, 2007 (at: http://www.wnd.com/?pageId=40073); "Pennsylvania Christians Face 47 Years in Prison for Reading Bible in Public," About.com, January, 2005 (at: http://urbanlegends.about.com/library/bl_christians_arrested.htm); Elizabeth O'Brien, "Christian minister arrested for praying near gay fest," Life Site News, July 10, 2007 (at: http://www.lifesitenews.com/news/archive/ldn/2007/jul/07071001); Jack Minor, "Kansas pastor arrested for Gospel tracts at mosque," Greeley Gazette, November 30, 2010 (at: http://www.greeleygazette.com/press/?p=6893); Bob Unruh, "Praying in park puts man in jail for 9 days," World Net Daily, March 24, 2010 (at: http://www.wnd.com/?pageId=131521); Lori Arnold, "Calif. Pastor Arrested for Reading Bible in Public," Christian Examiner Online, May 2011 (at: http://www.christianexaminer.com/Articles/Articles%20May11/Art_May11_23.html); Jack Minor, "Kansas Pastor Arrested for Gospel Tracts at Mosque," Greeley Gazette, November 30, 2010 (at: http://www.greeleygazette.com/press/?p=6893); "Four Christians Arrested Outside Arab Festival," Christian Examiner Online, June, 2010 (at: http://www.christianexaminer.com/Articles/Articles%20Jul10/Art_Jul10_01.html); etc.

73. For more examples, see the author's book Original Intent: The Courts, the Constitution, and Religion (Aledo: WallBuilder Press, 2011), 13–21. See also "Get Resources," Alliance Defense Fund (at: http://www.alliancedefensefund.org/About/Detail/4236); "Press Releases," American Center for Law and Justice (at: http://aclj.org/press-releases); "Newsletter Archive," Christian Law Associates (at: http://www.christianlaw.org/cla/index.php/articles/); "Press Release Archives," Liberty Counsel (at: http://www.lc.org/index.cfm?pid=14099); "Issues," Liberty Legal Institute (at: http://www.libertylegal.org/issues_main.php); "Resources," The National Legal Foundation (at: http://www.nlf.net/Resources/literature/Literature.htm); "Legal Battles," Pacific Justice Institute (at: http://www.pacificjustice.org/news); "Legal Landmines," Religious Organization Legal Defense Association (at: http://www.sharpefirm.com/rolda/landmines.html); "Press Room," Thomas More Law Center (at: http://www.thomasmore.org/qry/page.taf?id=20); "Religious Hostility in America," Family Research Institute, Liberty Council (at: http://www.religioushostility.org/); etc.

74. Thomas Jefferson, The Works of Thomas Jefferson (1904), Vol. II, 42, "Notice of Fast to the Inhabitants of the Parish of Saint Anne," June 1774.

75. Thomas Jefferson, The Papers of Thomas Jefferson, Julian P. Boyd, editor (Princeton: Princeton University Press, 1950), Vol. I, 105–106, "Resolution of the House of Burgesses Designating a Day of Fasting and Prayer," May 24, 1774.

76. Ibid., Vol. I, 116, to the Inhabitants of the Parish of St. Anne before July 23, 1774.

77. Ibid., Vol. I, 117n.

78. Ibid., Vol. I, 495, from "Report on a Seal for the United States, with Related Papers," August 20, 1776. See also John Adams, *Letters of John Adams*, Charles Francis Adams, editor (Boston: Charles C. Little and James Brown, 1841), Vol. I, 152, to Abigail Adams on August 14, 1776.

79. Thomas Jefferson, *The Writings of Thomas Jefferson* (1903), Vol. I, 62–74, "Autobiography," 1821.

80. Thomas Jefferson, *The Papers of Thomas Jefferson* (1950), Vol. II, 555, "A Bill for Punishing Disturbers of Religious Worship and Sabbath Breakers."

81. Ibid., Vol. II, 555, "A Bill for Appointing Days of Public Fasting and Thanksgiving."

82. Ibid., Vol. I, 556, "A Bill Annulling the Marriages Prohibited by the Levitical Law, and Appointing the Mode of Solemnizing Lawful Marriage."

83. Ibid., Vol. I, 553, "A Bill for Saving the Property of the Church Heretofore by Law Established."

84. Ibid., Vol. II, 555, "A Bill for Punishing Disturbers of Religious Worship and Sabbath Breakers," November 27, 1786.

85. Ibid., Vol. II, 556, "A Bill for Appointing Days of Public Fasting and Thanksgiving."

86. Ibid., Vol. II, 557, "A Bill Annulling the Marriages Prohibited by the Levitical Law, and Appointing the Mode of Solemnizing Lawful Marriage."

87. Ibid., Vol. I, 621, a "Bill for Establishing a General Court."

88. Ibid., Vol. 4, 35–36, "Robert Scot's Invoice for Executing Indian Medal, with Jefferson's Memoranda."

89. [Samuel Rutherford], *Lex, Rex: The Law and the Price. A Dispute for the just Prerogative of Kind and People* (London: John Field, 1644), 59–61 & passim; Jonathan Mayhew, *A Discourse Concerning Unlimited Submission and Non-Resistance to the Higher Powers* (Boston: D. Fowle, 1750), 28–29 & passim.

90. Thomas Jefferson, *The Papers of Thomas Jefferson* (1950), Vol. I, 495, from "Report on a Seal for the United States, with Related Papers," August 20, 1776. See also John Adams, *Letters of John Adams* (1841), Vol. I, 152, to Abigail Adams on August 14, 1776.

91. Dumas Malone, *Jefferson the Virginian* (Boston: Little, Brown and Co., 1948), Vol. I, 226.

92. *Federal Orrery* (Boston), July 2, 1795, 2, "Domestic Intelligence."

93. *Debates and Proceedings in the Congress of the United States* (Washington, DC: Gales and Seaton, 1851), 6th Cong., 797, December 4, 1800.

94. Bishop Claggett's letter of February 18, 1801, attests that while Vice-President, Jefferson attended church services in the House. Available in the Maryland Diocesan Archives.

95. Margaret Smith, *The First Forty Years of Washington Society* (New York: Charles Scribner's Sons, 1906), 13; James Hutson, *Religion and the Founding of the American Republic* (Washington, DC: Library of Congress, 1998), 84.

96. Rev. Manasseh Cutler, *Life, Journal, and Correspondence of Rev. Manasseh Cutler*, William Parker Cutler and Julia Perkins Cutler, editors (Cincinnati: Colin Robert Clarke & Co., 1888), Vol. II, 119, to Joseph Torrey on January 3, 1803.

97. Margaret Smith, *The First Forty Years of Washington Society*, 13.

98. Ibid.

99. Warren Throckmorton and Michael Coulter, *Getting Jefferson Right: Fact Checking Claims about Our Third President* (Grove City, PA: Salem Grove Press, 2012), 47–48.

100. Ibid., 48, n94.

101. See, for example, Rev. Manasseh Cutler, *Life, Journal, and Correspondence of Rev. Manasseh Cutler*, Vol. II, 119, to Dr. Joseph Torrey on January 3, 1803.

102. Ibid., Vol. II, 119, to Joseph Torrey on January 3, 1803.

103. Ibid., Vol. II, 114, diary entry for December 26, 1802.

104. James Hutson, *Religion and the Founding of the American Republic*, 89.

105. Margaret Smith, *The First Forty Years of Washington Society*, 14.

106. Ibid., 16.

107. John Quincy Adams, *Memoirs of John Quincy Adams*, Charles Francis Adams, editor (Philadelphia: J. B. Lippincott & Co., 1874), Vol. I, 265, diary entry for October 23, 1803, and Vol. I, 268, diary entry for October 30, 1803; *National Intelligencer*, December 9, 1820, 3. See also James Hutson, *Religion and the Founding of the American Republic*, 89.

108. James Hutson, *Religion and the Founding of the American Republic*, 96, quoting from a handwritten history in possession of the Library of Congress, "Washington Parish, Washington City," by Rev. Ethan Allen.

109. Ibid., 91.

110. Thomas Jefferson, *The Papers of Thomas Jefferson* (2008), Vol. 35, 202, to Bishop John Carroll on September 3, 1801.

111. Ibid., Vol. 30, 545, to Gouverneur Morris on November 1, 1801.

112. *Debates and Proceedings in the Congress of the United States* (1851), 7th Cong., 1st Sess., 1332, "An Act in Addition to an Act, Entitled, 'An Act in Addition to an Act Regulating the Grants of Land Appropriated for Military Services, and for the Society of the United Brethren for Propagating the Gospel Among the Heathen'," April 26, 1802; 7th Cong., 2nd Sess., 1602, "An Act to Revive and Continue in Force An Act in Addition to an Act, Entitled, 'An Act in Addition to an Act Regulating the Grants of Land Appropriated for Military Services, and for the Society of the United Brethren for Propagating the Gospel Among the Heathen,' and for Other Purposes," March 3, 1803; 8th Cong., 2nd Sess., 1279, "An Act Granting Further Time for Locating Military Land Warrants, and for Other Purposes," March 19, 1804.

113. Dorothy C. Bass, "Gideon Blackburn's Mission to the Cherokees," *Journal of Presbyterian History* (Fall, 1974), Vol. 52, num. 3, 209.

114. *American State Papers: Documents, Legislative and Executive of the Congress of the United States*, Walter Lowrie, editor (Washington, DC: Gales and Seaton, 1832), Vol. IV, 687, "The Kaskaskia and Other Tribes," October 31, 1803.

115. "Thomas Jefferson to the Nuns of the Order of St. Ursula on May 15, 1804," original on file with the New Orleans Parish.

116. *The American Diplomatic Code, Embracing a Collection of Treaties and Conventions Between the United States and Foreign Powers: From 1778 to 1834. With an Abstract of Important Judicial Decisions, On Points Connected with Our Foreign Relations*, Jonathan Elliot, editor (Washington, DC: Jonathan Elliot, 1834), Vol. I, 501, "Treaty of Peace and amity Between the United States of America and the Bashaw, Bey, and Subjects of Tripoli in Barbary," June 4, 1805, and Vol. I, 498, "Treaty of Peace and Friendship Between the United States of America and the Bey and Subjects of Tripoli of Barbary," November 4, 1796, signed January 4, 1797.

117. Ibid., Vol. I, 499, Art. 11, "Treaty of Peace and Friendship Between the United States of America and the Bey and Subjects of Tripoli of Barbary," November 4, 1796, signed January 4, 1797.

118. *The Debates and Proceedings in the Congress of the United States* (1852), 9th Cong., 1st Sess., 1238, "An Act for Establishing Rules and Articles for the Government of the Armies of the United States."

119. Thomas Jefferson, *The Writings of Thomas Jefferson* (1904), Vol. XVI, 291, to Captain John Thomas on November 18, 1807.

120. *Marsh v. Chambers*, 463 U.S. 783, 807 (1983) (Brennan, J. and Marshall, J., dissenting).

121. *Allegheny County v. Greater Pittsburgh ACLU*, 492 U.S. 573, 679, n. 8 (1989) (Kennedy, J., concurring and dissenting).

122. Thomas Jefferson, *Memoir, Correspondence, and Miscellanies* (1830), Vol. IV, 104, to Samuel Miller on January 23, 1808.

123. Thomas Jefferson, *The Works of Thomas Jefferson* (1904), Vol. I, 11, Jefferson's encouragement of a day for fasting and prayer for June 1, 1774, when the British blockaded Boston.

124. *Official Letters of the Governors of the State of Virginia*, H. R. McIlwaine, editor (Richmond: Virginia State Library, 1928), Vol. II, 65, Thomas Jefferson, "Proclamation," November 11, 1779; Thomas Jefferson, *The Papers of Thomas Jefferson* (1951), Vol. 3, 178, "Proclamation Appointing a Day of Thanksgiving and Prayer," November 11, 1779.

125. *Official Letters of the Governors of the State of Virginia* (1928), Vol. II, 65, Thomas Jefferson, "Proclamation," November 11, 1779; Thomas Jefferson, *The Papers of Thomas Jefferson* (1951), Vol. 3, 178, "Proclamation Appointing a Day of Thanksgiving and Prayer," November 11, 1779.

126. Thomas Jefferson, *The Writings of Thomas Jefferson* (1854), Vol. VIII, 45, Second Annual Address on March 4, 1805

127. Mark Beliles and Jerry Newcombe, *Doubting Thomas? The Religious Life and Legacy of Thomas Jefferson* (New York: Morgan James Publishing, 2015), 73.

128. Joseph J. Ellis, *American Sphinx: The Character of Thomas Jefferson* (New York: Vintage Books, 1998), 310.

LIE # 6

1. John E. Remsburg, *Six Historic Americans* (New York: The Truth Seeker Project Company, 1906), 78.

2. Farrell Till, "The Christian Nation Myth," The Secular Web (at: http://www.infidels. org/library/modern/farrell_till/myth.html) (accessed on March 4, 2013).

3. Andrew Preston, *Sword of the Spirit, Shield of Faith* (New York: Alfred A. Knopf, 2012), 88.

4. Bill Fairchild, "Thomas Jefferson and the 'Clergy'," The Painful Truth (at: http://www. hwarmstrong.com/thomas_jefferson_clergy.htm) (accessed on March 4, 2013).

5. Austin Cline, "What is Anti-Clericalism?" About.com (at: http://atheism.about.com/od/Criticism-Religious-Critique/f/Anti-Clericalism.htm) (accessed on March 4, 2013).

6. Thomas Jefferson, *The Papers of Thomas Jefferson*, Julian P. Boyd, editor (Princeton: Princeton University Press, 1953), Vol. 8, 468, to Chelier de Chastellux on September 2, 1785.

7. Ibid., Vol. 8, 468, to Chelier de Chastellux on September 2, 1785.

8. John Adams, *The Works of John Adams*, Charles Francis Adams, editor (Boston: Little, Brown and Company, 1854), Vol. IX, 637, to Benjamin Rush on August 28, 1811.

9. George Washington, *The Writings of George Washington*, Jared Sparks, editor (Boston: Ferdinand Andrews, Publisher, 1837), Vol. XII, 405–407, from Eleanor "Nelly" Parke Custis Lewis (Washington's adopted granddaughter, raised by him, and who lived twenty years at Mount Vernon) to Jared Sparks on February 26, 1833.

10. See, for example, Charles Warren, Odd Byways in American History (Cambridge: Harvard University Press, 1942), 127–128; Dumas Malone, *Jefferson and the Ordeal of Liberty* (Boston: Little, Brown and Company, 1962), Vol. Three, 481; Charles O. Lerche, Jr., "Jefferson and the Election of 1800: A Case Study in the Political Smear," *William and Mary Quarterly*, 3rd Series, Vol. V, No. 4, October 1948, 466–491.

11. Wilburn E. MacClenny, *The Life of Rev. James O'Kelly and the Early History of the Christian Church in the South* (Suffolk: Edwards & Broughton Printing Company, 1910), 171–173.

12. John Adams, *The Works of John Adams* (1854), Vol. IX, 636, to Benjamin Rush on August 28, 1811.

13. *Appleton's Cyclopedia* (New York: D. Appleton and Company, 1887), s.v. "Cotton Mather Smith."

14. Thomas Jefferson, *The Papers of Thomas Jefferson*, Barbara B. Oberg, editor (Princeton: Princeton University Press, 2005), Vol. 32, 58–59, from Uriah McGregory on July 19, 1800.

15. Thomas Jefferson, *Memoir, Correspondence, and Miscellanies*, Thomas Jefferson Randolph, editor (New York: G. & C. & H. Carvill, 1830), Vol. III, 438–440, to Uriah McGregory on August 13, 1800.

16. William Linn, *Serious Considerations on the Election of a President: Addressed to the Citizens of the United States* (New York: John Furman, 1800), 24, Evans No. 37835.

17. Ibid., 30.

18. John Mitchell Mason, *A Voice of Warning to Christians, on the Ensuing Election of a President of the United States* (New York: G. F. Hopkins, 1800), 22–23.

19. Ibid., 37–38.

20. Nathanael Emmons, *The Works of Nathanael Emmons, D. D., Late Pastor of the Church in Franklin, Mass., With a Memoir of His Life*, Jacob Ide, editor (Boston: Crocker & Brewster, 1842), Vol. II, 194, Sermon XIII, "Jeroboam. Annual Fast, April 9, 1801."

21. Ibid., Vol. II, 284–285, Sermon XIX, "Rights of the People. National Thanksgiving, November 25, 1813."

22. Thomas Jefferson, *Memoir, Correspondence, and Miscellanies* (1830), Vol. III, 478, to Levi Lincoln on August 26, 1801.

23. Claude G. Bowers, *Jefferson in Power – the Death Struggle of the Federalists* (Cambridge: The Riverside Press, 1936), 145.

24. Saul K. Padover, *Jefferson* (New York: Penguin Books, 1970; reprint of a 1942 original), 119.

25. Alan Heimert, *Religion and the American Mind* (Cambridge: Harvard University Press, 2006; reprint of 1966 original), 534–538.

26. *Dictionary of American Biography*, Dumas Malone, editor (New York: Charles Scribner's Sons, 1929), s.v. "Rev. John Leland.", 161.

27. John Leland, *The Writings of the Late Elder John Leland, Including Some Events in His Life, Written by Himself, With Additional Sketches*, L. F. Greene, editor (New York: G. W. Wood, 1845), 255 "A Blow at the Root."

28. Rev. Manasseh Cutler, *Life, Journals and Correspondence of Rev. Manasseh Cutler*, William Parker Cutler and Julia P. Cutler, editors (Cincinnati: Robert Clarke & Co., 1888), Vol. II, 54, editor's note in journal entry for January 1, 1802.

29. Charles Cist, *Cincinnati in 1841: Its Early Annals and Future Prospects* (Cincinnati: Published for the Author, 1841), 187; Dumas Malone, *Jefferson the Virginian* (Boston: Little, Brown and Co., 1948), Vol. I, 226.

30. Ellen M. Raynor and Emma L. Petitclerc, *History of the Town of Cheshire* (Holyoke, MA: Clark W. Bryan & Company, 1885), 87.

31. Rev. Manasseh Cutler, *Life, Journals and Correspondence*, Vol. II, 66.

32. Ibid., Vol. II, 66, to Dr. Torrey on January 4, 1802.

33. Ibid., Vol. II, 66–67, to Dr. Torrey on January 4, 1802.

34. Thomas Jefferson, *The Papers of Thomas Jefferson; Jefferson's Memorandum Books*, James Bear and Lucia Stanton, editors (Princeton: Princeton University Press, 1997), Vol. II, 1062, January 1, 1802.

35. Ibid., Vols. I–II.

36. Wilbur E. MacClenny, *The Centennial of Religious Journalism*, John Pressley Barrett, editor (Dayton: Christian Publishing Association, 1908), 250 and 265, "James O'Kelly: A Champion of Christian Freedom."

37. Thomas Jefferson, *The Papers of Thomas Jefferson* (1950), Vol. 2, 6, "Subscription to Support a Clergyman in Charlottesville" in February 1777.

38. Ibid.

39. Ibid., 7.

40. Ibid., Vol. 3, 67, "Testimonial for Charles Clay," August 15, 1779.

41. Ibid., Vol. 1, 23, to William Preston on August 18, 1768.

42. Thomas Jefferson, *The Papers of Thomas Jefferson* (2008), Vol. 35, 350–351, to Samuel Smith on September 26, 1801.

43. Mark A. Beliles, "Religion and Republicanism in Jefferson's Virginia," doctrinal dissertation for Whitefield Theological Seminary, 1993, 69–70.

44. Samuel Stanhope Smith, *The Divine Goodness to the United States of America – A Discourse on the Subjects of National Gratitude* (Philadelphia: William Young, 1795); Jonathan French, *A Sermon Delivered on the Anniversary of Thanksgiving, November 29, 1798* (Andover: Ames and Parker, 1799); Rev. Joseph Willard, *A Thanksgiving Sermon Delivered at Boston December 11, 1783* (Boston: T. and J. Fleet, 1784); William Hazlitt, *A Thanksgiving Sermon Preached at Hallowell, December 15, 1785* (Boston: Samuel Hall, 1786); Evan Johns, The Happiness of American Christians, *A Thanksgiving Sermon Preached on Thursday the 24th of November 1803* (Hartford: Hudson and Goodwin, 1804); Isaac Backus, *An Appeal to the Public for Religious Liberty* (Boston: John Boyle, 1773); etc.

45. See, for example, Christopher Reyes, *In His Name* (Bloomington, IN: AuthorHouse, 2010), 253; Mark Hulsether, *Religion, Culture and Politics in the 20th Century United States* (New York: Columbia University Press, 2007), 41; "Our Founding Fathers Were Not Christians," BibleTrash.com, July 4, 2000 (at: http://freethought.mbdojo.com/foundingfathers.html); Jim Walker, "Thomas Jefferson of Christianity and Religion," Nobeliefs.com (at: http://nobeliefs.com/jefferson.htm) (accessed on March 4, 2013).

46. Lorenzo Dow, *Biography and Miscellany* (Norwich, CT: William Faulkner, 1834), 242–243, "Appendix."

47. Thomas Jefferson, *Memoir, Correspondence, and Miscellanies* (1830), Vol. III, 441, to Dr. Benjamin Rush on September 23, 1800.

48. Thomas Jefferson, *The Writings of Thomas Jefferson* (1904), Vol. XV, 60, to Mrs. M. Harrison Smith on August 6, 1816.

49. Samuel Knox, *A Vindication of the Religion of Thomas Jefferson* (Baltimore: W. Pechin, 1800); Thomas E. Buckley, "Thomas Jefferson and Myth of Separation," Religion and the American Presidency (at: http://www.thedivineconspiracy.org/Z5212U.pdf) (accessed on March 4, 2013).

50. Fred Hood, *Reformed America: The Middle and Southern States, 1783–1837* (Tuscaloosa, AL: The University of Alabama, 1980), 83.

51. Elias Smith, *The Whole World Governed by a Jew, or, The Government of the Second Adam as King and Priest* (Exeter: Henry Ranlet, 1805), 34–35, 76–77.

52. See, for example, Mark A. Beliles and Jerry Newcombe, *Doubting Thomas? The Religious Life and Legacy of Thomas Jefferson* (New York: Morgan James Publishing, 2015), 21, 31–32, 51–52, 54, 94–95.

53. Thomas Jefferson, *The Papers of Thomas Jefferson*; Jefferson's Memorandum Books, Vol. I, 402, 403, 407; Vol. II, 1093, 1177, 1196, 1403, 1068, etc.

54. Ibid., Vol. II, 1070, 1144, 1146, 1180, 1403.

55. Ibid., Vol. II, 884.

56. Ibid., Vol. I, 285; Vol. II, 837, 1057, 1062, 1071, 1095, 1111, 1130, 1154, 1348, etc.

57. Some of Jefferson's quotes regarding this narrow type of clergy that are often extended to wrongly cover all clergy include: Thomas Jefferson, *The Works of Thomas Jefferson* (1904–5), Vol. 9, 146–149, to Benjamin Rush on September 23, 1800; Vol. 9, 346–347, to Attorney General Levi Lincoln on January 1, 1802; Vol. 9, 142–144, to Jeremiah Moor on August 14, 1800; and others.

58. John Leland, The *Writings of the Late Elder John Leland*, 484, "Which Has Done the Most Mischief in the World, The Kings-Evil or Priest-Craft?"

59. David Ramsay, *The History of the American Revolution* (Trenton: James J. Wilson, 1811), Vol. I, 305.

60. Thomas Jefferson, *The Works of Thomas Jefferson* (1905), Vol. IX, 393, to Elbridge Gerry on August 28, 1802.

61. Thomas Jefferson, *Memoir, Correspondence, and Miscellanies* (1830), Vol. III, 304–305, to Tench Coxe on May 1, 1794; Vol. III, 377–378, to James Madison on March 2, 1798; Vol. III, 461–462, to Doctor Joseph Priestly on March 21, 1801; Vol. IV, 204–206, to John Adams on August 22, 1813; Vol. IV, 274–277, to John Taylor on May 28, 1816; Thomas Jefferson, *The Works of Thomas Jefferson* (1905), Vol. XI, 351, to Baron von Humboldt on December 6, 1813; Vol. XI, 491, to Benjamin Waterhouse on October 13, 1815.

62. Thomas Jefferson, *The Writings of Thomas Jefferson* (1904), Vol. XIV, 119, to Horatio G. Spafford on March 17, 1814.

63. Fall rreTill, "The Christian Nation Myth," The Secular Web (at: http://www.infidels.org/library/modern/farrell_till/myth.html) (accessed on March 4, 2013).

64. *The Constitution of the Sixteen States* (Boston: Manning and Loring, 1797), 209, "The Constitution of Virginia" July 5, 1776, "...all ministers of the gospel, of every denomination, be incapable of being elected members..."

65. Thomas Jefferson, *The Papers of Thomas Jefferson* (1953), Vol. VIII, 470, to Chelier de Chastellux on September 2, 1785.

66. Thomas Jefferson, *The Works of Thomas Jefferson* (1905), Vol. IX, 143, to Jeremiah Moore on August 14, 1800.

67. Thomas Jefferson, *The Writings of Thomas Jefferson* (1903), Vol. VIII, 3–4, to Rev. Charles Clay on January 27, 1790.

68. Rev. John B. Turpin, *A Brief History of the Albemarle Baptist Association* (Richmond, VA: The Virginia Baptist Historical Society, 1891), 30–31.

LIE # 7

1.   Mark A Gifford, "Country Mouse and Town Mouse," hyerliterature.com, May 18, 2010 (at: http://www.hyperliterature.com/?p=1763), quoting from Joseph J. Ellis, *Founding Brothers* (New York: Vintage Books, 2000), 139.

2.   "Cloudy Judgment," Minds Alike, April 18, 2011 (at: http://mindsalike.co/2011/04/18/ cloudy judgement/).

3.   Paul O'Brien, "Jefferson," Paul O'Brien's Web (at: http://home.comcast.net/~pobrien48/ jefferson_Letters.htm) (accessed on March 4, 2013).

4.   "An Interview with Michael Weinstein of Military Religious Freedom Foundation," *Pagan + Politics*, February 26, 2010 (at: http://www.facebook.com/note.php?note_ id=360240177811).

5.   John E. Remsburg, *Six Historic Americans* (New York: The Truth Seeker Company, 1906), 65.

6.   "About," *The Freethinker*: The voice of Atheism Since 1881 (accessed January 25, 2013) (at: http://freethinker.co.uk/history/); "About Us," *Iowa Atheist and Freethinkers* (at: http://www.iowaatheists.org/about-us-1) (accessed March 4, 2013); "Atheism Basics," *Atheist, Agnostics, & Freethinkers at NYU* (at: http://www.nyu.edu/clubs/atheists/faqs. html) (accessed March 4, 2013).

7.   *Merriam Webster Dictionary of Synonyms* (Springfield: Merriam-Webster Incorporated, 1984), 71, s. v. "atheist."

8.   See, for example, Richard Losch, *The Many Faces of Faith* (Cambridge: Wm B. Eerdmans publishing Co., 2001), p.57; Valerii Kuvakin, *In Search of Our Humanity: Neither Paradise or Hell* (Amherst, NY: Prometheus Books, 2003), 29; Susan Jacoby, *Freethinkers: A History of American Secularism* (New York: Henry Holt and Company, 2005), 43.

9.   See, for example, Richard Hughes, The American Quest for The Primitive Church (Urbana, IL: Board of Trustees of the University of Illinois, 1988), 75; David Holmes, The Faith of the Founding Fathers (New York: Oxford University Press, 2006), p.80; Robert Johnson, The Deist Roots of the United States of America (at: http://www. deism.com/deistamerica.htm) (accessed March 4, 2013).

10.   Fredericksville Parish Vestry Book, 1742–1787, Rosalie David, editor (Manchester, Missouri, 1978), 88.

11.   Claude G. Bowers, *The Young Jefferson* (Boston: Houghton Mifflin Company, 1945), 312.

12.   Thomas Jefferson, *The Works of Thomas Jefferson*, Paul Leicester Ford, editor (New York: G. P. Putnam's Sons, 1904), Vol. II, 94, "Notes on Religion," October 1776.

13.   Ibid., Vol. II, 94–95, "Notes on Religion," October 1776.

14.   See, for example, *The New England Primer Improved For the more easy attaining the true reading of English* (Boston: Edward Draper, 1777), 16–17, and *The New England Primer: A History of its Origin and Development with a Reprint of the Unique Copy of the Earliest Known Edition and Many Fac-simile Illustrations and Reproductions*, Paul Leicester Ford,

editor (New York: Dodd, Mead and Company, 1897), 73–74, as printed in the 1727 *New England Primer* (online: https://books.google.com/books?id=NRwUAAAAIAAJ &pg=PA73#v=onepage&q&f=false).

15. In addition to attending three different Anglican schools (that of the Reverend William Douglass, the Reverend James Fontaine Maury, and then William and Mary), Jefferson affirms in his autobiography that at William and Mary, he and the other students "were required… to learn its Catechism [of the Church of England]." Thomas Jefferson, *Autobiography of Thomas Jefferson* (New York: G. P. Putnam's Sons, 1914), 76.

16. *The Book of Common Prayer, And Administration of the Sacraments, And Other Rites and Ceremonies of the Church According to the Use of The Church of England* (Oxford: T. Wright and W. Gill, 1771), iv, "A Catechism; that is to say, An Instruction, to be learned of every person, before he be brought to be confirmed by the Bishop" (online: https:// books.google.com/books?id=6Mo-AAAAcAAJ&pg=RA1-PR4#v=onepage&q&f=false). See, for example, *The Psalms of David with the Ten Commandment, Creed, Lord's Prayer &c. In Metre. Also the Catechism, Confession of Faith, Liturgy, & c. Translated from the Dutch,* Francis Hopkinson, editor and translator (New York: James Parker, 1767), 140, "The Confession of Faith, Composed in the Council of Nice, in the year of our Lord, 325."

17. Thomas Jefferson, *The Works of Thomas Jefferson* (1904), Vol. II, 255, "Notes on Religion," October 1776.

18. Ibid. Vol. II, 258, "Notes on Religion," October 1776.

19. John Adams, *The Works of John Adams,* Charles Francis Adams, editor (Boston: Little, Brown, and Company, 1856), Vol. X, 185, to Dr. Jedediah Morse on December 2, 1815; William Warren Sweet, *The Story of Religion in America* (New York: Harper & Brothers Publishers, 1950), 174–175; Will C. Wood, *Five Problems of State and Religion* (Boston: Henry Hoyt, 1877), 169; Thomas Kidd, *God of Liberty: A Religious History of the American Revolution* (New York: Basic Books, 2010) [chapter on appointing a bishop]. See generally, Carl Bridenbaugh, *Mitre and Sceptre: Transatlantic Faiths, Ideas, Personalities, and Politics: 1689–1775* (New York: Oxford University Press, 1962).

20. Thomas Jefferson, *The Works of Thomas Jefferson* (1904), Vol. II, 258, "Notes on Religion," October 1776.

21. Ibid., Vol. II, 261, "Notes on Religion," October 1776.

22. Sarah Randolph, *The Domestic Life of Thomas Jefferson* (New York: Harper & Brothers, 1871), 343–345, from Ellen Coolidge to Henry S. Randall.

23. Thomas Jefferson, *The Works of Thomas Jefferson* (1904), Vol. III, 244, to Francois Jean, Chevalier de Chastellux on November 26, 1782.

24. William Stoddard, *The Lives of the Presidents: John Adams and Thomas Jefferson* (New York: White, Stokes, & Allen, 1887), Vol. II, 270.

25. Sarah Randolph, *The Domestic Life of Thomas Jefferson,* 62–63, excerpt from Martha Jefferson Randolph's manuscript.

26. Ibid.

27. Henry Stephens Randall, *The Life of Thomas Jefferson* (New York: Derby & Jackson, 1858), Vol. III, 101–103, to Henry S. Randall on January 15, 1856.

28. "Devereux Jarratt," *Encyclopedia Virginia* (at: http://www.encyclopediavirginia.org/Jarratt_Devereux_1733-1801#start_entry) (accessed on March 10, 2015).

29. William H. B. Thomas, *Faith of our Fathers: Religion and the Churches in Colonial Orange County* (Orange, VA: Orange County Bicentennial Commission, 1975), 8,

30. See, for example, Nathaniel Appleton, *A Plain and Faithful Testimony against that Abominable, but Too Fashionable Vice of Profane Swearing: Being the Substance of Several Discourses from James V. 12 which came lately in Course to be Expounded* (Boston: R. & S. Draper, 1765); Isaac Backus, *Family Prayer Not to Be Neglected. A Discourse, Where is Opened, The Nature of Prayer and General and the Warrant for Family in Particular* (Newport, RI: Samuel Hall, 1766); Moses Baldwin, *The Ungodly Condemned in Judgment. A Sermon Preached at Springfield, December 13th, 1770. On Occasion of the Execution of William Shaw for Murder* (Boston: Kneeland and Adams, 1771); Samuel Davies, *Religion and Patriotism the Constituents of a Good Soldier. A Sermon Preached to Captain Overton's Independent Company of Volunteers, Raised in Hanover County, Virginia, August 17, 1755* (Philadelphia: 1756); Stephen Hales, *The Pernicious Practice of Dram-Drinking, Set Forth in its Proper Light* (Woodbridge, NJ: James Parker, 1759); Jonathan Mayhew, *God's Hand and Providence to be Religiously Acknowledged in Public Calamities. A Sermon Occasioned by the Great Fire in Boston, New-England, Thursday March 20, 1760 and Preached on the Lord's Day Following* (Boston: Richard Draper, et.al., 1760); Josiah Woodward, *A Kind Caution to Profane Swearers, by Josiah Woodward, D.D. Minister of Poplar* (Newport, RI: 1752).

31. See, for example, Charles Chauncy, *A Discourse On "the good News from a far Country." Delivered July 24th. A Day of Thanksgiving to Almighty God, throughout the Province of the Massachusetts-Bay in New-England, on Occasion of the Repeal of the Stamp Act* (Boston: Kneeland and Adams, 1766); Elihu Coleman, *A Testimony Against that Antichristian Practice of Making Slaves of Men. Wherein it is Viewed to be Contrary to the Dispensation of the Law and Time of the Gospel, and Very Opposite Both to Grace and Nature* (Boston: 1733); Jason Haven, *A Sermon Preached Before His Excellency Francis Bernard, Baronet, Governor: His Honor Thomas Hutchinson, Esq. Lieutenant Governor, the Honorable His Majesty's Council and the Honorable House of Representatives of the Province of the Massachusetts Bay in New England, May 31st, 1769* (Boston: Richard Draper, 1769); William Stith, *The Sinfulness and Pernicious Nature of Gaming: A Sermon Preached Before the General Assembly of Virginia: at Williamsburg, March 1st, 1752* (Williamsburg, VA: William Hunter, 1752).

32. John Woolman, *A Journal of the Life and Travels of John Woolman in the Service of the Gospel* (Lindfield: 1838), 77–81; John Woolman, *The Journal and Essays of John Woolman* (New York: The MacMillan Company, 1922), xix–xx for a list of works by John Woolman.

33. John Leland, *The Writings of the Late Elder John Leland, Including Some Events in His Life, Written by Himself, With Additional Sketches*, L. F. Greene, editor (New York: G. W. Wood, 1845), 98, from The Virginia Chronicle on "Of The Slaves."

34. William Maxwell, *A Memoir of the Rev. John H. Rice, D. D.* (J. Whetham: Philadelphia, 1835), 50–51, to Rev. Archibald Alexander on January 28, 1810.

35. Ibid., 51–52.

36. Edgar Woods, *Albemarle County in Virginia* (Charlottesville: Michie Company, 1901), 131.

37. Mark A. Beliles and Jerry Newcombe, *Doubting Thomas? The Religious Life and Legacy of Thomas Jefferson* (New York: Morgan James Publishing, 2015), 116–118, 63–64.

38. Robert Mallett, "What do you Mean, Restoration Movement?," The Christian Restoration Movement (at: http://www.thecra.org/restmovement.html) (accessed March 4, 2013).

39. Elias Smith, *The Life, Conversion, Preaching, Travels and Sufferings of Elias Smith* (Boston: 1840), Vol. I, 275.

40. See, for example, "James O'Kelly," The Restoration Movement (at: http://www.therestorationmovement.com/okelley,james.htm) (accessed March 4, 2013); B. J. Humble, "the Story of Restoration," lavozeterna.org (at: http://www.lavozeterna.org/estudios/storyrestoration.htm) (accessed March 4, 2013); "What do you Mean, Restoration Movement?," The Christian Restoration Movement (at: http://www.thecra.org/restmovement.html) (accessed March 4, 2013).

41. *Christian History Magazine* (Christian History Magazine, 1995), Issue 45, 23, "Christianity on the Early American Frontier: A Gallery of Trendsetters in the Religious Wilderness."

42. Wilburn E. MacClenny, *The Life of Rev. James O'Kelly and the Early History of the Christian Church in the South* (Suffolk: Edwards & Broughton Printing Company, 1910), 217–221, quoting from O'Kelly's "The Divine Oracles Consulted," 1820, and "The Prospect Before Us," 1824.

43. Thomas Campbell, On Religious Reformation (at: http://www.mun.ca/rels/restmov/texts/tcampbell/etc/ORR.HTM) (accessed March 4, 2013).

44. Wilburn E. MacClenny, *The Life of Rev. James O'Kelly*, 217, excerpt from "The Prospect Before Us," 1824.

45. Michael G. Kenny, *The Perfect Law of Liberty: Elias Smith and the Providential History of America* (Washington, DC: Smithsonian Institution Press, 1994), 93.

46. Ibid., 128. See also William B. Erdman, *Erdman's Handbook to Christianity in America*, Mark Noll, editor (Grand Rapids: William B. Erdmans Publishing Co., 1983), 210.

47. Alexander Campbell, "To Timothy," Memorial University, March 1, 1827 (at: http://www.mun.ca/rels/restmov/texts/acampbell/tcb/TCB410.HTM#Essay5).

48. Douglas Allen Foster, The Encyclopedia of the Stone-Campbell Movement (Grand Rapids: William B. Eerdmans Publishing, 2004), 356.

49. J. F. Burnett, *Elias Smith: Reformer, Journalist, Doctor; Horace Mann: Christian Statesman and Educator* (Dayton: The Christian Publishing Association, 1921).

50. In 1815 Thomas Jefferson sold a collection of books and pamphlets to the Library of Congress, a list of these works can be found here: *Selected Special Collections: Thomas Jefferson's Library*, Library of Congress (at: http://www.loc.gov/rr/rarebook/coll/130.html). Some of the books included in this collection that include views often associated with Primitivist or Restoration include: Ethan Allen, *Reason the Only Oracle of Man, or A Compendious System of Natural Religion* (VT: Haswell & Russell, 1784); Joseph Priestley, *An History of Early Opinions Concerning Jesus Christ* (London: Pearson and Rollason, 1736); Matthew Tindal, *Christianity as Old as the Creation* (London, 1732); William Wollaston, *The Religion of Nature Delineated* (Glasgow: R. Urie and Company, 1746); William Whiston, *Primitive Christianity Reviv'd* (London: 1711–1712).

51. Thomas Jefferson, "Thomas Jefferson Papers," Library of Congress, to Francis A. Van Der Kemp on July 9, 1820 (at: http://hdl.loc.gov/loc.mss/mtj.mtjbib023864).

52. Thomas Jefferson, *Memoir, Correspondence, and Miscellanies*, Thomas Jefferson Randolph, editor (New York: G. & C. & H. Carvill, 1830), Vol. IV, 353–354, to Doctor Benjamin Waterhouse on July 19, 1822.

53. Ibid., Vol. IV, 360–361, to James Smith on December 8, 1822.

54. Thomas Jefferson, "Thomas Jefferson Papers," Library of Congress, to Salma Hale on July 26, 1818 (at: http://hdl.loc.gov/loc.mss/mtj.mtjbib023250).

55. Thomas Jefferson, *Memoir, Correspondence, and Miscellanies* (1830), Vol. IV, 349, to Dr. Benjamin Waterhouse on June 26, 1822.

56. Thomas Jefferson, *Writings of Thomas Jefferson*, Andrew A. Lipscomb, editor (Washington, DC: The Thomas Jefferson Memorial Association, 1904), Vol. XV, 405–406, to Dr. Thomas Cooper on November 2, 1822.

57. Thomas Jefferson, *Memoir, Correspondence, and Miscellanies* (1830), Vol. IV, 358, to Doctor Thomas Cooper on November 2, 1822.

58. Ibid.

59. Thomas Jefferson, "Thomas Jefferson Papers," Library of Congress, to Ezra Styles Ely on June 25, 1819 (at: http://hdl.loc.gov/loc.mss/mtj.mtjbib023541).

60. Thomas Jefferson, *The Adams-Jefferson Letters*, Lester J. Cappon, editor (Chapel Hill: The University of North Carolina Press, 1959), Vol. II, 421, to John Adams on January 24, 1814.

61. Thomas Jefferson, *Memoir, Correspondence, and Miscellanies* (1830), Vol. IV, 321, to William Short on April 13, 1820.

62. Thomas Jefferson, *The Writings of Thomas Jefferson*, Henry A. Washington, editor (New York: Derby & Jackson, 1859), Vol. VII, 395, to General Alexander Smyth on January 17, 1825.

63. Thomas Jefferson, "The Thomas Jefferson Papers," Library of Congress, to Martha (Patsy) Jefferson on December 11, 1783 (at: http://hdl.loc.gov/loc.mss/mtj.mtjbib000839).

64. Thomas Jefferson, *Memoir, Correspondence, and Miscellanies* (1830), Vol. IV, 326, to William Short on August 4, 1820.

65. Ibid.

66. Thomas Jefferson, *The Works of Thomas Jefferson* (1904), Vol. 1, 69, "Autobiography."

67. Thomas Jefferson, "The Thomas Jefferson Papers," Library of Congress, to Ezra Styles Ely on June 25, 1819 (at: http://hdl.loc.gov/loc.mss/mtj.mtjbib023541).

68. Thomas Jefferson, *The Works of Thomas Jefferson* (1904), Vol. II, 260, "Notes on Religion," October 1776.

69. Thomas Jefferson, *The Papers of Thomas Jefferson*, Julian P. Boyd, editor (Princeton: Princeton University Press, 1950), Vol. 2, 6–7, "Subscription to Support a Clergyman in Charlottesville," February, 1777.

70. Henry S. Randall, *The Life of Thomas Jefferson* (New York: Derby & Jackson, 1858), Vol. III, 672, Appendix No. XXXVI, Thomas Jefferson Randolph to Henry S. Randall.

71. Thomas Jefferson, *Memoir, Correspondence, and Miscellanies* (1830), Vol. IV, 322, to William Short on April 13, 1820.

72. Thomas Jefferson, "The Thomas Jefferson Papers," Library of Congress, to Thomas B. Parker on May 15, 1819 (at: http://hdl.loc.gov/loc.mss/mtj.mtjbib023495).

73. Thomas Jefferson, "The Thomas Jefferson Papers," Library of Congress, to Salma Hale on July 26, 1818 (at: http://hdl.loc.gov/loc.mss/mtj.mtjbib023250).

74. Thomas Jefferson, *Memoir, Correspondence, and Miscellanies* (1830), Vol. IV, 358, to Dr. Benjamin Waterhouse on June 26, 1822.

75. Ibid.

76. Ibid., Vol. IV, 363, to John Adams on April 11, 1823.

77. Thomas Jefferson, *The Writings of Thomas Jefferson* (1899), Vol. X, 144n, to William Short on October 31, 1819.

78. Thomas Jefferson, *Memoir, Correspondence, and Miscellanies* (1830), Vol. IV, 366, to John Adams on April 11, 1823.

79. *The Concise Columbia Encyclopedia*, Judith S. Levey, editor (New York: Avon Books, 1983), 872.

80. See, for example, *Rev. Charles Buck, A Theological Dictionary Containing Definitions of All Religious Terms* (Philadelphia: Edwin T. Scott, 1823), 582; An Answer to the Question, Why do you attend a Unitarian Church? (Christian Register Office, circa 1840); Daniel Rupp, *An Original History of the Religious Denominations at Present Existing in the United States* (Philadelphia: J. Y. Humphrys, 1844), 711; etc.

81. Daniel Rupp, *An Original History of the Religious*, 711.

82. *Dictionary of American History*, James Truslow Adams, editor (New York: Charles Scribner's Sons, 1940), s.v. "Unitarians."

83. *Dictionary of Christianity in America*, Daniel G. Reid, editor (Downers Grove, IL: InterVarsity Press, 1990), 1196–1198, "Unitarian Universalist Association"; Engaging Our Theological Diversity (Boston: Unitarian Universalist Association, 2005), 17–26, "History: Where Do We Come From?"

84. John Quincy Adams, *Memoirs of John Quincy Adams*, Charles Francis Adams, editor (Philadelphia: J. B. Lippincott & Co., 1875), Vol. VII, 324, diary entry on August 13, 1827.

85. Ibid.

86. *The Living Age*, Eliakim Littell, editor (Boston: Littell, Son, and Company, 1865), Vol. 86, 200, "The Anti-Slavery Revolution in America."

87. Samuel J. May, *Some Recollections of Our Antislavery Conflict* (Boston: Fields, Osgood, & Co., 1869), 335.

88. See, for example, Thomas Jefferson, *Memoir, Correspondence, and Miscellanies* (1830), Vol. IV, 206, to John Adams on August 22, 1813; Thomas Jefferson, *The Writings of Thomas Jefferson* (1903), Vol. XV, 1, to Francis A. Van Der Kemp on April 25, 1816; etc.

89. See, for example, Thomas Jefferson, *The Works of Thomas Jefferson* (1905), Vol. IX, 459n; Thomas Jefferson, *Memoir, Correspondence, and Miscellanies* (1830), Vol. IV, 320, to William Short on April 13, 1820; Benjamin Rush, *Letters of Benjamin Rush*, L. H. Butterfield, editor (Princeton: Princeton University Press, 1951), Vol. II, 863–864, to Thomas Jefferson on May 5, 1803; Thomas Jefferson, *Memoir, Correspondence, and Miscellanies* (1830), Vol. IV, 44–49, to William Duane on March 22, 1806, and Vol. III, 413, to Elbridge Gerry on January 26, 1799; Thomas Jefferson, *The Works of Thomas Jefferson* (1904), Vol. 4, 413, to James Madison on May 11, 1785; Vol. VIII, 130, to James Cheetham on January 17, 1802; etc.

90. Thomas Jefferson, *The Works of Thomas Jefferson* (1905), Volume IX, 459n, "Syllabus of an Estimate of the Merit of the Doctrines of Jesus, Compared with those of Others," draft of letter to Levi Lincoln on April 26, 1803.

91. Thomas Jefferson, *Memoir, Correspondence, and Miscellanies* (1830), Vol. IV, 361, to James Smith on December 8, 1822.

92. Ibid., Vol. IV, 360, to James Smith on December 8, 1822.

93. Ibid., Vol. IV, 350, to Dr. Benjamin Waterhouse on June 26, 1822.

94. Wilburn E. MacClenny, *The Life of Rev. James O'Kelly*, 217, excerpt from "The Prospect Before Us," 1824.

95. Thomas Jefferson, *The Writings of Thomas Jefferson* (1904), Vol. 14, 385, to Charles Thompson on January 9, 1816.

96. Thomas Jefferson, *Memoir, Correspondence, and Miscellanies* (1830), Vol. III, 506, to Benjamin Rush on April 21, 1803.

97. Thomas Jefferson, *The Writings of Thomas Jefferson* (1859), Vol. VII, 127, to Ezra Styles on June 25, 1819.

98. Dumas Malone, *Jefferson the President, First Term 1801–1805* (Boston: Little Brown & Co., 1970), Vol. Four, 205.

99. Ibid., Vol. Four, 202.

100. Benjamin Rush, *The Autobiography of Benjamin Rush. His "Travels through Life" Together with His Commonplace Book for 1789–1813*, George W. Corner, editor (Princeton: Princeton University Press, 1948), 152, "Characters of the Revolutionary Patriots."

101. Benjamin Rush, *Letters of Benjamin Rush*, Vol. II, 864, to Thomas Jefferson on May 5, 1803.
102. Ibid.
103. Thomas Jefferson, *The Writings of Thomas Jefferson*, Vol. VII, 281, to John Adams on April 11, 1823.
104. *The American Heritage Dictionary* (New York: Dell Publishing, 1983), s.v. "Deism"; *The American College Dictionary*, Clarence L. Barnhart, editor (New York: Random House, 1947), s.v. "Deism."
105. See, for example, Thomas Jefferson, *Notes of the State of Virginia* (Philadelphia: Matthew Carey,1794), 236–237, "Query XVIII The particular customs and manners that may happen to be received in that state?"; Thomas Jefferson, *The Works of Thomas Jefferson* (1905), Vol. XI, 419–420, to Edward Coles on August 25, 1814; Vol. XI, 471, to David Barrow on May 1, 1815; and others.
106. Thomas Jefferson, *The Writings of Thomas Jefferson* (1897), Vol. VIII, 347–348, "Second Inaugural Address," March 4, 1805.
107. See, for example, Thomas Jefferson, *Memoir, Correspondence, and Miscellanies*, (1829), Vol. III, 439, to Uriah McGregory on August 13, 1800, and Vol. IV, 23, to Mrs. John Adams on July 22, 1804; Thomas Jefferson, *The Works of Thomas Jefferson* (1905), Vol. XII, 474n, to Henry Lee Jr. on May 15, 1826; etc.
108. Henry S. Randall, *The Life of Thomas Jefferson*, Vol. III, 672, Appendix No. XXXVI, Thomas Jefferson Randolph to Henry S. Randall.

CONCLUSION: THOMAS JEFFERSON: AN AMERICAN HERO

1. *Everson v. Board of Education*, 330 U.S. 1, 33 (1947)
2. On February 12, 2008, in a Westlaw search of legal cases (both state and federal) undertaken for the author, some 2,851 cases specifically cited the language of the First Amendment (search string was "respecting an establishment . . . "), but 4,189 cases cited the phrase "wall separating church and state," or a close variation of that language. Thus in cases specifically addressing First Amendment issues, the First Amendment itself was quoted much less often than the separation metaphor, which was regularly used as judicial replacement language for the First Amendment.
3. *ACLU of Ky. v. Mercer County, Ky.*, 432 F.3d 624, 638 (6th Cir. 2005) (Judge Richard Suhrheinrich's opinion stating "The ACLU's argument contains three fundamental flaws. First, the ACLU makes repeated reference to "the separation of church and state." This extra-constitutional construct has grown tiresome. The First Amendment does not demand a wall of separation between church and state.")
4. *Wallace v. Jaffree* (472 U.S. 38, 1985), at 106–107, 112, Rehnquist, J. (dissenting).
5. Henry S. Randall, *The Life of Thomas Jefferson* (New York: Derby & Jackson, 1858), Vol. III, 673, from Thomas Jefferson Randolph to Henry S. Randall.

6. *The Debates, Resolutions, and Other Proceedings, in Convention, on the Adoption of the Federal Constitution*, Jonathan Elliot, editor (Washington, DC: Printed for the Editor, 1828), Vol. II, 281, James Madison on June 14, 1788.

7. Thomas Jefferson, *The Works of Thomas Jefferson*, Paul Leicester Ford, editor (New York: G. P. Putnam's Sons, 1904), Vol. V, 332, to Joseph Jones on August 14, 1787.

8. Caitlin Macneal, "RNC Condemns AP Exam's 'Radically Revisionist View' of U.S. History," TPM, August 13, 2014 (at: http://talkingpointsmemo.com/livewire/rnc-ap-exam-revisionist-history); "College Board Moves to 'Clarify' New AP History Test," *Daily Caller*, August 12, 2014 (at: http://dailycaller.com/2014/08/12/college-board-moves-to-clarify-new-ap-history-test/).

9. Sheldon and Jeremy Stern, "The State of State U.S. History Standards in 2011," Thomas Fordham Institute, February 2011 (at: http://www.edexcellencemedia.net/publications/2011/20110216_SOSHS/SOSS_History_FINAL.pdf), These findings are based on the published scope and sequence of history standards for the various states. States that require high school students to learn only from 1900 forward are: California, Connecticut, Nevada, North Dakota, Oregon, and Washington (1890–present). States that require high school students to learn from Reconstruction forward are: Colorado, Delaware, Florida, Hawaii, Indiana, Kansas, Kentucky, Louisiana, Maryland, Michigan, Missouri, New Mexico, Ohio, South Dakota, Tennessee, Texas, and Utah.

10. Paul Vitz, *Censorship: Evidence of Bias in our Children's Textbooks* (Ann Arbor: Servant Books, 1986), 80.

11. Ibid., 77.

12. James Madison, *The Papers of James Madison*, Henry D. Gilpin, editor (Washington: Langtree and O'Sullivan, 1840), Vol. II, 985, Benjamin Franklin on June 28, 1787.

13. Jedidiah Morse and Elijah Parish, *A Compendious History of New England* (Charlestown: S. Etheridge, 1820), xiii.

14. Daniel Webster, *The Works of Daniel Webster* (Boston: Little, Brown, and Company, 1881), Vol. II, 399, "Reception at Savannah," originally printed in the Savannah Republican, June 3, 1847, part of a speech by Justice James Moore Wayne.

15. George Bancroft, *Memorial Address of the Life and Character of Abraham Lincoln, Delivered at the Request of Both Houses of the Congress of America, Before Them, in the House of Representatives at Washington, on the 12th of February, 1866* (Washington DC: Government Printing Office, 1866), 3.

16. George Bancroft, *History of the United States* (Boston: Little, Brown, and Company, 1874), Vol. I, 4.

17. Charles Coffin, *The Story of Liberty* (New York: Harper & Brothers, 1878), 9.

18. Sarah Randolph, *The Domestic Life of Thomas Jefferson* (New York: Harper & Brothers, 1871), 38.

19. Henry S. Randall, *The Life of Thomas Jefferson*, Vol. III, 675, from Thomas Jefferson Randolph to Henry S. Randall; Sarah Randolph, *The Domestic Life of Thomas Jefferson*, 337.

20. Thomas Jefferson, *The Works of Thomas Jefferson* (1904), Vol. V, 128, to Mrs. Maria Cosway on October 12, 1786.
21. Sarah Randolph, *The Domestic Life of Thomas Jefferson*, 289–290.
22. Ibid.
23. Henry Stephens Randall, *The Life of Thomas Jefferson*, Vol. I, 490–491, quoting from an article in *Harper's Magazine* entitled "Social Hours of Daniel Webster," July, 1856.
24. Henry S. Randall, *The Life of Thomas Jefferson*, Vol. III, 671, from Thomas Jefferson Randolph to Henry S. Randall.
25. Sarah Randolph, *The Domestic Life of Thomas Jefferson*, 344–345, from Ellen Coolidge to Henry S. Randall.
26. Ibid.
27. Henry S. Randall, *The Life of Thomas Jefferson*, Vol. III, 673, from Thomas Jefferson Randolph to Henry S. Randall.
28. Sarah Randolph, *The Domestic Life of Thomas Jefferson*, 394–395, "Dr. Dunglison's Memoranda," 1825.
29. Calvin Coolidge, "Address Before the Congress Sitting in Joint Session in the House of Representatives," American Presidency Project, February 22, 1927 (at: http://www.presidency.ucsb.edu/ws/index.php?pid=418&st=&st1=#ixzz1PNL7rdMJ).

INDEX

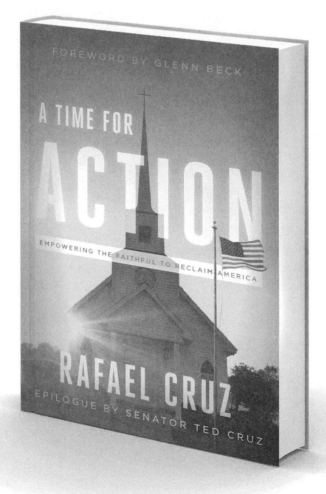

A TIME FOR ACTION is more than the story or one man's quest for refuge from Cuban persecution to realizing the American dream. It is a wake-up call to the faithful across the land to step up to the challenge of entering the public arena and taking on the forces at work to destroy the guiding principles that made this country great. Our mission is "to declare," as St. Paul said, "the whole counsel of God." If we instead remain silent, we have to answer to God for our silence. Let's not be politically correct. Let's be biblically correct.

WND BOOKS • WASHINGTON DC • WNDBOOKS.COM

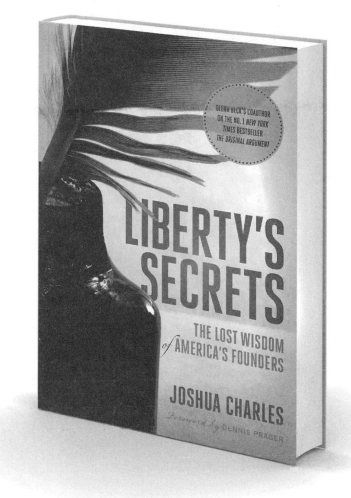

LIBERTY'S SECRETS exposes readers to the Founding Fathers as never before. They believed in God, Judeo-Christian values and the freedom and necessity of religion in order to have a free and prosperous society. They believed in a free press and knew, as John Adams argued, that "when a people is corrupted, the press may be made an engine to complete their ruin." They believed in a limited government, strong education and private property.

WND Books • WASHINGTON DC • WNDBOOKS.COM

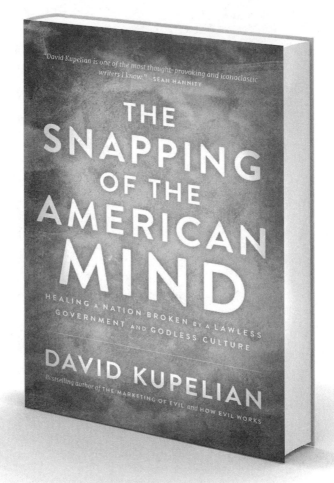

In THE SNAPPING OF THE AMERICAN MIND, bestselling author and journalist David Kupelian shows how the secular left – which has come to dominate most of America's key institutions, from the news and entertainment media to education to government itself – is accomplishing much more than just enlarging government, enacting progressive redistributionist policies and de-Christianizing the culture. It is also, whether intentionally or not, promoting widespread dependency, family breakdown, crime, corruption, addiction, despair, and suicide.

WND Books • WASHINGTON DC • WNDBOOKS.COM

No publisher in the world has a higher percentage of *New York Times* bestsellers.